Chess Stars Openings

The Modern Triangle

Semko Semkov

Chess Stars
www.chess-stars.com

Chess Stars Publishing
Current Theory and Practice Series

The Modern Triangle

Cover design by Kaloyan Nachev, Semko Semkov

Printed in Bulgaria
ISBN: 978-619-7188-27-1

Contents

Bibliography

Books

The Triangle System, Ruslan Scherbakov, Everyman Chess 2012

The Triangle Setup, Michal Krasenkow, ChessBase 2015

Playing 1.d4, Lars Schandorff, Quality Chess 2012

Attacking the English/Reti, Alexander Delchev and Semko Semkov, Chess Stars 2016

A Practical Black *Repertoire with d5, c6. Volume 1: The Slav*, Alexei Kornev, Chess Stars 2017

The Meran & Anti-Meran Variations, Alexey Dreev, Chess Stars 2011

Periodicals

Chess Informant

New in Chess Yearbook

Internet resources

Databases

The Week In Chess (www.theweekinchess.com)

Chess Publishing (www.chesspublishing.com)

Introduction

This book is devoted to the Triangle set-up, which arises after **1.d4 d5 2.c4 e6 3.♘c3/♘f3 c6**.

I have been playing it all my life, at first in OTB tournaments, then in blitz.

My concept for the Triangle set-up can be summarised in 3 principles:

1. We do not plan to entrench ourselves around the d5-square. On the contrary – we aim to take on c4 in order to play double-edged positions with open centre and asymmetrical pawn structures.
2. We do not cling to the extra c4-pawn. It serves us only to distract the opponent's forces from the centre. In many lines we return it with ...c5 to open our bishop.
3. We never play ...f5 or any form of the Stonewall.

I understand that Number 3 of this list is controversial. It implies that if White defends c4 with e3, we should enter the Meran. On the other hand, I do not regard that as a drawback. The Meran is one of the most solid and theoretically sound systems in chess. You can study it from Chess Stars' book *The Meran & Anti-Meran Variations by* Alexey Dreev. And if you want a more lazy way to build up a complete repertoire around the Triangle System, you should look at Kornev's book *A Practical* Black *Repertoire with d5, c6. Volume 1.* It offers a Black repertoire with 4.e3 ♘f6 5.♘f3 a6.

Why am I against the Stonewall? I must admit that I played it many times with good results against e3. However, compared to the Meran, it is a second-rate opening. Against a really strong opponent, you are likely to struggle for many moves, with poor chances to win. Even more importantly, playing the Stonewall could hamper you to improve your chess understanding as you'd be getting one and the same closed pawn structure all the time. The spirit of the Triangle is quite the opposite – we seek sharp unbalanced play.

So I omitted 4.e3, but paid enough attention to the Marshall, the Noteboom, and all the other 4th moves after 3.♘f3 c6 – 4.♘bd2, 4.♕c2, 4.♕b3, 4.g3, 4.♗g5, 4.b3, the Carlsbad structure with cxd5.
I also added a chapter on the Reti and the King's Indian Attack, although it is beyond the scope of the Triangle System.

What do we gain with the Triangle move order?

We avoid:
the Slav and the Exchange Slav;
the Botvinnik Variation;
the tremendously popular Catalan;
the Queen's Gambit Declined;
the Classical Carlsbad with 3...♘f6 4.cxd5.

We also set a psychological trap: Many players believe that the Noteboom is clearly better for White. This is a very old myth. As you will see, Black does not have any theoretical problems. Furthermore, statistics show that after 1.d4 d5 2.c4 e6 3.♘c3, 3...c6 is the best scoring move for Black. Then 4.♘f3 dxc4 brings Black 54.2%!

In blitz I often meet players who stubbornly repeat some poor Noteboom line only because some book promised them an advantage! But if you look closely in the database, you could notice that top players choose 3.♘f3 c6 and now almost everything but 4.♘c3.

I especially like the fact that the Triangle is effective against the Catalan. It is always difficult to impose double-edged play against the fianchetto, but 3.♘f3 c6 4.g3 dxc4! is again the best practical decision.

The open centre promises lively play with plenty of tactical tricks.

I tried to explain the most important plans and key positions in the "Main Ideas" sections, so please do not skip them! Anyway you will not be able to memorize the variations from the "Step by Step" sections, although I selected only the most topical information.
On the opposite, some annotated games present alternative lines, which could enrich your repertoire, but are not vital for the start.

Now I'd like to present you the most unusual game in my career. Besides the fun, it displays the enormous potential of the Triangle System to face White with nontrivial strategic tasks. I won both my Triangle games in this closed GM tournament, and that was decisive to share first place with Bareev.

P.Lukacs – Semkov
Vrnjacka Banja 1987

1.d4 d5 2.♘f3 c6 3.c4 e6 4.♘c3 dxc4 5.♗g5

5...f6

My opponent was a decent grandmaster, famous with his erudition in the openings. So it was impractical to enter the Botvinnik Variation. Nowadays I'm wiser, so I recommend 5...♗e7. Instead I decided to create more imbalances.

6.♗d2 a6 7.g3?! (7.a4! e5) **7...b5 8.♗g2 ♘e7 9.0-0 ♘d5 10.b3 ♘xc3 11.♗xc3 b4 12.♗e1 c3**

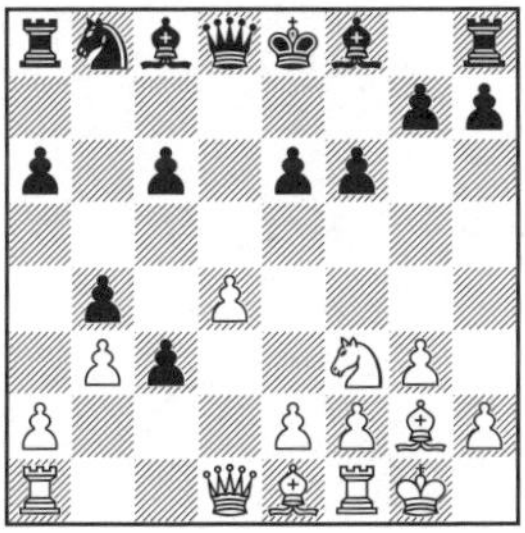

It looks like Black forgot how the pieces moved... But I was already happy with my position.

13.♕c2? (13.a3 c5 14.♕c2 ♖a7 15.dxc5 ♗xc5) **13...a5 14.a3 ♖a6! 15.♖d1 ♗e7 16.♘h4**

This is the first line of Houdini, so do not condemn this move.

16...c5 (16...g5! 17.♘f3 0-0) **17.d5 ♖d6 18.e4**

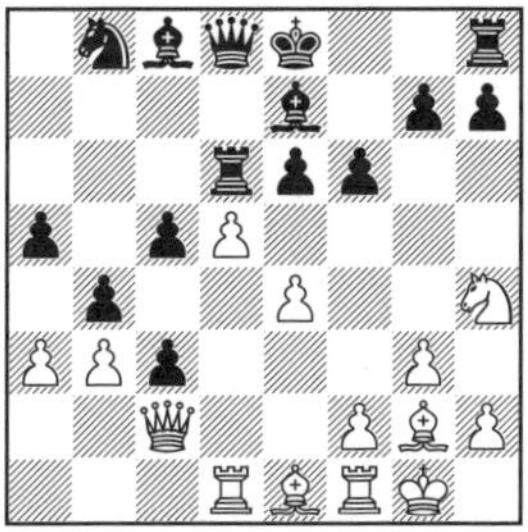

18...g5!

Mirroring the queenside pawn storm to the other wing.

19.e5 (desperation) **19...fxe5 20.f4 exf4 21.♘f3 ♖xd5 22.♗f2 g4 23.♘e5 f3–+ 24.♗h1**

An amazing picture! I won the game almost without my minor pieces.

24...♖d2 25.♖xd2 ♕xd2 26.♕e4 ♕d5 27.♕e3 ♖f8 28.h3 ♖f5 29.♘xg4 ♗g5 30.♕e1 ♗d2 31.♕b1 ♗a6 32.♖d1 ♕d3 33.♕a1 e5 34.axb4 c2 0-1

Chapter 1. The Noteboom System – Sidelines

Main Ideas

The Noteboom System arises after:
1.d4 d5 2.c4 e6 3.♘f3 c6 4.♘c3 dxc4

It is one of the most extraordinary openings. In many senses the Noteboom defies the classical rules of positional chess. It is the antipode of Botvinnik's principle that if Black bolstered up the d5 square against 1.d4, he should maintain even chances. Furthermore, Black neglects development!
The move 4...dxc4 breaks the symmetry and begins the fight for an opening advantage! That is not the way to play for a half point. You should display ingenuity and concrete thinking.

The obvious aim of our last move is to hang to the c4-pawn with ...b5. White can still regain the pawn by 5.a4 ♗b4 6.e3 b5 7.♗d2 a5! 8.axb5 ♗xc3 9.♗xc3 cxb5 10.b3 ♗b7 11.bxc4 b4 12.♗b2 ♘f6, but at the cost of accepting two connected passed pawns on the queenside. That is the main line, and we are going to study it in the next chapter.
In this chapter I'll confine myself to variations where White plays in a gambit style with e4. Let's consider:
5.e4 b5 6.♗e2 ♗b7 7.0-0 ♘f6

The most popular approach is to lead out the bishop – 8.♗g5?!. White hopes to see ...♗e7, when e5 will trade bishops and White will get the d6-square at his full disposal. That is not too dangerous, but Black will have to defend passively, which is not in our plans. As a rule, we should meet ♗g5 by 8...

♘bd7 (planning ...h6). Then 9.e5 h6 10.♗h4 g5 11.♗g3 ♘d5 is excellent for us.

An alternative way is 8.♕c2 ♗e7 9.e5 ♘d5 10.♘e4

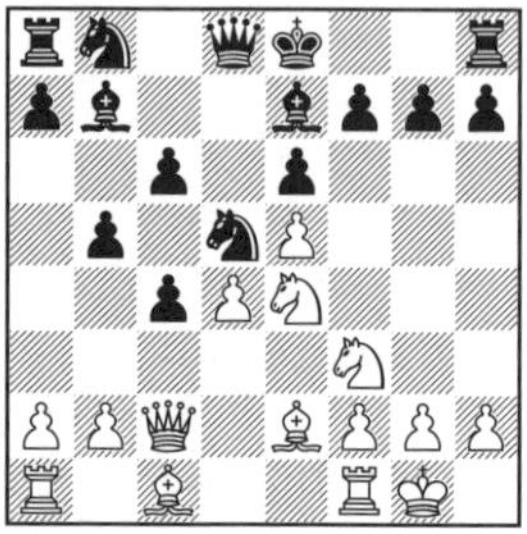

I suggest to treat this pawn structure with 10...h6. It looks dangerous to provide a lever on the kingside, but my idea is to quickly undermine the e5-pawn with ...f6 or ...f5:

Analysis

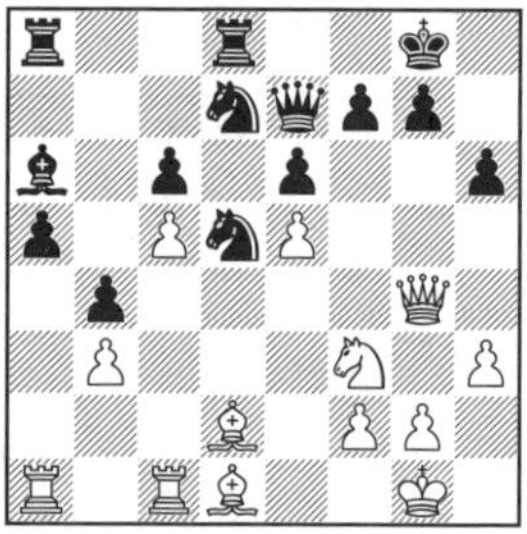

20...f5! 21.exf6 ♘5xf6↑.

In this example White activated his queen via e4-g4. He might also build the battery ♗d2+♕c1 with the unequivocal intention to take on h6. It is often impossible to calculate all the consequences of such sacrifice.

I suggest to save this effort and simply answer ♗xh6 with ...f6:

Analysis

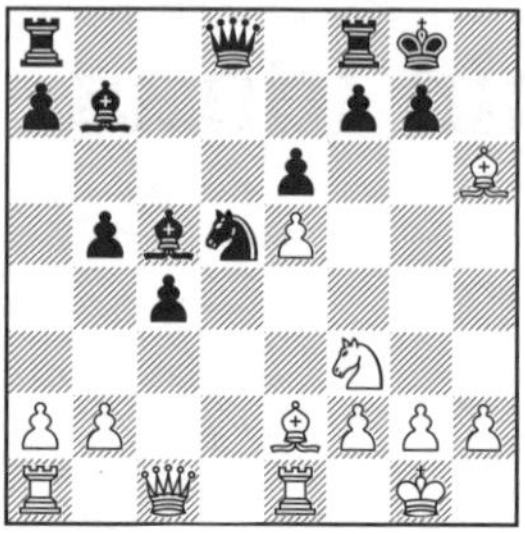

16...f6! 17.exf6?! (17.♗d2 ♕b6↑) 17... gxh6∓.

Analysis

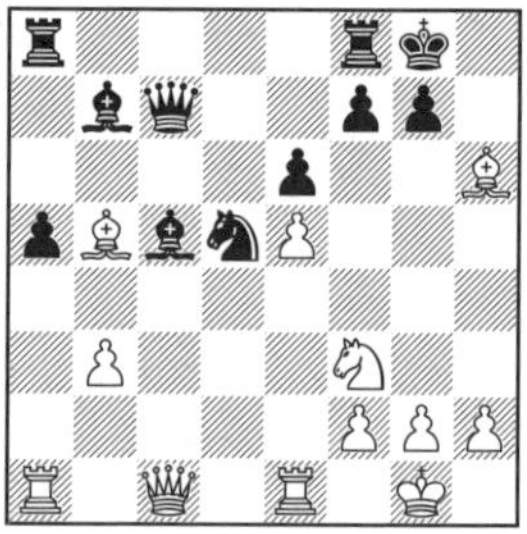

19...f6↑.

The bottom line of the above explanations is that White lacks enough resources to decide the game solely on the kingside, mostly because his light-squared bishop cannot join the attack. Therefore, he should undermine the c4-pawn with a4 and b3.

5.a4 ♗b4 6.e4

Here a reliable equaliser is 6...♘f6 7.♗g5 ♗xc3+!, which is a sideline of the Botvinnik Variation. I suggest to stay true to the Noteboom spirit with **6...b5!**. Then we have to deal with the following pawn structures:

After 7.♗d2 a5 8.axb5 ♗xc3 9.bxc3 cxb5 10.♕b1

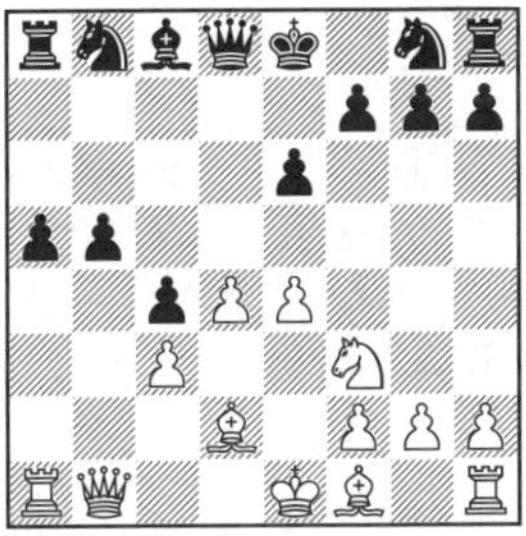

Although ...♗a6 is possible, I suggest in such situation to always keep the bishop closer to the kingside: 10...♗d7.

Another typical pawn structure is:

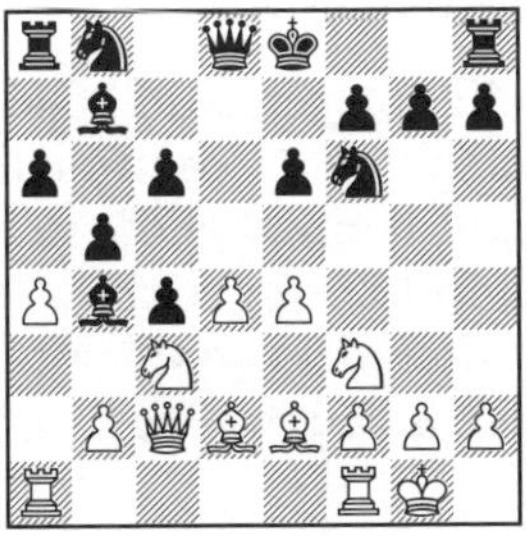

My recommendation is to open the b7-bishop as early as possible: 10...c5!? 11.dxc5 0-0.

Always prefer counter-attack rather than a passive stand even when the engines claim the opposite.

Here is more of the same:

Analysis

11...c5! 12.dxc5 ♘d7↑.

Analysis

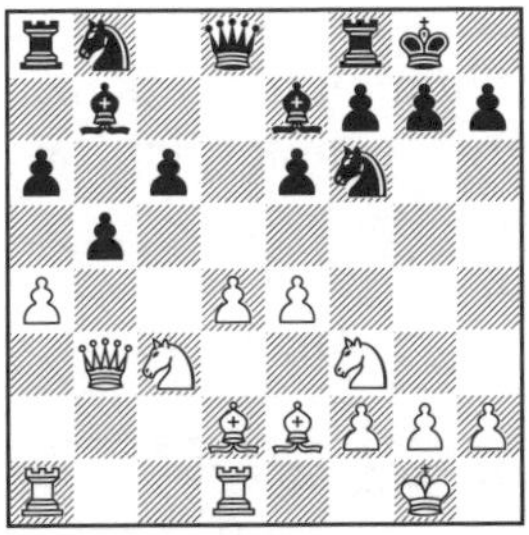

15...c5!?=.

Analysis

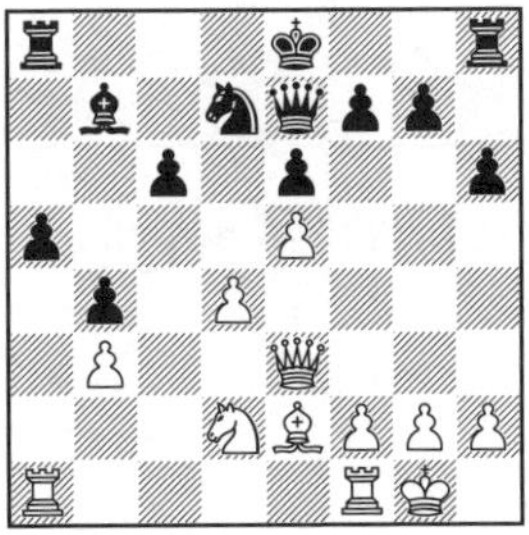

17...c5! 18.dxc5 0-0!∓.

After b2-b3 we often can take over the initiative with a break in the centre:

Analysis

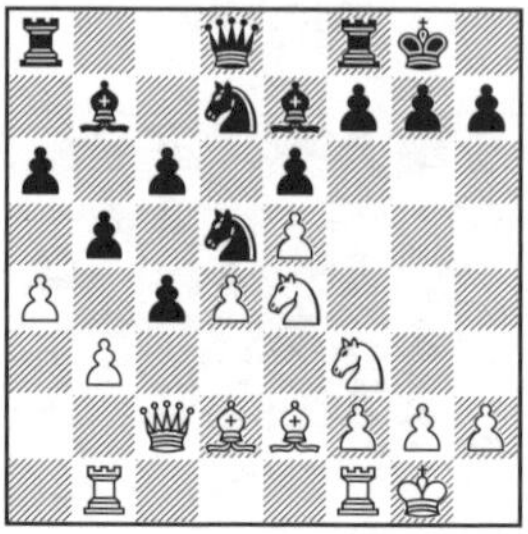

14...c3! 15.♗xc3 c5!↑. Or 15.♘xc3 c5.

Sometimes the engines prefer to keep the extra pawn, relying on their amazing defensive capabilities. However, we should take into account human limitations and opt for active counterplay whenever possible:

Analysis

The best practical approach is 10...b4! 11.♘e4 ♗a6 12.♗g5 f6 13.exf6 gxf6.

The passive alternative 10...♗d7 (or 10...a6) preserves the status quo on the queenside, but gives White a lasting initiative. For instance, he could play 11.h4 a5 12.♖h3 h6 13.♖g3 ♔f8 14.h5 ♘a6 15.♔f1 ♘ab4 16.♔g1 ♘xc3 17.bxc3 ♘d5 18.♕e4 ♔g8 19.♕g4 ♗f8 20.♘h2 ♖b8 21.♘f1 ♕c7 22.♘e3

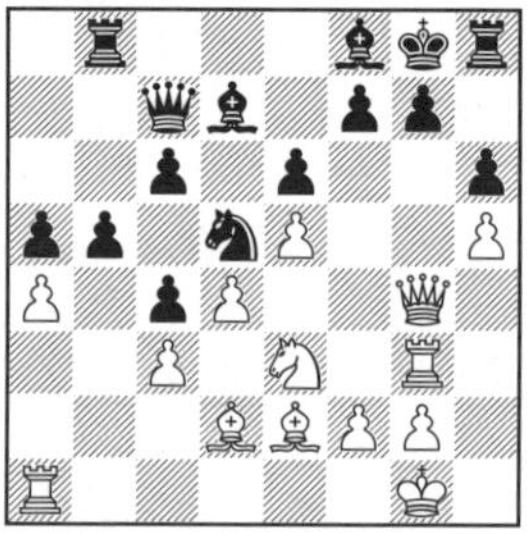

Black lacks any constructive plan, while the opponent has several ways to improve his pieces. For instance, ♖b1, ♗d1-c2, ♘g4.

Theoretical status

Many club players still believe that the Noteboom is positionally dubious and happily allow it. That is our chance! Statistics show 46% for White after 5.a4, 44% after 5.e3, and mere 38% after 5.e4.

Step by Step

1.d4 d5 2.c4 e6 3.♘f3 c6 4.♘c3 dxc4

White might prefer to play a real gambit without making a hole on b4 – **A.** 5.e4, or regain the pawn with **B.** 5.a4.

5.e3 b5 6.a4 ♗b4 transposes to line B. The only independent line is

6.♘e5?! ♘d7! 7.♘xc6 ♕b6 8.♘e5 ♘xe5 9.dxe5 ♗b7 10.♗d2 (Aiming to enable b3. Or 10.♕c2 a6 11.b3 cxb3∓) 10...♘h6 11.a4 a6 12.axb5 axb5 13.b3 ♗e7 14.bxc4 b4∓.

5.♗g5 ♗e7 6.♗xe7 ♘xe7 is seldom seen, but it deserves special attention.

7.a4

7.e4 b5 transposes to A1.

7.e3 b5 8.a4 ♘d5 keeps the extra pawn.

7...♘d5

7...c5!? is obviously fine for Black, but the text is more challenging.

8.a5 c5 9.e4 ♘b4 10.d5!? exd5 11.♘xd5 ♘8c6 12.♗xc4 ♘xa5 13.♕a4+ ♘ac6 14.0-0 0-0 15.♕b5

Or 15.♖fd1 ♘xd5 16.♗xd5 ♕b6=.

15...♗g4! 16.♕xc5 ♗xf3 17.gxf3 ♘xd5 18.♗xd5 ♕f6=.

5.g3 b5 is covered in Chapter 4.

A. 5.e4 b5

Now we have a split:

A1. 6.♗g5; **A2.** 6.♗e2
6.a4 ♗b4 is covered in line B.

A1. 6.♗g5 ♗e7!

I won against grandmasters Peter Lukacs and Dusan Rajkovic with 6...f6, but during the game with Rajkovic I painfully felt the weaknesses on g6 and e6, which he underlined with 7.♗f4 a6 8.♗e2 ♘e7 9.h4!?, followed by h5, ♘h4.

7.♗xe7

7.h4 is pointless as we could answer 6...h6 or simply ignore the g5-bishop.

7...♘xe7 8.a4

8.♗e2 ♘d7 9.0-0 ♖b8 neutralises the threat d4-d5 and prepares ...c5 with good timing.

8...♗b7

This is the safest solution!
8...♗d7!? keeps the pawn, but Black remains passive. Overall, Black gets a firm position, but with little chances to win after 9.♗e2 0-0 10.0-0 a5 11.e5 ♘a6 12.♕d2 ♘b4 13.♘e4 ♘f5 14.h3 h6.

Another decent answer is 8...a6 9.axb5 cxb5 10.♘xb5 axb5! 11.♖xa8 ♗b7 12.♖a1 ♗xe4. A similar sacrifice is known from the QGA, but it is stronger here. Still, White has a draw with 13.b3! ♘bc6 14.bxc4 ♘b4 (14...♗xf3=) 15.♖c1 ♘a2 16.♖a1.

9.axb5

In practice White prefers to take a grip on the dark squares with 9.e5?!, but his task should be difficult after 9...a6 10.♘e4 0-0 11.♘d6 ♕c7 12.g3 (12.g4 c5) 12...♘f5∓.

9...cxb5 10.♘xb5 ♗xe4 11.♗xc4 ♘bc6 12.0-0 ♗xf3

12...0-0!? 13.♘e5 a6 14.♘c3 ♘xe5 15.dxe5 ♗b7 is also slightly better for Black, Damaso-Flores, Linares 2019.

13.♕xf3 0-0 14.♖fd1 ♕b6 15.♕a3 ♖fd8 16.♕a6!

White should be able to achieve a draw.

A2. 6.♗e2 ♗b7 7.0-0 ♘f6

Do not waste time on ...a6 unless it is absolutely obligatory!

8.♗g5?!

This is the most frequent move, but it does not achieve its aim – to trade dark-squared bishops.

8.♕c2 ♗e7 9.e5

9.b3 b4 10.e5 ♘d5 11.♘xd5 cxd5 12.bxc4 dxc4 13.♗xc4 0-0∓.

After 9.♗g5 h6 10.♗h4 we should not fear a bishop trade, provided that we activate our b7-bishop on time – 10...♘bd7 11.e5 ♘d5 12.♗xe7 ♕xe7 13.b3 ♘xc3 14.♕xc3 cxb3 15.axb3 b4 16.♕e3 a5 17.♘d2 (or 17.♖fc1 0-0 18.♘d2 c5!) 17...c5! 18.dxc5 0-0!∓.

The insertion of 9.a4 a6 does not change much.

9...♘d5 10.♘e4

Against 10.♕e4, 10...0-0 is possible, but Black should quickly counterattack in the centre. For instance: 11.♗d1 c5!?. I believe that it is wiser to refrain from castling. A set-up like ...h5, ...♔f8 would keep us on the safe side. We can start with either of these moves.

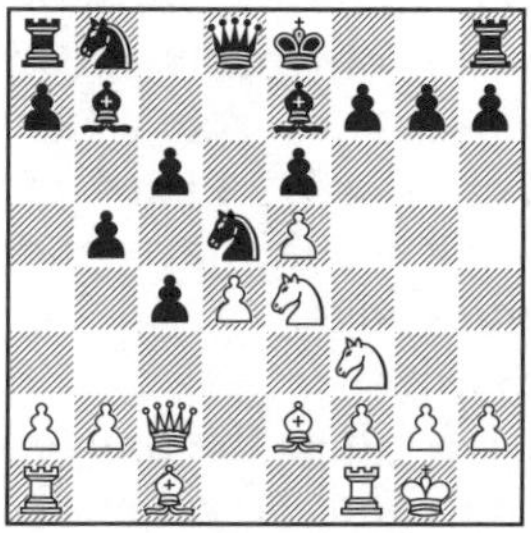

10...h6 – see **Game 2** Guerreiro-Tropf, ICCF 2017.

8.♖b1!?. The idea of this mysterious move is to enable b3, eliminating the answer ...b4 in view of bxc4. If Black took on b3, White's rook would join in the kingside attack via the third rank. Thus we should plan how to meet this positional threat.

8...♘bd7!?

The engines like 8...a6 9.b3 cxb3, but in my opinion White gets sufficient compensation following 10.♖xb3! ♗e7 11.e5 ♘fd7! (preparing ...c5) 12.h4! h6 (12...c5 13.d5 h6 14.♖e1; 12...0-0 13.♘g5 h6 is dangerous – 14.♗d3 or even 14.♘xe6!? fxe6 15.♗g4.) 13.♘e4 c5 14.♘d6+ ♗xd6 15.exd6, then ♘e5, ♗f3, ♖g3.

9.b3 ♗b4! 10.♕c2

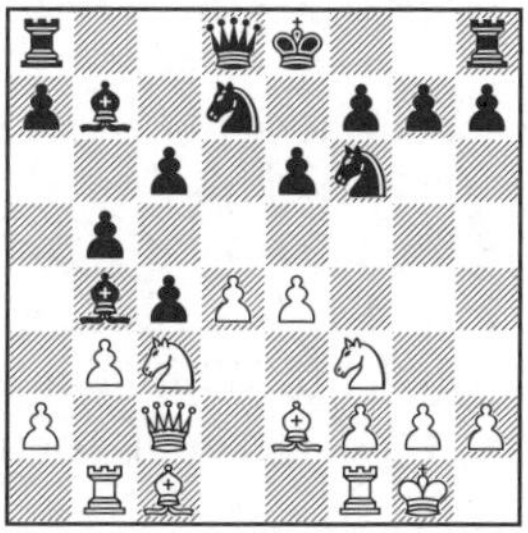

10...♗xc3!

The only high-level game, Dubov-Inarkiev, Moscow 2019, saw the obviously inconsistent 10...0-0 11.e5 ♗xc3 12.exf6 b4 13.fxg7 ♔xg7 14.bxc4 c5, when 15.♘g5! would have underlined White's edge.

11.♕xc3 cxb3

11...c5!? plugs the dangerous diagonal and is generally safer. After 12.bxc4 b4 13.♕e3 ♗xe4 14.♖b2 a5 15.dxc5 ♕c7 16.a3 ♕xc5 17.axb4 axb4 18.♕xc5 ♘xc5 19.♘e5! ♘fd7 20.♘xd7 ♘xd7 21.♖xb4 ♔e7 White has a bishop pair, but Black's pieces are active and the material is limited. A draw is the most likely result.

The text looks risky, but Black has a streamlined way to neutralise the pressure:

12.♕xb3 ♘xe4 13.♗a3 a5 14.d5!

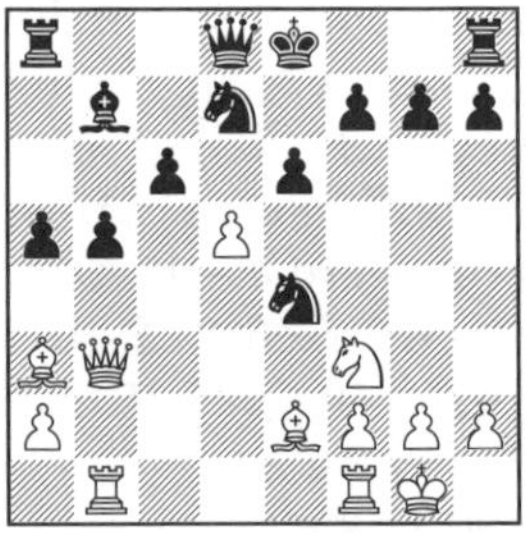

This resource keeps White in the game:

14...b4 (14...exd5 15.♗xb5!!=∞) 15.dxe6 fxe6 16.♗b2 ♕e7 17.♘d4!? ♘d2 18.♕h3 0-0 19.♘xe6 ♖f6. Again, it looks that Black emerges with an edge, but White has enough powder in his arsenal to make a draw:

20.♘g5 ♖h6 21.♕g3 ♖g6 22.h4 ♘xb1 23.♗c4+ ♔h8 24.♖xb1 ♘f6 25.♕e5! ♕xe5 26.♘f7+ ♔g8 27.♘xe5+ ♘d5 28.♘xg6 hxg6 29.♖e1 (to drag the king to the 7th rank) 29...♔f7 30.♖c1=. The g7- and a5-pawn are weak.

8...♘bd7!?

This is my favourite approach to ♗g5 in various settings. We preserve our bishop from exchange.

9.e5 h6 10.♗h4 g5 11.♗g3 ♘h5 12.♘d2 ♘xg3 13.hxg3

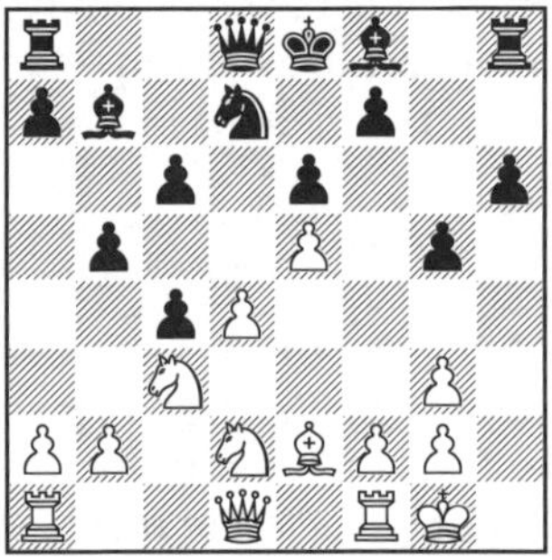

The engines are a bit overoptimistic about Black's chances. I think that White has fair compensation with best play. The most natural approach is to hit d4:

13...♕b6

13...♗e7!?, planning short castling, keeps things more tangled. Perhaps it is Black's best chance to play for a win:

14.♕c2 0-0 15.♖ad1 ♕b6 16.♘de4

c5 17.d5 ♘xe5 18.d6 ♗d8 19.f4 ♘d3 20.f5

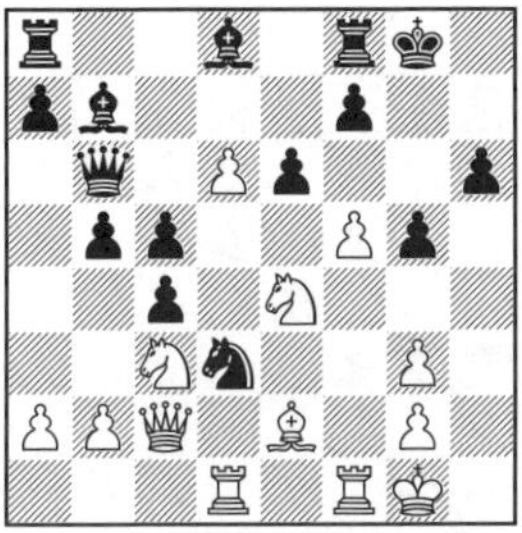

Despite the two extra pawns, the position remains extremely complex. One greedy move like:

20...b4? 20.fxe6 fxe6? and Black is lost after 21.♖xf8+ ♔xf8 22.♖f1+ ♔g7 23.♘a4. Best is:

20...♗d5 21.♔h2 b4 22.fxe6 bxc3 23.e7 ♗xe7 24.♘xc3 ♕xd6 25.♗xd3 cxd3 26.♖xd3 ♗b3! 27.axb3 ♕g6 28.♕e2 with sufficient compensation for the pawn.

14.a4!

White's only chance is to open files on the queenside. The speculative sacrifice 14.♗h5 ♕xd4 15.♗xf7+? ♔xf7 16.♕h5+ ♔g7 17.♖ad1 proved to be hopeless after 17...♘xe5 18.♘f3 ♕g4 19.♖d7+ ♔g8 20.♘e4 ♗g7 21.♕xg4 ♘xg4–+, Piket-Gelfand, blindfold, Monte Carlo 2000.

14...♕xd4

14...♗e7 15.axb5 cxb5 16.♗f3 ♖d8 17.♗xb7 ♕xb7 18.b3 generates enough counterplay for a draw – 18...cxb3 19.♕xb3 0-0 20.♕xb5 ♕xb5 21.♘xb5 ♘xe5 22.♖xa7=.

15.axb5 ♘xe5 16.♘xc4 ♕xd1 17.♖fxd1 ♘xc4 18.♗xc4 ♗c5 19.♘e4 ♗b4 20.♖d4 ♗e7 21.♘d6+ ♗xd6 22.bxc6 0-0-0 23.cxb7+ ♔xb7

White's active rooks and opposite-coloured bishops provide excellent chances for a draw despite the missing pawn.

B. 5.a4 ♗b4

B1. 6.e4; **B2.** 6.e3

6.♗d2 is best met by 6...a5

I played against Pogorelov 6...c5 by analogy to 6.g3, but White is better developed following 7.dxc5 ♗xc5 8.e4!. (My opponent preferred 8.♘e4 ♗e7 9.♕c2 ♘f6 10.♘xf6+ ♗xf6 11.e4 ♘c6 12.♗xc4 ♗d7=.)

7.♕b1 (7.e3 and 7.e4 transpose to the main lines) 7...b6!? 8.e3 ♗a6 9.♘e5 b5 10.♕e4 ♗xc3 11.bxc3 ♘f6 12.♕f3 ♕d5 13.♕g3 0-0 14.f3 ♖fc8! is more pleasant for Black.

14...♕d8, followed by ...♘e8 and ...f6, is also fine for Black.

15.♗e2 ♕d8 16.e4 (16.0-0 ♘bd7) 16...b4↑ (or 16...c5).

6.g3 does not transpose to Chapter 4 since the move ♗b4 does not combine well with ...b5 against White's fianchetto. We should change our plans accordingly:
6...c5! 7.♗g2 ♘c6 8.♗e3

Black has a pleasant choice now between 8...♘f6 9.dxc5 ♘d5, 8...cxd4 9.♘xd4 ♘ge7, and 8...♘ge7 9.dxc5 ♘d5 with a balanced game in all cases.

B1. 6.e4 b5

6...♘f6 7.♗g5 is a well known sideline of the Botvinnik Variation. The only drawback of this line is the rather drawish character of the main equaliser – see **Game 1** Kir. Georgiev-Banusz, Plovdiv 2012.
The two seventh move White's alternatives offer Black excellent chances to fight for a full point:

a) 7.e5 ♘d5 8.♗d2 b5 9.axb5
9.♘g5 offers two good options: 9...h6 10.♘ge4 0-0 11.axb5 (11. g3 c5! 12.dxc5 ♘d7↑) 11...cxb5 12.♘xb5 ♕h4 13.♘ed6 (13.♘g3) 13...♗xd6 14.exd6 a6 15.♘a3 ♘c6 16.♗c3 e5 17.dxe5=;
9...♗e7!? 10.♕h5 g6 11.♕h6 b4!

12.♘ce4 (Black's edge is overwhelming after 12.♕g7 ♖f8 13.♘xd5 ♕xd5 14.♘xh7 ♘d7 15.♗e3 c3∓) 12...c3 13.bxc3 bxc3 14.♗e3 ♗f8! [14...♕b6 15.♕g7 ♖f8 (15...♕b2=) 16.♗e2 ♗a6 17.♘xh7 ♘d7 18.♘xf8 ♗xf8 19.♘d6+ ♗xd6 20.exd6 0-0-0=] 15.♕h3 h6 (15...♗e7=) 16.♗d3 ♗e7 17.0-0 ♗a6∓.
9...♗xc3 10.bxc3 cxb5 11.♘g5

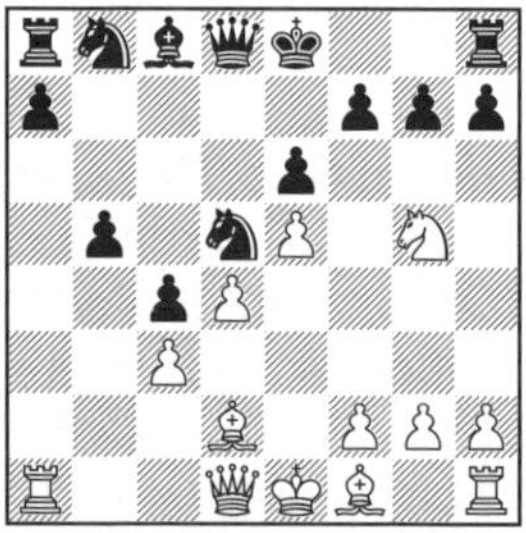

11...♗b7
Computers like 11...h6, but human logic suggests that the bishop does not have a better place than b7 anyway, while ...h6 could be postponed or avoided altogether. I admit I would feel safer without it.

12.♕h5 ♕e7 13.♗e2 ♘d7 14.♗f3 ♘7b6

Naturally, it is pointless to stay "solid" on the queenside. Our plan is ...b4, so 14...a5! was more straightforward.

15.0-0 a5! 16.♖ab1 ♗c6 17.♖fe1 ♔f8!

In such positions it is wise to leave the rook on the h-file and castle "by hand" with ...h6, ...g6, ...♔g7. The game Wagner-Grandelius, Minsk 2017, saw the nervous reaction 17...a4 18.♘e4 0-0 19.♗g5 f6, when White found a juicy target on e6 following 20.exf6 gxf6 21.♗h6 ♖f7 22.♘c5±.

18.♘e4 b4 19.♘d6 b3. White will need miracles of ingenuity to stay in the game.

b) 7.♕c2 b5 8.♗e2 ♗b7 transposes to the main line.

7.♗e2

7.♗d2 can be met by 7...a5 in true Noteboom spirit.

7...♘f6 8.e5! ♗xc3 9.bxc3 ♘e4 is sufficient for equalisation only. Scherbakov suggests 10.♕c2! (10.♕b1 ♕d5 11.♗e2 ♗b7 12.0-0 ♘d7 is pleasant for Black.), when play is balanced following 10... ♘xd2 11.♘xd2 ♘d7 12.g3 ♘b6 13.♗g2 ♘d5 14.♘e4 0-0 15.0-0 a5 16.♖fb1 ♗d7. Both sides lack clear plans. Black can even push ...f5, without altering this evaluation – 17.♘c5 ♕e7 18.♘b7 ♖fb8 19.♘d6 h6 20.h4 ♕f8 21.♔h2 f5=.

8.axb5

The idea of ...a5 is seen after 8.♗e2 ♗a6! (If we wanted to play 8...♘f6, it was better to do it on the previous turn. Besides, 8...♘e7 is an interesting alternative.) 9.d5 (Or 9.axb5 cxb5 10.d5 exd5 11.♘xd5 ♘c6 12.b3 ♘f6. The plan with 9.h4!? ♘e7 ♖h3 is entirely unexplored.) 9...exd5 10.exd5 cxd5 11.♗g5 ♘f6∓.

8...♗xc3 9.bxc3!

9.♗xc3 cxb5 10.b3 ♘f6 underlines the drawback of 6.e4. The e4-pawn is hanging and White must spend a tempo – 11.♕b1 cxb3 12.♗xb5+ ♗d7∓.

9...cxb5 10.♕b1

10...♗d7

10...♗a6 protects everything, but the bishop looks rather clumsy on that square. After 11.g3 ♘f6

12.♗g2 ♘bd7 13.0-0 0-0 play may be equal, but Black's set-up is passive.

11.g3

Meet 11.♘e5 by 11...♘e7 – note that in this line ♘f6 would be bad owing to the pin ♗g5!

11.h4 ♘e7 12.h5 h6 13.♖h3 is totally unexplored.

11...♘e7 12.♗g2 ♘bc6 13.0-0 a4

Enabling 14.d5 ♘a5. Black is well protected against a kingside offense, thanks to the ♗d7 which may go to e8. White can change plans with:

14.♗c1 0-0 15.♗a3, but he lacks serious threats.

7...♘f6

It would be good to define the pawn structure in the centre before playing moves like 7...a6 8.0-0 ♗b7, when we could face 9.♗d2 ♘f6 10.e5 ♘d5 11.♘e4. The difference with the main line is that we have already taken a passive stand on the queenside.

8.♕c2

8.e5 ♘d5 9.♗d2 ♗e7! has been tested in several games. Black frees b4 for the pawn:

10.♕b1

Or 10.♘e4 ♘d7 (10...a5!?; 10...h6!?) 11.♗g5 f6∓, Granda Zuniga-Bruzon Batista, La Roda 2010.

10...b4 11.♘e4 ♗a6 12.♗g5 f6 13.exf6 gxf6 14.♗h6 c3! 15.♗xa6 ♘xa6 16.0-0 ♕a5. Black's king will feel comfortable at d7.

8...♗b7 9.0-0!

9.e5 is harmless with a queen on c2 because White lacks the threat ♘g5+♕h5. Now we should only watch out for ♕e4. Black has good chances for intercepting the initiative. For instance:

9...♘d5 10.0-0 a6 11.♘e4 ♘d7 12.♗d2 ♗e7 13.♖ab1 0-0 14.b3 c3! 15.♗xc3 c5!↑.

9.♗g5 h6 10.♗h4 ♘bd7 11.e5 (11.0-0 ♕b6∓) 11...g5 12.♗g3 ♘d5 13.0-0 a6 transposes to the main line.

9...a6 10.♗g5

10.b3!? can be met in two ways:

a) 10...cxb3 11.♕xb3 ♗e7 is relatively simpler (11...♗xc3 is more risky) 12.axb5 cxb5 13.d5 exd5 14.e5 ♘e4 15.♘xe4 dxe4 16.♖d1 ♕c7! (White won a correspondence game after 16...♕b6)

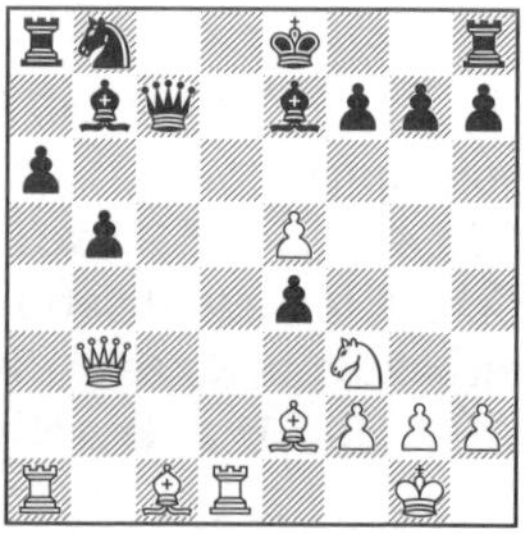

White has fair chances to hold after 17.♘g5 0-0 18.e6 ♗xg5 19.♗xg5 fxe6 20.♕xe6+ ♕f7 21.♕b6 ♗d5 22.♗e3⩲. He could also try 17.e6, when 17...0-0 is similar to the previous line, while 17...exf3 18.exf7+ ♔f8 19.♗xf3 ♘c6∞ is more double-edged.

b) 10...♕a5 11.e5

11.♘a2 cxb3 12.♕xb3 ♗e7 13.♗d2 ♕d8 14.♘c3 0-0 15.♖fd1 c5 or 15...b4 is balanced.

11...cxb3 12.♕xb3 ♗xc3 13.exf6 gxf6 14.♖a2 c5 15.axb5 ♕b4 16.♕c2 axb5 17.♖xa8 ♗xa8 18.♗f4 ♘c6. White can now force a draw with 19.♗xb5 (19.♗d6 ♕b2 is no better) 19...♕xb5 20.♕xc3 cxd4 21.♘xd4 ♘xd4 22.♕xd4 ♕d5=.

10.♗d2 could be thematically met by the freeing 10...c5!?, but Black could aspire for the edge with:

10...♗e7! 11.e5 ♘d5 12.♘e4 ♘bd7 13.b3 (13.♗g5 0-0) 13...cxb3 14.♕xb3 0-0 15.♖fc1 ♖c8. White can hardly prevent ...b4 + ...c5 with a clear extra pawn.

10...h6 11.♗h4 ♘bd7 12.e5 g5 13.♗g3 ♘d5 14.♘e4

14...g4! 15.♘h4 h5∓

Black castled long and went on to win. See **Game 3** Rogos-Oreopoulos, ICCF 2014.

B2. 6.e3 b5 7.♗d2

7.♘d2 opens a path to the kingside for the white queen.

7...♘e7 8.axb5 ♗xc3 9.bxc3 cxb5 10.♕f3 (10.♗a3 ♗d7!, intending 10...♗c6.) 10...♘bc6 11.♗a3 ♗d7 12.♕h5 a5 is possible, but I do not see how to win this position with passive pieces. Perhaps:

7...♕d7 offers more chances, preserving the dark-squared bishop, even for a while:

8.♕f3 ♗b7 9.♕g3 f5!

Scherbakov recommends 9...♔f8, but the text is more challenging. The king gets a perfect place on f7.

10.axb5 ♗xc3 11.bxc3 cxb5 12.♗a3 ♘f6

White does not have full compensation for the pawn. For instance:

13.h4 ♔f7 14.h5 h6! 15.♕g6+ ♔g8 16.♗e2 ♕f7 17.0-0 a6 18.♖fb1 ♗d5∓.

Or 13.♖b1 ♔f7 14.♗e2 a6 15.f3 ♖c8 16.e4 ♔g8∓, castling "by hand".

7.♘e5 (planning ♕f3) 7...♘f6 8.♗d2!

Instead 8.♕f3?! 0-0! (Note this move! My hand tends to play automatically 8...♕d5.) 9.axb5 ♘d5 is clearly better for Black, as Scherbakov points out.

8.g4 is another dubious idea – 8...♗b7 9.♗g2 ♘d5 10.♗d2 ♘d7 11.0-0 ♘xe5 12.dxe5 ♗xc3 13.bxc3, Vunder-Burmakin, St Petersburg 1998, when simplest is 13...♕c7 14.e4 ♘b6∓.

8...a5. Play transposes to the main line with 8.♘e5.

7...a5

7...♕b6?! 8.♘e4 ♗e7 9.b3 cxb3 10.♕xb3 offers White a stable pull.

7...♗b7? is a wrong move order. White regains the pawn following 8.axb5 ♗xc3 9.♗xc3 cxb5 10.d5 ♘f6 11.dxe6 ♕xd1+ 12.♖xd1±.

7...♕e7 8.axb5 ♗xc3 9.♗xc3 cxb5 was popular 20 years ago, then it suddenly disappeared without an obvious reason.

Black scored rather well after 10.d5 ♘f6 11.d6 ♕b7 12.b3, although the engines claimed that White was clearly better. I did not dig deeper since:

10.♗d2!? ♘f6 (10...♕b7 keeps the extra pawn at a high positional cost.) 11.b3 0-0 12.bxc4 bxc4 13.♗xc4 assures White of a small but stable advantage.

8.axb5

8.♘e5 threatens ♕f3 with a double hit on f7 and a8. It is natural to answer 8...♘f6 9.♕f3

9.axb5 ♗xc3 10.♗xc3 (for 10.bxc3 – see the main line, 9.bxc3) 10...cxb5 11.b3 (11.♕f3 ♖a6) 11...♗b7 12.bxc4 b4 13.♕a4+ is the only way to exploit the early ♘e5, but it turns out that 13...♘fd7 14.♘xd7 ♘xd7! 15.♗b2 0-0 16.c5 ♘b8! blocks the c-pawn and frees the queen to pop up on g5 or h4.

9...♖a7

10.axb5

10.♘xc6 leads by force to a Black's edge – 10...♘xc6 11.♕xc6+ ♗d7 12.♕f3 bxa4 13.♗xc4 a3 14.bxa3 ♗xc3 15.♗xc3 ♕c8 16.♕e2 ♖c7

17.♗a6 ♕a8 18.♗d2 ♕xg2 19.♕f1 ♕c6∓, Kozlov-Burmakin, St Petersburg 1995.

10.♗e2 0-0 11.0-0 ♖b7! pursues similar ideas – 12.♘xc6?! ♘xc6 13.♕xc6 ♖b6 14.♕f3 ♗b7 15.♕h3 bxa4!.

10...♗xc3 11.♗xc3

11.bxc3 cxb5 12.♖b1 ♗b7! 13.♕f4 0-0 14.♖xb5 a4 takes over the initiative.

11...cxb5 12.♕g3 0-0 13.♘xc4

White regained the pawn and the chances are even after 13... bxc4 14.♕xb8 ♕d7 15.♗e2 ♖b7.

13...♗a6 14.♗xa5 ♕e7

White is lagging behind in development, but he can survive:

15.♘d6

Or 15.♘d2 ♗b7 16.♗xb5 ♖xa5 17.♖xa5 ♕b4 18.♕c7 ♗xg2↑.

15...♖d7 16.♗d3 ♕xd6 17.♕xd6 ♖xd6 18.♗b4. The rook + pawn balance Black's 2 minor pieces. Perhaps best retreat now is 18...♖b6=.

I would not have paid any attention to 8.♖b1 if it were not for Schandorff recommending it in his repertoire book. White's rook takes aim at the b5-pawn. The safer answer is:

8...♕b6 9.axb5 cxb5 10.b3 ♗xc3 11.♗xc3 cxb3 12.♕xb3 b4 13.d5 ♘f6 14.♕a4+ (Scherbakov's suggestion. Schandorff gives 14.♗d4?! ♕b7 15.♗xf6 gxf6 16.♗c4, when Black is not forced to castle. Instead 16... ♘d7 17.0-0 ♘b6 18.♗b5+ ♗d7 19.♗xd7+ ♕xd7 20.♖bd1 exd5 21.♖d4 ♖c8 clearly favours him.) 14...♘bd7 (14...♗d7 15.♕a1 ♘xd5 16.♗xg7∞) 15.♗d4 ♕d6 16.dxe6 ♕xe6 17.♖xb4 – White regained the pawn with balanced play.

I propose to show some nerve and cling to the extra pawn:

8...♗d7! 9.♘e5 ♘f6 10.♕f3 ♖a7 11.♗e2 0-0 12.0-0 ♗e8

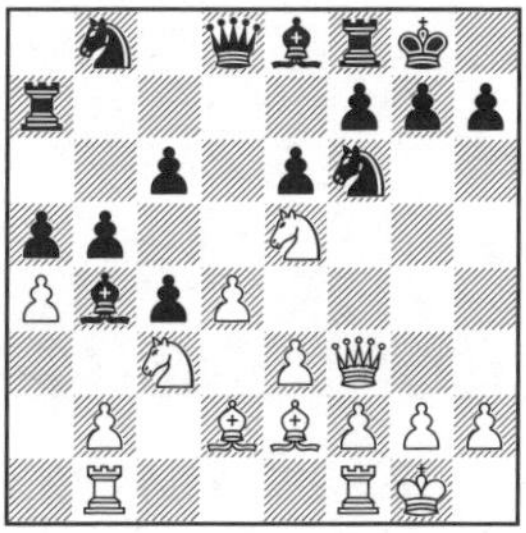

Black's queenside offensive looks more tangible than anything White could oppose on the other wing. For instance:

13.♖fd1 ♗d6 14.e4 b4 15.♘a2 c5 16.♘xc4 ♗e7∓. Obviously White should catch the chance that Black cannot take on d4, and open the d2-bishop:

13.e4! ♖b7

Threatening d4. I have found 13...♘fd7!? 14.♘xd7 ♖xd7 15.♕g3 ♖xd4 16.♗h6 ♕f6 17.♗f4 to be only equal – 17...♘d7 18.♗g5 ♕g6 19.axb5 cxb5 20.♗e3 ♕xg3

21.hxg3 ♖d6 22.♘xb5 ♖c6 23.♖fc1 ♘e5 24.♘d4=.

After the rook move White can hardly generate serious threats:

14.♖fd1 ♕xd4 15.♕g3 ♘xe4 16.♘xe4 ♕xe4 17.♗xb4 axb4 18.♗f3 ♕f5 19.axb5 c3∓ or:

14.♗g5 h6 15.♗e3 ♘fd7 16.♘xd7 ♘xd7 17.♕g3 ♔h8 18.♗f3 ♘b6 19.axb5 cxb5 20.♕h3 f6∓.

8...♗xc3 9.♗xc3

9.bxc3 cxb5 10.♘e5 ♘f6 11.♕b1 with a pleasant choice:

11...♕d5 12.♗e2 ♘e4 13.♗f3 f5 blocks the centre, keeping a healthy extra pawn.

11...♗a6 is more flexible, although I prefer to avoid this move if I have an alternative. Black is better following 12.♗e2 0-0 13.0-0 ♘fd7.

9...cxb5 10.b3

10.d5?! ♘f6 11.dxe6 ♕xd1+ 12.♔xd1 ♘c6! assures Black of a strong attack.

10...♗b7 11.bxc4

You'll rarely meet 11.d5 ♘f6 12.bxc4 b4 13.♗xf6 ♕xf6 14.♕a4+ ♘d7 15.♘d4.

It was popular in the 80ies, until Black discovered that 15...♔e7 16.d6+ ♔xd6 17.♖d1 ♔c7 or 17...♘c5 was playable. Lately Black has found an even better and far less stressing defence:

15...♕e7! 16.♕b5 ♖b8. As simple as that! Now Black castles and the tables turn abruptly:

17.♕xa5

Nobody has played 17.♗e2 0-0 18.0-0, but that may be the best way to bail out – 18...♗xd5 19.♕xa5 ♗e4 20.f3 e5 21.fxe4 exd4 22.♕a7 dxe3 23.♖ad1 ♖fd8 24.c5 ♖bc8 25.♕b7 ♖xc5 26.♕xb4, struggling for the draw.

17.♖xa5 ♗xd5 18.♕a4 is hopeless due to 18...♗e4 19.f3 e5.

17...0-0 18.♖b1 exd5 19.♕xb4 ♕e4 20.♖d1

20.♘b5 ♗a6 21.cxd5 ♕g6 22.h4 ♖b6 23.h5 ♕c2 24.♖h4 ♗xb5 25.♗xb5 ♖fb8 26.♖c4 ♖xb5 27.♖xc2 ♖xb4 and Black is a piece up, Palliser-Haria, Hull 2019.

20...♘f6

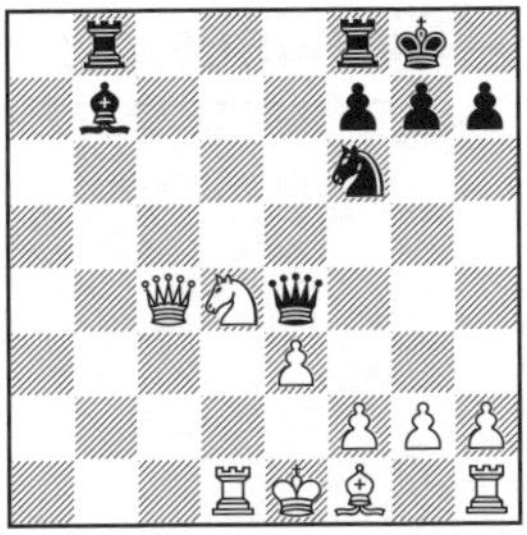

White has never survived from here in correspondence games.

11...b4 12.♗b2 ♘f6

We have reached the main tabiya of the Noteboom System. It is the subject of Chapter 2.

Chapter 1. The Noteboom System – Sidelines

Annotated Games

1. Kiril Georgiev – Banusz
Plovdiv 27.03.2012

1.d4 d5 2.♘f3 ♘f6 3.c4 c6 4.♘c3 dxc4 5.a4 e6 6.e4 ♗b4 7.♗g5

7...♗xc3+!

7...♕a5 8.♗d2 c5 9.♗xc4 cxd4 10.♘xd4 looks close to equal, but in practice Black faces unexpected problems:
10...0-0

10...♕c5!? 11.♗b5+ ♗d7 12.♘b3 ♕c7 13.0-0 0-0 might be equal.

11.♘c2 ♘c6 12.♘xb4 ♕xb4 13.b3 ♖d8 14.0-0 ♕e7 15.♕c2!?

Nacamura beat Giri with 15.♖e1, when correct is 15...b6!=.

15...b6 16.♖fd1 ♗b7 17.f3 ♕c5+ 18.♔h1 ♕f2 19.♕a2 ♘e5 20.♗f1 ♘d3 and both correspondence games ended in a draw. Anyway, the text is a smoother equaliser.

8.bxc3 ♕a5 9.e5 ♘e4 10.♗d2

10.♖c1 allows 10...b5 11.♕c2 ♘xg5 12.♘xg5 ♘d7!? with complications where White is struggling to keep the balance.

12...♕xa4 13.♕xa4 bxa4 14.♗xc4 ♘d7 15.♘e4 ♔e7 16.0-0 a5=.

13.♘e4 0-0 14.♘g5 g6 15.axb5 cxb5 16.h4 h6

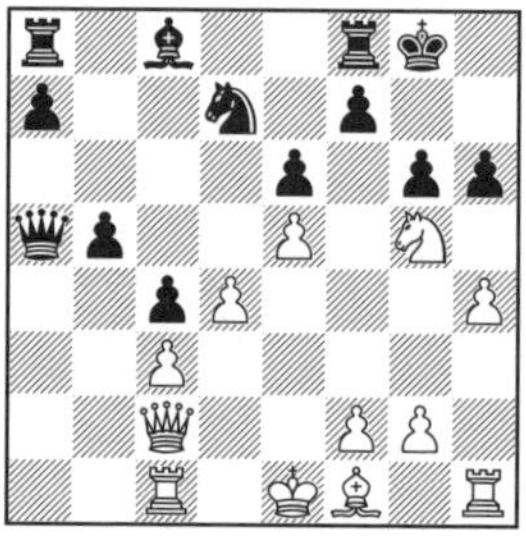

17.h5

17.♘e4 ♗b7 18.♘d6 ♗c6 19.h5 g5 looks safe enough for Black.

17...hxg5 18.hxg6. Here Black should choose between the safer

18...♘xe5= and 18...f5 19.♕d1 g4 20.♕d2 f4=.

10...c5!

Forcing an exchange of queens. 10...♕d5?! gives White an attack after 11.♕c2 or 11.♗e3!?.

11.♗xc4 ♘xd2!

11...cxd4 12.cxd4 ♘xd2 is less precise as White can keep the queens with 13.♘xd2!.

12.♕xd2 cxd4 13.cxd4

13...♘c6!=

13...♕xd2+ only helps White's development, although White still does not have much after 14.♔xd2 ♘c6 15.♖hc1 ♔e7 16.♖ab1 ♖b8 17.♔e3 f6 18.exf6+ gxf6, and Ipatov-Smeets, Wijk aan Zee 2013, was eventually drawn.

14.d5

14.♗b5 ♗d7 15.♕xa5

15.♗xc6 ♕xd2+ 16.♘xd2 ♗xc6 17.♘c4 0-0 18.f3 ♗xa4=, Ipatov-Thorhallsson, Tromsoe 2014.

15...♘xa5 16.♔e2 ♖c8 (16...♖d8) 17.♖hd1 ♔e7 18.d5 ♖hd8 19.d6+ ♔e8 20.♖ac1 ♘b3 21.♗xd7+ ♔xd7 22.♖b1 ♖c3 occurred in Ikonnikov-Smeets, Dieren 2012. Although White won, play is double edged, e.g.23.♘g5!? ♖dc8.

14...exd5 15.♗xd5

15.♕xa5 ♘xa5 16.♗xd5 ♔e7 17.♖c1 ♗d7 is even more pleasant for Black. Fier-Motylev, Moscow 2011, concluded with 18.♘d4 ♖ac8 19.♔e2 ♖hd8 20.♔e3 g6 21.f4 b6 22.♖xc8 ♖xc8 23.♘b5 ♖c5 24.♔d4 ♗xb5 25.axb5 ♖xb5 26.♖c1 ½-½.

15...♕xd2+

15...♕a6!? is more ambitious. Black won both computer games after 16.♗xc6+ bxc6 17.♕b4 ♕b6 18.♖ab1 ♕xb4 19.♖xb4 ♗a6, using the power of his long-range pieces.

16.♔xd2

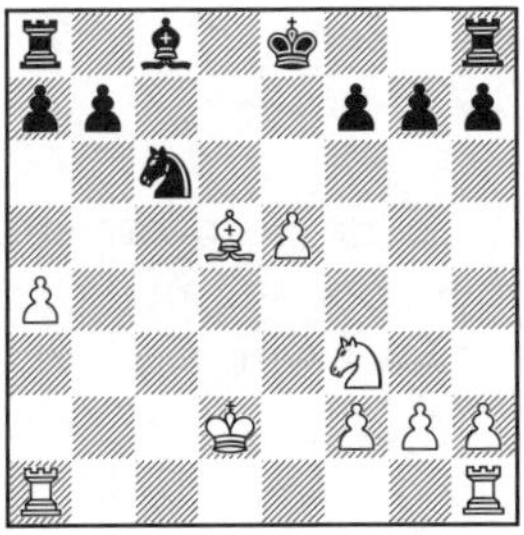

16...♗d7

Computers prefer 16...♗e6 17.♗xc6+ bxc6 18.♘d4 ♗d5= and J. Geller drew with 16...♗f5, but the text is more solid. ♗alck avoids any weaknesses in his pawn structure. Even such a famous endgame technician as Georgiev fails to pose any problems.

17.♔e3 ♔e7 18.♖hb1 ♖ab8 19.a5 ♖hc8 20.♖a3 h6 21.h3

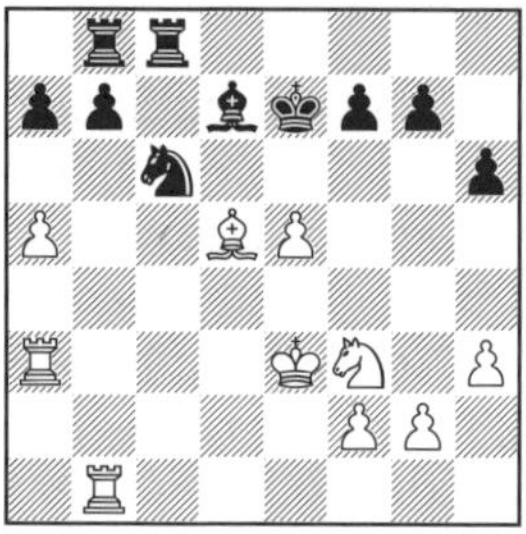

21...f6?!

It was unnecessary to exchange the weak pawn. Now White takes the initiative thanks to his more active rooks. A natural follow up was 21... b5! 22.axb6 ♖xb6=.

22.exf6+ ♔xf6 23.♘d2 ♗f5 24.♖b5 ♖e8+ 25.♘e4+ ♗xe4 26.♗xe4 ♖e5 27.♖xe5 ♘xe5 28.♖c3 ♘f7 29.f4

Now Black has to overcome some difficulties, but the material is insufficient for a win.

29...♘d6 30.♗d5 g5 31.♔f3 ♖e8 32.a6 ♘b5 33.♖c4 bxa6 34.♖c6+ ♔g7 35.♖xa6 ♖f8 36.g3 gxf4 37.gxf4 ♖f6 38.♖a1 a6 39.♗c4 ♖c6 40.♗d3 ♘d4+ 41.♔g4 ♖d6 42.♖a3 ♖f6 43.♖a5 ♖d6 44.♗xa6 ♖g6+ 45.♔h4 ♘e6 46.f5 ♖g5 47.♗e2 ♘d4 48.♗g4 ♔f6 49.♖a6+ ♔g7 50.f6+ ♔g6 51.f7+ ♔xf7 52.♖xh6 ♘f5+ 53.♔xg5 ♘xh6 54.♔xh6 ♔g8 ½-½

---

2. Guerreiro – Tropf
ICCF, 15.12.2017

1.d4 d5 2.c4 c6 3.♘c3 dxc4 4.e4 b5 5.♘f3 ♘f6 6.♕c2 e6 7.♗e2 ♗b7 8.0-0 ♗e7 9.e5 ♘d5 10.♘e4 h6

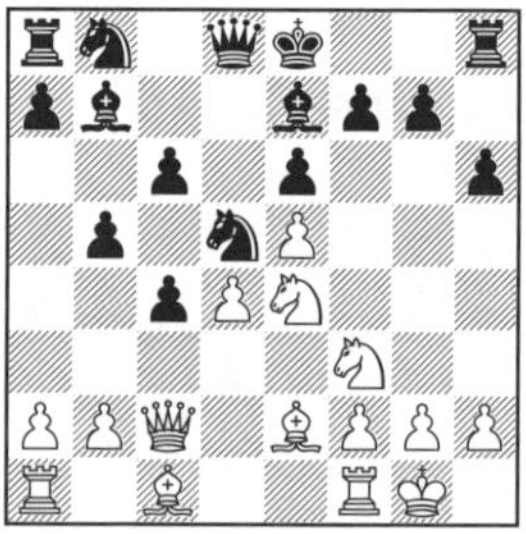

11.b3

White cannot decide the game only on the kingside, mostly because the c4-pawn deprives his bishop of the d3-square. Moreover that Black has not committed his king with a short castle yet, so White lacks a target. For instance, 11.♘g3 ♘d7 12.♘h5 could be met by 12...♔f8, followed by ...c5, or 12...g5 13.a4 a6 14.♗d2 ♕b6, leaving the option of ...0-0-0 open. If White awaits castling, Black can simply attack the centre – 11.♗d2 ♘d7 12.♖fe1 c5, although even 12...0-0 is fine. The point is that 13.♕c1 c5 14.dxc5 ♘xc5 15.♘xc5 ♗xc5 16.♗xh6 stumbles into 16... f6! 17.exf6 (17.♗d2 ♕b6 18.♖f1 fxe5)

17...gxh6. Therefore, b3 is without alternatives.

11...cxb3 12.axb3 a5

This is the favourite set-up of the engines. Now that ...c5 seems a mirage, Black enables ...b4, ...♗a6 to get rid of the bad bishop. At the same time the queen's knight goes to d7, to be closer to the kingside. Besides, 12...♘a6 is also possible – the knight replaces the c4-pawn to watch out for ♗d3. After 13.♗b2 ♘ab4 14.♕d2 0-0 15.♖fc1 a5 16.♘c5 ♕c7 White found enough counterplay using the c5-square – 17.♕d1 ♖fd8 18.♘d2 ♘f4 19.♘de4 ♘a6∓. Black returns the pawn to remain with the better bishop. 20.♘xb7 ♕xb7 21.♖xa5 ♘b4 22.♖xa8 ♘xe2+ 23.♕xe2 ♖xa8 24.♕g4 ♘d5 25.♖d1 ♕c7 26.g3 ♖a2 27.♗c1 ♔f8 28.♕f3 ♕a5 29.♗d2 ♕a3 30.♗c1 ♕a7 31.h4 ½-½, Babychuk-Tkachenko, ICCF 2016.

13.♗d2 ♘d7

It is pointless to play 13...♕b6 as 14.♘d6+ ♗xd6 15.exd6 ♕d8 16.♘e5 gives White enough threats – 16...♕xd6 17.♖xa5 ♖xa5 18.♗xa5 ♘d7 19.♘xd7 ♔xd7 20.♗f3 ♖a8 21.♗d2=.

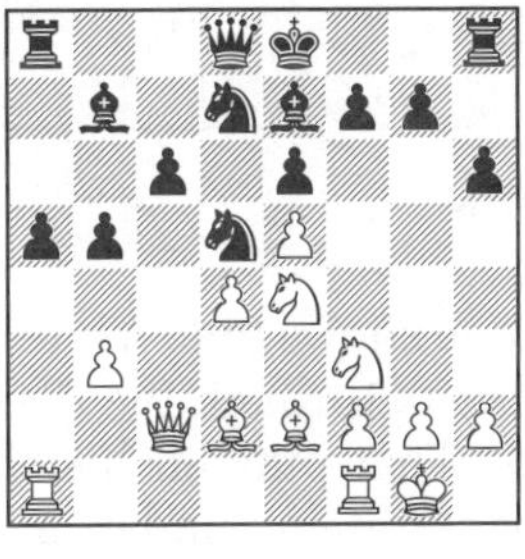

14.♖fe1

White anticipates a possible ...f5. 14.h4 0-0 15.♕c1 could be neutralised with 15...f5 16.exf6 ♘5xf6 17.♘xf6+ ♖xf6. If White built a battery along the b1-h7 diagonal, e.g. 18.♗c3 ♗d6 19.♕e3 ♗f4 20.♕e4 ♕c7 21.♗d3, the simple 21...♘f8∓ would protect h7.
The same defence works against 14.♘c5 ♗xc5 15.dxc5 b4 16.♖fc1 ♕e7 17.♕c4 0-0 18.♗d1 ♖fd8 19.♕g4 – 19...f5!∓.

14...b4

Black faced an important choice. 14...0-0 looked most natural, but how to meet 15.♕c1 with the unequivocal plan to take on h6?

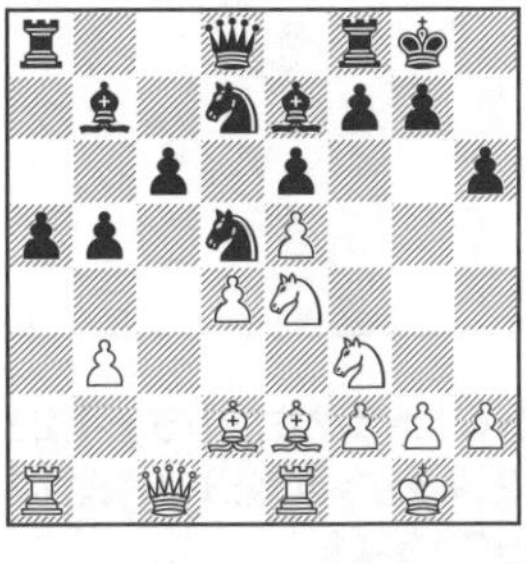

15...♗b4?! does not solve the problem owing to 16.♘d6 ♗xd6 17.exd6 ♘7f6 18.♗xh6 with an attack.

We could recall the rule that attack is the best defence and try: 15...c5 16.dxc5 (16.♗xh6? ♖c8) 16...♕c7 17.♗xb5 (17.♗xh6 ♘xc5) 17...♘xc5 18.♘xc5 ♗xc5 19.♗xh6! f6, but this looks equal – 20.♖a4! ♖ac8 21.♖g4 ♗xf2+ 22.♔f1 ♘e3+ 23.♗xe3 ♕xc1 24.♖xc1 ♗xe3. Apparently it is early for ...0-0, so Black should devise some active idea on the queenside.

Another option was 14...♕c7 15.♕c1 a4 16.bxa4 ♖xa4 17.♖xa4 bxa4 18.♕c2 a3 19.♘d6+ ♗xd6 20.exd6 ♕xd6 21.♕b3 ♗a8, when 22.♘e5 0-0 23.♕g3 ♘xe5 24.dxe5 ♕c7 25.♗xh6 f5 is also equal.

In many variation the b5-pawn is hanging, so Black decides to protect it first. However, I do not believe he could win with that backward extra pawn on a5.

15.♗c4 0-0 16.♖ad1 c5 17.♕c1 a4 18.bxa4 ♖xa4

19.♗xh6 ♖a3 20.♗b5 c4 21.♗xd7 ♘c3 22.♘xc3 ♖xc3 23.♕f4 ♕xd7 24.♗xg7 ½-½

24.♕g4 g6 25.♘g5 or 25.d5 ♗xd5 26.♘g5 ♖a8 27.♕h4 f5 is also a draw.

---

3. Rogos – Oreopoulos
ICCF 2014

1.d4 d5 2.c4 c6 3.♘f3 e6 4.♘c3 dxc4 5.a4 ♗b4 6.e4 b5 7.♕c2 ♘f6 8.♗e2 ♗b7 9.0-0 a6 10.♗g5 h6 11.♗h4 ♘bd7 12.e5 g5 13.♗g3 ♘d5 14.♘e4 g4 15.♘h4 h5

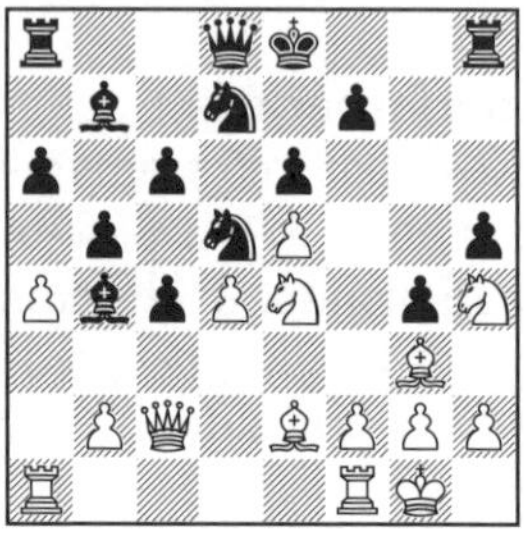

The pawn structure reminds me of the Moscow Variation. 16.♘g6? is senseless in view of 16...♖g8 17.♘f4 h4, so White's knight is doomed to stay at the rim. Another try is to open the queenside with:
16.b3 c3 17.♗c4!?, but Black simply ignores the bishop 17...♕b6! 18.♖fd1 a5, threatening to take on c4.
Thus Rogos decides to postpone the important decisions.

16.♖fe1 ♕b6 17.♖ed1 0-0-0 18.b3 c3 19.♗c4

19...♔b8

This game shows that White is unable to break through the queenside fortress. That puts all his sluggish opening strategy under a strong doubt. The desperate attempt to open the f-file is also unsuccessful.

20.♘g5 ♖df8 21.♗xd5 cxd5 22.axb5 ♕xb5 23.f4 ♖hg8 24.♘h7 ♖e8 25.f5

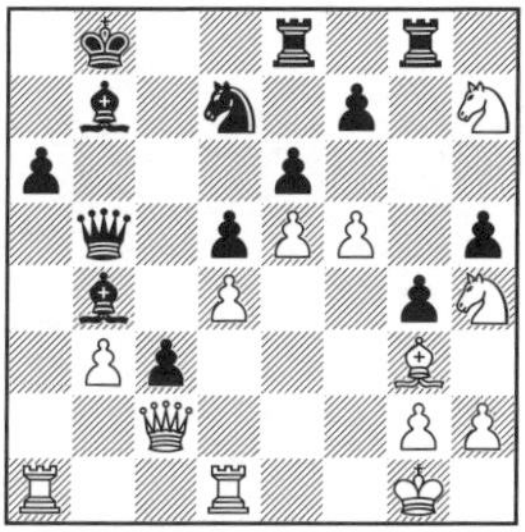

25...♕b6

It turns out that 26.fxe6 ♖xe6 27.♘f5 ♔a7 28.♔h1 f6 is lost for White. His heavy pieces are very passive and the d4-pawn is weak.

26.♔h1 ♔a7 27.♖dc1 ♖g7 28.♘f6 ♘xf6 29.exf6 ♖gg8 30.♗e5 exf5 31.♕xf5 ♖e6 32.♕xh5

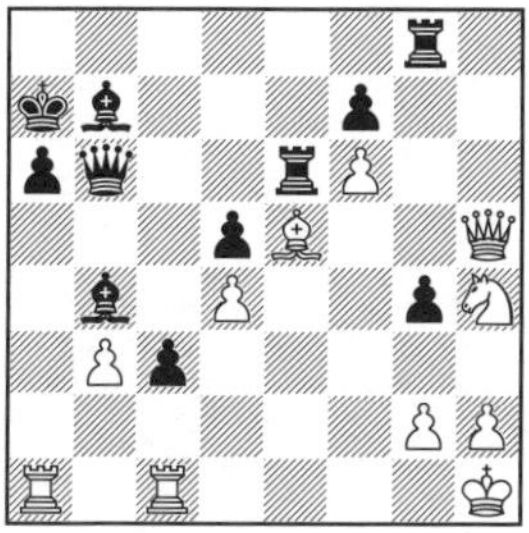

32...♖xf6! 33.♕h7

Or 33.♗xf6 ♕xf6 34.♖f1 ♕xd4. The central pawns, supported by a bishop pair, are unstoppable.

33...♖c8 34.♗xf6 ♕xf6 35.♖f1 ♕xd4 36.♖xf7 ♕b6 37.♕c2 ♕e6 0-1

Chapter 2. The Noteboom System – Main Line

Main Ideas

In this chapter we deal with the main line of the Noteboom System: **1.d4 d5 2.c4 e6 3.♘f3 c6 4.♘c3 dxc4 5.a4 ♗b4 6.e3 b5 7.♗d2 a5 8.axb5 ♗xc3 9.♗xc3 cxb5 10.b3 ♗b7 11.bxc4 b4 12.♗b2 ♘f6**

At this point White should decide what pawn structure he would like to reach. His decision would imply different plans and different targets for attack.

For instance, 13.c5 0-0 14.♗b5 assumes that White will play in the centre, while ♗d3+e3-e4 would designate the black king as the main aim. White's mediocre results in both plans have called for a new approach lately – the modern trend is to postpone the decision, adapting it to Black's set-up, especially the placement of his king's rook.

At first White tried the most straightforward idea:

13.♗d3 ♘bd7 14.0-0 0-0 15.♕c2 ♕c7 16.e4

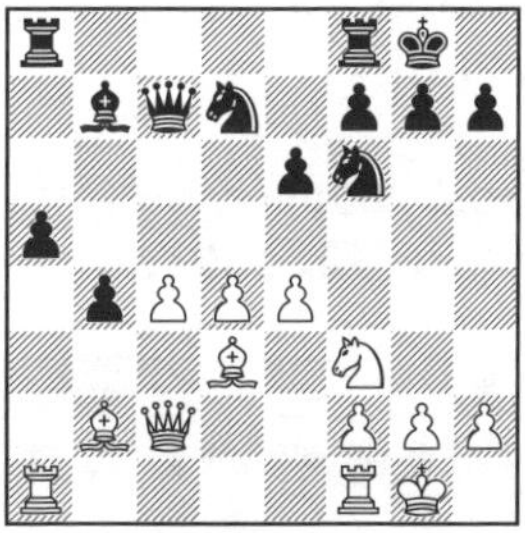

It turned out that **16...e5!!** effectively stops White's attack. This positional sacrifice is the first thing you should learn about the Noteboom! It is the foundation of all the system. The "tiny" detail which tips the balance in Black's favour is that the queen is misplaced on c2. After 17.d5 ♖fe8 it hinders the regrouping ♘d2+♗d3-c2-a4.

Logically, first players turned to another way of preparing e3-e4: **15.♖e1**.

Now we should not ignore e4 anymore. Both **15...♗e4** and 15...♘e4 lead to similar positions since in the latter case White could trade bishops in other ways after c4-c5. The critical position arises after 16.♗xe4 ♘xe4 17.♕c2 f5 18.c5

I consider the plans in this pawn structure later in this section. See also **Game 5** Sakaev-Kharlov, Tomsk 2001.

The most dangerous move has proved to be **15.♘d2!?**.

Have in mind that the real threat is not f2-f4. We can even provoke it with 15...♕c7. For simplicity, I will assume that Black answers **15...h6**, as it is always a useful move in the Noteboom. At the same time it denies 16.f4 owing to 16...♘c5. Instead White follows his waiting strategy with **16.♗c2**, heading for a4. After **16...♕c7** the following important position arises:

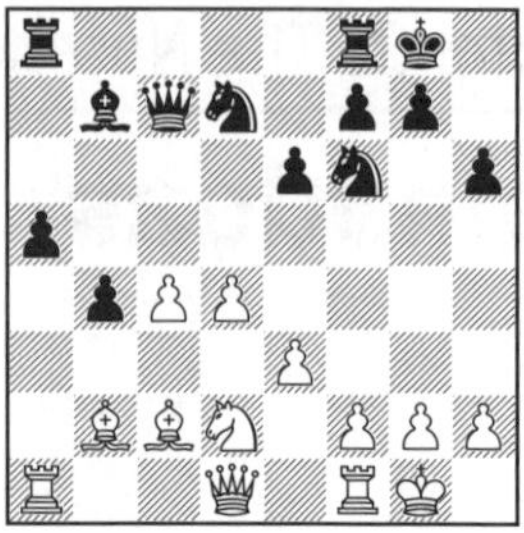

It has occurred in only two OTB encounters, but I have seen hundreds of correspondence and computer games. It is so flexible, and the pawn centre so fluid, that it is impossible to encompass all the variations which could ensue from it. Instead I will confine myself to commenting on the main pawn structures:

Pawn structure with c4-c5

The main danger for Black is the advance d4-d5 – with, or without the help of a pawn on e4!

Lomineishvili-Melnikova
Dresden 2004

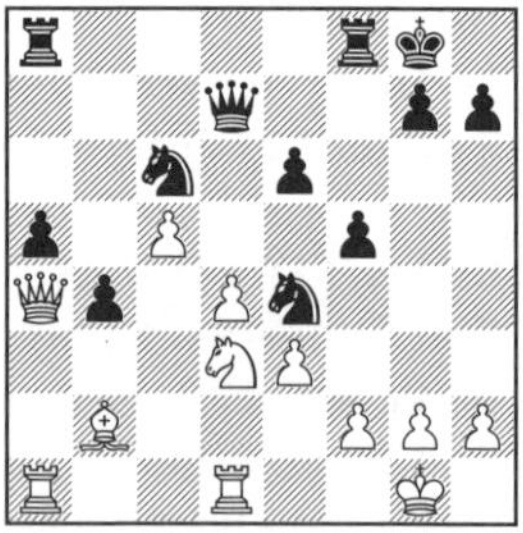

White should have played 21.d5! exd5 22.♘f4±.

The d5-square should be under

constant surveillance, or even better, firmly blocked. In such events our passers commonly find somehow their way to conversion:

Analysis

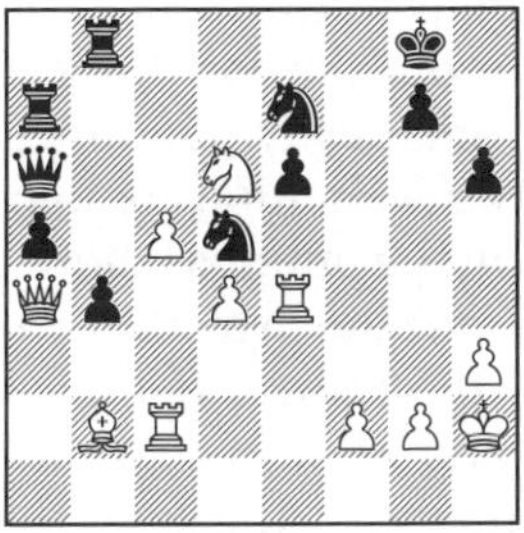

27...♕c6!. The pawns do not count here as Black's queenside passers decide the game.

When White thrusts c4-c5, he usually trades light-squared bishop through e4 or b5, and queens through a4. The following diagram represents the general case of a queenless middlegame:

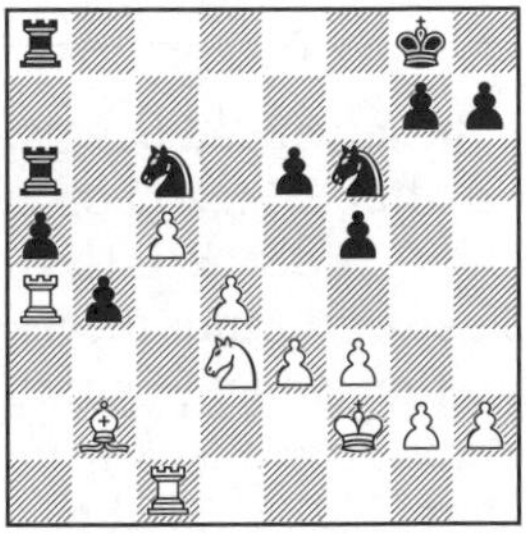

Chances are even. Black has counterplay against the d4-pawn. Accordingly, his best set-up on the kingside is with g5 (to undermine the base of the pawn chain with ...f5-f4). The rooks could be activated with ♖d8+♖d7 or ♖d8+♖b8, anticipating the opening of the centre. See **Game 5** Sakaev-Kharlov. Note that until White keeps his knight, ...e5 is generally not a very good idea unless it is winning, as in the following example:

Analysis

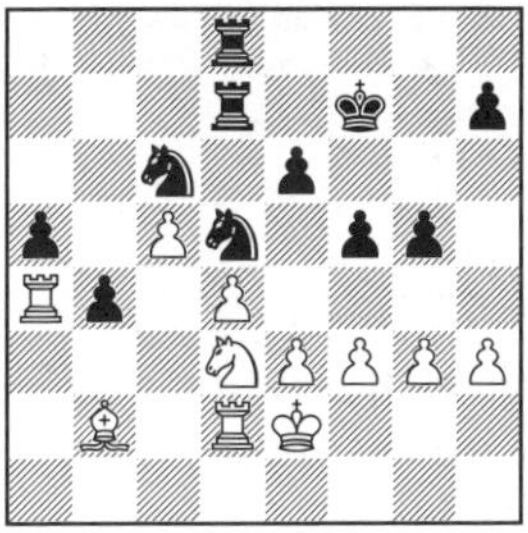

34...e5!–+.

If White trades his knight, the plans of both sides change significantly. White's king gets a free path to c4. If it arrives there, the effect on the centre would be devastating – nothing would stop e4 and d5. In such piece configuration, we must quickly create concrete threats in the centre with ...e5!

Analysis

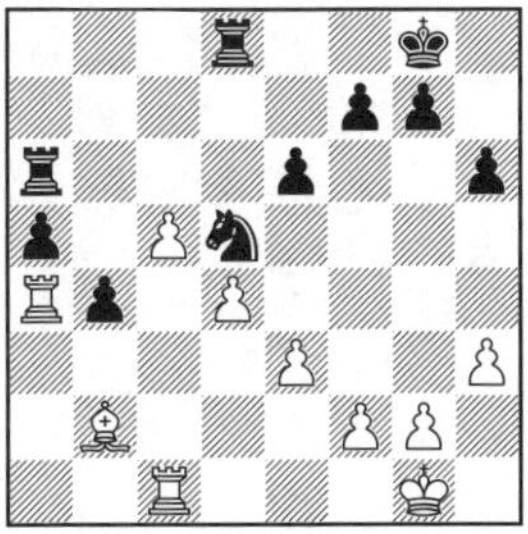

Do not waste time, play 24...e5!=

now or on the next turn! If White stays, we could attack the d4-pawn:

Serradimigni-Oreopoulos
ICCF 2012

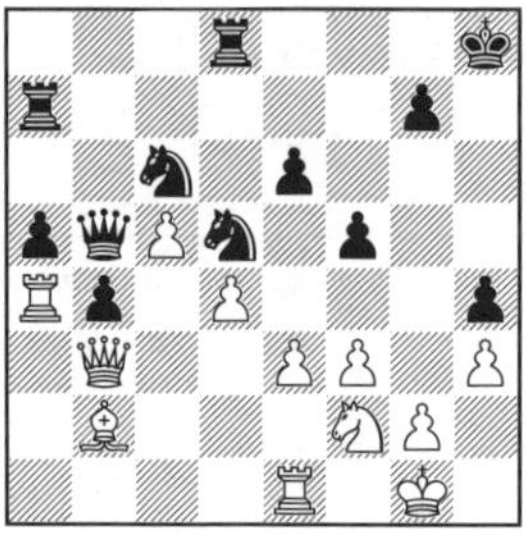

Here White has weakened his pawn chain with the move f3, so 37...f4!∓ destroys its base.

A golden rule in the Noteboom is: exchanges favour Black.

That is a natural effect of White's space advantage.
Now let's pay attention to complex positions with queens. The most obvious reason behind 15.♘d2 is to plant a knight on d6. Yet it turns out that it is totally harmless from there.

Analysis

Black's chances are at least equal here. We do not risk much when the b2-bishop is securely blocked. At the same time we have a clear objective to push ...a4. A possible follow up is 24.g3 ♕d7 25.f4 ♘ge7 26.♕g4 g6 27.♕h4 h5.
You should be aware that even if our pawns cross the forth line, it does not automatically guarantee us an edge. The evaluation commonly depends on the options before the b2-bishop and the availability of open files in the centre. If the centre is closed and a1 is free so the bishop can remain on the long diagonal, the position remains unclear.

Analysis

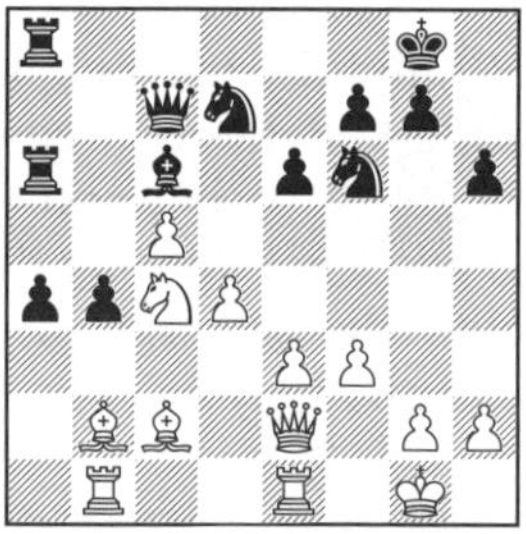

Despite the advanced pawns, play is balanced after 20...♗b5 or 20...♖b8 or even 20...♖d8. White's central pawns keep our minor pieces at bay. Imagine the same position without ♗c2 and ♗c6. Black would have been clearly better. That evaluation would have been even more valid if we removed a pair of knights, for instance, ♘c4 and ♘d7.

Finally, here are two **tactical motifs** which are typical for this pawn structure:

Analysis

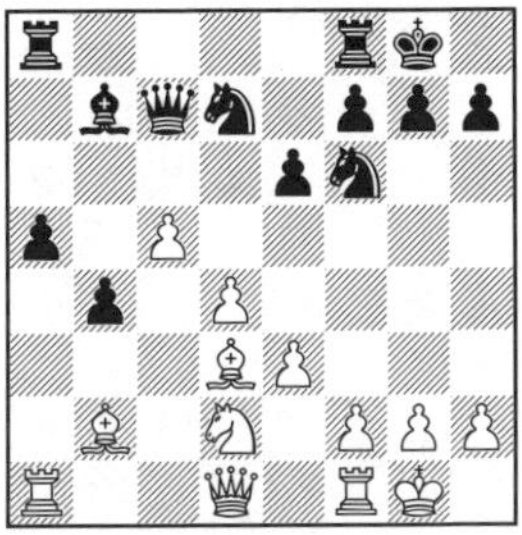

16...a4! 17.♖xa4?? ♕c6.
This double hit explains why in so many games White plays f3. But it has other drawbacks, notably the weakness of the g1-a7 diagonal.

Analysis

20...e5 is a good way to open a second front since the opponent lacks d4-d5.

Analysis

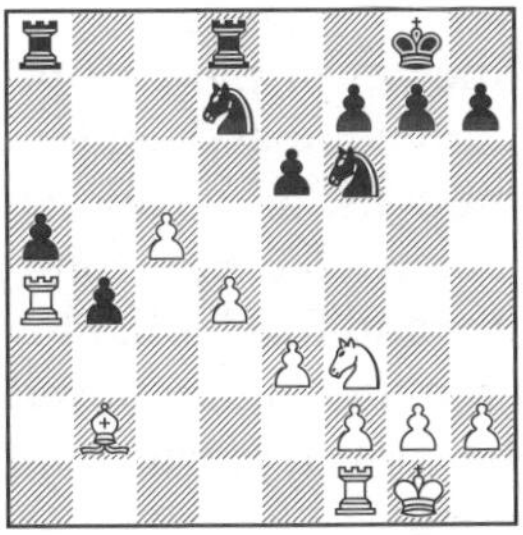

In an endgame Black's passed pawns gain in strength and are commonly stronger than a piece:
20...♘e4! and Black meets almost any move by ...♘dxc5!.

Pawn structure with e4, d5, c4

This pawn configuration could be dangerous for us when it arises after 15.♘d2, followed by ♗c2. In that event we should not play ...e5 too early, especially while the rook is still on f1. The reason is that White would easily open the f-file. That would give him an initiative, even at the cost of a pawn:

Analysis

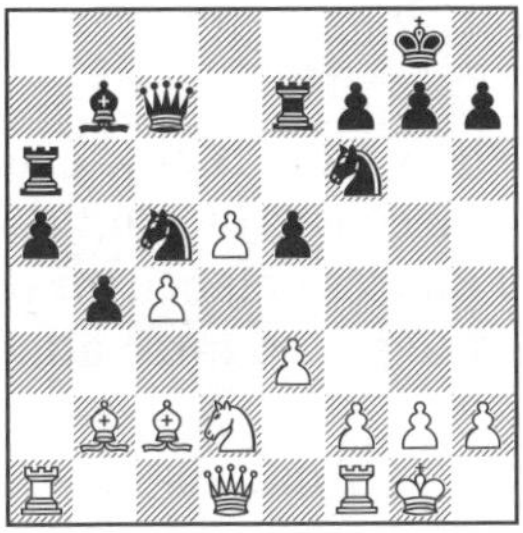

22.f4! exf4 23.♖xf4! ♖xe3 24.♕f1↑.

Note that the early ...e5-thrust is recommended by many commentators and Scherbakov, and it is often seen in practice. My opinion is that we should refrain from it, in favour of ...♖a6, ...♖fc8, seeking a way to advance our a-pawn. Only then could we think of ...e5.

Do not thrust ...e5 while the white rook is still on f1!

Of course if White advances e3-e4, we stop it by ...e5. Then White will try to break through with f4:

Analysis

I prefer to treat this position dynamically, taking on f4 instead of trying to passively hold the blockade with ...♘c5, ...♘fd7, ...f6: 21...exf4! 22.e5 ♘xd5!∓.

I can show you many examples, when a piece sacrifice on d5 is the point of Black's defence (or perhaps it is right to say counter-attack):

Analysis

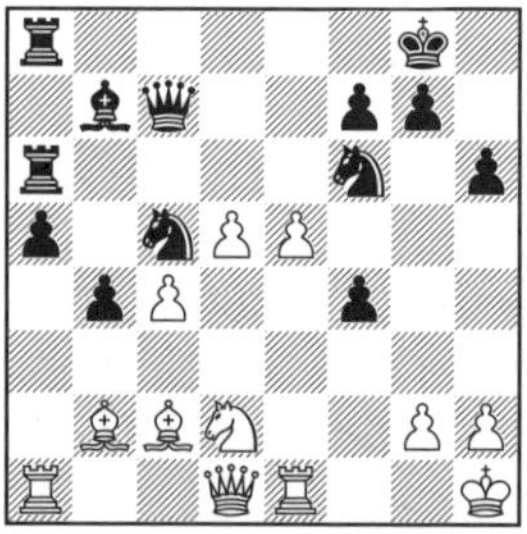

23...♘xd5! 24.cxd5 ♗xd5, and White should seek counterplay to stay in the game – 25.♘e4 ♘xe4 26.♗xe4 ♗xe4 27.♖xe4 ♖d8 28.♕e2 ♖c6 29.e6!=.

Analysis

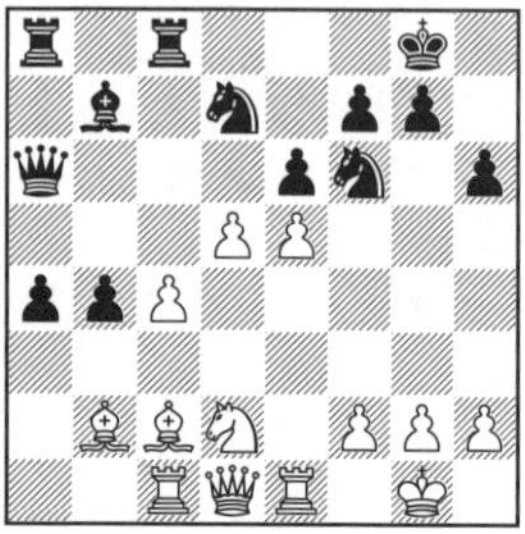

Here the sacrifice on d5 is less obvious, but not less effective:
21...♘xd5! 22.cxd5 ♗xd5 23.♖e3 a3 24.♗d4 ♘f8=∞.
In such positions only computers are able to keep White in the game.

Daus-Filipchenko
ICCF 2015

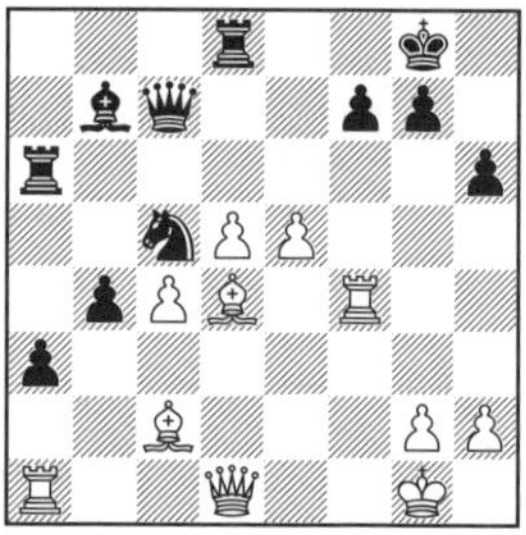

27...♗xd5!=∞ 28.cxd5 ♖xd5 29.♕f3 ♘e6 30.♕xd5 ♘xf4 31.♕e4 ♖c6 32.♗b3 ½-½.

Sometimes even pawns on b3 and a4 cannot combat White's forces. That happens in positions where White's pieces have a strong grip on the centre and Black's light-squared bishop remains unemployed on b7. Then the central pawns tend to roll unimpeded:

Pierzak-Oreopoulos
ICCF 2018

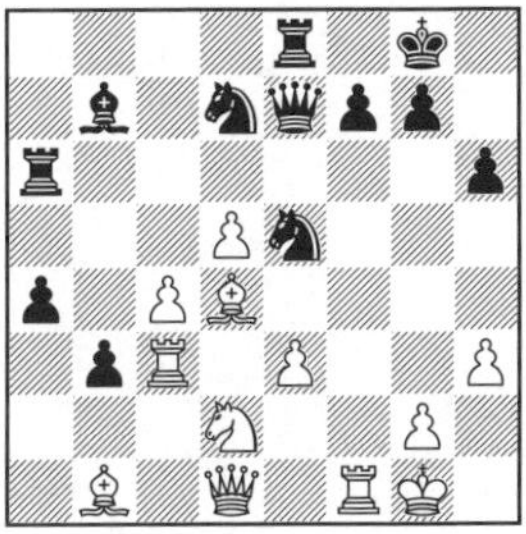

29.♘f3 ♖f6 30.♘xe5 ♘xe5 31.♖xf6 ♕xf6 32.e4, and Black cannot stop c4-c5±.

Typical tactical motifs

Sacrificing material to destroy the enemy centre is very common in the Noteboom. We often see White hiding behind the central pawns, while his pieces are busy blockading the flank. That creates ground for various destructive blows:

Analysis

White's king is exposed in the centre. Both 28...♖xd4!= and 28...♘c6! 29.c5 ♕b4 30.♕xc6 ♕d2+ 31.♗e2 ♕xb2 32.♕xe6+ ♔h8 33.♕g6! ♘xf4+ 34.gxf4 ♖xd4= do the job.

Kalashnikov-Agaltsov
ICCF 2017

20...a4!∞.

Kurbasov-Gromov
ICCF 2012

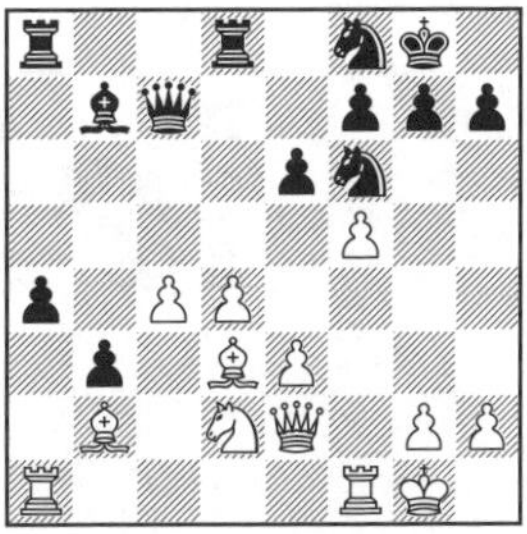

20...e5! 21.dxe5 ♘6d7∞.

Conclusion

The modern Noteboom is one of the most destructive Black's weapons against 1.d4. In OTB games draws are really scarce. At highest level practically nobody allows 4...dxc4 anymore. After 1.d4 d5 2.c4 e6 3.♘f3 c6 strong players try all kind of deviations from the main line Noteboom, such as 4.g3, 4.♘bd2, 4.e3, 4.♕c2, 4.♕b3, even 4.b3!?. I think that is the strongest proof of the soundness of Black's provocative set-up!

Step by Step

1.d4 d5 2.c4 e6 3.♘f3 c6 4.♘c3 dxc4 5.a4 ♗b4 6.e3 b5 7.♗d2 a5 8.axb5 ♗xc3 9.♗xc3 cxb5 10.b3 ♗b7 11.bxc4 b4 12.♗b2 ♘f6

13.♗d3

13.c5 0-0 14.♗b5 is a rare but important line. Instead of attacking the kingside White aims to block the enemy passed pawns on the light squares and eventually push d5.

a) 14...♗c6 15.♗a4

I have also met 15.♕a4 ♕d5 16.0-0 ♗xb5 17.♕xb5 ♘c6 18.♘d2 ♖fb8 19.♕a4, when both 19...e5 and 19...♘e4 offer Black a comfortable game.

15...♗xa4 (or 15...♕c8 16.♘e5 ♗xa4) 16.♕xa4

The first thing we should do is to get a clear notion of which pieces we should trade, and most importantly, to evaluate the chances after a possible exchange of queens.

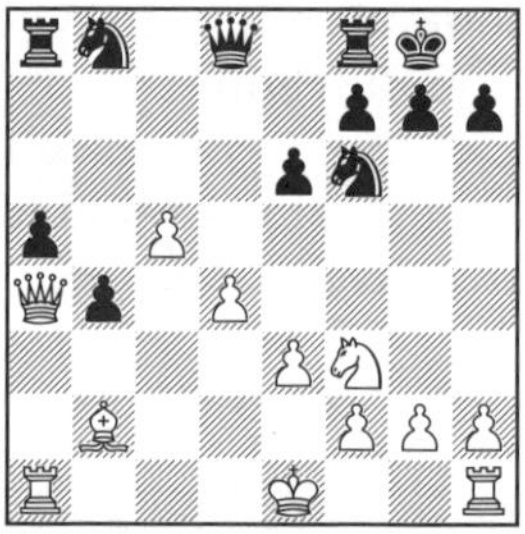

A queenless middlegame could arise in many Noteboom lines (for instance, in line B), so we must be familiar with it. I discuss it in the "Main Ideas" section. My conclusion is that it is comfortable for Black, provided that he mounts pressure against d4 quickly. Perhaps the best set-up is:

a1) 16...♕c8!? 17.0-0 ♘c6, followed by ...♕a6, ...♘d5. I discuss it in the annotations to **Game 4** Rawlings-Smythe, ICCF 2013.

a2) In practice Black chooses 16...♕d5, which provokes e4. Still, I do not see problems for Black following 17.0-0 ♘c6 18.♖fd1 ♖fc8, but he should avoid weakening his kingside with ...f5:

19.♘e5

19.♘d2 ♘e4 20.♘f1 e5! is a good illustration of my advice. We do not passively block the centre, but attack it, e.g. 21.f3 ♘c3 22.♗xc3 bxc3 23.e4 ♕d8 24.d5 ♘d4 25.c6 ♖ab8↑.

19...♘e8 20.♘xc6 ♖xc6 21.f3

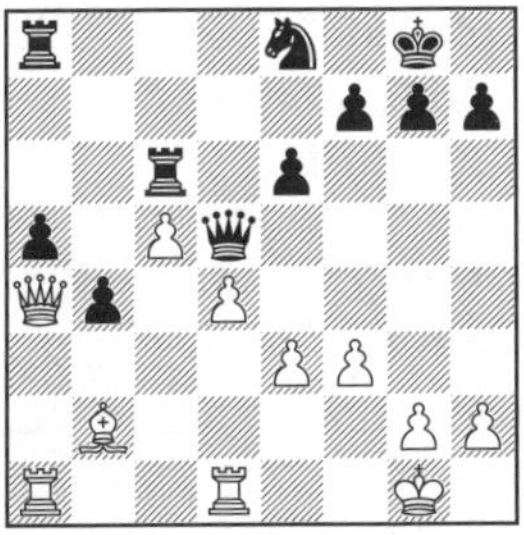

21...♖cc8!

Again, I recommend to refrain from 21...f5. In such unbalanced positions it only pours oil into the fire. Although 22.e4 fxe4 23.fxe4 ♕xe4 24.♖e1 ♕d5 25.♖e5 ♕d7 26.d5 ♖c7 27.d6 ♕xa4 28.♖xa4 ♖c6 29.♖xe6 ♖xc5 30.d7 ♔f7! was a draw in L'Ami-Krasenkow, Hoogeveen 2013, I do not like 29.♖a1! a4 30.♖xe6 a3 31.♗d4 with active pieces.

22.e4 ♕c4 23.♔f2 ♘c7 24.♖ac1 ♕b5 25.♕xb5 ♘xb5 26.d5 exd5 27.exd5 f6. Both sides cleared the obstacles before their passers, but it turns out that this is a draw! The game Nataf-Perry, ICCF 2015, went on:

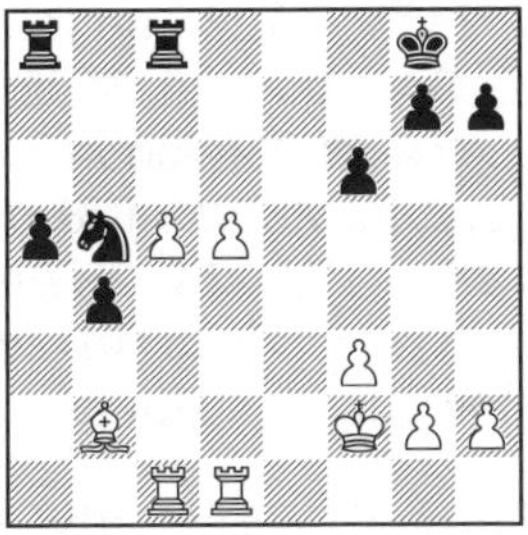

28.c6 ♘d6 29.♗d4 b3 30.♗c5 ♘b5, and both opponents have to sacrifice a piece to stop the pawn marches. The resulting rook endgame is drawn.

b) 14...♕d5!? 15.0-0 ♘c6 does not look consistent at first glance as Black avoids exchanges being cramped in the centre.

However, the battery on the long diagonal pins the f3-knight. Thus Black hampers both active plans of White – the manoeuvre ♘f3-d2-c4 and f3+e4. Besides, he has not renounced on trading bishops.

For instance, 16.♘e1?! would be met by 16...♗a6 17.♗xa6 ♖xa6 18.♕a4 e5∓.

Or 16.♕c2 ♘e7 17.♖fe1 ♖fb8 18.♗a4 ♗c6, when 19.e4 ♗xa4 20.♖xa4 b3 21.♕d3 ♕c6 22.♕c4 is not dangerous – both 22...

♘g6 23.♘d2 ♘f4 and 22...♘xe4 23.♘e5 ♕d5 24.♕xd5 exd5 25.♘d7 ♖d8 26.♘b6 ♖a7 27.♖a3 [27.♖e2 h5 28.♖a3 (28.f3 ♘d6) 28...a4=] 27...♘d2 28.♗c3 ♘c4 29.♖xb3 f6∞ lead to complex double-edged positions.

16.♖e1 ♘e7 17.♕c2 ♖fb8 18.♗a4 h6 19.♗b3 ♕e4 20.♕xe4 ♘xe4 21.♘e5 ♘d2 22.♗a4 ♗d5= occurred in Amico-Gerasimov, ICCF 2018.

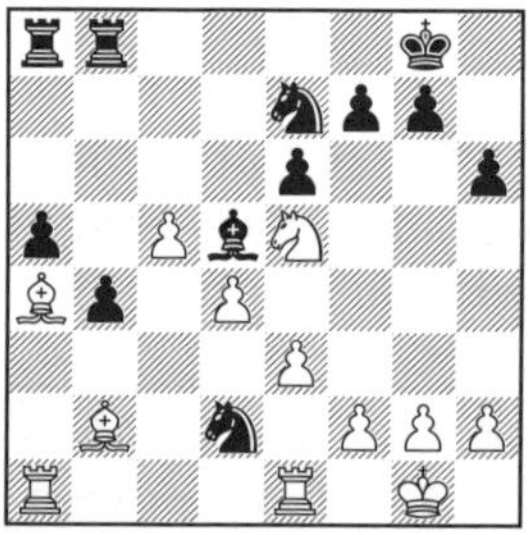

The game went on 23.♗c1 ♘b3 24.♖b1 ♘xc1 25.♖exc1 ♖a7 26.f3 f6 27.♘d7 ♖d8 28.♘b6 ♗c6 29.♗b3 ♔f7 30.♖a1 ♗d5 31.♗d1 f5 32.♔f2 f4! – the typical break I mentioned in the "Main Ideas" – and soon finished in a draw.

The most frequent answer is:

16.♕e2 ♘e7 17.♖fc1

Or 17.♖fe1 ♖fb8 18.♗c4 ♕h5 19.♗b3 ♗c6.

17...♗c6

17...♖fb8 also deserves attention.

Schandorff mentions only 17...♖fc8, which is pointless. Black lost a tempo after 18.♕f1 ♗c6 19.♘e5 ♗xb5 20.♕xb5 ♖cb8, although play remains unclear after 21.♕a4 ♘g6.

18.♗c4 ♕h5 19.♗b5 ♕d5 20.♗a4 ♘e4 21.♘e1 ♗xa4 22.♖xa4 ♘c6, with a comfortable position for Black, Serradimigni-Oreopoulos, ICCF 2012.

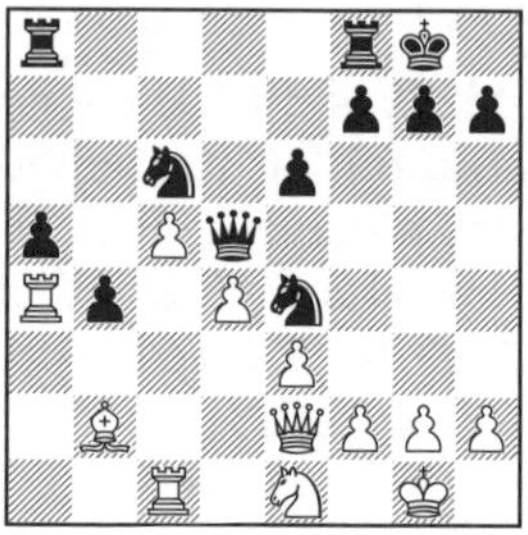

White played 23.♕c2 ♖fd8 24.f3 ♘f6 25.♘d3 and waited, to see Black preparing ...f5-f4.

13.♘e5?! 0-0 14.f3 ♘bd7 15.♘d3 leaves White's king's bishop unemployed. Black should attack c4 with 15...♕c7 16.♖c1 ♗a6 or 15...♗a6 16.♖c1 ♕b8 17.♕b3 ♖c8. The point is that the advance c4-c5 would invite the black knight to d5, pinpointing the weakness on e3.

13...♘bd7

We are not striving to trade light-squared bishops via e4 at any cost, although it is a sound positional idea. We can resort to it in the event White prepares e4 with ♖e1.

14.0-0

Occasionally White prepares e4 with 14.♕c2. The problem is if he fulfils his plan after 14...0-0 – 15.e4?! would be a serious mistake due to the unexpected 15...♘h5! (human players automatically answer 15...e5, which is less clear), followed by ...f5. 16.♗c1 does not help due to 16...♕c7! 17.e5? ♗xf3 18.gxf3 ♘xe5–+.

14...0-0

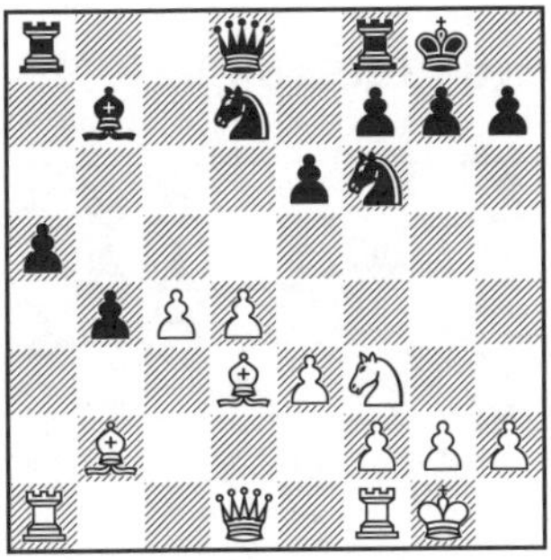

We have reached the main tabiya of the Noteboom.

A. 15.♕c2; **B.** 15.♖e1; **C.** 15.♘d2

15.c5 is rarely seen.

One reason is the hanging state of the d3-bishop – after 15...♗xf3 White must recapture 16.gxf3, and it is unclear what active plan he would be able to devise with his static pawns following 16...♘d5 17.♗b5 ♘7f6 18.♔h1 ♘h5 19.♖g1 ♕h4 20.♕f1 g6. The same could be said about Black though. So I recommend something more straightforward:

15...♗c6

Also in the Noteboom spirit is 15...♖a7!? 16.♗c2 ♕a8 17.♗a4 ♖d8 – see line C for ideas.

16.♗c2 ♕c7 17.♗a4. Black has a healthy extra tempo in comparison to the line 13.c5 0-0 14.♗b5 ♗c6 15.♗a4.

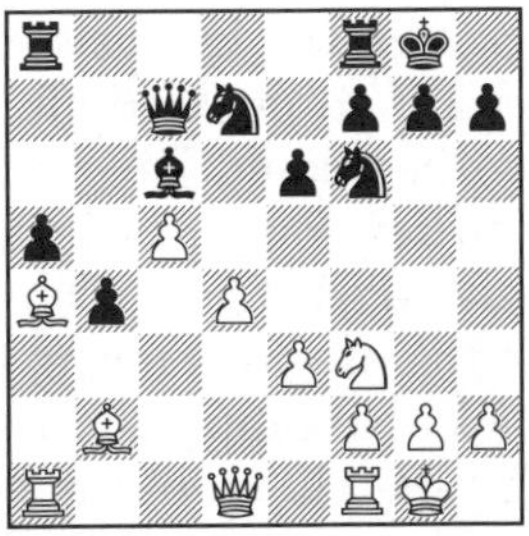

He could use it for 17...♘e4 18.♕c2 f5 with excellent results, but, again, I prefer the more active:

17...♖fd8 (aimed against 18.♘d2 – 18...♗xa4 19.♕xa4? ♘xc5) 18.♗xc6 ♕xc6 19.♕a4 ♕xa4 20.♖xa4 ♘e4, planning to meet almost any move by ...♘dxc5. White should show good defensive capabilities to hold.

A. 15.♕c2

This is the old approach to the Noteboom. White counts on e3-e4, but we'll see that ...e5 neutralises efficiently this advance. Besides, 15...♗xf3 16.gxf3 ♕c7 is difficult to break. White scores less than 50% in both computer and practical chess. However, I preach a more dynamic approach to the Noteboom.

15...♕c7! 16.e4

Note that 16.♘e5? ♘xe5! 17.dxe5 ♘d7 18.♗xh7+ ♔h8 has been known to be clearly better for Black ever since the 80ies, but many players keep on falling in this positional trap.

16.c5 is at least inconsistent. Its main idea is to push c6 after ♖fc1, but then he should have played it earlier, to develop the bishop on b5. Although 16...♗xf3 is even better than on the previous move, I think that Black's best approach is to support the march of his queenside pawns with ...♗c6 or ...♖fb8. For instance:
16...♖fb8 17.e4 (17.♖fc1 ♗c6) 17...h6 18.♘d2 ♗c6∓.

16...e5!

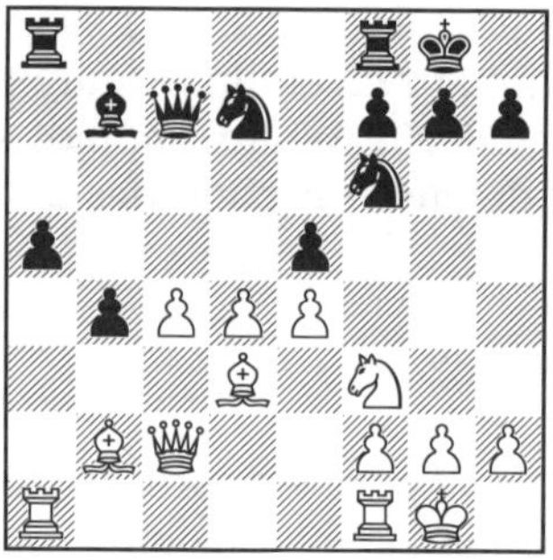

In our particular case this blockade is all the more effective as we should not worry about the principled 17.d5 since White lacks the blockading manoeuvre ♗c2-a4. Things are much more complicated if White had ♘d2 instead of ♕c2, as we'll see in line C.

17.c5

17.♖fe1 is 3 times less frequent. Then 17...♖fe8 (or 17...h6) 18.c5 exd4 19.♗xd4 h6, transposing to the main line, has proved to be good enough, but perhaps 17...♖fc8!? is more challenging. The game Pálsson-Owen, ICCF 2016, went 18.c5 exd4 19.e5 ♕xc5 20.♕d2 ♗xf3 21.♗xd4 ♕xd4 22.♗xh7+ ♘xh7 23.♕xd4 ♗c6, and White held the draw.

17...exd4 18.♗xd4 h6

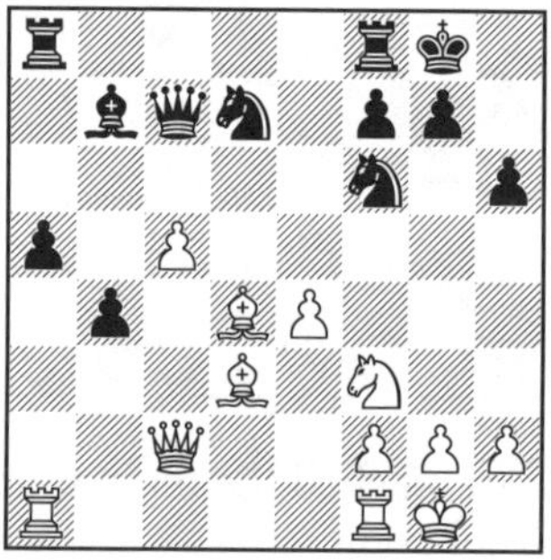

The main position for the 16.♕c2 line. Objectively it should be balanced, but in practice Black's task proves to be easier.

19.♖ac1!?

The king's rook is the last hope to generate threats against the black king. Therefore, 19.♖fc1 ♗c6 20.♕b2 is dubious – 20...♖fe8 21.e5 (21.♖e1 ♗xe4∓, Dragiev-Semkov, Elenite 1993) 21...♘g4 22.♗f5 ♘dxe5–+, Haba-M.Kuijf, Germany 1997.

White has also tried 19.♖fe1 ♖fe8 20.h3 ♗c6 21.e5 ♘d5 (21...♘h5, preventing the piece sac, is safe, too.) 22.e6 ♖xe6 23.♖xe6 fxe6 24.♗h7+ ♔h8 25.♗xg7+ ♔xg7 26.♕g6+ ♔h8 27.♕xh6 ♘f8 28.♗f5+ ♘h7 29.♗xh7

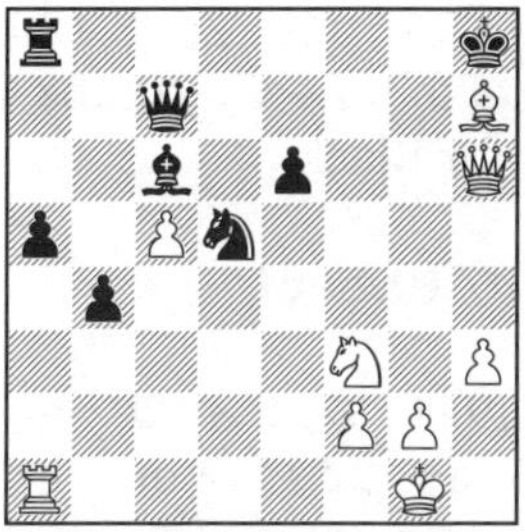

This sacrifice first occurred in Neverov-Kramnik, Moscow 1991. The future world champion took the bishop and went on to win, but it was much stronger to trade queens with 29...♕g7!!. Then the remote passers quickly decide the game.

19...♗c6 20.♖fe1 ♖fe8 21.♗a1!

The only way to maintain the intrigue. The model game for this line, Spraggett-Semkov, Manresa 1993, went 21.h3?! a4 22.e5 b3 23.♕b1 ♘h5!? with a big advantage for Black.

21...♖ab8

Scherbakov recommends 21...♘g4, when 22.h3 ♘ge5 23.♘d4 a4 and 22.♗c4 a4 or 22...♕f4 are unclear.

22.e5!

Scherbakov mentions only 22.♘d4 ♘e5 23.f3 a4 24.♗f1 ♕d7 "with good counter-chances". I would add 24...♘h5!∓.

22...b3

Or 22...♘g4 23.♗c4 ♗xf3 24.♗xf7!+ ♔xf7 25.♕b3+ ♗d5 26.♕xd5+ ♖e6 27.♕f3+ ♘df6 28.♕b3! ♘d7=.

23.♕b2 ♘h5 24.e6 ♖xe6 25.♖xe6 fxe6 26.♘d4 e5 27.♘b5 ♕d8=.

B. 15.♖e1

The idea of this move is that the thematic retort 15...♕c7? 16.e4 e5 is bad owing to 17.c5 exd4 18.♖c1 ♘e5 19.c6±. Therefore, we have no choice but block the e-pawn.

15...♗e4

This looks straight enough if you want to equalise before all. 15...♘e4!? keeps more tension and is preferred in practice. To be fair, White can still trade bishops. For instance:

16.♕c2

> 16.♘d2 ♘xd2 17.♕xd2 removes the light squares blockade, but in correspondence chess White scores badly after 17...♕g5 18.f4 ♕e7 19.♗c2 (19.e4 a4 20.♖eb1 ♖fb8) 19...♖fc8 or 19...♖fd8. It seems that the knight is more

useful than the bishop in this closed position.

16...f5 17.c5 ♕c7 18.♗c4 ♗d5 19.♗b3 ♗xb3 20.♕xb3 ♕c6=. Play is similar to the main line.

16.♗xe4

16.♗c2 ♕c7 17.c5

17.♘d2 ♗xc2 18.♕xc2 ♕c6 19.e4 a4 unblocks the pawns.

17...♖fd8 18.♗a4 ♗c6 with typical play. A correspondence game successfully tested 18...e5 19.♘g5 ♗g6 (19...♗c6!?) 20.♖c1 ♘f8 21.c6 e4 22.f3 ♖d5, intending to sacrifice the exchange in order to keep the blockade. It looks a bit too committal to me.

16...♘xe4 17.♕c2

Or 17.c5 ♕c7 18.♕a4 ♖fc8 19.♖ec1 ♕c6 20.♕xc6 ♖xc6 21.♖a4 e5!=, Kantsler-Haba, Pardubice 2016.

17...f5

18.c5

It is risky for White to keep the centre undefined for long since 18.♖ec1 ♕c7 19.♘e1 a4!? 20.f3 (20.♖xa4? b3! 21.♕xb3 ♘ec5) 20...b3 cannot be bad for Black.

18...♕c7 19.♖ec1

After 19.c6?! ♖fc8 20.♖ec1 ♘b6 21.♘e5 a4 22.f3 ♘d6 the black pawns are more menacing.

19...♕c6 20.♕a4 ♖fc8 21.♕xc6 ♖xc6=. See **Game 5** Sakaev-Kharlov, Tomsk 2001.

C. 15.♘d2 ♕c7

This is a provocation! Black challenges the opponent to enter the sharp line 16.f4. If you are scared of it or simply want to save extra learning time, **I suggest a convenient way to sidestep it**:

15...h6!?

Scherbakov recommends 15...e5? 16.♗c2 ♕c7 17.d5 ♖fe8 18.♗a4 ♖e7

The drawback of an early e5 is that it allows White to open the f-file: 19.f4! exf4 20.♖xf4 ♖xe3 21.♕f1 ♖e7 22.♗d4±.

16.f3

The catch is 16.f4?! ♘c5, while 16.♗c2 ♕c7 transposes to the main line.

16...♕c7

16...e5 is already playable, but 17.d5 ♕b6 18.♖e1 ♖fe8 19.h3, inthending ♔h2+f4, is still slightly better for White – 19...♘c5 20.♗c2 ♗a6 21.♔h2. Now 21...♖ad8?! stumbles into 22.f4 b3 23.♗b1 a4 24.fxe5 ♘fd7 25.♘f3 ♗xc4 26.e6, so Black should relieve the tension with 21...b3 22.♘xb3 ♘xb3 23.♗xb3 ♖ab8 24.♖a3 ♗xc4 25.♗xc4 ♕xb2 26.♖xa5 e4 27.f4 ♕c3. White's extra pawn is hardly convertible.

17.♗c2 ♖fd8. See **Game 6** Dhanish-Evtushenko, ICCF 2015, for details.

15...♖fe8 has ...e5 in mind, but my suggestion is to postpone this break for later stages.

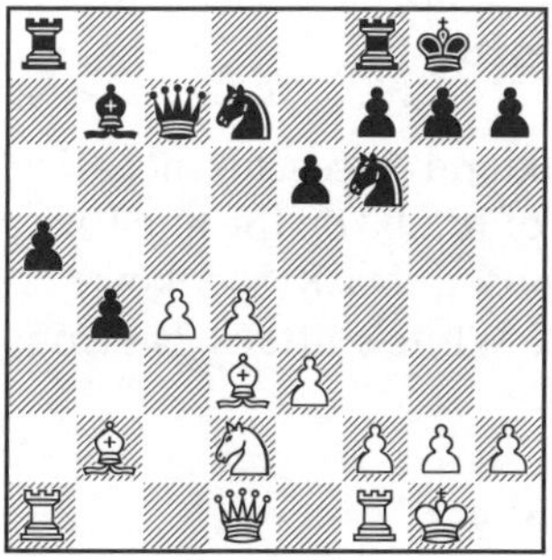

C1. 16.f4; **C2.** 16.♗c2

16.f3 is a frequent response, but it is a fairly useless move in my opinion. It does prevent 16...a4, which would be possible in the event of 16.c5 in view of the double hit ...♕c6. However, it weakens both the g1-a7 diagonal and the base of the pawn chain e3 – it could be attacked in an endgame by ...f5-f4. You could answer 16...h6 to transpose to 15...h6 after 17.♗c2. However:

16...♗c6!? 17.♗c2 ♕a7 is a more concrete approach. The threat ...a4 practically forces 18.♗a4 ♕a6 (or 18...♗xa4 19.♕xa4 ♖fb8 20.c5 ♘d5 21.♘c4 ♘xc5 22.dxc5 ♕xc5 23.♖ac1 ♘xe3 24.♘xe3 ♕xe3+ 25.♔h1 ♖d8 26.♖ce1 ½-½, Malin-Perry ICCF 2019), when 19.e4 faces Black with a choice.

Although 19...♗xa4 20.♕xa4 ♖fd8 is possible, I think that we should stick (for consistency sake) to the thematic:

19...e5. Correspondence games go from here:

20.♘b3 ♗xa4 21.♖xa4 ♕xc4 22.♖xa5 exd4=, Wharrier-Korovnik, ICCF 2019.

C1. 16.f4 a4!

This is the price White must pay for the "luxury" of forbidding ...e5. The pawn is indirectly protected by the double hit ...♕c6.

17.♖b1

Kasparov played in a simultaneous game 17.e4?, which is horrible for White after 17...a3 18.♗c1 ♕d6. Obviously, White must free the a1-square for the bishop.

17.♖c1 leaves the b-pawn undisturbed, so we should focus on its advance – 17...a3! (17...♖fd8 might be inaccurate here.) 18.♗a1 ♗c6

In two games Black set up the positional trap 18...♖fb8!? 19.e4?! b3!. White should have prepared e4 with 19.♕e2 ♗c6 20.♖b1 a2 21.♖b3 (21.♖b2 ♖a3) 21...♗a4 22.♖b2 b3 23.e4

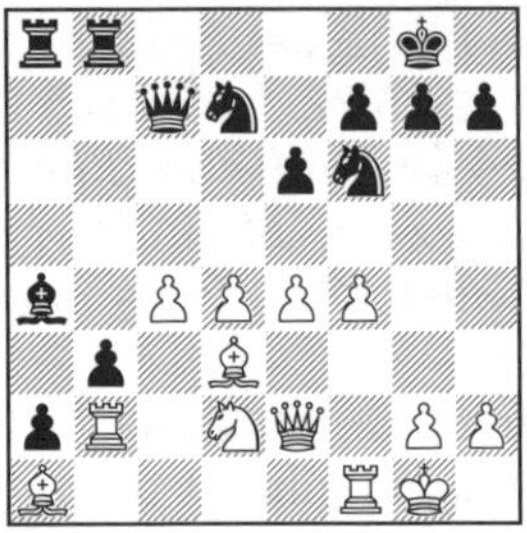

I have never seen a similar position in the opening! It is difficult to evaluate, but Black should have decent counter-chances, based on the weak spot d4 after 23...♕b6 or 23...♕a7.

19.e4 ♕b7 20.♖e1 (20.d5? ♗a4; 20.e5?! ♘e4 21.♘b3 f5) 20...♖fb8 21.e5 b3! 22.exf6 b2, when White has a draw with 23.♗xh7+! ♔xh7 24.♕h5+ ♔g8 25.fxg7 ♔xg7 26.f5.

17...♖fd8 18.♕e2 b3

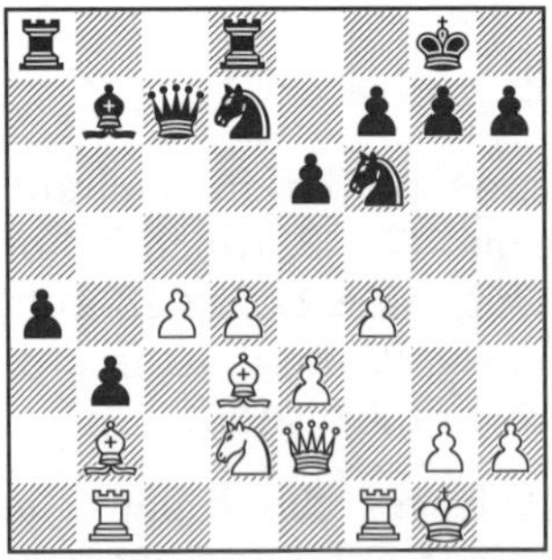

Shankland awards this move with a "?" mark, but after all, he has never played the Noteboom with any colour, at least according to databases!

19.♖a1

Several strong GMs chose to stop the black pawns with 19.♗a1. Then we have nothing concrete, so we should start rearranging our pieces. At first we should improve the placement of our d7-knight. The safest manoeuvre is 19...♘f8!

19...♘b8 (going to c6) is also met – 20.f5 ♕e7 21.fxe6 fxe6 22.e4 e5 23.dxe5, and the game Dorner-Sabaev, ICCF 2016 was suddenly interrupted by a draw agreement. After 23...♘fd7 24.e6! ♕xe6 25.e5 Black's kingside looks alarmingly naked to me.

20.e4 ♘g6∞.

19...♘f8!

Shankland bases his negative opinion of 18...b3 on the line 19...♘b8?! (proposed by Krasenkow) 20.f5!, when White's attack is strong, indeed.

20.f5

The other way to attack is 20.e4 ♕b6! (hoping for ...♖xd4) 21.♘f3 (21.e5 a3!), when Black has an original way to open a second front – 21...h5!?. See **Game 7** Oreopoulos-Oseledets, ICCF 2012.

Stepanov-Johansen, ICCF 2018, saw 20.♖a3 ♘g6 21.♖fa1 ♗c6 22.g3 h5 and only now did White play 23.f5. The game went on 23...♘f8 24.fxe6 ♘xe6 25.d5 ♘c5 26.♗d4 ♗b7∞ to finish in a draw.

20...e5! 21.dxe5 ♘6d7 22.e6 ♘c5! 23.♗b1

23.exf7+ ♕xf7 24.♗b1 ♘fd7 25.e4 ♖e8 stalls the attack.

23...fxe6 24.f6

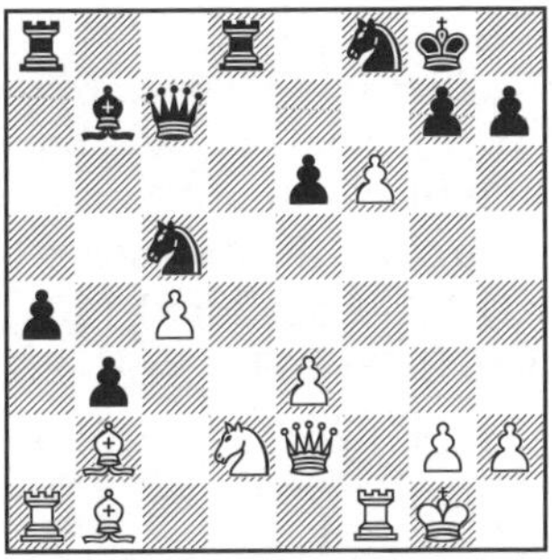

This position firstly occurred in Kurbasov-Gromov, ICCF 2012. It continued 24...e5 25.fxg7

White lost both correspondence games after 25.f7+ ♔h8 26.♘f3 ♘cd7.

25...♕xg7 26.♘f3 ♕g4 27.h3 ♕h5 28.♕e1! ♘g6∞. Here White parted with one of his bishops to eliminate a key defender – 29.♗xg6 ♕xg6 30.♘h4 ♕g7 31.♗a3 ♘d3 32.♕e2 ♔h8 33.♘f5 ♕g6 34.e4 ♕c6. The position remains tangled, although the engines evaluate it as 0.00.

In the diagram position I prefer the untested **24...♖d7!?** to include the rook in the defence.

Obviously 25.fxg7 ♖xg7 26.♗xg7 is not an option as it removes the blockade of the black passers.

Therefore, White should go:

25.♘f3 gxf6 26.♗xf6 ♖f7∞. A curious line is 26...♖g7!? 27.♕b2 ♖d8!∞, completely ignoring the white bishop.

C2. 16.♗c2!

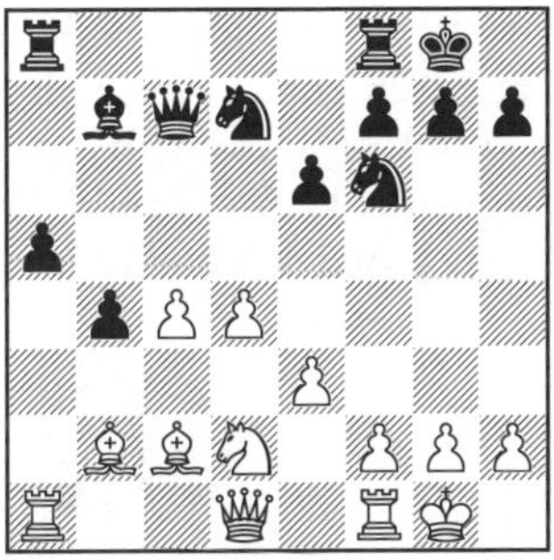

This cunning move has multiple purposes. The most obvious is to stop securely the a5-pawn. A less conspicuous aim is to anticipate ...e5, which will be answered by d4-d5 and ...♘c5 will be without a tempo. Finally, ♗c2 could be the first link of White's waiting strategy, which also comprises h3, ♖e1.

16...h6

Some explanation is needed at this point. The last few moves create the impression that White is playing a game of cat and mouse. He actively occupied the centre with his pawns and, all of a sudden, he started retreating his pieces. Amazingly, but that is the last word of theory in the Noteboom. And what is Black doing in response?! He is paying the opponent with the same coin! The catch is in the fact that Black's main active plan is to open the centre with ...e5, but it is less effective while the rook remains on f1 as White will open the f-file with f4 later. So both sides are lying in wait to see who will move his e-pawn first.

The situation with the c-pawn is similar. White is not too keen on playing c4-c5 early, as it will allow us to counterattack with ...e5. On the opposite, White would like to reach this pawn structure:

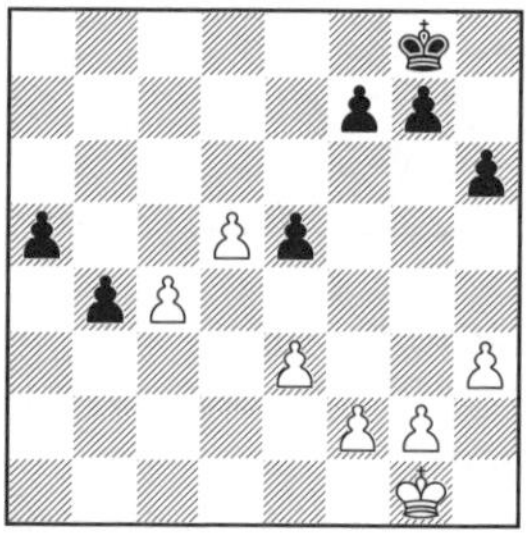

Here it is easier for him to remove the blockade, compared to set-ups with c5+d4. He would follow with f2-f4xe5, ♗d4, ♘b3 with a combined attack on c5 and e5. You may argue that Black could wait with some developing move, as:

16...♖fd8. Indeed, it is frequently played, and Black achieves about 60% with it! However, I believe that the rook is slightly displaced on d8. For instance, I analysed the line 17.h3 h6 18.♖e1 ♖a6 (to control the 6th line or double the rooks on the a-file) 19.e4 e5 20.d5 ♘c5 21.f4! ♘fd7 22.fxe5 ♘xe5 23.♗d4

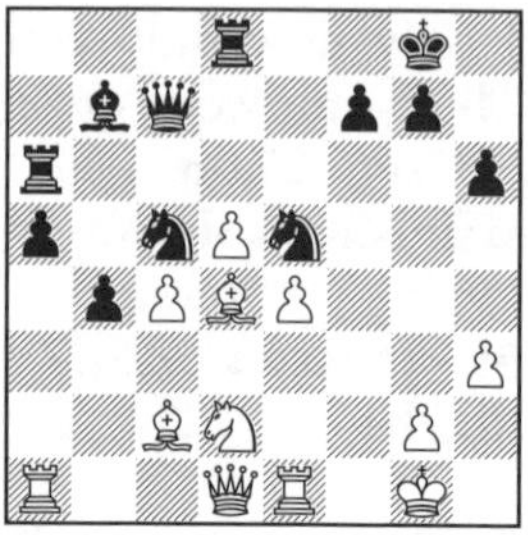

Both sides have followed their plans to reach this position. It is slightly better for White! For instance: 23...f6 (23...♘e6 24.♗f2 ♘c5 25.♘b3) 24.♔h1!

> Or 24.♘b3 ♘cd7! (24...♘e6 fails to 25.dxe6 a4 26.♗xe5! when Black cannot recapture by queen since the d8-rook is hanging!) 25.♘xa5 ♖da8! (25...♖xa5 26.d6±) 26.♘xb7 ♖xa1 27.♗xa1 ♖xa1 28.♕xa1 ♘f3+! 29.♔f1 ♘xe1 30.♕a8+ ♔h7 31.♔xe1 ♕g3+ 32.♔d1 ♘e5=.

24...♖c8 25.♘f3 ♔h8 26.♘h4 ♖d8 27.♕h5±.

The bottom line of my analysis was that a passive stand where Black tries to block the c4- and e4-pawn is not entirely satisfactory.

That made me look for an active approach. Instead of blocking the pawn at c4, we could attack it. For that, our rook should be on c8. It would also enable tactical devices based on the hanging c2-bishop. Thus:

16...♖fc8!? is a fair option which is not worse than 16...h6. The trick behind this move order is 17.f4 ♘b6 18.c5 a4!∓. The waiting 17.h3 also allows 17...♘b6 18.c5 a4, e.g. 19.♖c1

b3 20.♗xb3 ♕c6! 21.f3 axb3 22.cxb6 ♕xb6 23.♖xc8+ ♖xc8 24.♕xb3 ♕xb3 25.♘xb3 ♖b8 26.♘xc5 ♗xf3=.
17.♖e1 e5 (17...h6 transposes to 16...h6) is an interesting independent line – see **Game 8** Andriuschenko-Karpenko, ICCF 2016.
Still, it could be useful not to define the rook's placement yet. In some lines with ...e5 the rook would be better off on e8, and after 17.c5 the best answer is 17...♖d8! (to be fair, Black is doing fine in this position after 18.♖e1 h6 or 18...e5).

Of course, all this elaboration on the waiting strategy would have been superfluous if the active plan with 16...e5?! were good. In fact, Krasenkov and many other GMs stick to it. Scherbakov also regards it as the only option. Unfortunately, the pawn structure after 17.d5 favours White, as I pointed out above. Neither 17...♖fc8 (mentioned by Scherbakov) 18.♗a4 (or 18.♔h1, intending f4) nor 17...♖fe8 18.♗a4 could suit Black:

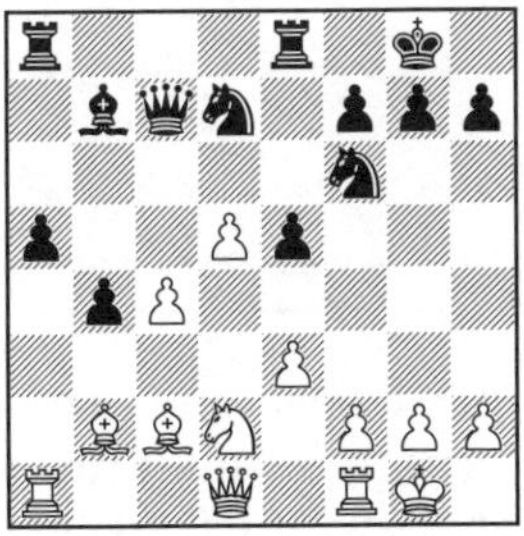

The point is that 18...♖e7 19.f4 exf4 will be met by 20.♖xf4! (missed by Scherbakov) 20...♖xe3 21.♕f1 ♖e7 22.♗d4 is positionally hopeless for Black.

Another author on the Triangle set-up tried 18...♕b6 19.♔h1 ♖e7 20.f4 ♕xe3 21.♘f3 exf4 22.♗d4 ♕e2, Smirnov-Krasenkow, Canberra 2017, when 23.d6! ♖e4 24.♕xe2 ♖xe2 25.♖fe1± would have led to total domination.

17.f3

In correspondence chess this is by far the most frequent continuation. However, White has a wide choice of other logical moves:

17.c5?! shows the merit of the waiting move ...h6. Black can put his rook on the best place d8 without losing a tempo on ...♖f-c8-d8. He is even better after 17...♖fd8 18.♖e1 e5.

17.e4!? is a very rare move, but it is not without venom. We answer 17...e5 18.d5, and we face a choice.

Of course we can block the pawns with ...♘c5, ...♘fd7, ...f6, and 18...♘c5 would not be a mistake. Still, in the Noteboom we should always think concretely and grasp every chance to pose some problems:

18...♗a6!? 19.♕e2

19.f4 exf4 20.♗d4 ♖ac8 21.♗a4 ♘c5 22.♗xf6 ♘xa4! is equal – 23.e5 gxf6 24.♕g4+ ♔h8 25.♕xf4 ♕xe5 26.♕xh6+ ♔g8 27.♖xa4 ♕d4+ 28.♔h1 ♗xc4 29.♖f3 ♗d3=.

19...♖fc8

As a rule, 19...♖fe8 is dubious in this structure in view of the pin 20.♗a4! ♖e7 21.♕e3±.

20.♖fc1 ♘c5 21.f4 ♘fd7 22.fxe5 b3!

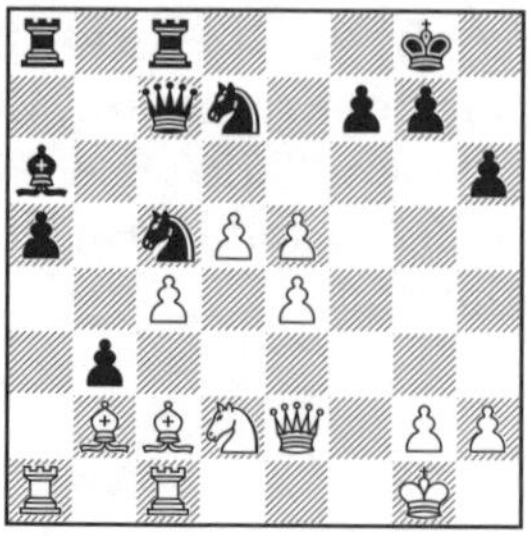

Disrupting the coordination of the enemy pieces. This *intermezzo* is a common tactical motif in the Noteboom. We can survive the attack after 23.♗xb3 ♘xb3 24.♘xb3 ♕b6+ 25.♗d4 ♕xb3 26.♖c3 ♕b4! 27.e6 (27.♖ac1 ♘f8) 27...fxe6 28.♕g4 ♕e7 29.d6 ♘f6! 30.♕g3 (30.♕h4! ♕f7 31.c5∞, e.g. 31...e5!? 32.♗xe5 ♘d7 33.♗d4 ♘f8 34.c6 ♘e6=, or 31...a4!?) owing to the trick 30...♕f7 31.♖f1 e5! 32.♗xe5 ♕a7+ 33.♔h1 ♘xe4∓.

23.e6 fxe6 24.dxe6 bxc2 was harmless in Shatkovsky-Moiseev, ICCF 2014.

23.♗d1 a4

A typical extremely sharp Noteboom position has arisen. 24.♘f3 ♕b6 25.♔h1

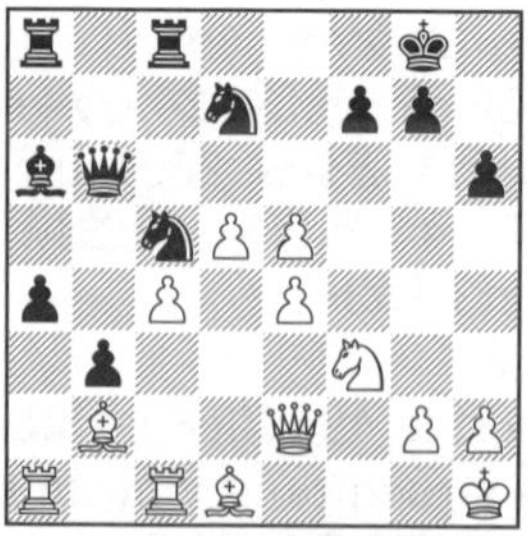

25...♕g6! (The engines recommend 25...♖e8 26.♕e3 f6 27.h3 ♘xe5 28.♘xe5 ♖xe5!, but White will not take the exchange – 29.♗f3 ♖c8 30.♕d4, remaining the active side.) Black seizes the initiative – a spectacular line is 26.♘d2 ♕g5 27.♖c3 ♘xe5 28.♘f3 ♗xc4!! 29.♖xc4 ♘xc4 30.♘xg5 ♘xb2, when the only move is 31.♘xf7! ♘bd3 32.♘xh6+=.

In Díaz-Fernández, ICCF 2018, White preferred to open the long diagonal at once:

24.e6 fxe6 25.♕e3 ♖f8 26.♖c3 with a balanced game after 26...♕f4. Sharper is 26...exd5 27.cxd5 ♕b6.

17.h3!?

A little prophylaxis before ♖e1, e4, followed by f4. Perhaps this is the sternest test of Black's setup.

17...♖fc8! 18.♖e1 e5

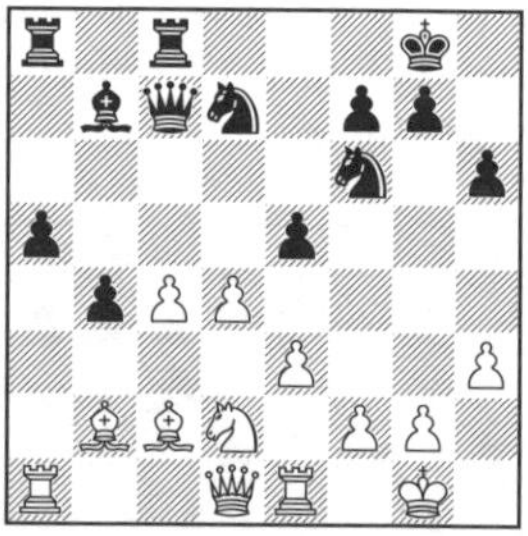

This typical position deserves detailed scrutiny. See **Game 9** Tauber-Kurtenkov, ICCF 2018.

17.♖e1 ♖fc8 18.h3 transposes to 17.h3, while the independent lines:

18.♖c1 ♕c6 19.e4 a4 20.d5 ♕a6 21.e5 ♘xd5! 22.cxd5 ♗xd5

23.♖e3 a3 24.♗d4 ♘f8⩲ and: 18.c5 ♖d8 19.♖c1 ♗c6 20.♗a4 e5, Merrell-Korovnik, ICCF 2019, are nice to play with Black.

17...♖fd8!?

White is going to play in the centre, so it is consistent to put the rook exactly on d8. I regard this option of another argument in favour of the move order with 16...h6 instead of 16...♖fc8.

18.♖f2

White removes the rook from the pin along the diagonal f1-a6, keeping it on the f-file.
For 18.♖e1 ♖a6!? see **Game 6** Dhanish-Evtushenko, ICCF 2015.

18...♖a6

“The voice of the people is the voice of God.” Black prefers this move in the majority of the games, so I consent with the public opinion. The rook could be always handy on the 6th rank.

Besides, 18...♘b6 is also consistent:
19.c5

19.♗b3 ♕c6 20.e4 a4 21.d5 exd5 22.exd5 ♕c7 23.♗xa4 ♘xc4 24.♘xc4 ♕xc4 25.♗b3 ♖xa1 26.♗xa1 ♕f4 27.♖d2 ♕g5 28.♗b2 ♘xd5 29.h4 ♕f5 30.♕e1 ♖c8 31.♕e5 ♕xe5 32.♗xe5 ♖d8 33.♖d4 ♔h7

19...♘bd7

Normally we should prefer 19...♘bd5 in such positions, enabling the blockading manoeuvre ...♘c7 in emergency cases. Indeed, it is a good move and Black is fine, e.g. 20.♕e1 ♗a6 21.♘e4 ♘e8!? 22.♗a4 f5 23.♘g3 f4. However, in the concrete position we can aspire for more with ...e5, to fix the pawns securely. For that we need the knight back to d7.

20.♗a4 e5 21.♘b3 exd4. Now 22.exd4 ♘d5 favours Black, while 22.♗xd4 ♘d5 or 22...♘e5, heading for c6, is also easy to play.

19.♔h1

White makes all possible improvements before defining the pawn structure. 19.e4 e5 20.d5 ♘c5 21.♘b3 ♘xb3 22.♗xb3 ♘d7 23.f4 occurred in several games.

Although 23...f6 24.fxe5 fxe5 25.♔h1 ♘c5 26.♗c2 a4 27.♕h5 ♕e7 28.♖af1 ♘d7 29.c5 ♖f6 30.♖xf6 ♘xf6 31.♕e2 a3 32.♗b3 ♔h7 33.♗a1 ♕xc5 34.♗xe5 ♖f8=, Stuart-Tombette, ICCF 2017 is possible, I prefer to avoid passive defence in favour of the counter-attacking approach:

23...exf4 24.e5 ♘c5 25.♗c2 a4 26.♖xf4 a3 27.♗d4

27...♗xd5!=∞ 28.cxd5 ♖xd5 29.♕f3 ♘e6 30.♕xd5 ♘xf4 31.♕e4 ♖c6 32.♗b3 ½-½, Daus-Filipchenko, ICCF 2015.

19...e5

The last White's move allows us to strike first in the centre. Now we should not worry about d4-d5 anymore since 20.d5 ♖c8! 21.♖c1 ♖ca8 would display the venom behind 18...♖a6.

20.♗b3

We can speak of a dynamic balance here. Black should prepare ...a4. The latest word in this line has been Egoshin-Shapiro, ICCF 2016:

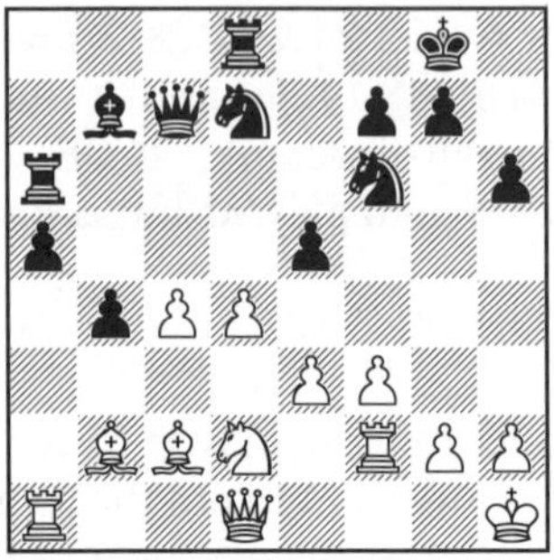

20...♘b6 (Evtushenko prefers the move order 20...♖da8 21.♖e2 exd4 22.exd4 ♘b6.) 21.♖e2 exd4 22.exd4 ♖da8 23.c5 ♘bd5 24.♘c4 ♗c6 25.♘d6 a4. White must be careful: 26.♗c4 ♖6a7 27.♖e5 ♖d8 28.♘f5 ♘f4 29.♕e1 ♘g6 30.♘d6 ♘xe5 31.dxe5 ♘d5 32.e6 ♖xd6 33.exf7+ ♔xf7 34.cxd6 ♕xd6 35.♕e4 ♔g8 36.♖e1 ½-½.

Annotated Games

4. Rawlings – Smythe
ICCF 2013

1.d4 d5 2.c4 c6 3.♘f3 e6 4.♘c3 dxc4 5.a4 ♗b4 6.e3 b5 7.♗d2 a5 8.axb5 ♗xc3 9.♗xc3 cxb5 10.b3 ♗b7 11.bxc4 b4 12.♗b2 ♘f6 13.c5 0-0 14.♗b5 ♗c6 15.♗a4

15...♗xa4

Black may try 15...♕c8 first, intending to meet 16.♘e5 by 16...♗xa4 17.♖xa4 (17.♕xa4 is dubious in view of 17...♕a6) 17...♕b7 18.f3 ♘c6 19.♘c4 ♕e7 20.♖a1 e5!=. However, 16.0-0! ♗xa4 transposes to the game.

16.♕xa4 ♕c8!?

Krasenkow prefers 16...♕d5 17.0-0 ♘c6 18.♖fd1 ♖fc8 19.♘e5 ♘e8 20.♘xc6 ♖xc6=.

17.0-0 ♘c6 18.♘d2 ♕a6

With this move Black accepts an exchange of queens. 18...♘d5 retains more tension. However, 19.♘c4 f5 20.♖ac1 ♘ce7 21.♖fe1 ♖a7 may be equal according to engines, but Black lacks an active plan and must only stay and wait.

19.♖fc1 ♘d5

This knight must always stay in contact with the critical square d5. 19...♖fc8 20.♘c4 ♘fd7? would face 21.e4±.

20.♘c4 ♖fd8

It is logical to put the rook on the most critical file. 20...♖fb8 is possible since 21.e4 ♘c3 (21...♘f4 22.♕d1) 22.♗xc3 ♕xc4 23.d5 ♕b5! evens the chances, but White also has 21.♘b6. See the next paragraph.

21.h3

21.♘b6!? is already critical, but the inclusion of h3 does not change the character of the position. 21.e4 ♘f4 is of course pointless for White.

21...h6 22.♖c2

White listens to the engines, which claim 0.00 after 22.♘b6!? ♘xb6 23.♕xc6 ♘d5 24.♕xa6 ♖xa6 25.♖a4

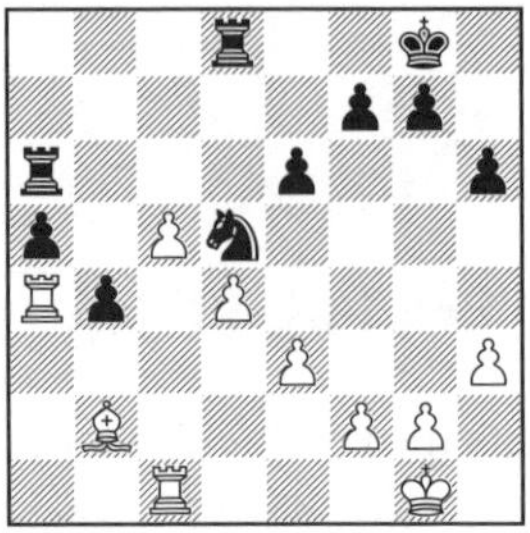

Chances may really be even, but Black must know what to do from here. Otherwise White could bring his king to c4 and push e4+d5.

Look at the following example:

Lomineishvili-Melnikova
Dresden 2004

The most straightforward and easy approach is to kill the possibility of e4 and d5 at once with 31...e5! 32.dxe5 ♘d7 or 32...♘fd5. Instead Black just stayed on: 31...♖fd8?! 32.♘f4 ♖a6 (again 32...e5! was essential) 33.♖ea1 ♖da8 34.♘d3 ♘c6 35.♔f2 ♔g8 36.♔e2 ♔f7 37.♔d2 ♖6a7 38.♔c2 ♖b8?! 39.♔b3 g5 40.♖e1 (40.♘e5+±) 40...♖d7 41.♔c4 ♔e7

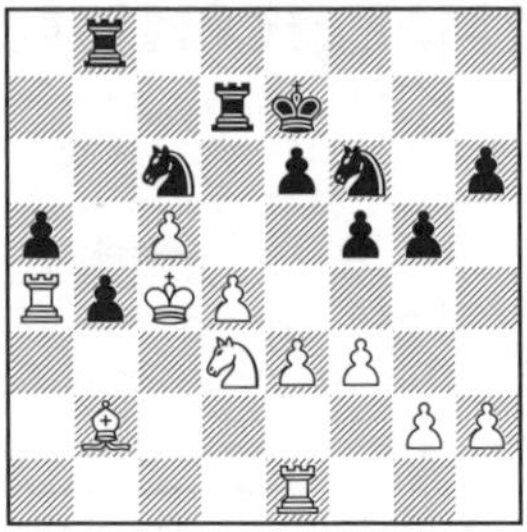

Remember this diagram! 42.e4± fxe4 43.fxe4 ♔f7 44.♖f1 ♔g6 45.♖xf6+ ♔xf6 46.d5+ ♔e7 47.dxc6 ♖a7 48.♗e5 1-0. None of this would have been possible without the e-pawns.

Let's now return to our analysis after 25.♖a4. Although the computer does not have any problem to hold things together with 25...f5 26.♔f1 ♔f8 27.♔e2 ♔e8 28.♔d3 ♔d7 29.♖ca1 ♖da8 30.♔c4 h5, I think that it is safer to define the centre right away with 25...e5!

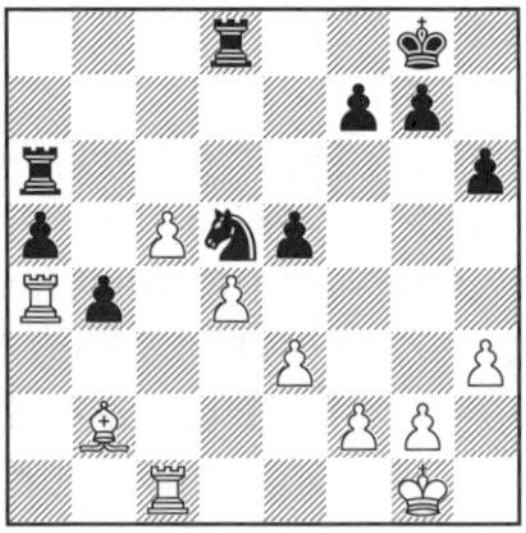

26.dxe5 (or 26.♖ca1 exd4=) 26...♘e7 27.♔f1 ♘c6. Despite the extra pawn, it is White who should be careful when Black's king arrives at c6.

22...♖db8 23.♘d6

23.♘b6? does not work anymore as the c2-rook is hanging – 23...♘xb6 24.♕xc6 ♖c8.

23...f5 24.♖e1

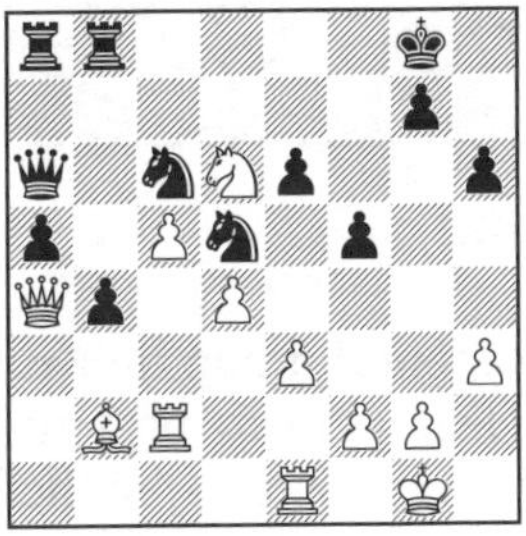

24...♘d8

A solid move, which anticipates the threat of e4. 24...♘ce7!? was more provocative, luring the opponent into complications following 25.♕d7 ♖f8 26.♕xe6+ ♔h7. Black's pawns are dangerous and force White to find only moves.

25.♖a1

Acknowledging the fact that White has no plan. After the text Black could have made a final improvement of his position before forcing play with ...b3 – 25...♔h7!, when 26.c6 b3 27.♖c5 ♖b4 28.♕xa5 ♕xa5 29.♖axa5 ♖xa5 30.♖xa5 ♘xc6 assures Black of some edge owing to the the b-passer. Instead Black rushed things with:

25...b3 26.♖cc1 ♔h7 27.♖c4 ♖a7

Preparing ...♘f7. White finds a way to kill the advanced pawn:

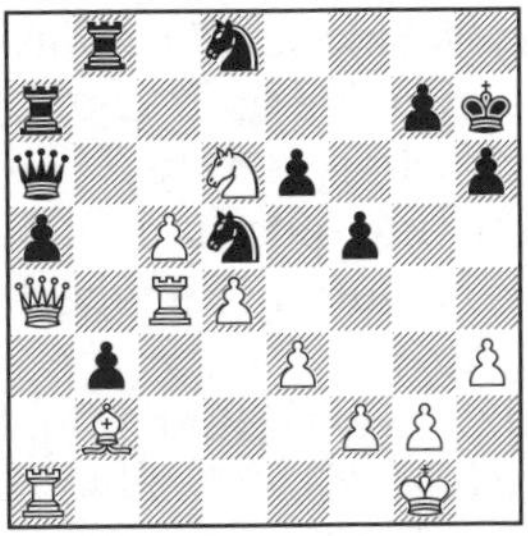

28.♖b1 ♘f7 29.♘xf7 ♖xf7 30.♗a3 ♖fb7 (30...f4!?) **31.c6 ♖b5 32.c7 ♖c8 33.♖xb3 ♖xb3 34.♕xb3 ♖xc7 35.♖c5 ♖b7 ½-½**

---

5. Sakaev – Kharlov
Tomsk 16.05.2001

1.d4 d5 2.c4 e6 3.♘c3 c6 4.♘f3 dxc4 5.a4 ♗b4 6.e3 b5 7.♗d2 a5 8.axb5 ♗xc3 9.♗xc3 cxb5 10.b3 ♗b7 11.bxc4 b4 12.♗b2 ♘f6 13.♗d3 ♘bd7 14.0-0 0-0 15.♖e1 ♗e4 16.♗xe4 ♘xe4 17.♕c2 f5 18.c5 ♕c7 19.♖ec1 ♕c6 20.♕a4 ♖fc8 21.♕xc6 ♖xc6 22.♘e1

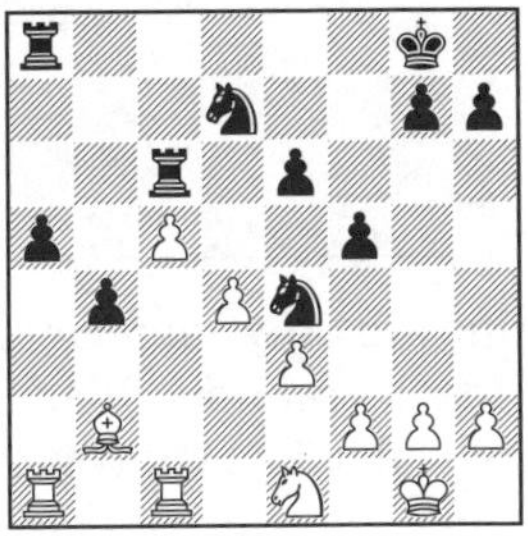

22...♘b8!?

Remember that the critical point in White's position is d4! Kharlov revives his awkward knight in an exemplary fashion. His approach is most instructive as it could be applied in various settings.

The concrete position allows yet another solution, suggested by Scherbakov:

22...♘d2!. Now 23.♖a4 looks natural, when 23...e5 24.♘d3 ♖cc8 25.h4 is about equal. The knight looks astray on d2, but concrete calculation proves that it is amazingly nippy from there. The point is that White's king cannot attack it since 25.f3 fails to 25...f4. And 25.♖d1 ♘b3 26.♔f1?! (26.♘c1 ♘xc1 27.♗xc1=) could be attacked by 26...♖d8 27.♔e2 exd4 28.exd4 ♖e8+.

23.♘d3 ♖ca6 24.f3 ♘f6 25.♔f2

The game Jordaan-Wenger, IECC 2012, saw 25.♘e5 ♘c6 26.♘xc6 ♖xc6 27.♖a4

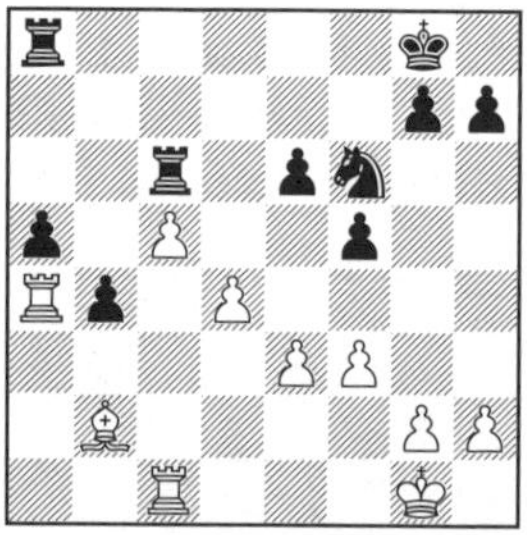

According to my advice in the "Main Ideas" section, Black could now safely play 27...e5! (or 27...♔f7 28.♔f2 e5!) to ensure a firm blockade on the light squares – 28.dxe5 (28.♔f2? e4!) 28...♘d7 29.♗d4 ♘b6=.

25...♘c6 26.♖a4

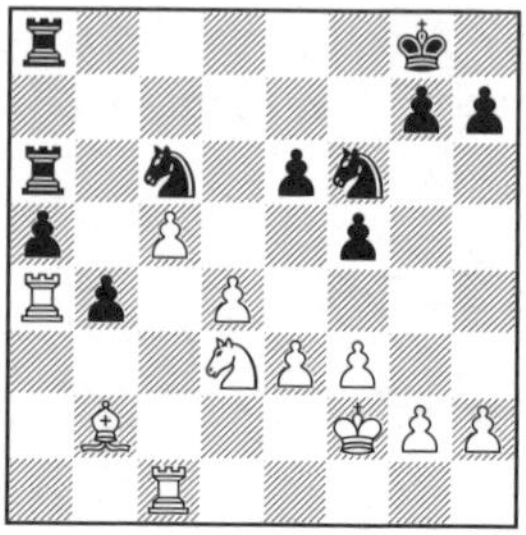

26...♖d8!

A consistent human move. Black has a clear plan to pressurise d4, and he takes the bull by the horns. Halliwell-Schmidt, ICCF 2012, went 26...♔f7 27.♖ca1 ♖6a7 28.♔e2 g5 29.♔d2 ♔e7 30.♖e1 ♖d7 31.♔c2 ♔d8 32.♔b3 ♔c7 33.♗a1 ♘d5 34.h4 h6 35.hxg5 hxg5 36.e4 ♘de7 37.♔c4 ♖ad8 with an eventual draw. The problem of this approach is that any miscalculation could have put Black in a hopeless situation. It is safer to anticipate the march of White's king to c4.

27.♖ca1 ♖aa8 28.♔e2 ♘d5 29.h3

Curiously, Scherbakov evaluates Black's position as "slightly worse, but defendable". I'm not that sure he is the defending side though...

29.♘e5 ♘xe5 30.dxe5 wins the a5-pawn, but 30...f4! levels the game – 31.e4 ♘e3 32.♖xa5 ♖xa5 33.♖xa5 ♘c4 34.♖b5 ♘xb2 35.c6 ♘d1= with a perpetual.

If White prevents the blow ...f4 with 29.g3, Black will prepare to defend a5 twice – 29...♖a7. In that event

30.e4 fxe4 31.fxe4 ♘f6= would give him counterplay.

29...♖ab8!?

Again Kharlov opts for the most active set-up of his rooks. He enables the threat ...♘c3 in some lines. Also good was 29...g5.

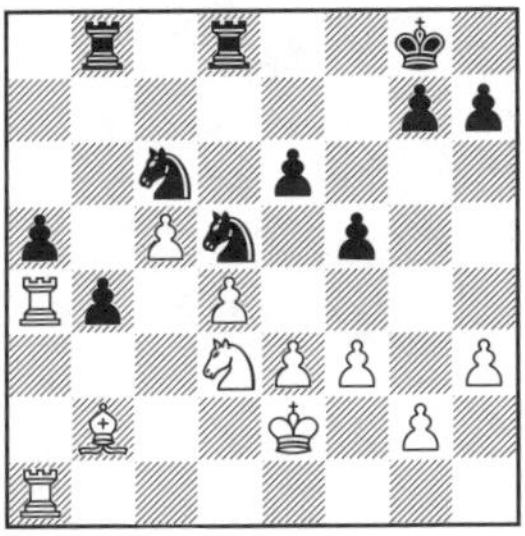

30.♖d1?!

White acknowledges the fact that he lacks a constructive plan and beats the retreat. He obviously did not like 30.e4 ♘c3+ 31.♗xc3 bxc3 32.♔e3 ♖b3↑, but he could have tried 30.g4 g6=. Black could also force a draw with 30...f4 31.♘xf4 (31.exf4 ♖f8) 31...♘xf4+ 32.exf4 ♘xd4+ 33.♗xd4 ♖xd4 34.♖xa5 ♖xf4=.

30...♖b5

Kharlov has conducted the game at highest level so far, and after Sakaev's hesitant last move he could have gained the initiative with 30... g5!↑ 31.g3 ♔f7 32.♖d2 ♖d7, doubling rooks on the d-file – 33.♖d1 ♖bd8 34.♖d2 e5.

31.e4 (31.g4 g6=) **31...♘c3+ 32.♗xc3 bxc3 33.♔e3**

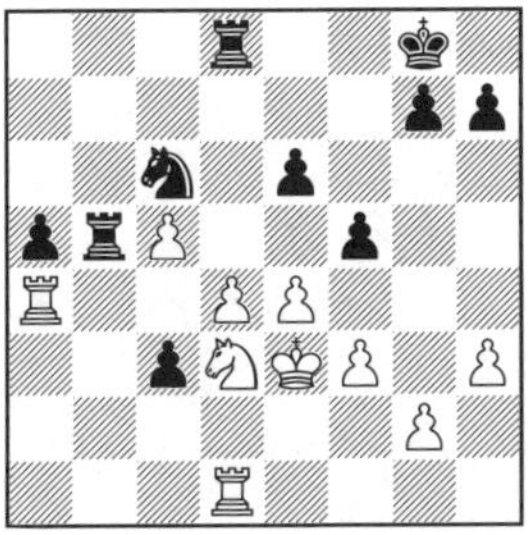

33...c2

33...g5! 34.g3 ♖b3 would have posed problems to White.

34.♖c1 ♖b3?! (34...f4+ 35.♘xf4 ♖b3+ 36.♘d3 ♘e5=) **35.exf5?!**

35.♖xc2 ♘xd4 36.♖xd4 f4+ 37.♔xf4 ♖xd4 38.c6 ♖d8 39.♘c5 ♖b6 40.♘xe6 ♖c8 41.♘d4 a4 is a draw, according to engines, but White's play is undoubtedly easier.

35...e5 36.♔e4?

And this ruins the game. 36.♖xc2 ♘xd4 37.♖d2 ♘xf5+ 38.♔e4 ♘g3+ 39.♔xe5 ♖bxd3 40.♖xd3 ♖xd3 41.♖xa5 was enough for a draw.

36...exd4 37.♖xc2 ♘b4 38.♘xb4 axb4 39.c6 ♖e8+ 0-1

---

6. Dhanish – Evtushenko
ICCF 2015

1.d4 d5 2.c4 c6 3.♘f3 e6 4.♘c3 dxc4 5.a4 ♗b4 6.e3 b5 7.♗d2 a5 8.axb5 ♗xc3 9.♗xc3 cxb5 10.b3

♗b7 11.♗b2 ♘f6 12.bxc4 b4 13.♗d3 0-0 14.0-0 ♘bd7 15.♗c2 ♕c7 16.♘d2 h6

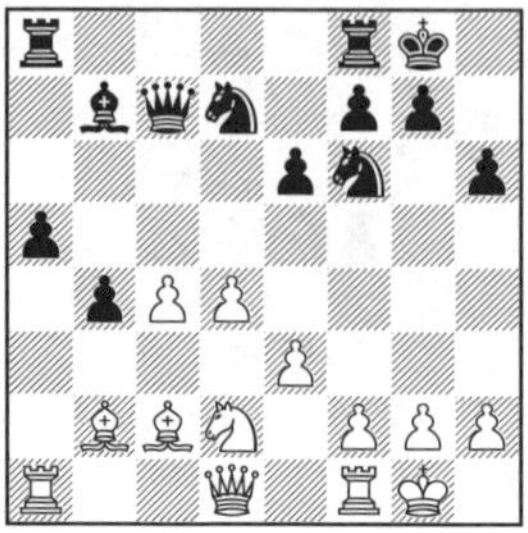

17.f3

We frequently see this stand in practice, although I do not grasp its design – White can easily push e4 without any pawn help. The waiting strategy with ♖e1, h3 is more cunning, avoiding any weaknesses.

17...♖fd8 18.♖e1 ♖a6!?

Black was at a crossroads.
The thematic 18...e5 is controversial, as usual. Although Black drew all the correspondence games after 19.d5 ♖e8 20.♗a4 ♖e7 – 21.♗c2 ♖c8; 21.♖e2 ♘b6; 21.♖f1 ♘b6, White retains a slight pull due to his stable space advantage.

The only other plan is to prepare ...a4, and the game move is a step in that direction – Black intends to double his rooks on the a-file. In practice we see much more often the other approach:
18...♗c6!? 19.e4 ♘b6 20.c5

20.♔h1 (20.d5 ♗e8) 20...♘fd7 21.♕e2 a4 22.c5 ♘c8 23.d5 exd5 24.exd5 ♗xd5 25.♕d3 ♘f8 26.♕d4 (26.♘e4 ♕f4!) 26...♘e6 27.♕d3=, Rivera De León-Marbourg, ICCF 2017.

20...♘bd7 21.e5 ♘d5 (21...♘e8 also holds) 22.♘e4 ♘f8 23.♘d6 ♘g6 24.g3 ♕d7 25.f4 ♘ge7 26.♕g4

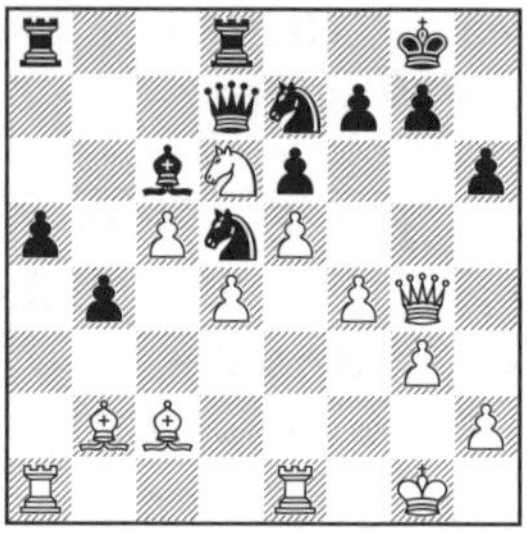

Black's position is very resilient. The game Oliveira-Privara, ICCF 2016, went 26...g6 27.♕h4 h5 28.♕g5 and White eventually found a way to force a draw with a perpetual. 26...♘c7!?, threatening ...b3, would have faced him with more problems. If he pushed 27.f5, Black's knight would find a perfect stand on e6.

19.♔h1

The game Legemaat-Panman saw the timid 19.♕e2. Black followed his plan – 19...♖da8 20.c5 a4

This advance is undoubtedly a serious achievement, but it is commonly not enough to win the game as White easily blocks the pawns on their next step. For obtaining a decisive advantage, Black should break through the centre anyway. Therefore, 20...e5 was a notable alternative.

19...♖da8

19...e5 is also consistent.

In Debnár-De Paz González, ICCF 2018, White quickly became worse after 20.♗a4 ♘b6 21.♗b5 ♖aa8 22.c5 ♘bd7 23.♘b3 ♗d5 24.♗a4 exd4 25.exd4 ♘f8∓. The manoeuvre ♗a4 is a fair option against ♖e8, but here it just wasted tempi. Perhaps White should try:

20.d5!, when Black has nothing better than the defensive stand ...♖fc8, ...♘c5, ...♘fd7, f6. Thus the game course looks more principled.

20.e4

White cannot wait much longer as ...♗c6 would ensure the advance of the pawns.

20...e5 21.♘f1

I think that 21.d5 ♘c5 22.f4 is more critical.

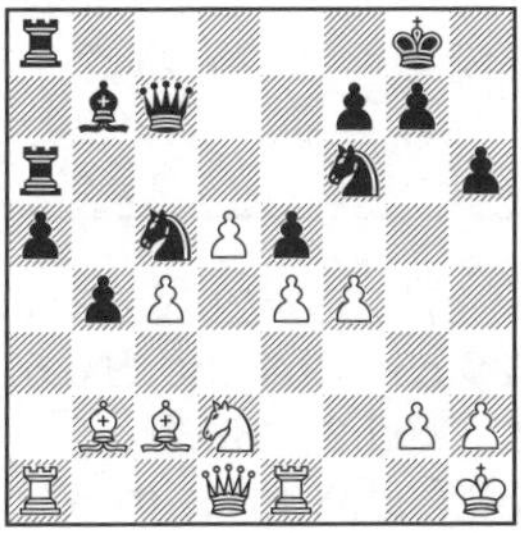

In this pawn structure White can play for e4-e5 or c4-c5 and his pieces are quite active. For instance, 22...♘fd7 23.fxe5 ♘xe5 24.♗d4, followed by ♘f3, retains some pressure, e.g. 24...a4 25.♘f3 f6 26.♘xe5 fxe5 27.♗xc5 ♕xc5 28.♖xa4 ♖xa4 29.♗xa4 ♕xc4 30.h3 – the protected passed pawn at d5 is a bit stronger than the one on b4.

In the Noteboom it is often better not to block White's centre but to attack it:

22...exf4!? 23.♘b3 (23.e5 ♘xd5! 24.cxd5 ♗xd5⩱) 23...♘xb3 24.♗xb3 a4 25.♖xa4 ♖xa4 26.♗xa4 ♕xc4 27.♗b3 ♕c5 28.♕f3 ♖e8!⇄ 29.♕xf4? ♗xd5.

21...exd4 22.♗xd4 ♘c5 23.♘e3 ♘fd7 24.♖b1 ♖b8

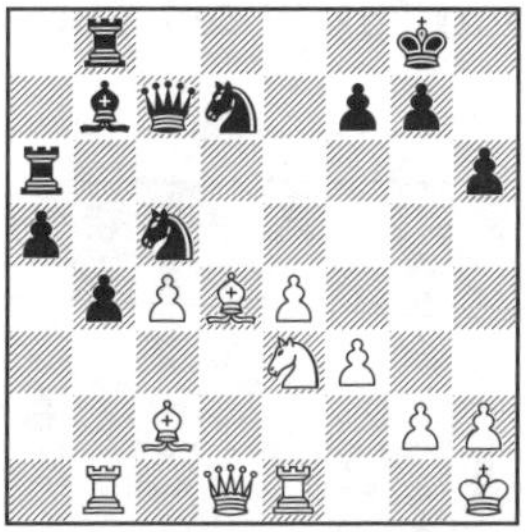

25.♕e2

A later game saw 25.♘d5 ♗xd5 26.exd5 ♕d6 27.f4 ♕xf4 28.♖f1 ♕h4 29.♖e1 ♕f4 30.♖f1 ♕h4 31.♖e1 ½-½, Shulman-Geier, ICCF 2017. The text also allows exchanges which facilitate Black's task:

25...b3 26.♗xb3 ♗xe4 27.♗c2 ♖xb1 28.♖xb1 ♗xc2 29.♘d5 ♕d6= 30.♕xc2 a4 31.h3 a3 32.♗c3 ♘b6 33.♗b4 a2 34.♖a1 ♘xd5 35.cxd5 ♕e5 36.♖xa2 ♖xa2 37.♕xa2 ♘d3 38.♗d2 ♕d4 39.♕a5 ♘f2+ 40.♔h2 ♘d3 41.♕d8+ ½-½

7. Oreopoulos – Oseledets
ICCF 2012

In this game we'll meet with the typical scenario when White lets the black pawns cross the fourth line, but he occupies the whole broad centre in return.

1.d4 d5 2.c4 c6 3.Nc3 e6 4.Nf3 dxc4 5.a4 Bb4 6.e3 b5 7.Bd2 a5 8.axb5 Bxc3 9.Bxc3 cxb5 10.b3 Bb7 11.bxc4 b4 12.Bb2 Nf6 13.Bd3 Nbd7 14.0-0 0-0 15.Nd2 Qc7 16.f4 a4 17.Rb1 Rfd8 18.Qe2 b3 19.Ra1 Nf8 20.e4 Qb6 21.Nf3 h5!?

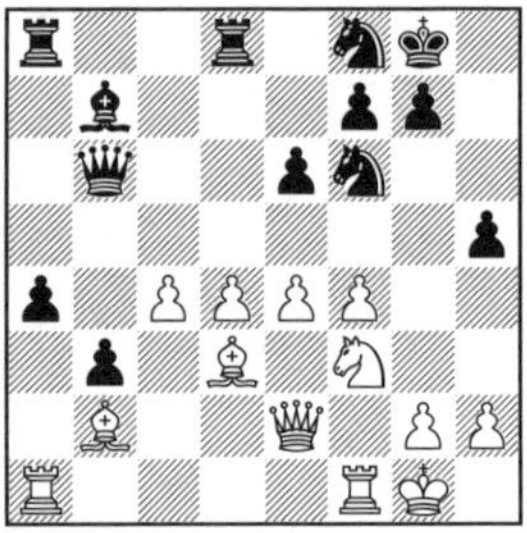

This advance seems to defy one basic rule of the positional chess – not to make weaknesses where the opponent is stronger. On a deeper level, we may notice that in fact we have more pieces on the kingside than White! Furthermore, our queen and b7-bishop are also targeted at the white king. The four pawns are controlling everything and are keeping Black's forces at bay, so the only way to break through is with the help of the h-pawn. The idea is to weaken the g3- and g4-square and eventually achieve the stab ...f5. All in all, most variations favour Black and one small mistake could tip the fragile balance.

22.Ra3 Ng6 23.g3 h4 24.Rc1

The thrust of the c-pawn was ineffective – 24.c5 Qb4 25.Qe1 Qxe1 26.Rxe1 Ne7! 27.Nxh4 Nc6 28.Nf3 Nb4 29.Bb1 Rdb8 30.Nd2 Nc2 gives Black an initiative, so White supports the pawn to have c5-c6 in the above line.
He could have acted on the kingside, but 24.Nxh4? Nxh4 25.gxh4 stumbles into 25...Rxd4.
If White tried to escape the X-ray from the queen with 24.Kg2 Nh5 (or 24...Ra5 25.c5 Qc6 26.Nd2) 25.Qe3, 25...f5! raises up the tension:

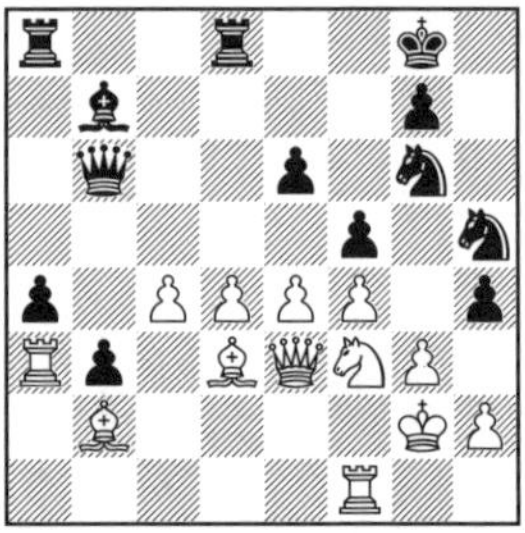

26.e5 Ne7 27.Kf2! Bxf3 28.Qxf3 Nc6! 29.c5 Qb4 30.Qxc6 Qd2+ 31.Be2 Qxb2 32.Qxe6+ Kh8. Now 33.Qxf5? loses to 33...hxg3+ 34.hxg3 Qxe2+!, but 33.Qg6! should draw – 33...Nxf4+ 34.gxf4 Rxd4=. This line pinpoints the most sensitive spot in White's position – the d4-square.

Here is another illustration of the merits of ...h5 – 24.Rfa1 Bc6 25.Bc3 Rab8 26.Re1 Qa7 27.c5 h3!, and the

pawn has great potential if Black infiltrates through the light squares after a bishop trade.
An example of my blitz game:

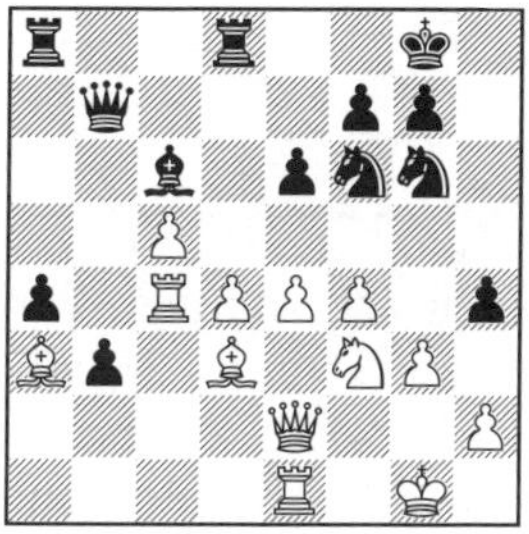

My opponent was obviously perplexed by the arrogant thrust of the h-pawn and thought up the manoeuvre ♖c1-c4-b4. However, 26.♖b4?! ♕d7! (protecting the bishop) would have left him without many useful moves. I chose instead 26...♕e7 and went on to win in the complications. It is horrible to have such a position with White in a rapid game – he has too many options to blunder.

24...♗c6 25.♖aa1 ♖a5

I guess that the AI Alpha Zero would have played here 25...h3! without much hesitation. This type of moves have too long horizon for the conventional engines.

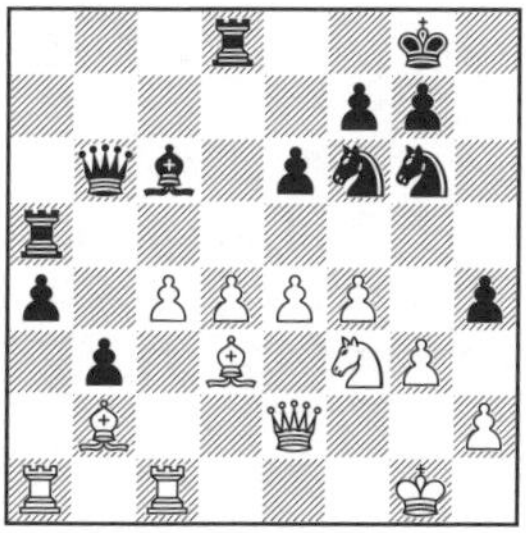

26.♔f1?!

This looks unaesthetic, and the engines also do not approve of it. 26.♔g2 was more natural.

26...♘h5?!

Black could have punished White's mistake more energetically with 26...♕a7! 27.d5 (27.♖a3 ♖h5 28.♔g2 ♕d7–+) 27...a3 28.♗d4 ♕a8.

27.♕f2 ♕a6 28.♖a3 ♘f6 29.♕e2 ♖h5 30.d5 hxg3 31.hxg3 ♗e8 32.♖aa1 ♕c8 33.♔f2 ♗d7

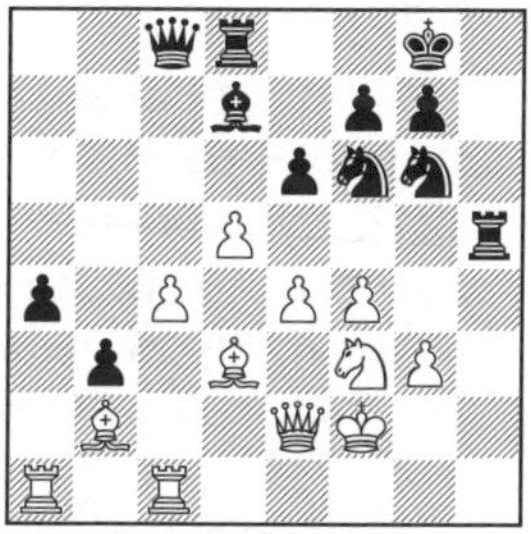

White's last 10 moves turned out to be a waste of time, to say the least. Still, he had to pursue his plan with 34.e5 ♘g4+ 35.♔g2 with a dangerous, but probably balanced position. For instance, 35...♖e8!? 36.d6 ♗c6 37.♗e4 f5 38.exf6 e5!↑.
Instead White enters a losing line:

34.♔g2? ♖e8 35.d6 e5 36.f5 ♖xf5! with a debacle. **0-1**

8. Andriuschenko – Karpenko
ICCF 2016

1.d4 d5 2.c4 c6 3.♘f3 e6 4.♘c3

dxc4 5.a4 ♗b4 6.e3 b5 7.♗d2 a5 8.axb5 ♗xc3 9.♗xc3 cxb5 10.b3 ♗b7 11.bxc4 b4 12.♗b2 ♘f6 13.♗d3 ♘bd7 14.0-0 0-0 15.♘d2 ♕c7 16.♗c2 ♖fc8 17.♖e1

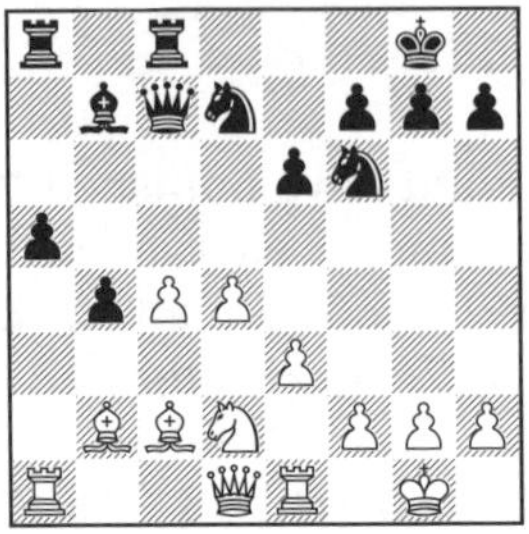

17...e5

Lately Black has discovered alternative plans, but opening the centre remains one of the main Black's weapons in the Noteboom.
17...h6 transposes to 16...h6, which is the main line in the "Step by Step" section.

The thematic idea behind 16...♖fc8 – the hit on c2 – does not work well because Black lacks the pin along the f1-a6 diagonal after 17...♘b6?! 18.c5 a4 19.♖c1 b3 20.♗b1 ♘bd5 21.♘c4±.

18.c5

Perhaps critical for 17...e5 is 18.♖c1 ♖e8 (18...h6 19.d5) 19.d5!

The most dangerous structure! 19.♖f1 ♖a6! 20.f3 h6 21.♔h1 ♖ea8 22.♖a1 ♖c8 should be fine for Black.

19...♘c5 20.f4

It looks like White has won the opening battle.

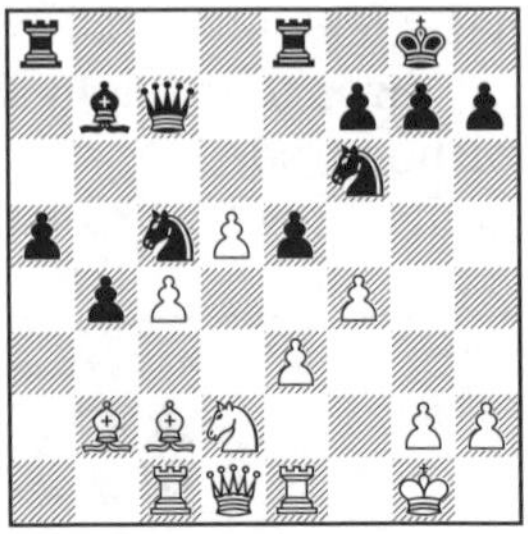

20...♘fd7?! cannot keep the blockade due to 21.fxe5 ♘xe5 22.♘e4, when c5 is cracking. However, material is only a secondary factor in such asymmetrical positions.

20...a4! 21.fxe5 ♖xe5 22.♖b1! ♖h5

A handy tempo! Now we can understand why lately White often prefers to put in h3 before embarking on concrete actions in the centre. 23.♗xf6 ♕xh2+ 24.♔f2 gxf6 is unclear.

23.♘f1 b3 24.♗xb3 ♘xb3 25.♗xf6 ♖h6 26.♗b2

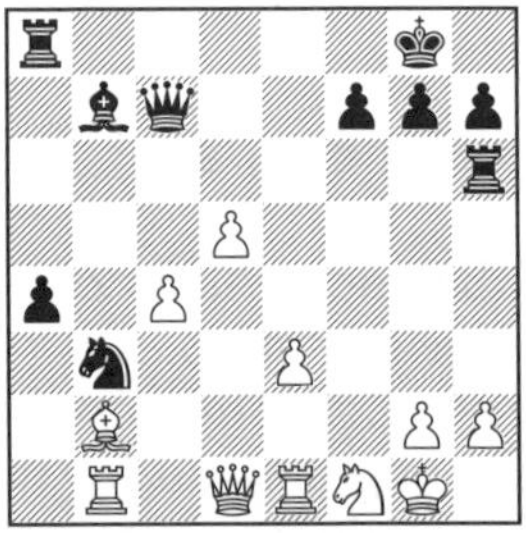

Black is beyond danger here. He can play 26...♖g6 27.♗a3 (27.♕d3 ♗a6) 27...♕xc4 or:

26...♕xc4 27.e4 ♕b4 28.♕f3 ♗c8 29.♔h1 ♖g6, and the game Kalashnikov-Agaltsov, ICCF 2017, was drawn on move 43.

18...♖d8!

Black should feel relieved to see the opponent building the “wrong” pawn structure with c5. Now the control of d5 becomes decisive.

19.♗b3 exd4

Shulman-Stieger, ICCF 2015, saw Black inserting 19...♗c6 20.♕c2, and only now 20...exd4 21.♗xd4 (21.exd4 ♕f4) 21...♘g4=. The game went on 22.f4 a4 23.♗xa4 ♗xa4 24.♖xa4 ♖xa4 25.♕xa4 ♘xc5 26.♕c2 ♘e6 27.♕xc7 ♘xc7 28.♘b3 h5 29.h3 ♘f6= to finish in a draw.

20.exd4 ♕f4 21.g3 ♕f5 22.♗a4

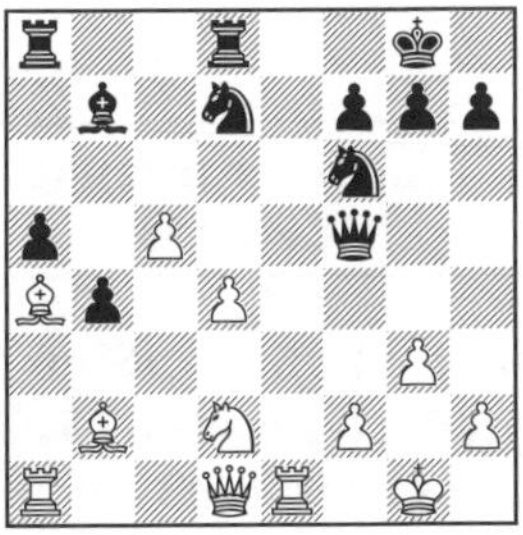

22...♕d5

The black queen was perfectly placed on f5 – eyeing both d5, h3 and f5. An additional resource for the attack is ...h7-h5-h4. Therefore, 22...♗d5 deserved attention. Here are some examples:
23.♗b5 ♖db8 24.♗c4 b3 25.♖e3 a4↑; 23.♕b1 ♕h3 24.f3 h5 25.♖e3 h4 26.♕f1 ♕f5 27.♖ae1 hxg3 28.hxg3 ♘f8 29.♘e4 ♘e6↑.

23.f3 ♗c6 24.♗xc6 ♕xc6 25.♕b3 ♘d5 26.♕a4 ♕g6

White’s king is very weak and the threat of invasion along the second rank is in the air. Black could have retreated the queen to c8, the point being 26...♕c8!? 27.♘b3 h5! 28.♘xa5?

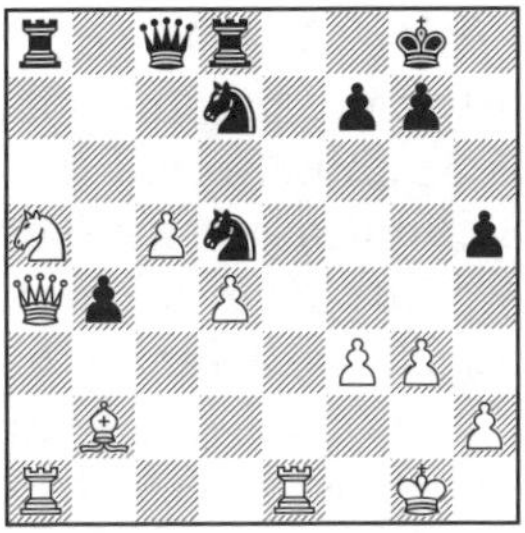

28...♘xc5! 29.dxc5 ♕xc5+ 30.♔h1
Or 30.♔g2 ♘b6–+, followed by a check from d2.
30...♕f2–+.

27.♕b3 ♘7f6 28.♘c4

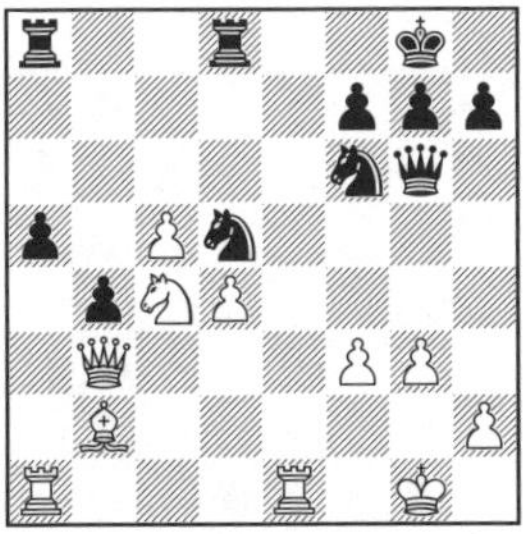

28...a4!? 29.♖xa4 ♖xa4 30.♕xa4 ♕d3 31.♕a2

White’s defence is bothersome. All his pieces, but especially his king, are awkwardly placed. Black’s biggest problem is that he has too many tempting options. Even in a correspondence game, it is difficult to make the best practical choice. For instance, 31...♕xf3 regains the pawn, but allows White to set up some coordination following 32.♘e5 ♕f5 33.♕b1∓.

Without rooks White would be unable to defend his king, but 31...♖e8 could be answered with 32.♖f1 ♕e2 33.♖f2 ♕d1+ 34.♖f1 ♕c2 35.♖c1, constantly harassing the queen.

Perhaps 31...h5!? would have been the most unpleasant try. The game move would have been justified only if Black was winning by force. Otherwise it only helps White's defence. It seems that Andriuschenko simply followed the first line of Stockfish, without elaborating too much on the position.

31...♘c3?! 32.♗xc3 ♕xc3 33.♖d1 ♕xf3 34.♕c2 ♘g4 35.♖e1 g6 36.♘d6 b3 37.♕e2 ♕c3 38.♘b5 ♕b4 39.c6

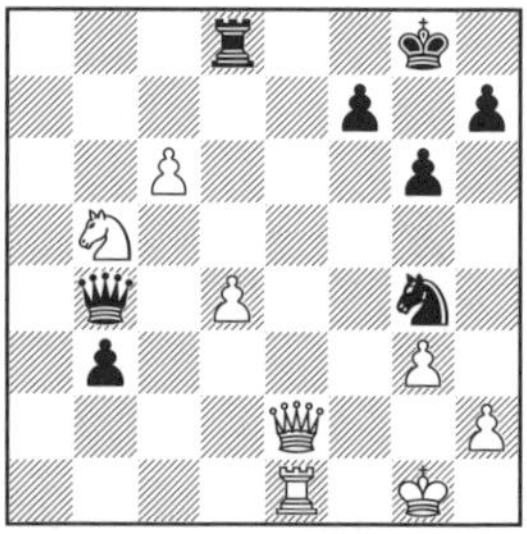

White got some play, too, and the climax is close. Now the outcome is a matter of calculation.

39...♖a8 40.c7 ♔g7 41.♖b1 h5 42.h3 ♖a2 43.♖b2 ♖xb2 44.♕xb2 ♕e1+ 45.♔g2 ♘e3+ 46.♔h2 ♘d1 47.♕g2 b2 48.c8=♕ b1=♕

White's king is weaker, but it turns out that Black cannot break through.

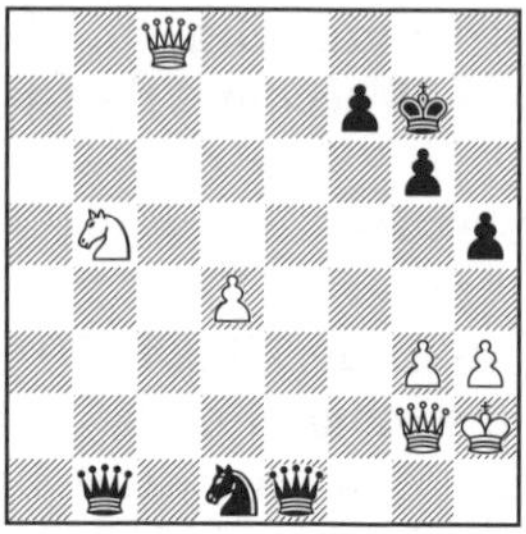

49.♘d6 ♕e7 50.♘e8+ ♔h7 51.♕gc2 ♕xc2+ 52.♕xc2 ♕e1 53.♘f6+ ♔g7 54.♘e8+ ♔f8 55.♘f6 ♘c3 56.♕b2 ♕e2+ 57.♕xe2 ♘xe2 58.d5 ♔e7 59.♘e4 f5 60.♘g5 ♘c3 61.g4 ♘xd5 ½-½

---

9. Tauber – Kurtenkov
ICCF 2018

1.d4 d5 2.c4 c6 3.♘f3 e6 4.♘c3 dxc4 5.a4 ♗b4 6.e3 b5 7.♗d2 a5 8.axb5 ♗xc3 9.♗xc3 cxb5 10.b3 ♗b7 11.♗b2 ♘f6 12.bxc4 b4 13.♗d3 0-0 14.0-0 ♘bd7 15.♘d2 ♕c7 16.♗c2 h6 17.h3

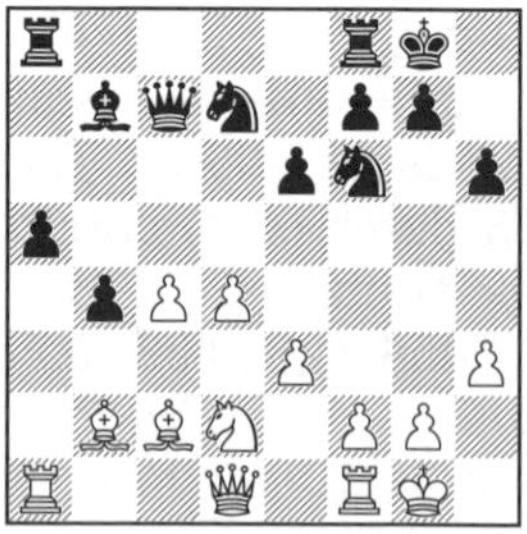

17...♖fc8!

Everybody puts the rook on d8 or e8, but I reached to the conclusion

that the best place for it against a waiting strategy is c8. The idea is to pressurize the c4-pawn, disturbing the harmony of White's pieces.
After 17...♖fd8 18.♖e1 (waiting!) 18...♘b6 19.♖c1! a4 20.c5 ♕c6 21.e4 ♘bd7 22.♗d3 or 22.♗b1 White's centre looks more dangerous than the queenside passers.
17...♖fe8 18.♖e1 e5 19.d5 ♘b6 occurred in Haugen-Johansen, ICCF 2019. White obtained an initiative following 20.♖c1 ♘fd7 21.f4 a4 22.♗a1 b3 23.♗b1 ♖ac8 24.♕e2 ♗a6 25.♕g4 ♕b8 26.♕f5 g6 27.♕g4 ♔h7 28.f5. The more straightforward approach 20.e4 ♖ec8 21.♗b3 ♘fd7 22.f4 f6 23.♘f3∞ is also dangerous.

18.♖e1

The key of Black's design is to counter-attack 18.e4 e5 19.d5 by 19...♗a6 20.♖c1 ♘b6, intending to meet 21.f4 by 21...♘xc4 22.♘xc4 ♕xc4∞.

18...e5

Practice has only seen this thematic break, but I was curious to investigate what could happen if we waited for e4 – 18...♖a6!? 19.e4 (19.♗a4 ♗c6) 19...e5 20.d5 ♘c5 21.f4 ♘fd7 22.♕h5 f6 23.♘f3 a4

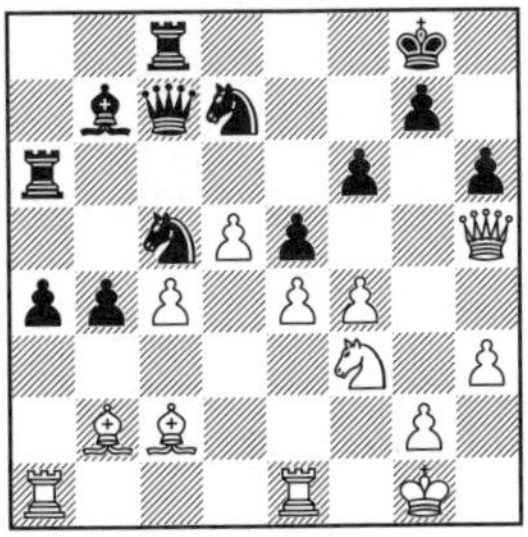

It seems that this position is the maximum White could reach, but the endgame after:
24.fxe5 fxe5 25.♘xe5 ♘xe5 26.♗xe5 g6 27.♗xc7 gxh5 28.♗e5 ♘d7 29.♗d4 ♖xc4 30.♗xa4 ♖xd4= can be calculated up to a draw. One sample variation is 31.♗xd7 ♖xe4 32.♗e6+ ♔g7 33.♖xe4 ♖xa1+ 34.♔f2 ♖a2+ 35.♔e3 ♖a5 36.♔d4 b3 37.♖e2 ♖a2 38.♖e3 ♖d2+ 39.♔e5 b2 40.♖g3+ ♔h7 41.♖b3 ♗a6 42.♗f5+ ♔g7 43.d6 ♗c4 44.♖b7+ ♔f8 45.♖b8+ ♔f7 46.d7 ♖d5+ 47.♔f4 ♗d3=.
The merit of 18...♖a6 is that in the event of e4 White clogs himself his potentially very nasty light-squared bishop.

19.♖c1

19.c5 ♖d8 20.♗b3 exd4 21.exd4 offers Black a perfect square for the queen – 21...♕f4! with ...♗d5 or ...♕g5 coming next.

19...♖e8!

What's this?! The rook went to c8 only two moves ago! I see two reasons for the return:

1. The white rook went to e1, which makes the f4-break less dangerous.

2. 19.♖c1 eliminated our threats down the c-line. However, that was at a cost – it would be easier now to achieve ...a4.

Actually I chose to annotate this game, because Kurtenkov shows a method – how to hold the centre. It may be passive, but you can rely on it. I would like very much to treat this position more concretely, trying to advance the queenside pawns. However, I have realised that even with a pawn on b3 things are not all rosy for Black:

19...♖a6. Doubling rooks to threaten ...a4 and defending the 6th rank.

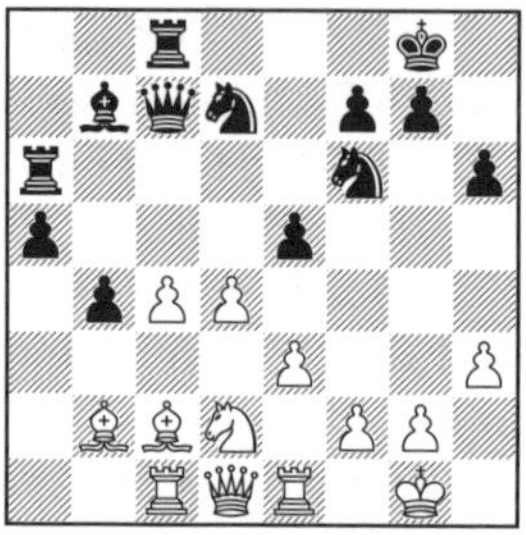

The critical structure arises after:

20.d5!

If White keeps on waiting, we play for ...a4 – 20.♗a1 ♖ca8 21.♗d3 e4 22.♗e2 a4 23.♖b1 b3 24.♕c1 ♖c6 25.♕b2 ♕a5∞.

The structure with 20.c5 is also very sharp – 20...exd4 [We can already play 20...♖d8 21.♗d3 ♖e6 22.♗f5 (22.♗c4 ♖ee8) 22...♖a6.] 21.♗xd4 (21.exd4 ♘d5∞) 21...♖d8 22.♗f5 ♖c6 23.♘f3 ♘xc5 24.♘e5

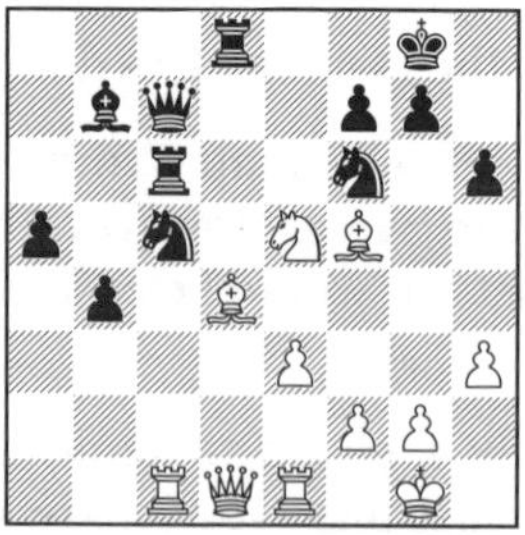

It seems that White is winning something, but time and again we observe that material is irrelevant in the Noteboom:

24...♖d5! 25.♘xc6 ♖xf5 26.♘d8! ♖xf2! with an attack.

20...♖ca8 21.f4

White cannot prevent ...a4 with 21.♖a1 due to 21...♘b6 22.e4 ♘fd7 23.♖e3 a4, e.g. 24.♖g3 a3 25.♗c1 ♔h8∞.

Only 21.♗a4 ♘c5 22.♕c2 stops the pawn, but 22...♘fd7 23.f4 ♘xa4 24.♕xa4 ♖g6 is unclear.

21...a4

It is risky to open more lines with 21...exf4 – 22.exf4 a4 23.♘e4 ♘xe4 24.♗xe4 a3 25.♗a1.

22.fxe5 ♘xe5 23.♗d4 b3 24.♗b1

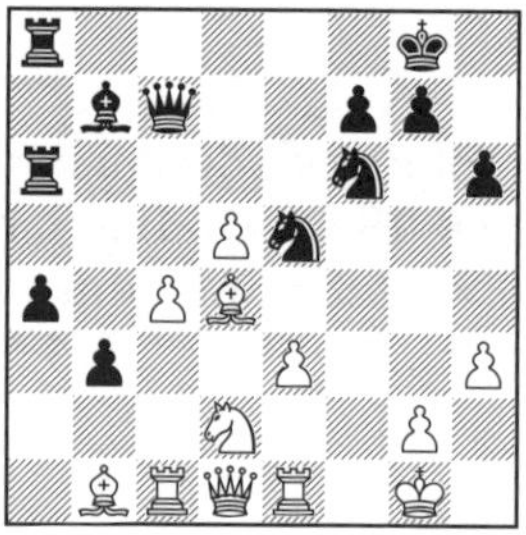

This position occurred in Pierzak-Oreopoulos, ICCF 2018. Black spent a tempo on:

24...♕e7 25.♖f1 ♘fd7 26.♖c3 (In Esposito-Ingersol, ICCF 2019, Black survived after 26.♕h5 ♖e8 27.♕f5 ♖g6, but I still do not like his position.) 26...♖e8 (26...♖c8 27.♕h5) 27.♘f3 ♖f6 28.♘xe5 ♘xe5 29.♖xf6 ♕xf6 30.e4 ♖d8 (30...♗a6 31.c5 ♕f4 32.c6 ♘c4 33.♖f3 ♕d6 34.♔h1±) and got smashed following 31.c5. He should have tried:

24...♘fd7!? 25.♖f1 ♖e8 and Black is holding the blockade, but still White's chances remain somewhat preferable after:

26.e4!

26.♖c3 ♖ea8 (26...♖f6 27.♗f5) 27.♘f3 (27.♗e4 ♘c5 28.♗b1 ♘cd7; 27.♗f5) 27...♖f6 28.♘xe5 ♖xf1+ 29.♕xf1 ♘xe5 30.♕f4 f6 31.♕f5 b2 32.♕h7+ ♔f8 33.e4 ♘f7 34.c5 ♘g5 35.♕f5 a3 36.♗a2 b1=♕+=;

26.♖f5 ♖f6 27.♖xf6 ♘xf6 28.e4 ♗a6 29.c5 ♗d3 30.d6 ♕c6 31.♗xe5 ♗c2 32.♗xc2 ♕xc5+ 33.♔h1 ♕xe5=.

26...♘c5 27.♖c3 ♗c8 28.♕e2 f6 29.♕f2±.

20.d5 ♘c5 21.♖a1

Of course, the most principled approach was 21.f4!? a4 22.fxe5

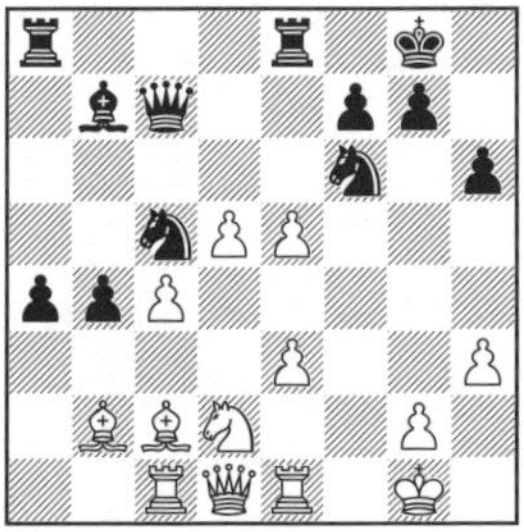

22...♘fd7!

We have seen this trick in a similar position in the "Move by move" section (22...♖xe5 23.♗d4!).

23.♗d4

Or 23.e6 fxe6 24.♕g4 e5 25.♖f1 ♖a6 26.♕f5 ♘f6 27.♕g6 ♖e7 28.♖xf6 ♖xf6 29.♕h7+ ♔f8 when White has a perpetual.

23...b3 24.♗b1 ♘xe5 25.♖f1 ♖a6 26.♖c3 ♗c8 27.♕h5 ♖e7∞. Everything is covered and any mistake could cost White dearly. The a-pawn is hanging like the sword of Damocles over White's position.

21...♕d6 22.f3 ♘fd7 23.♖f1 ♘b6!

Black consistently prepares ...a4. The only other logical move is 23...♖a6, but it fails tactically to 24.f4 e4?! 25.♗d4 ♘b6 26.♘b3+–.

After the text this variation would not be possible since Black would have 25...a4!.

24.f4 e4

24...exf4?? would be a losing mistake due to 25.♕g4 g6 26.♖xf4 with a debacle.

Less obvious is 24...a4?, but again White's attack is crushing after 25.fxe5 ♖xe5 26.♕f3 f6 27.♕f4 b3 28.♗g6+–. Th b6-knight does not help in the defence.

25.♕g4 ♕f8 26.♗d4 ½-½

The peace treaty comes unexpectedly. The position remains tangled and perhaps more precarious for White after 26...a4 27.f5 f6 or 27.♕f5 ♗c8.

Chapter 3. The Marshall Gambit

Main Ideas

1.d4 d5 2.c4 e6 3.♘c3 c6 4.e4

The Marshall Gambit, which arises after 4...dxe4 5.♘xe4 ♗b4+ 6.♗d2, has always been considered by theory as harmless. Yet it brings White 57% (compared to only 46% after 4.♘f3 dxc4). My own experience also confirms that Black's task is not easy. My first test (without any preparation!) concluded with a debacle:

Donchev-Semkov

Bul. ch. Sofia 1985

1.c4 e6 2.d4 d5 3.♘c3 c6 4.e4 dxe4 5.♘xe4 ♗b4+ 6.♗d2 ♕xd4 7.♗xb4 ♕xe4+ 8.♗e2 ♘a6 9.♗d6 b6 10.♕d2 ♗b7 11.♘f3 ♖d8? 12.0-0-0 ♕f5

The game has barely begun, but White has already a decisive edge. That is a typical scenario in the Marshall Gambit. Just one mistake, often not too obvious, and Black's position is defenceless. The finish was:

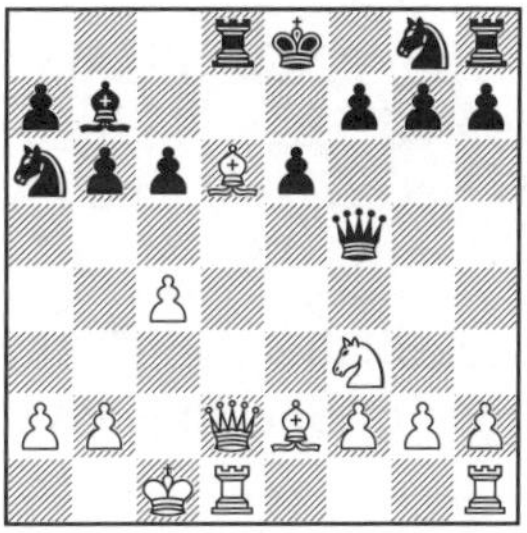

13.g4! ♕a5 14.♕f4! f6 15.♗a3 b5 16.♖xd8+ ♕xd8 17.♖d1 ♕c8 18.♗d6 ♘e7 19.♔b1 ♘g6 20.♕e3 b4 21.♘d4 ♔f7 22.c5 ♘e7 23.♗xe7 ♔xe7 24.♘f5+ ♔f8 25.♘d6 ♕d7 26.♘xb7 1-0.

Since then I began playing the gambit with White, and was impressed how stable and difficult to neutralise his initiative was. In the following example my opponent was a well prepared GM. Although he survived the opening, he has never tamed the bishop pair:

Semkov-Spassov

Bul. chT Sofia 1991

1.d4 d5 2.c4 e6 3.♘c3 c6 4.e4 dxe4 5.♘xe4 ♗b4+ 6.♗d2 ♕xd4 7.♗xb4 ♕xe4+ 8.♗e2 ♘a6 9.♗c3 e5 10.♕d6 ♘e7 11.♖d1 ♗e6 12.♘f3 ♘f5 13.♕xe5 ♕xe5 14.♗xe5 f6 15.♗c3 c5 16.g4 ♘e7 17.g5 ♔f7 18.gxf6 gxf6 19.♘h4 h5 20.f4 ♘c7

21.f5! ♘xf5 22.♘xf5 ♗xf5 23.♖f1 ♔e6 24.♖d5! ♗g4 25.♖xf6+ ♔e7 26.♖xc5 ♘e6 27.♖e5!, and I went on to win on move 47.

This "lyrical diversion" aimed to underline my following advice:

Do not try to play the Marshall Gambit without a thorough preparation!

Unlike the Noteboom, where a few key strategic ideas should be enough for obtaining decent results, here you'll need to remember the main lines move by move. There is really no ground for improvisation. I've boiled the vital information down to 12 pages in the "Step by Step" section, so it should not be a Sisyphean task.

Move orders

After **4.e4** we take the gift – **4...dxe4**. You may have seen many games with 4...♗b4. It would have made sense to study its numerous branches only if we wanted to meet 5.♗d2 by 5...dxc4 6.♗xc4 ♕xd4. I feel that this variation is more dangerous for Black than the main line. At least 4...dxe4 is well tested and you can follow proven paths, while here White still has many unexplored possibilities.

Thus I will focus on **5.♘xe4 ♗b4+ 6.♗d2**.

6.♘c3 is a harmless way to bail out. It is enough to remember that we attack the centre with 6...c5 7.a3 ♗a5 8.♗e3 ♘e7 (planning ...♘f5), or 8.♘f3 ♘f6.

6...♕xd4 7.♗xb4 ♕xe4+

The main answer is 8.♗e2, but recently I have been observing a turn towards **8.♘e2**. After it we cannot avoid the equal endgame which occurs in different settings, e.g. 8...♘a6 9.♗f8 ♘e7 10.♗xg7 ♘b4! 11.♕d6 ♘d3+ 12.♔d2 ♘f5 13.♕xd3 ♕xd3+ 14.♔xd3 ♘xg7.

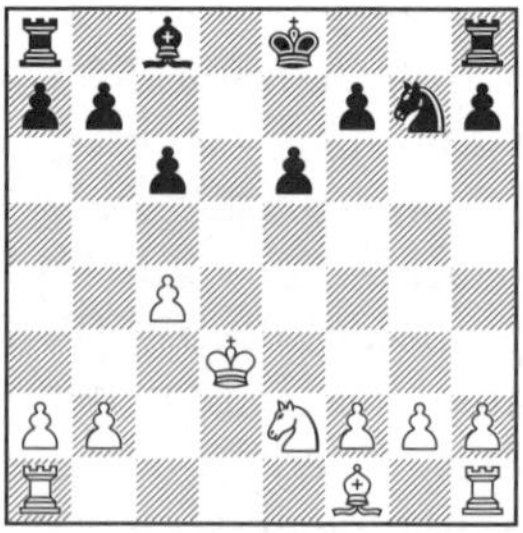

Black's best plan is ...b6, ...♗b7 (not ...e5), ...0-0-0, then he tries to get rid of the h-pawn with ...h5.

8.♗e2 ♘a6 leads us to the main split in the Marshall Gambit:

9.♗d6 and 9.♗a5 have been dominating lately, although:
9.♗c3 is hardly any worse. I recommend to meet it by 9...f6, followed by ...♘e7 and ...0-0 if White castles short, or ...♔f7, ...♖e8 if White plays ♕d6.

9.♗a5 b6 10.♕d6 ♗d7 11.♗c3 f6 is a more sophisticated version of 9.♗c3.

Before settling down on the main diagonal, the bishop provoked ...b6. That could be a useful move, if Black could follow with ...♗b7, but in connection with ...♗d7 it just weakens c6. That forces some corrections in our set-up. Our knight goes to h6, but more importantly, our king may have to stay on e8 or even hide on the queenside in lines like 12.♘f3 ♘h6 13.♖d1 ♖d8 14.♕a3 ♗c8 15.♖xd8+ ♔xd8.

In both 9.♗c3 and 9.♗a5 lines White commonly has sufficient long-term compensation for the pawn. Sometimes it is due to the awkward knight on a6, in other games Black suffers from a weak seventh rank. Thus play is balanced, with heavy calculation. Do not overestimate your chances in endgames with an extra pawn!
Sometimes even two extra pawns are not enough to claim a Black's advantage.

Analysis

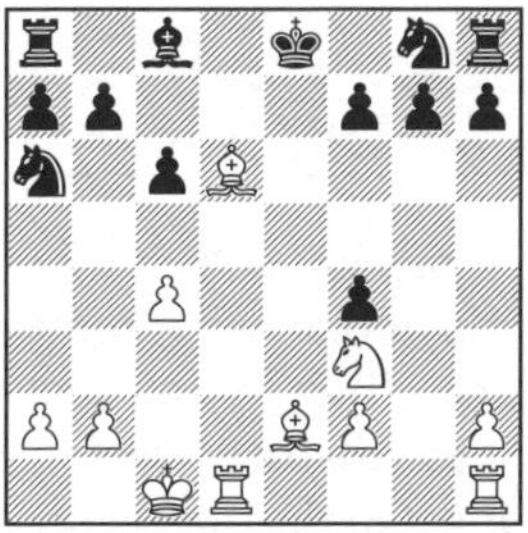

Black can just maintain the balance with 14...♘h6 15.c5 ♘b4 16.♖he1 ♗e6=.

Important decisions

It is fashionable for Black to try ...a5 in many lines of the Marshall Gambit. I do not like this move at all.
We should prefer a set-up with ...c5+...b6 rather than ...a5+...b5 in order to activate our bishop.
Compare the following two diagrams. In the first one Black comfortably completes development and puts a rook on d8:

Analysis

Analysis

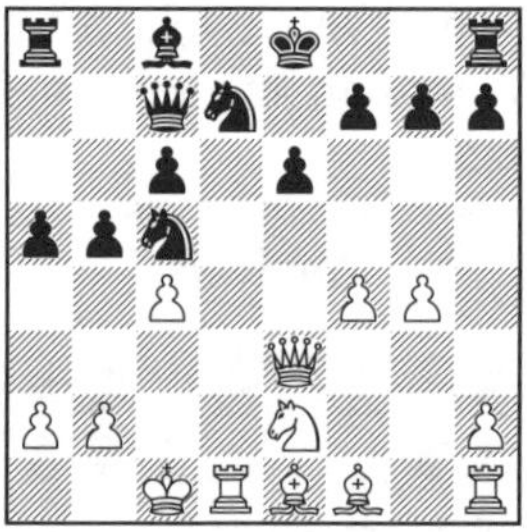

Here Black's activity on the queenside looks very tempting at first glance, but his pieces are too passive to disturb seriously the white king. On the opposite, White's pawn storm on the other wing is more dangerous and does not demand difficult decisions.

Even if Black castles short, trouble could still await him.

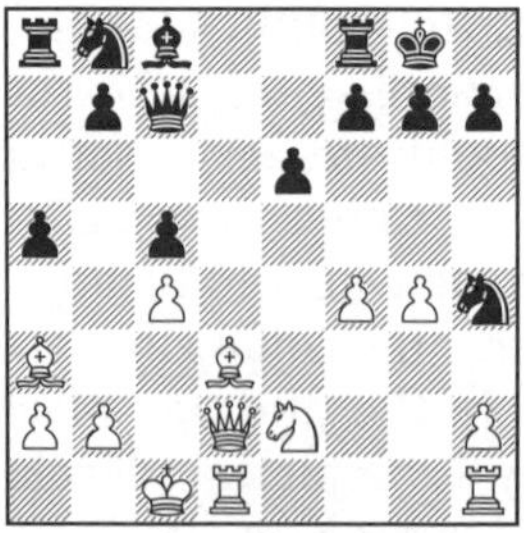

In this typical position White has a strong initiative all over the board.

Another important moment is when to play ...e5. Several decades ago Black was trying to solve his problems with an early ...e5, even as a counter-sacrifice. My treatment is to avoid this move at the early stage of the game, except for the line 9.♗d6. The reason is that ...e5 often gives White a lever for an attack. You should constantly calculate blows on e5:

Analysis

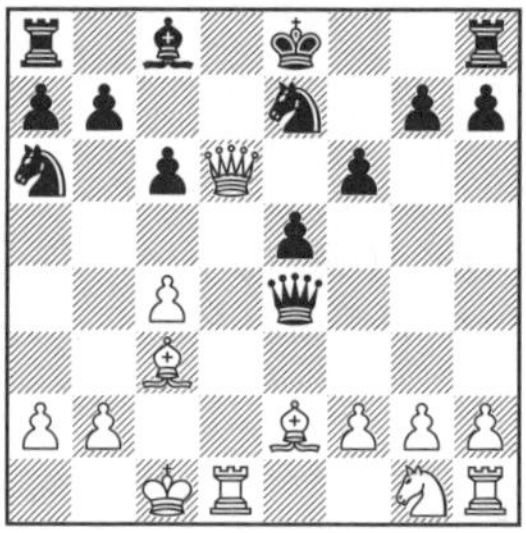

12.♘f3! ♕xe2 13.♖he1 ♕xf2 14.♖xe5! 0-0 15.♕xe7 ♗g4 16.♖d2 ♕xd2+ 17.♘d2 ♖f7 18.♘e4↑.

Analysis

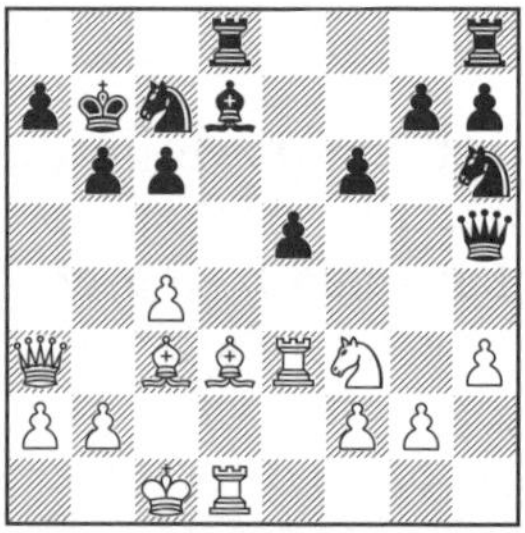

19.♘xe5!! fxe5 20.♗xe5 with an attack, e.g. 20...a5 21.♗e2 ♕g6 22.♖b3.

Analysis

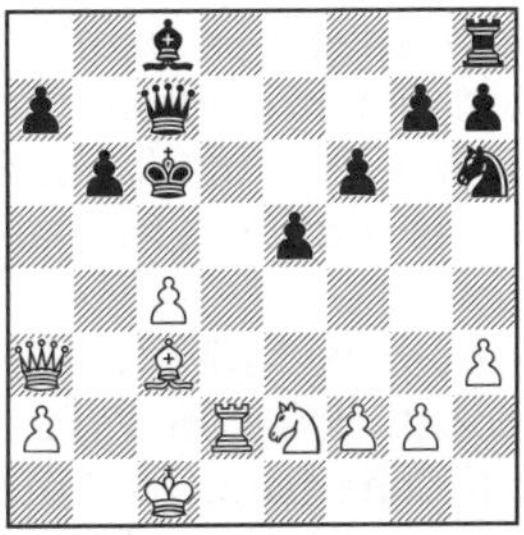

24.♗xe5! ♕xe5 25.♕xa7 ♘f5 26.g4=, regaining the piece.

The main line 9.♗d6

9.♗d6 ♕xg2! considerably differs from the other 9th move options.

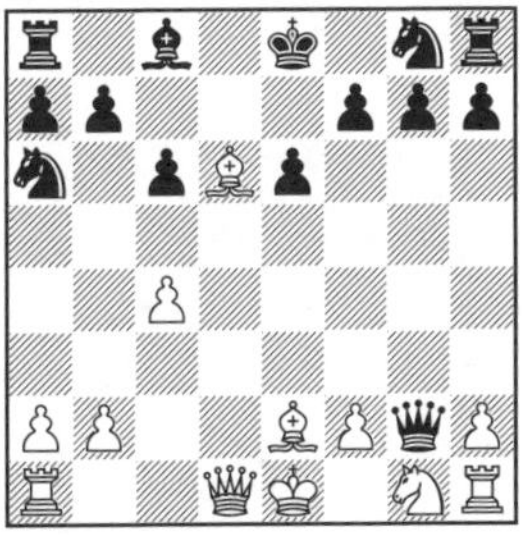

The bishop plugs the d-file and that gives Black time to grab a second pawn. The subsequent play is forced, so the general principles from the other lines are irrelevant. White's main retort is **10.♕d2**.

10.♗f3 ♕g5 11.♘e2 ♘e7 12.♘g3! is rare, but not bad. For consistency with the main line you could remember 12...e5!=.

10...e5!?

This is the surprise I have in store. The well known equaliser is 10...♘f6. See **Game 14** Denisov-Kurbasov, ICCF 2015.

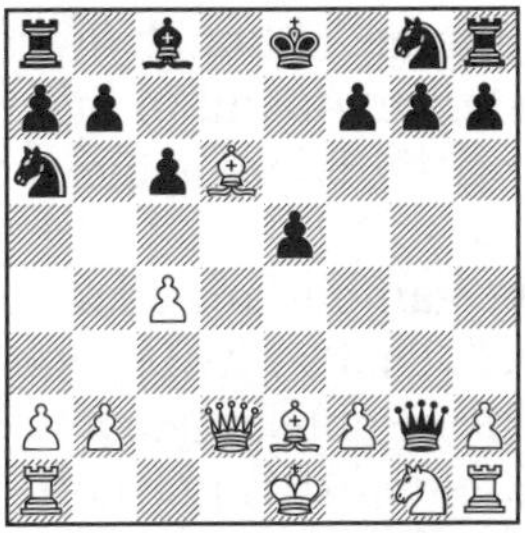

This position is almost unexplored, and you should have a serious practical edge over your unsuspecting opponents. The idea is to attack White's long castle along the diagonal b1-h7 with ...♗f5, ...♕e4. Remeber the correct move order – 11.♗xe5 ♗f5, but 11.0-0-0 must be met by 11...♕e4!. Otherwise White can cut off our queen from the centre with ♘f3 and we'd risk to co-author a miniature, as in:

Steneskog-Eriksson
Linkoping, 1996

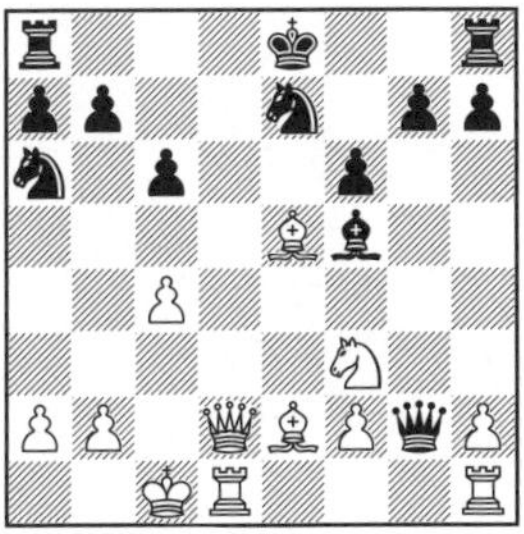

14.♖hg1 ♕h3 15.♖xg7 fxe5 16.♖xe7+ ♔xe7 17.♕d6+ 1-0.

For the rest, you better study carefully the "Step by Step" section.

Theoretical status

The Marshall Gambit has always been regarded by theory as insufficient for an advantage, although owing to different variations throughout the years. For instance, Anand in his world title match against Kramnik provoked it choosing the Triangle move order. Clearly, he was confident in Black's position.
Still, the gambit fans count on practical chances, since "initiative is an advantage". That's why I propose the rare counter-attack 9.♗d6 ♕xg2 10.♕d2 e5!?. ChessPublishing.com ignores it at all, while Scherbakov just mentions that 11.♗xe5 ♗f5 is playable. Hopefully, your opponents would not be prepared for this turn of events.

Chapter 3. The Marshall Gambit

Step by Step

1.d4 d5 2.c4 e6 3.♘c3 c6 4.e4

4.♗f4?! dxc4 5.e3 b5 6.a4 counts only the trap:

6...♗b4? 7.axb5 cxb5 8.♕f3 ♕d5 9.♕g3 with a double hit on g7 and b8. The careful answer is:

6...♕b6! 7.♗e2 ♘f6∓.

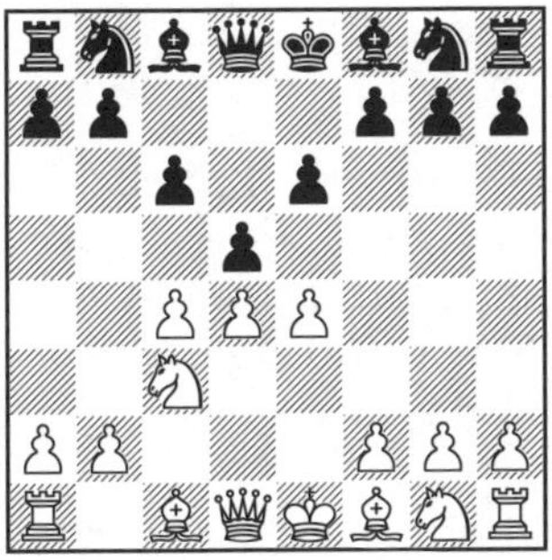

4...dxe4

4...♗b4?! is less explored so it might look suitable to play for a win. However, I do not see any chess arguments in its favour. For instance, you should study the unpleasant retorts 5.e5, 5.cxd5, 5.♗d3, even 5.exd5, and when (and if) you finally feel fully prepared, your opponent suddenly answers:

5.♗d2!?. The only way to justify the effort you invested in 4...♗b4 is to deviate from the main line with:

5...dxc4 6.♗xc4 ♕xd4 (or 6...♘f6 7.♕e2 ♕xd4) 7.♕e2 ♘f6, to enter another gambit, which in my opinion gives White more chances than the true Marshall.

White has plenty of ways to attack with natural moves. Even if we play the most obvious ones:

8.♘f3 ♕d8

8...♕b6 is better, but the plan with e4-e5 remains effective, although White must spend a tempo to defend b2 after ...♗b4-e7.

9.e5 ♘d5 10.0-0 ♗e7 11.♕e4, Black's defence is not trivial at all. The computer suggests:

11...♔f8, but Black will never connect his rooks after it. White can continue with simple, typical moves:

12.h4 ♘d7 13.h5 h6 14.♖ad1 ♘c5 15.♕g4 ♕c7 16.♖fe1 b5 17.♗f1 b4 18.♘e4 ♘xe4 19.♖xe4 ♗b7 20.♕g3 ♔g8 21.♖g4

22.♗c1, intending ♘d2, also deserves attention.

21...♗f8 22.♘d4

I have followed all the way the first line of the engines for Black, to reach an extremely unpleasant position. White plays with an extra rook on the queenside.

In short, my advice is: 4...♗b4 is not worth the pain.

5.♘xe4

5.♗e3 is almost unknown, but it is not a mistake.

We should not try to refute it with jerky actions like 5...f5 as 6.f3 would give White what he wanted. Instead we develop our pieces:

5...♘f6 6.♕c2

6.f3 is well met by 6...♗b4 7.♕c2 (7.a3? ♗xc3+ 8.bxc3 ♕a5 9.♕c2 c5) 7...0-0 8.0-0-0 (8.♘ge2 exf3 9.gxf3 b5∓) 8...♗xc3 9.♕xc3 (9.bxc3 b5 10.fxe4 bxc4 11.♗xc4 ♕a5∓) 9...b5∓.

6...♗b4

Putting pressure on the centre. 6...♘bd7 7.0-0-0 ♗e7 8.♘xe4 ♘xe4 9.♕xe4 ♘f6 10.♕c2 b5 is possible, but 11.c5 leaves us with a bad bishop on c8, e.g. 11...♘d5 12.♘f3 a5 13.h4∞. I'd rather try to push ...e5.

7.♘ge2 0-0 8.a3 ♗e7 9.♘xe4 ♘xe4 10.♕xe4 ♘d7

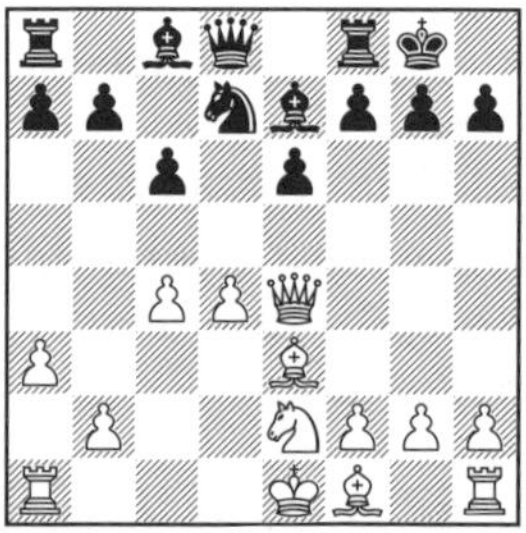

11.♕c2

11.0-0-0 ♘f6 12.♕c2 b5 is already good since a3 gives us a tempo for 13.c5 b4 14.a4 ♗a6.

11...e5 12.0-0-0 ♗g5 with a good, balanced game.

5...♗b4+

Kramnik's 5...c5?! does not work owing to 6.♘xc5 ♘c6 7.♘f3 ♘xd4 8.♕xd4 ♕xd4 9.♘xd4 ♗xc5 10.♘b5 ♔e7 11.♘c7! ♖b8 12.♗f4 ♗b4+ 13.♔e2 ♗d6 14.♗xd6+ ♔xd6 15.♘b5+ ♔c5 16.♘xa7 ♗d7 17.♔d2±.

6.♗d2

6.♘c3 is an attempt to bail out from

the theoretical dispute. The most challenging retort is:

6...c5

6...e5 7.dxe5 ♕xd1+ 8.♔xd1 ♗f5 is only good to eventually make a draw, e.g. 9.♘f3 ♘d7 10.♘h4 ♗e6 11.f4 ♘h6 12.♔c2 0-0-0 with compensation for the pawn.

7.a3

In some positions with doubled pawns on c3 and c4 White could be better off without a3. For instance: 7.♘f3 ♘f6 8.♗e3 cxd4 (8...0-0= is a fair alternative. 8...♕a5 is an attempt to exploit the absence of a3, but it is unclear what we gain after 9.♗d2 cxd4 10.♘xd4 ♕e5+ 11.♗e3) 9.♘xd4 (9.♕xd4 ♕a5) 9...0-0 10.♗e2

10...♗xc3+!? (10...e5 may be more sound, although not so easy to play: 11.♘db5 ♘c6 12.a3 ♗xc3+ 13.♘xc3 ♗e6 14.0-0 ♕c8 15.♘d5 ♗xd5 16.cxd5 ♖d8. The d5-pawn is doomed, but White will enjoy sufficient compensation due to his bishop pair – 17.♗c4 h6 18.♖c1 ♕f5 19.f3 ♘e7 20.d6 ♘c8 21.♖f2∞. You'll have to calculate much more in this line.) 11.bxc3 a6 12.♕b1 ♕c7 13.0-0 e5 14.♘f5 ♗xf5 15.♕xf5 ♘bd7. It would be difficult for White to create the smallest threat.

7...♗a5

7...♗xc3+ 8.bxc3 ♘f6 9.♘f3 ♕a5 10.♗d2 ♘e4 11.♗d3 ♘xd2 12.♕xd2 0-0! 13.0-0 cxd4 14.♕c2! dxc3 15.♗xh7+ ♔h8 leaves White some initiative, although both correspondence games finished in a draw.

8.♗e3

8.♘f3 accepts doubled pawns on the c-file – 8...♘f6 (8...♘e7 is pointless here as White has not committed his bishop to e3 – 9.♗e2 cxd4 10.♕xd4 ♕xd4 11.♘xd4 ♘bc6 12.♘xc6 ♗xc3+ 13.bxc3 ♘xc6 14.♖b1 with subsequent c4-c5.) 9.♕d3!? (Preventing ...♘e4 – 9.♗e2 ♘e4; 9.♗e3 ♘e4 10.♕c2 ♘xc3 11.bxc3 cxd4 12.♗xd4 0-0 13.♗d3 g6 is double-edged, with mutual chances. A safer solution is: 9...0-0! 10.♕d3 cxd4 11.♘xd4 e5 12.♘db5 a6 13.♘d6 ♗xc3+=.) 9...0-0 (9...cxd4 10.♘xd4 0-0 11.b4 ♗c7 12.♘db5 ♗e5 13.f4 ♕xd3 14.♗xd3 ♗xc3+ 15.♘xc3±) 10.dxc5 ♕xd3 11.♗xd3 ♗xc3+ 12.bxc3 ♗d7 with an excellent game. Black leads out his knight on a6 – 13.♘e5 ♘a6 or 13.♗e3 ♘a6 14.♘e5 ♖fc8. Another good set-up is 13.♗e3 ♖d8 14.0-0-0 ♘c6.

8...♘e7

8...♘f6 9.♘e2 cxd4 is more frequent (a recent game went 9.♘ge2 cxd4 10.♕xd4 ♕xd4 11.♗xd4 ♘c6 12.b4 ♘xd4 13.♘xd4 ♗c7 14.♗e2 ½-½, Markus-Berkes, Subotica 2019), but I want to have the threat ...♘f5 in our disposal.

9.♘ge2 cxd4 10.♕xd4 ♘f5 11.♕e4 (11.♕xd8+ ♗xd8=) 11...♘xe3. Black has a comfortable position. See **Game 10** Bär-Glatthaar, ICCF 2017.

6...♕xd4 7.♗xb4 ♕xe4+

A. 8.♘e2; **B.** 8.♗e2

A. 8.♘e2 ♘a6

8...♘d7 9.♕d6 ♕e5! is also possible. Note that I'm always against 9...a5? in the Marshall Gambit.

In my opinion we should choose plans with ...c5 rather than ...a5 – 10.♗a3 (10.♗c3 ♘gf6=) 10...♕e5 11.♕d2

Black lacks exactly one tempo to conclude development: 11...♘gf6 12.f4! ♕b8 13.♘c3 c5 14.g4 0-0 15.♗e2 ♖d8 16.g5 b5 17.♘xb5 ♘e4 18.♕e3 f5 19.0-0-0 ♗a6 20.♖he1±;

11...c5 12.f4 ♕b8 13.0-0-0 b6 14.g4 ♖a7 15.♘c3 ♗a6 16.♘e4 ♘df6 17.♘d6+ ♔e7 18.b4!! axb4 19.♗b2 ♖d7 20.♗e5 ♕d8 21.f5 ♘e4 22.♕f4 f6 23.fxe6 ♖xd6 24.♗xd6+ ♘xd6 25.h4± with total domination.

Scherbakov recommends 9...c5 at once, but after 10.♗c3 ♘e7 11.0-0-0 e5 12.♘g3 ♕f4+ he misses 13.♗d2! with an edge, e.g. 13...♕h4 (13...♕d4 14.♕c7) 14.♕c7 0-0 15.♗e3 f5 16.♖xd7 ♗xd7 17.♕xd7 ♖ad8 18.♕e6+ ♔h8 19.♕xe5 ♘g6 20.♕c3 f4 21.♗xc5±.

10.♕d2

White keeps the queens. This option is the difference (I do not mean it is a drawback!) in comparison to 8...♘a6.

10.♕xe5 ♘xe5 11.♗c3 (White does not have enough compensation following 11.♘g3 ♘f6 12.♗c3 ♘ed7 13.♗e2 b6 14.♘h5

♖g8 15.♘xf6+ gxf6 16.0-0-0 ♔e7 17.g3 ♗b7 18.♖d2∓) 11...f6 12.♗xe5 fxe5 13.♘c3. Black's crippled pawn structure balances the extra pawn – 13...♘f6 14.♗d3 b6 15.0-0-0 ♔e7 16.♖he1 ♘d7 17.f3 ♗b7 18.♘e4 c5 19.♘f2 ♖af8 20.♘g4 ♖f4 21.♘xe5 ♘xe5 22.♖xe5 ♖d8 23.♖e3 ♖d6=.

10...♘gf6 11.0-0-0

11.♗d6 ♘e4 12.♗xe5 ♘xd2 13.♗xg7 ♖g8 14.♔xd2 ♖xg7 15.g3 b6 16.♗g2 ♗b7 leads to the same structure as in the main line – 17.♔c3 0-0-0 18.♖hd1 c5=.

11.f4 ♕b8 12.♘c3 is ineffective as 12...c5 is with a tempo – 13.♗a3 b6 14.♘b5? ♘e4 15.♕e3 a6∓.

11...♘e4 12.♕e3

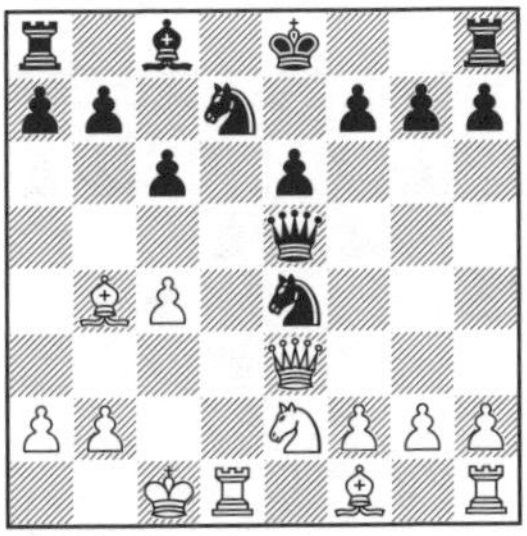

12...♘ef6

Again 12...a5 offers White an initiative – 13.f4 ♕c7 14.♗e1 ♘ec5 15.g4 b5 16.♘g3 0-0 17.♘h5 ♔h8 18.h4 ♖g8 19.g5 ♗a6 20.♗c3 bxc4 21.f5 e5 22.f6 g6 23.♘g3 h5 24.♘xh5 gxh5 25.♕e2↑.

13.♕f3 ♕e4 14.♕b3 c5 15.f3 ♕c6 16.♗e1 0-0 17.♗g3 b6 18.♕e3 ♗b7 19.♘c3 ♖fd8∞.

8...♕xc4? is too greedy. Black is horribly lagging behind in development after 9.♕d6 ♘d7 10.♘c3 ♕h4 11.♗a3, followed by ♗d3, 0-0 (or 0-0-0).

9.♗f8

9.♗a5!? is a fresh idea which needs more tests. Perhaps the safest answer is:

9...♕h4!

9...b6?! 10.♗c3 offers decent compensation. More interesting is:

9...♗d7 10.♕d2 (10.♕d6 ♘f6) 10...♘f6 11.f3 ♕xc4 12.♘f4 ♕c5 13.♗xa6 bxa6 14.♗b4 with equal chances, according to engines. However, Black's dark squares will be permanently weak.

The text defends d8 and prepares ...0-0. The c8-bishop may find good prospects on b7.

10.♕d2

Or 10.♘g3 ♘h6 11.♕d6 ♕e7.

10...♘h6 11.0-0-0 0-0 12.♘g3, Utnasunov-Kezin, rapid, Sochi 2017. Now 12...b6 13.♗c3 ♗b7 or 12...f6, intending ...e5 or ...♘f7, favour Black.

White has no threats after 9.♗c3 f6 10.♕d2 e5 11.♖d1 ♗e6 12.b3 ♘e7 13.f3 ♕h4+ 14.g3 ♕h5.

White is still to prove enough compensation for the two pawns after 9.f3 ♕xc4 10.♗c3 ♘f6 or 10...f6.

9...♘e7

9...♕e5? is awful after 10.♕d2 ♗d7 11.♗d6 ♕e4 12.0-0-0.

10.♗xg7

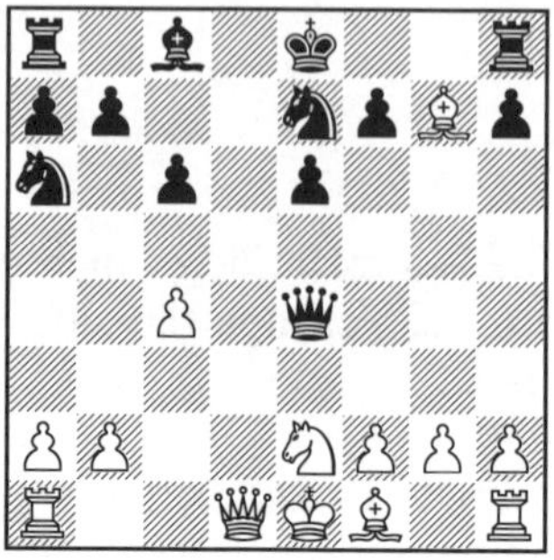

10...♘b4 11.♕d6

11.♗xh8 e5 12.♕d6

White is under attack following 12.♕b3 ♘d3+ 13.♔d2 ♗f5 14.f3 ♕h4.

12...♘c2+ 13.♔d2 ♗f5 14.♘g3 is a draw – 14...♕f4+ 15.♔c3 ♘d5+ 16.cxd5 ♕d4+ 17.♔b3 ♘xa1+ 18.♔a3 ♘c2+=.

11...♘d3+ 12.♔d2 ♘f5 13.♕xd3 ♕xd3+ 14.♔xd3 ♘xg7 15.♔c3

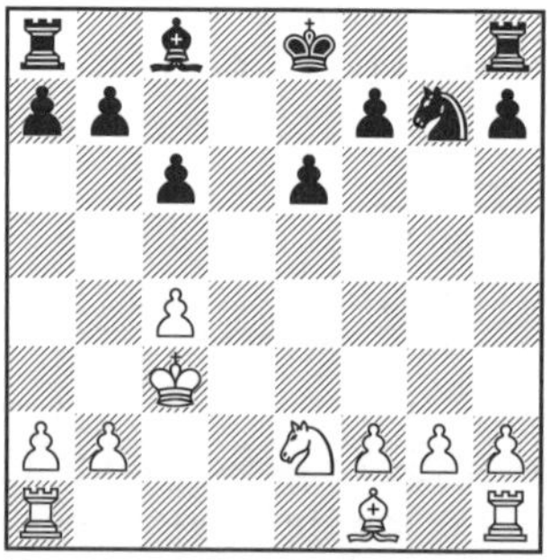

White has a tiny structural advantage as the h7-pawn is cut off from the rest of the chain. Still, a couple of precise moves should level the chances. It suffices to say that Black has not lost a single game according to my correspondence/computer database, and the OTB encounters are also in Black's favour. See **Game 11** Wojtaszek-Giri, Biel 2014.

B. 8.♗e2 ♘a6

8...a5 marked some initial success, but It seems that White has pinpointed the best retort:

9.♗d6 ♘h6 10.♕d2!

The speculative sacrifice 10.♘f3 ♘f5 11.0-0?! leads nowhere after 11...♘xd6 12.♕xd6 ♕xe2 13.♖ad1 ♘d7 14.b3 ♕b2 15.♘d4 ♖a6∓ (15...♕c3 also deserves attention).

10...♘f5 11.♗a3

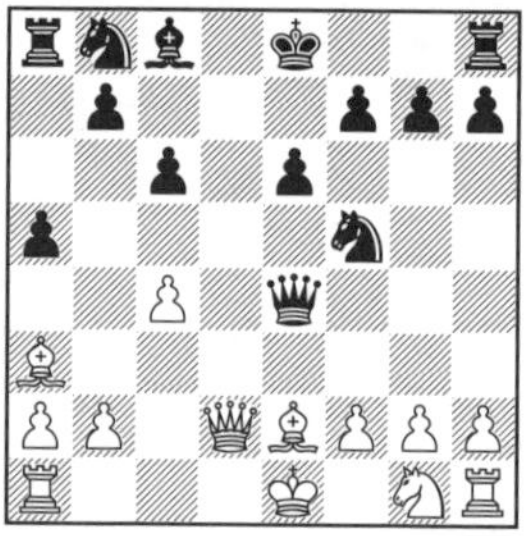

11...♕d4

11...♕xg2 12.0-0-0 ♘d7 13.♗f3 ♕g6 14.♗e4 f6 15.♘e2 ♔f7 16.f4 ♖e8 offered White many attacking possibilities. Jensson-Kolehmainen, ICCF 2017, saw:

17.♖hg1 ♕h6 18.♗xf5 exf5 19.♘g3 ♘f8 20.♖de1 ♖xe1+ 21.♖xe1 ♘g6 22.♔b1 ♘xf4 23.♕d8 with a catastrophe on the last two ranks.

17.♘g3 ♘f8 18.♖he1, intending to trade the last defenders, is similar.

11...♘d7 12.0-0-0 ♕h4? lost on the spot following 13.g4 ♘e7 14.♘f3 ♕f6 15.♘g5 0-0 16.♘xh7! ♔xh7 17.g5, Dambacher-Klein, Limburg 2018.

12.♗d3 ♕e5+ 13.♘e2 c5 14.0-0-0 0-0 15.g4 ♘h4 16.f4 ♕c7. White has the better game owing to his dominance on the d-file.

Curiously, Rogozenco-Lupulescu, Baile Govora 2017, stopped abruptly after 17.♖hf1 f5?!, draw?! In fact Black is almost lost, e.g. 18.gxf5 ♘xf5 19.♘c3 ♘a6 20.♗xf5 ♖xf5 21.b3±. Also good is:

17.♗e4 ♘a6 18.♘c3 ♘b4 19.b3 f5 20.gxf5 ♘xf5 21.♘b5 ♕e7 22.♖hg1 e5 23.♗b2±.

The old recommendation 8...c5 9.♗xc5 ♕xg2 is inferior. White has several promising continuations, e.g. 10.♗f3 ♕g5 11.♕d6 ♘d7 12.♗a3.

Let's now return to the move which stood the test of time:

Here White tried almost all legal retreats:

B1. 9.♗c3; **B2.** 9.♗a5; **B3.** 9.♗d6

9.♗a3? is a mistake as 9...c5 (or 9...♗d7 10.♘f3 c5) shuts down the bishop.

9.♗f8?! also sends the bishop to a precarious place – 9...♕xg2 10.♕d6 ♗d7 11.♗f3 ♕g5 12.♘h3 ♕f6 13.0-0-0 0-0-0.

B1. 9.♗c3 f6

9...♘e7 is also solid, but the text is more challenging.

10.♘f3

10.♕d6 should be met by 10...♘e7.

10...♘h6?! stumbled into 11.♗xf6! gxf6 12.0-0-0 ♕g6 13.♕d8+ ♔f7 14.♕xh8 ♘b4 15.♗h5 ♘xa2+ 16.♔d2 ♕xh5 17.♕xh7+ ♔f8 18.♘f3 e5, Nakamura-Tomashevsky, Elancourt 2013, when 19.♔e2 leads to an amazing 20-move drawing variation, but 9.h3!! e4 10.♖he1 gives White the upper hand. 10...♘e7 prevents this sacrifice.

11.0-0-0 (11.♖d1!?) 11...♔f7

11...e5 is not a mistake, but 12.♘f3! ♕xe2 13.♖he1 ♕xf2 14.♖xe5!! 0-0 15.♕xe7 ♗g4 16.♖d2 ♕xd2+ 17.♘xd2 offers White some initiative.

12.♗d3 ♕xg2 13.♘e2

We have reached a typical position for the Marshall Gambit. White undoubtedly has considerable compensation for the two pawns, and only concrete analysis could tell the correct evaluation. The rule is that if White does not win by force, all three results are possible. The most natural follow up is to check from g5:

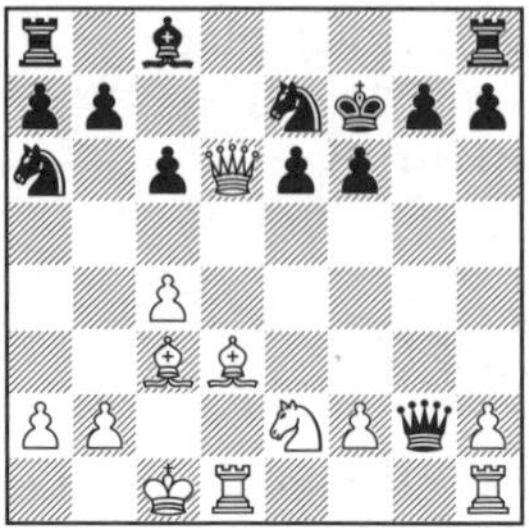

13...♕g5+!? 14.♖d2! (14.♔b1 e5! – leave the queen to defend the kingside, the point being 15.♖hg1 ♘f5!∓. In a blitz game I made the mistake 14...♕c5? and was worse after 15.♕g3 e5 16.♖hg1 g6 17.♕f3!, enabling ♘g3-e4.) 14...♕h6 15.f4 ♗d7 16.c5 ♖ad8 17.♗xa6 ♗c8 18.♕c7 ♖xd2 19.♗xd2 bxa6 20.♘c3 f5 21.h4 ♖e8 22.h5. White has full compensation and perhaps the cost of his mistakes is not so high.

But this is the only option which does not lead to a forced draw.

13...♖e8 14.♖hg1 ♕h3 transposes to 12...♕h3, but we also have to investigate the tangled line 14.f4 ♕h3 15.♘d4 ♕e3+ 16.♔b1 e5 17.fxe5 ♕xe5 18.♘b5 ♕h5 19.♖hg1⩲. Perhaps we should limit the opponent's options by:

13...♕h3

Now 14.♘f4 would fail to 14...♘f5, so the only sensible move is:

14.♖hg1 ♖e8

White has several ways to make a draw:

15.♖xg7+

Or 15.♘f4 ♕h4 (15...♘f5 16.♘xh3 ♘xd6 17.♗xh7 ♖h8=) 16.♖g2 g5 [16...♘c5!? does not escape from the draw – 17.♕xc5 ♕xf4+ 18.♗d2 ♕h4 19.♖dg1 g6 20.♖g4 (20.f4? ♘f5) 20...♕xh2 21.♗f4 ♕h3 22.♖4g3=.] 17.♖dg1 ♕xf4+ 18.♕xf4 gxf4 19.♖g7+ ♔f8 20.♗xf6 e5 21.♖xh7 ♘f5=.

15...♔xg7 16.♖g1+ ♔f7 17.♗xf6! ♘f5 18.♗xf5 ♕xf5 19.♗e5 ♖g8 20.♖xg8 ♔xg8 21.♕d8+ ♕f8 22.♕g5+ ♔f7 23.♘c3 ♘c5 24.♕h5+=. Eventually White gives perpetual check.

10...♘e7 11.0-0

11.♕d6 is already pointless on account of 11...♘g6 12.♘d2 ♕f4 13.♕a3 ♕c7 or 13...c5.

11...0-0 12.♖e1

12.b4 is much less frequent, but I think it is more useful than the rook move. At least it limits Black's options to 12...e5 13.♖e1 ♘g6, transposing to line a) below.

13.b5?! is premature as Black's

queen is still controlling b4 – 13...cxb5 14.cxb5 ♘c7.

Let's now return to 12.♖e1:

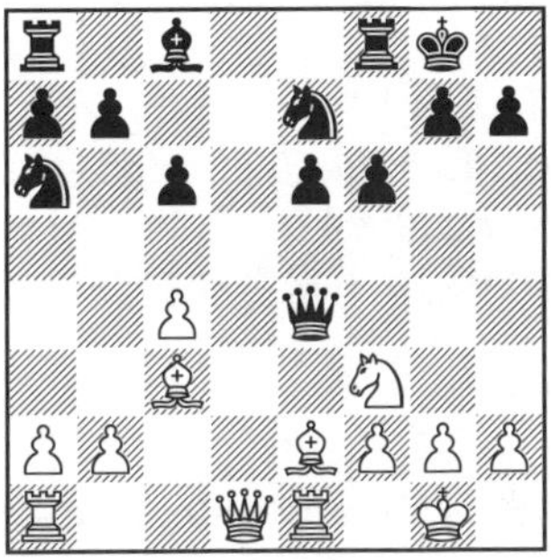

White's plan with short castling steered the game into a calm positional course. The focus of his actions will be the queenside, where b2-b4-b5 will open up a new operating diagonal for the c3-bishop. All Black's pieces are unstable, especially the queen and the e7-knight, which is threatened by a pin from b4. We have several ways to set-up coordination between them:

a) 12...♘g6 13.b4

Aleksandrov recently played 13.g3. We answer 13...e5 14.h4 ♗g4 15.♘g5 ♗xe2 16.♘xe4 ♗xd1 17.♖axd1. White has active pieces, but our extra pawn looks healthy.

13...e5

13...♘f4 14.♗f1 ♕g6 is also possible.

14.b5 ♘c7!

This leaves a weak pawn on c6, but neutralises the threat of ♗b4. For example, White retains some pressure following 14...cxb5 15.cxb5 ♘c5 16.♗f1 ♕g4 17.h3 ♕d7 18.♗b4 b6 19.♗c4+ ♔h8 20.♕xd7 ♗xd7 21.♗xc5 bxc5 22.♖ad1 ♗f5 23.♖d6.

15.♘d2 ♕f5 16.bxc6 bxc6 17.♗f3 ♘f4 18.♗xc6, Byrne-Conde Poderoso, ICCF 2019, 18...♖b8 19.♗e4 ♕g5 with complex play.

b) 12...♕g6 13.b4!?

13.♘h4 ♕h6 14.♕d6 ♖e8 15.g3 e5∞.

13.♗d3 ♕f7 14.♕e2 ♘g6 15.g3 e5 16.♘d2 ♘c5 17.♗c2 occurred in Rain-Villarreal, ICCF 2017. Now instead of the slow 17...a5, Black should have opted for 17...♗h3! 18.♗b4 b6↑.

13...♕f7 14.♘d2 ♖d8

It is safer to sit tight. It is pointless to give space to White's bishops until we are undeveloped – 14...e5 15.♘e4 ♘f5 16.b5 gives enough compensation.

15.f4 b5 16.♕c2 ♘c7 17.♘b3 bxc4 18.♗xc4 ♗a6=. Once we kill one of the bishops, life will be much easier.

B2. 9.♗a5 b6

The other critical line is :

9...f6 10.♘f3 b6

10...e5? 11.0-0 is bad for Black.

11.♘d2 ♕f5

11...♕f4 12.♗h5+ g6 13.♗f3 ♕e5+.

12.♗h5+ g6 13.♗f3 ♕e5+ 14.♔f1 ♕c7 15.♗c3 e5 16.♘e4 ♔f7 (16...h5!?) 17.b4 ♘e7 18.♕e2 ♘f5 19.h4 h5 20.♖e1 ♕e7! 21.g4 hxg4 22.♗xg4

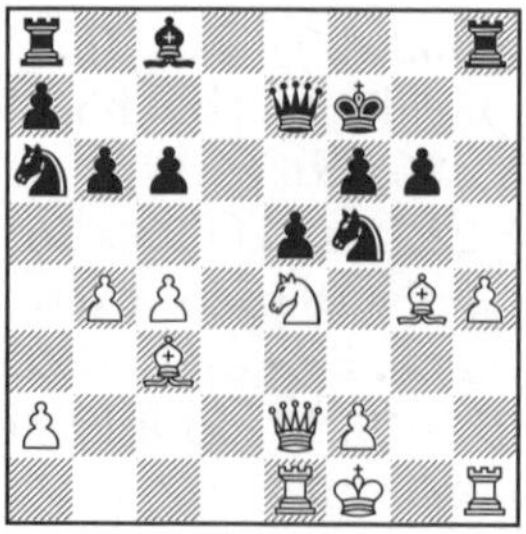

22...♘d6

22...♖xh4 23.♖xh4 ♘xh4 24.f4 also promises good compensation, although Black should be able to hold with 24...♘c7.

23.h5 ♗xg4 24.♕xg4 gxh5 25.♕f3 ♘xe4 26.♖xe4⩱. The game Lounek-Privara, ICCF 2016, ended in a draw, but it is easier to err with Black in this sharp position.

10.♕d6

10.♗c3 would make White's previous move pointless – 10...♗b7 11.♕d2 ♖d8 12.♕g5 ♘e7 13.f3 ♕c2 14.♘h3 ♖g8. The text forces the bishop to a passive place.

10...♗d7

11.♗c3

So the bishop went to the normal square c3, having provoked ...b6 and ♗d7. That is not necessarily in his favour though.

The inclusion of 11.0-0-0 0-0-0 favours Black – 12.♗c3 ♘f6 13.♕a3 ♔b7 14.♗f3 ♕f4+

Or 14...♕h4 15.g3 ♕g5+ 16.♖d2 e5 17.♗g2 e4∓.

15.♔b1 e5 16.♘e2 ♕xc4∓.

11...f6

11...♘f6 is already dubious owing to 12.♘f3!± and White castles short – 12...c5 13.♘d2 ♕g6 14.a4 (threatening a5) 14...♖d8 15.♗f3.

12.♘f3

The other plan is to castle queenside 12.0-0-0 0-0-0 13.♕a3 ♔b7 14.♗f3 ♕f4+ 15.♖d2 ♕c7 16.♘e2 e5 17.♖hd1 (17.♘g3 ♘h6) 17...♘h6

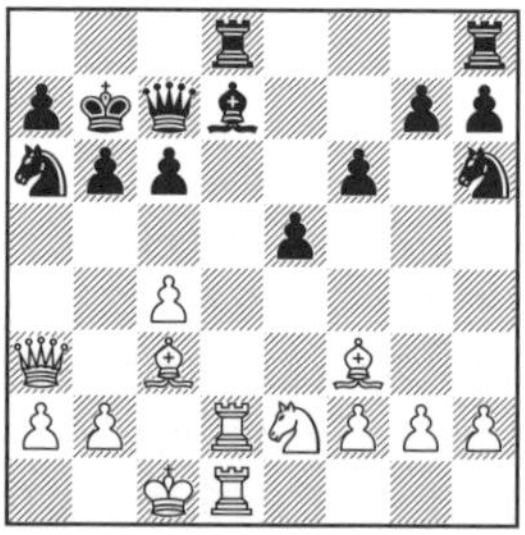

18.♘g3

The knight is heading for e4-d6. 18.b4 is not too menacing on account of 18...♘b8 19.b5 ♗g4 20.bxc6+ ♘xc6 21.♗xc6+ ♔xc6 22.h3 ♖xd2 23.♖xd2 ♗c8 24.♗xe5! ♕xe5 25.♕xa7 ♘f5 26.g4=.

18...♗g4=

Simplifying the defence. We could keep more pieces with: 18...♘f7 19.b4 ♘b8! 20.b5 f5 21.♘h5 ♗c8 22.bxc6+ ♘xc6 23.♗d5 ♖xd5 with sharp play. Or 18...♗c8!? 19.♘e4 ♘f5 20.♗g4 ♖xd2 21.♖xd2 ♔a8 22.♗xf5 ♗xf5 23.♘d6 ♗c8 24.♘xc8 ♕xc8, but it would be technically impossible to win with a weak seventh rank – 25.♕e7 ♕f8 26.♕xf8+ ♖xf8 27.♖d7 ♖g8 28.b4=.

19.♗xg4 ♘xg4 20.♘e4! ♖xd2 21.♖xd2 ♖d8 22.c5!, equalising – 22...♖xd2 23.♗xd2 ♘xc5 24.♘xc5+ bxc5 25.♕b3+ ♔c8= 26.♕c4 ♕d7 27.♕xc5 ♘xh2.

12.♕g3?! is pointless owing to 12...♕g6 13.0-0-0 ♘h6 14.♗d3 ♕xg3∓.

12...♘h6

The best square for the knight. 12...♘c5 13.♗b4 ♘e7 14.♖d1 ♖d8 15.♗xc5 bxc5 16.♕xc5 ♘g6 fails to achieve its goal in view of 17.g3! when 17...♘e5? 18.♘xe5! ♕xh1+ 19.♔d2 ♕e4 20.♖e1 suddenly turns the tables in White's favour. To be fair, 17...e5! 18.♕xa7 ♗g4 19.♕e3 ♖xd1+ 20.♗xd1 ♕xc4 21.♗b3 ♕b4+ is enough to hold the balance.

13.♖d1

13.0-0-0!? is best met by 13...♘c5 – to cut off the queen's retreat to a3.

13...0-0-0 14.♕a3 ♔b7 15.♖he1 ♘c7 is dangerous – 16.♗d3 ♕g4 17.h3 ♕h5 18.♖e3!, when the natural 18...e5 would give White additional attacking resources – 19.♘xe5!! fxe5 20.♗xe5→ a5 21.♗e2 ♕g6 22.♖b3.

14.♖he1 0-0-0 15.♗f1. Black has not less than three decent options, but all of them should lead to a draw if both sides play with computer precision:

15...♕f5 16.♘d4 ♕xf2 17.♘xc6 ♗xc6 18.♕xc6+ ♔b8 19.b4 ♕f4+ 20.♗d2 (20.♔c2 ♖xd1 21.♖xd1 ♘f5) 20...♖xd2 21.♖xd2 ♖d8 22.♖ed1 ♖xd2 23.♖xd2 ♘e4 24.♕e8+ ♔b7 25.♕e7+ ♔b8=;

15...♘f5!? 16.♕d2 ♕g4 17.h3 ♕g6 18.g4 ♘e7 19.♗b4 ♘e4 20.♖xe4 ♕xe4 21.♗xe7 ♕xf3 22.c5 ♔b7 23.♗c4 ♕xh3 24.♗xd8 ♖xd8 25.cxb6 axb6 26.♗xe6 ♗xe6 27.♕xd8 ♕xg4 28.♕e7+ ♔a6 29.♕a3+ ♔b7=.

15...♕g6 – this option is less attractive since White retains slight pressure with 16.♘e5! fxe5

16...♕e8 17.♘xd7 ♕xd7 18.♕xd7+ ♖xd7 19.b4 ♘a4 20.♗a1 could be dangerous only for Black owing to his knight being at the rim.

17.♗xe5 ♔b7 18.b4 ♘a6 19.b5 cxb5 20.cxb5 ♘f7 21.bxa6+ ♔a8 22.♕d3!, although the exchanges should allow Black to hold the draw (Scherbakov).

13...♖d8 14.♕a3 ♗c8 15.♘d2

15.♖xd8+ ♔xd8 16.♕d6+ ♗d7 does not achieve much since White must lose a tempo to castle.
See **Game 12** Sakaev-Bukavshin, Taganrog 2011.

15...♕f4 16.0-0

16.♗h5+!? ♘f7 17.0-0

17...c5

Laukola-Fagerström, ICCF 2019, saw 17...♕d6 18.b4 0-0 19.♘e4 ♕e7 20.c5 ♖d5 21.♗e2 b5 22.♖de1 ♘c7 23.♕b2 f5 24.♘d2 e5, and a draw was signed 6 moves later.

18.♕a4+ ♔e7 19.♖fe1 has been tested in several correspondence games. Forced play is over and Black can take a relieved breath. He has many decent continuations – 19...♖he8, 19...♖hf8, 19...♖d3.
Here is a relatively fresh example:
19...♘g5

Taking e4 under control. Previously Evtushenko tried 19...♖he8, so we should consider this an improvement.

20.♖e3 ♖d6 21.♖de1 ♖hd8

22.♘e4

22.♘f3 ♔f8 23.h3 ♘xf3+ 24.♗xf3 ♘b4 25.♕xa7 ♘c2 26.♖e4 ♕h6=, Rezzuti-Crielesi, ICCF 2018.

22...♘xe4 23.♖xe4 ♕h6 24.♗f3 ♔f8 25.♗g4 ♘b4 26.♗xe6 ♖xe6 27.♖xe6 ♗xe6 28.♖xe6 a5 29.h3 draw, Riedener-Evtushenko, ICCF 2017.

16...c5 17.♕a4+

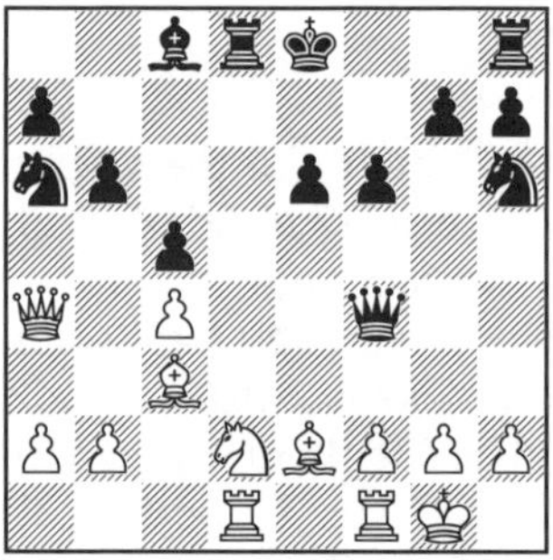

17...♔e7

17...♔f7!? 18.h3 ♘f5 looks at least as good, preparing castling by hand. However, in both practical games Black preferred leaving the king in the centre. Perhaps the idea was to trade rooks on the d-file with ...♖xd1, followed by ...♖d8.
Anyway, Black has consolidated and his plan is clear – to double

rooks on the d-file. Of course, his clumsy knight on a6 offers White probably enough compensation, so the position remains double-edged. See **Game 13** Volkov-Bukavshin, Taganrog 2013.

B3. 9.♗d6 ♕xg2!

9...e5 10.♘f3 ♗g4 11.0-0 0-0-0 12.b4! is pleasant for White.

12.♗d3 ♕f4 13.♗xe5 ♕xe5 14.♘xe5 ♗xd1 15.♗f5+ ♔c7 16.♘xf7 ♘h6 17.♘xh8 ♘xf5 18.♘f7 ♖d7 19.♘e5 ♗e2 20.♘xd7 ♗xf1 21.♘e5 ♗e2 22.f4 is about equal, although I'd take White.

12...♘f6 13.c5 ♘e8 14.♗d3 ♕f4 15.♗xe5 ♕xb4 16.♖b1 ♕a5

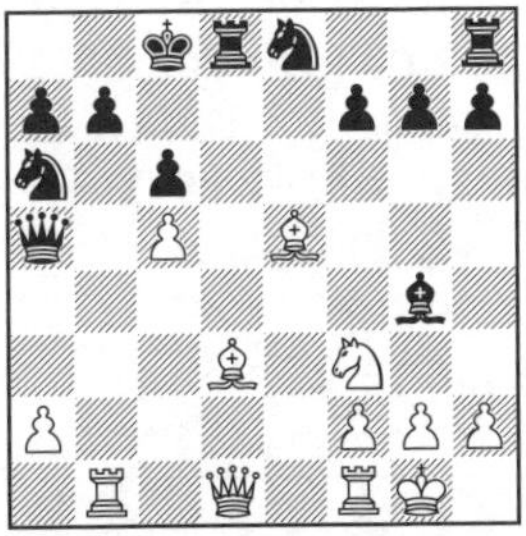

17.♗xa6! (Scherbakov prefers 17.♕c2) 17...♕xa6 18.♕b3 f6 19.♗g3 ♘c7 20.♖fe1 ♘d5 21.♘d4 ♖he8 22.h3±. Black might find it difficult to hold his position without computer help.

9...b6?! has faded out of fashion in view of 10.♘f3 ♗b7 11.0-0 ♖d8 12.♘g5 ♕g6 13.f4 or 12.♕d2 c5 13.♖ad1 with excellent attacking prospects.

10.♕d2

10.♗f3 has a bad reputation due to 10...♕g5 11.♘e2 ♘e7 12.♖g1?! ♕a5+ 13.♘c3 ♘f5.
However, 12.♘g3! is practically unexplored.

It is better to target e4, leaving the knight on the kingside. 12.♘c3 ♕a5 13.a3 ♘f5 was satisfactory for Black in a correspondence game. Besides, all the engines suggest 12...e5 13.♘e4 ♕f4 14.♗xe7 ♗g4!∓.

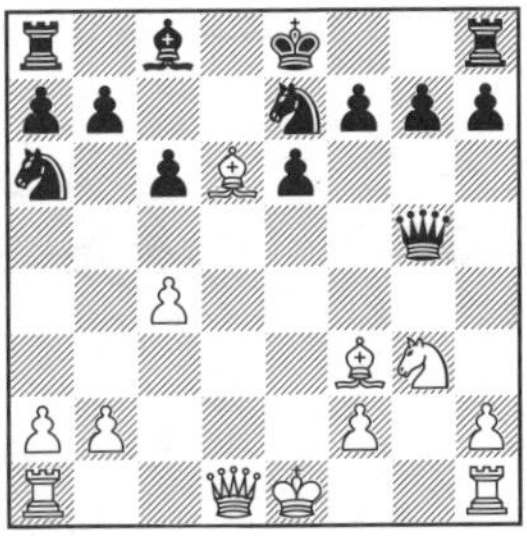

In this position the engines find two curious perpetual checks:

12...e5 13.♕b3 (13.♘e4?! transposes to 12.♘c3) 13...♘g6 14.♖d1 ♘h4 15.♗e2 ♘g2+ 16.♔f1 ♗h3 17.♕xb7 ♘f4+=;

12...0-0 13.♘e4 ♕a5+ 14.b4 ♕d8 15.♕d2 ♘f5 16.♗xf8 ♕xf8 17.0-0-0 e5!

Be careful with the last rank! 17...♘xb4?? loses to 18.♘f6+! gxf6 19.♖hg1+ ♔h8 20.♕h6!!.

18.♕d8 ♗e6 19.♘f6+ gxf6 20.♖hg1+ ♔h8 21.♕xf6+ ♘g7 22.♖xg7 ♕xg7 23.♖d8+ ♖xd8 24.♕xd8+ ♕g8 25.♕f6+=.

10...e5!?

Opening the c8-bishop. The well known equaliser is 10...♘f6. See **Game 14** Denisov-Kurbasov, ICCF 2015.

The text is objectively not worse than 10...♘f6, and it could be surprising for your opponent. That is a serious argument in its favour. Provided that you had done carefully your homework! Improvising in such positions would most probably end with a catastrophe since Black's path to a safe position is narrow.

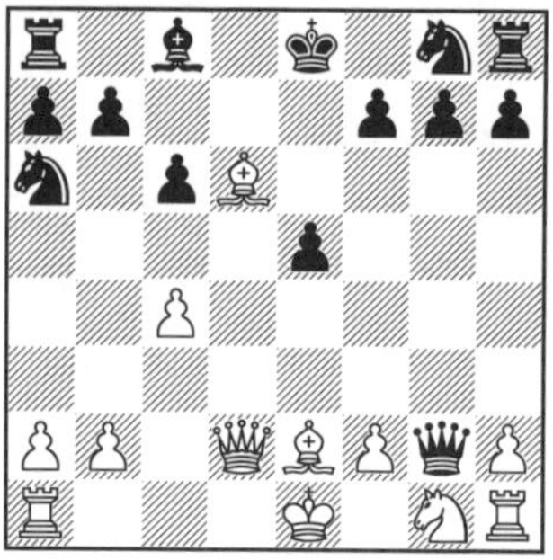

11.♗xe5

11.0-0-0 should be met by 11...♕e4! (11...♗f5? 12.♘f3±) 12.♗xe5

12.♕g5 ♕f4+ 13.♕xf4 exf4 14.♘f3 is harmless. Black can always return the loot to stay on the safe side. For instance: 14...♘h6 15.c5 ♘b4 16.♖he1 ♗e6 17.♗c4 ♘f5 18.♘g5 ♘d5 19.♗xd5 cxd5 20.♖xd5 0-0-0 21.♘xe6 fxe6 22.♖xe6 ♘xd6 23.cxd6 ♔d7 24.♖e7+ ♔c6 25.♖d4 ♖d7 26.♖xf4 ♖hd8=.

12...♗f5 13.♗d3 ♕xd3 14.♕xd3 ♗xd3 15.♗xg7 ♘b4!

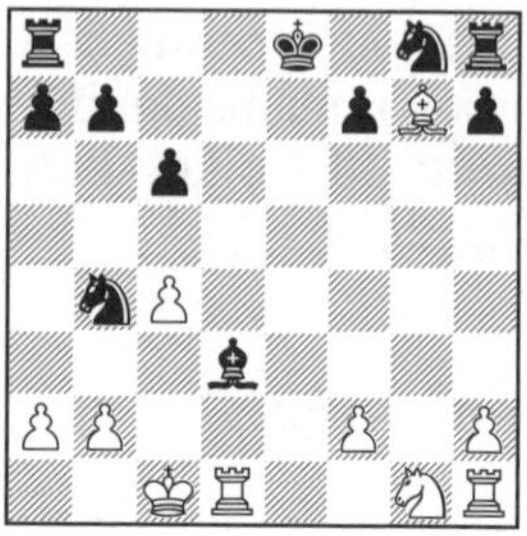

The point of Black's play. It transpires that White is unable to grab smoothly the h8-rook. 16.♗xh8?! ♘xa2+ 17.♔d2 ♗xc4 offers Black two pawns and an initiative for the exchange. The attempt to give only one pawn is sufficient only for equality:

16.b3 (16.a3 ♘a2+ 17.♔d2 0-0-0 18.♔e1 ♖e8+= or 18...♘h6=) 16...♗e4 17.f3 ♘d3+ 18.♔d2 ♗f5 19.♗xh8 ♘f2 20.♖e1+ ♘e7 21.♔c3 ♘xh1 (Or 21...♖d8 22.♗d4 ♘xh1 23.♘e2 b6=) 22.♗f6 ♗e6 23.♖f1=.

11.♗f3 ♕g6 12.♗xe5

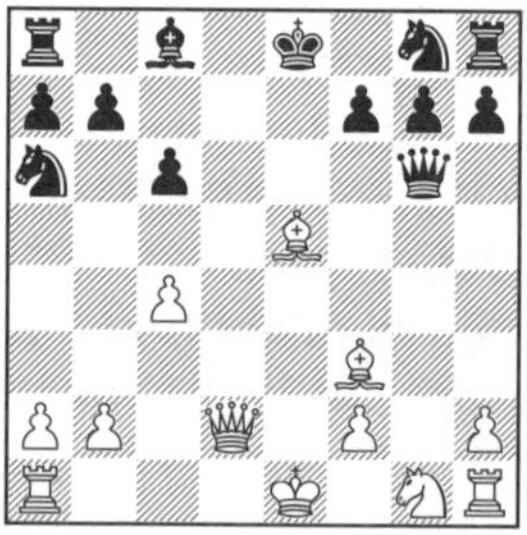

Play could transpose to the main line after:

12...♗f5, while Sengupta played 12...♗e6 13.0-0-0 ♘f6 14.♘e2 ♕f5, transposing to 10...♘f6.

However, this move order offers Black an independent option: 12...♕e6!? 13.0-0-0 ♕xc4+ 14.♗c3 ♗e6 followed by ...♘e7 and short castling.

11...♗f5

This may lead to multiple exchanges and a draw. 11...♘e7, intending a short castle, is more tangled, yet also more risky – 12.♗f3

12.0-0-0 allows 12...0-0 13.♘f3 ♘g6 and Black should not have any problems. Feldborg-Lakatos, ICCF 2017, went further: 14.♖hg1 ♕h3 15.♖g3 ♕f5 16.♗c3 ♘c5 17.♕e3 ♘a4 (17...f6=) 18.♗d3 ♕e6 19.♕xe6 ♗xe6 20.♗d4 c5 21.♗e3 ♖fd8 22.♖d2 f6 23.b3 ♘c3 24.♔b2 ♖xd3 25.♖xd3 ♘e2 26.♖xg6 ½-½.

12...♕g6 13.♘e2 f6 14.♗d6 ♕f7 15.0-0-0 0-0 16.b3. Black will complete development with 16...♖e8 and ...♖ad8, but he lacks stable stands for his pieces. Although the engines do not see anything dangerous, I thing that in a practical game White's chances should be higher.

12.♗f3

12.0-0-0 ♕e4 transposes to 11.0-0-0 ♕e4.

12...♕g6 13.0-0-0 ♘c5 14.♕e3 ♗b1 15.♖d2

15.♗d6+ ♘e6 16.♕b3 0-0-0 17.♗xc6 ♘c5 is a forced draw – 18.♗xc5 ♖xd1+ 19.♕xd1 ♕xc6 20.♕g4+ ♔c7 21.♕f4+ ♔c8 22.♔xb1 ♕xh1 23.♕g4+ ♔d8 24.♕d4+ ½-½ Dannehr-Hildebrand, ICCF 2017.

15...♗xa2 16.♗d6+ ♘e6 17.♗e4 ♕h6 18.f4

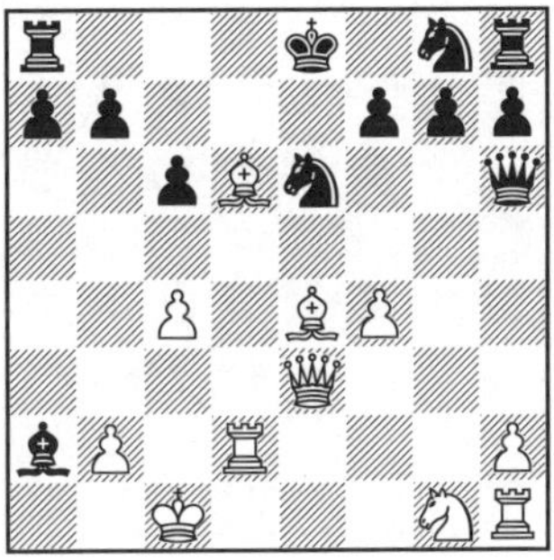

This position looks critical for 11...♗f5.

18...♘f6 19.♘f3 ♗xc4

If you want a simpler solution, 19...♘xe4!? 20.♕xe4 0-0-0 21.♘e5 ♖he8 is a better choice.

21...♕f6 22.♘xc6 ♖xd6 23.♘xa7 ♔b8 24.♖xd6 ♘c5 (24...♕xf4+)=.

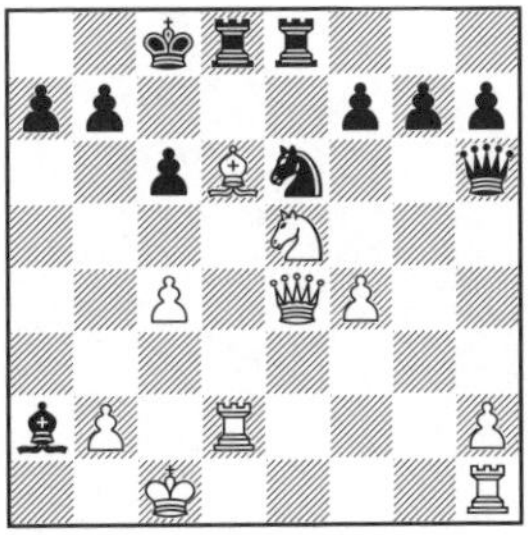

22.♘xc6 (22.♘xf7 ♘d4 23.♕xd4 ♕g6=) 22...♖xd6 23.♖xd6 ♕xf4+ 24.♕xf4 ♘xf4 25.♘xa7+ ♔b8 26.♘b5 ♗xc4 27.♘c3 ♘d3+=. Both sides could play on here, while the main line is a perpetual.

20.♖e1

20.♗f5!? throws in another pawn. 20...♘d5 21.♕a3 ♘dxf4 22.♖e1 ♕f6 with unclear consequences.

20...0-0-0!

Of course not 20...♘d5? 21.♗xd5 ♗xd5 22.♖xd5! cxd5 23.♕c5.

21.♗xc6

Or Black will take the lead after 21...♘d5.

21...bxc6

21...♗a6?? 22.♘g5 ♘xg5? 23.♗d7+!! is mate in four – 23...♔xd7 24.♕e7+ ♔c6 25.♕c7+ 1-0, Bacrot-Morozevich, Biel 2012.

22.♕xa7 ♖xd6 23.♕a8+

23.♖xd6? ♕xf4+ 24.♖d2 ♘c7 defends everything.

23...♔c7 24.♕a7+

With perpetual check, Kudas-Watorek, Koszalin 2012.

Chapter 3. The Marshall Gambit

Annotated Games

10. Bär – Glatthaar
ICCF 2017

1.d4 d5 2.c4 e6 3.♘c3 c6 4.e4 dxe4 5.♘xe4 ♗b4+ 6.♘c3 c5 7.a3 ♗a5 8.♗e3 ♘e7 9.♘ge2 cxd4 10.♕xd4 ♘f5 11.♕e4 ♘xe3 12.♕xe3 ♘c6

13.♖b1

The necessity for this move allows Black to complete development. The key point is 13.b4? ♗xb4! 14.axb4 ♘xb4 with a double threat.

13...0-0 14.b4 ♗c7 15.g3 ♘e5

Black grasps the chance to reduce the material on the queenside with concrete play. Besides, the normal 15...b6 16.♗g2 ♗b7 17.0-0 ♕c8 is also solid.

16.♖d1 ♕f6 17.♘d4 a5 18.♗e2 axb4 19.axb4 ♘c6 20.♘xc6 bxc6

The forced operation is over. The pawn majority on the queenside would have assured White of a slight edge if he had a bishop instead of a knight, for instance on e3. The actual position is totally equal as neither of White's pawns cant cross the fifth rank.

21.0-0 ♖b8 22.b5 cxb5 23.♘xb5 ♕e5 24.♘xc7 ♕xc7 25.c5 ♗b7=

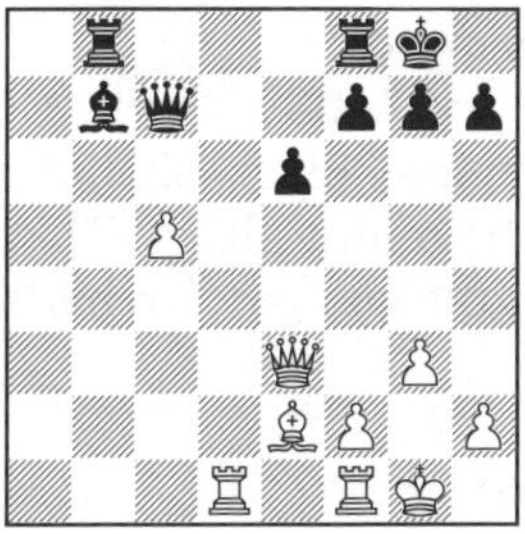

26.♖d6 ♗c6 27.♖fd1 ♖b4 28.♗f1 h6 29.♕c3 ♖fb8 30.♗g2 ♖b1 31.♗xc6 ♖xd1+ 32.♖xd1 ♕xc6 33.h4 ½-½

11. Wojtaszek – Giri
Biel 2014

1.d4 d5 2.c4 e6 3.♘c3 c6 4.e4 dxe4 5.♘xe4 ♗b4+ 6.♗d2 ♕xd4 7.♗xb4 ♕xe4+ 8.♘e2 ♘a6 9.♗f8 ♘e7 10.♗xg7 ♘b4 11.♕d6 ♘d3+! 12.♔d2 ♘f5 13.♕xd3 ♕xd3+ 14.♔xd3 ♘xg7

15.♔c3

Another possible set-up is 15.♘g3 c5

> Krasenkow disapproves of 15...b6 in view of 16.c5, but this move offers Black the d5-square – 16...♔e7 17.♔c3 ♘e8!, heading for d5. White should continue instead 16.♗e2, when 16...c5 transposes.

16.♗e2 b6 17.♗f3 ♖b8 18.♔c3 ♗b7=. In principle Black should aim to trade the minor pieces. That would reduce the danger for his split h-pawn.

15...b6!

It is a good idea to shift the queenside pawns to dark squares, having a light-squared bishop. 15...e5 gives White a target – 16.♖e1 0-0 17.♘g3 f6 18.♗d3 ♗d7 19.♖hf1, planning f2-f4.

16.g4

White's only chance for an edge is to do something on the kingside. 16.g3 is more flexible, but 16...c5 17.♗g2 ♖b8 is fine for Black.

16...♗b7 17.♗g2 0-0-0 18.♖ad1

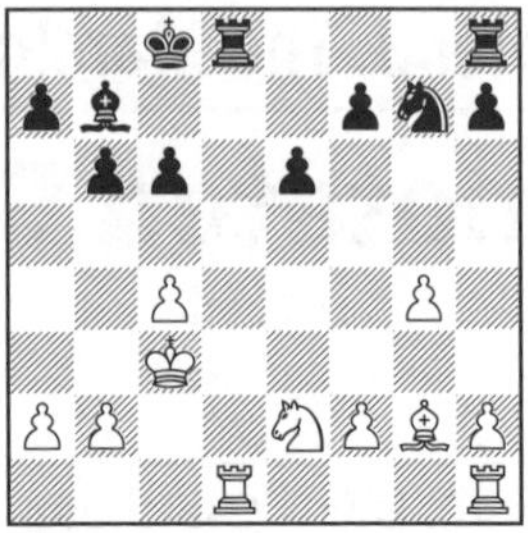

18...h5?!

A correct idea in imperfect execution. 18...c5 is a smoother equaliser – 19.♗xb7+ ♔xb7 20.♘f4 and only now 20...h5!=.

19.g5 c5 20.♗xb7+ ♔xb7 21.♘f4

Black's premature thrust on the 18th move allowed 21.h4! ♘f5 22.♘g3 ♘d4 23.♔d3!, when the strong knight on d4 would not entirely compensate the weakness of the h5-pawn.

21...♘f5

The simplest solution. This sacrifice was tested in 3 games. All of them finished in a draw.

22.♖xd8 ♖xd8 23.♘xh5

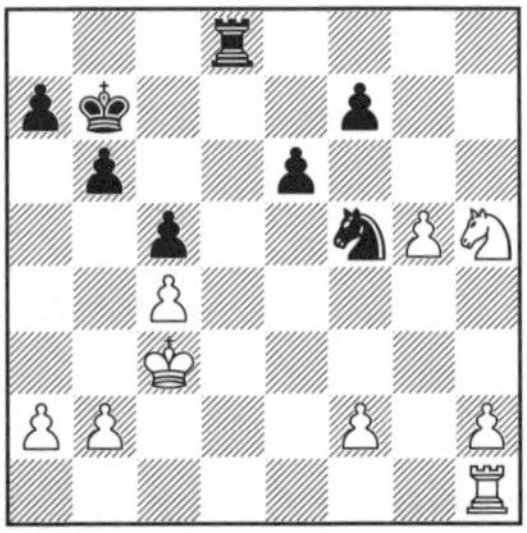

23...♖g8

This finesse was not obligatory. 23...♖h8 24.♘g3 ♖h3 would have done the job, too, but the text is more forcing.

24.h4

It transpires that 24.f4?! ♖h8 25.♘g3 is impossible, and 25.♘f6 ♖h3+ is pleasant for Black.

24.♖g1 ♖h8 25.♘g3 ♖xh2 26.♘xf5 exf5 27.♖e1 ♖xf2 led to a draw in Timofeev-Frolyanov, Tyumen 2012.

24...♖h8 25.♘g3 ♖xh4 26.♖xh4 ♘xh4

The rest is of no interest.

27.♘e4 ♔c6 28.♔d3 ♘g6 29.♔e3 ♘e5 30.b3 ♔d7 31.♘f6+ ♔e7 32.♔e4 ♘c6 33.♘g4 ♘d4 34.b4 ♘e2 35.bxc5 bxc5 36.a3 ♘d4 37.♘e5 a6 38.f4 a5 39.a4 ♘e2 40.♘c6+ ♔d6 41.♘d8 (41.♘xa5 ♘c3+ 42.♔d3 ♘xa4=) **41...♔e7 42.♘b7 ♘c3+ 43.♔e5 ♘xa4 44.♘xa5 ♘b6 45.♔e4 f6 46.♘c6+ ♔f7 47.♘d8+ ♔g6 48.♘xe6 fxg5 49.fxg5 ♘xc4 50.♘xc5 ♔xg5 ½-½**

---

12. Sakaev – Bukavshin
Taganrog 22.06.2011

1.d4 d5 2.c4 e6 3.♘c3 c6 4.e4 dxe4 5.♘xe4 ♗b4+ 6.♗d2 ♕xd4 7.♗xb4 ♕xe4+ 8.♗e2 ♘a6 9.♗a5 b6 10.♕d6 ♗d7 11.♗c3 f6 12.♘f3 ♘h6 13.♖d1 ♖d8 14.♕a3 ♗c8 15.♖xd8+ ♔xd8 16.♕d6+ ♗d7 17.♕d1

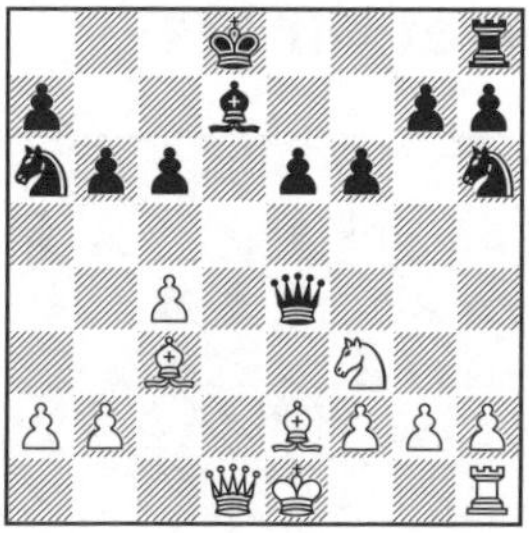

17...c5

Black chose in the game to leave the king on the queenside, but 17...♔e7 18.0-0 c5 19.♗d3 ♕g4 20.h3 ♕h5 21.♗e4 ♖d8=, Pert-Hawkins, Aberystwyth 2014, was also possible.

18.0-0 ♕f4

The queens was not threatened, so 18...♔c8 was more logical – 19.♗d3 (19.♘d2 ♕f4 20.♗f3 ♘f5∓) 19...♕f4

19...♕b7 20.♖e1 e5 gives White play on the light squares – 21.♘h4 ♘b4 22.♗e4 ♗c6 23.♘f5 ♘xf5 24.♗xf5+ ♗d7 25.♗e4 ♕c7 26.♗xb4 cxb4 27.♕d5=. Paradoxically, White is happy to trade minor pieces as they defend the weak pawns.

20.♕e2 ♘f7 21.♖d1 ♘c7 22.♘e1 e5. White still has to prove his compensation.

19.g3 ♕c7 20.♕d2?!

A strange decision from Sakaev. He manoeuvres the queen to e3 instead of putting it on the diagonal b1-h7, perhaps on b1. It was natural to gain space with a3 and b4.

20...♘f5 21.♖d1 ♔c8

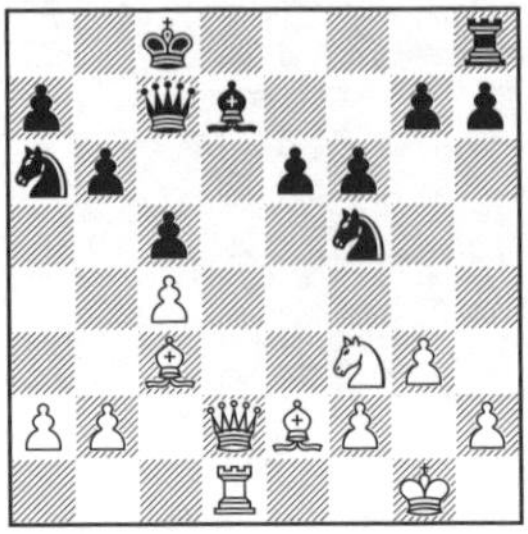

Black's advantage takes shape. His extra pawn assures him of the better control of the centre. Sakaev's jerky attempts to obtain counterplay only aggravate his situation.

22.g4 ♘e7 23.♕e3 ♘c6 24.g5 e5 25.gxf6 gxf6 26.♕h6 ♘d4 27.♗xd4 exd4 28.♕xf6 ♖g8+ 29.♔f1 ♖e8 30.♔e1?

Black would have had to work longer to cash in after 30.a3 ♘b8 31.♕h4.

30...♘b4 31.♔d2 b5 0-1

32.a3 ♕a5 decides.

---

13. Volkov – Bukavshin
Taganrog 19.01.2013

1.d4 d5 2.c4 e6 3.♘c3 c6 4.e4 dxe4 5.♘xe4 ♗b4+ 6.♗d2 ♕xd4 7.♗xb4 ♕xe4+ 8.♗e2 ♘a6 9.♗a5 b6 10.♕d6 ♗d7 11.♗c3 f6 12.♘f3 ♘h6 13.♖d1 ♖d8 14.♕a3 ♗c8 15.♘d2 ♕f4 16.0-0 c5 17.♕a4+ ♔e7 (17...♔f7!?)

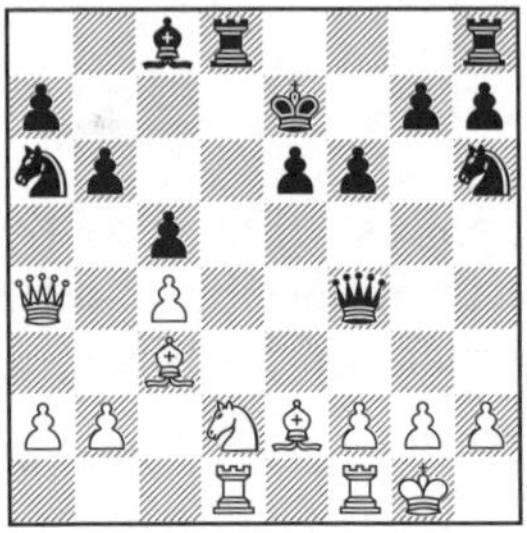

Both sides have played more or less forced moves, and now White faces a choice. The thematic plan is: 18.a3 ♘f5 19.b4, but in Lysyj-Yudin, Khanty-Mansiysk 2013, White obviously did not like 19...♘d4, so he opted for:

> 19.♘f3?! ♖xd1 20.♖xd1 ♖d8 21.♖e1. The tempo gave Black an initiative, and following 21...♗b7 22.♗f1 ♖d7 23.b4 ♗xf3 24.♕xa6 he could have won with 24...♘h4!.

Volkov anticipates the manoeuvre ...♘f5-d4 by preparing ♗e4.

18.♗f3 ♕c7

Evacuating the queen to a safer place before pushing ...e5.

19.♖fe1 ♘f5 20.♗e4 ♘d4

20...♔f7! 21.a3 ♖d6 was more precise, and White still has to prove enough compensation. For instance: 22.b4 ♖hd8 23.♖c1 ♔f8 24.h3 ♗b7, or 22.♘f3 ♖xd1 23.♕xd1 ♖d8 24.♘d2 ♔g8.

21.♘f3 ♘xf3+

Black keeps the extra pawn, but the position opens up. 21...e5 was wiser – 22.♘xd4 cxd4 23.♗xd4 ♖xd4 24.♖xd4 exd4 25.♗b7+ ♔f7 26.♗xa6 ♗xa6 27.♕xa6 ♖d8 with some initiative for Black.

22.♗xf3 ♖xd1 23.♕xd1 ♘b4 24.♕b1

24...♘c6

The first of a series of small imprecisions, which eventually ruin Black's game. 24...♔f7! denied 25.♕e4 as the a2-pawn was hanging.

25.♕e4 ♘e5 26.♗h5 ♘f7

26...♘g6 27.h4 ♔f7=.

27.f4 g6

It was better to avoid new weaknesses with 27...♖f8 28.♗g4 (28.♕xh7 ♕xf4 29.♕xg7 e5=) 28...♖e8 or 27...♕b7 28.♕d3 ♕c7, but perhaps Black did not realise in time that he should think about drawing.

28.♗f3 a5 29.h4?!

White is impatient. A solid preparatory move was 20.♕e3, creating the threat of ♗g4.

29...♖g8 30.g4 h6?!

Black misses his chance to exploit the hasty pawn storm with 30...♘d6 31.♕e2 ♘f5! 32.♗d5 ♕xf4 with a perpetual.
After the text 31.♗g2! would have neutralised such tactics.

31.♔g2?!

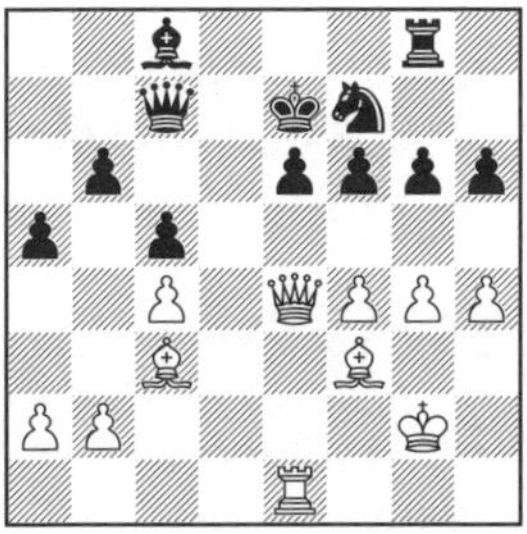

31...f5?

A positionally horrible move. Now the long diagonal is gaping open. 31...♘d6!, going for f5, was still working.

32.♕e3 g5 33.fxg5 hxg5 34.h5 ♘h6 35.♗e5 ♕d7 36.♖d1 ♕a4 37.♕d2+– ♔f7 38.♕d6 ♕e8 39.♕xb6 ♕e7 40.♗d6 ♕d8 41.♕xc5 fxg4 42.♗c6 ♗d7 43.♕a7 ♔e8 44.♗xd7+ ♕xd7 45.♕xd7+ ♔xd7 46.♗f8+ 1-0

14. Denisov – Kurbasov
ICCF 2015

1.d4 d5 2.c4 e6 3.♘c3 c6 4.e4 dxe4 5.♘xe4 ♗b4+ 6.♗d2 ♕xd4 7.♗xb4 ♕xe4+ 8.♗e2 ♘a6 9.♗d6 ♕xg2 10.♕d2 ♘f6

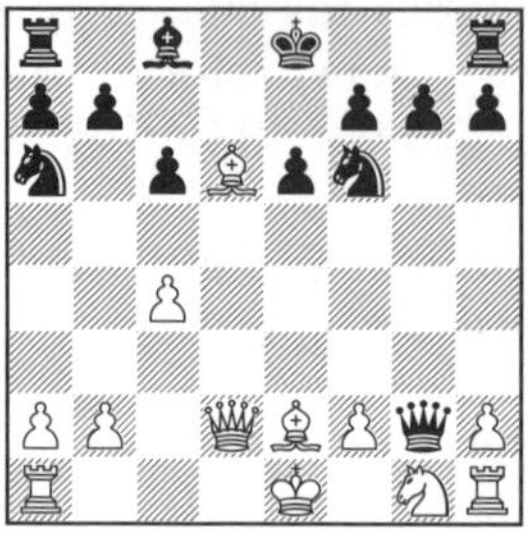

White has not found more than equality in this line. The next series of moves is forced:

11.♗f3 ♕g6 12.♘e2

12.0-0-0 e5 13.♗xe5 ♗e6 transposes to the game.

12...e5 13.♗xe5

13.0-0-0 allows, besides 13...♗e6, 13...♗g4 14.♗xg4 ♘xg4 15.f3 ♘f2 16.♗xe5 ♘xd1 17.♖xd1 ♘c5

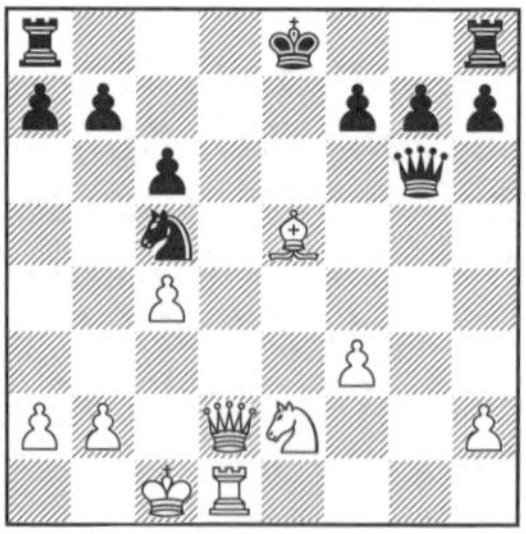

A dozen of games have proved that White's initiative is enough for a draw. For instance, 18.b4 ♕f5 19.♗xg7 ♖g8 or 18.♕e3 ♘e6.

Only Potkin won after:

18.♕d4 b6?,

when 19.♗xg7 ♖hg8 20.♗f6 decides. The only correct answer is:

18...♕g5+!, intending to defend the knight from e7. For instance:

19.f4 ♕e7 20.♗xg7 ♘e6, or 19.♗f4 ♕e7 20.♕xg7 ♖f8 21.♗h6 ♘e6 22.♕xh7 ♘g5= (22...♕h4!?).

13...♗e6 14.0-0-0 ♕f5 15.♗f4

15.♗c3? stumbled into 15...♘b4! in Lupulescu-Naningue, Romania 2012.

15...♗xc4! 16.♘d4

White can win the exchange in another way – 16.♘g3 ♕c5 17.♖he1

In 2008 Gupta won with 17.♗e3 ♕b4 18.♘f5 ♕xd2+ 19.♖xd2 ♗d5? 20.♘xg7+±, but several correspondence games of 2012 proved that after the cold-blooded 19...♔f8! White's limit is a draw, e.g. 20.♗f4 h5 21.♖hd1 ♔g8=.

17...♗e6+ 18.♔b1 0-0 19.♗d6 ♖fd8 20.♗xc5. The play is similar to the main game, as well as the evaluation – chances are even.

16.♕e3+?! ♗e6 17.♗d6 ♘d5 favours Black.

16.♖hg1 ♗xa2! 17.♕e3+ ♕e6! 18.♗e5 ♕e7 19.♕g5

Or 19.♘c3 ♗b3 20.♘b5 cxb5 21.♕xb3 0-0=.

19...♘d7 20.♕xe7+ ♔xe7 21.♗d6+ ♔f6= was first tested in Doric-Pavasovic, Slovenia 2011, which finished in a draw after 22.♘c3 ♗b3 23.♘e4+ ♔e6 24.♘g5+ ♔f6 25.♘e4+ ♔e6 26.♘g5+ ♔f6 27.♘e4+ ♔e6 28.♘g5+ ♔f6 29.♘e4+ ♔e6. Later 22.♗g3 ♔e7 23.♘d4 ♘dc5 has also proved to be balanced.

16...♕c5

17.♘c2

Or 17.♖he1+ ♗e6+ 18.♘c2 (18.♔b1? allows 18...0-0-0) 18...0-0, when Jianu and Mastrovasilis, Arad 2019, signed a draw. Thus the main game is the only example of play with an exchange for two pawns. These positions are vital for the 10...♘f6 line, as they could occur in various settings.

17...0-0

This sacrifice completely changes the course of the game and brings it down to a calm endgame. This is a sound practical decision, but the correspondence game Zakharov-Evtushenko, ICCF 2012, showed an alternative approach:

17...♗e6 18.♖hg1 ♘d5 19.♗xd5 ♕xd5 20.♕e3 ♕c5 21.♖d4 ♖d8 22.b4 ♕b6 23.♖xg7 c5 24.bxc5 ♕xc5 25.♖g5 ♕b6 26.♖xd8+ ♔xd8 27.♕c3 ♖e8 28.♖g3 h6 29.♖d3+ ♗d7 30.♗e3 ♕c6 31.♕xc6 bxc6 ½-½.

18.♗d6 ♖fd8 19.♗xc5 ♖xd2 20.♖xd2 ♘xc5

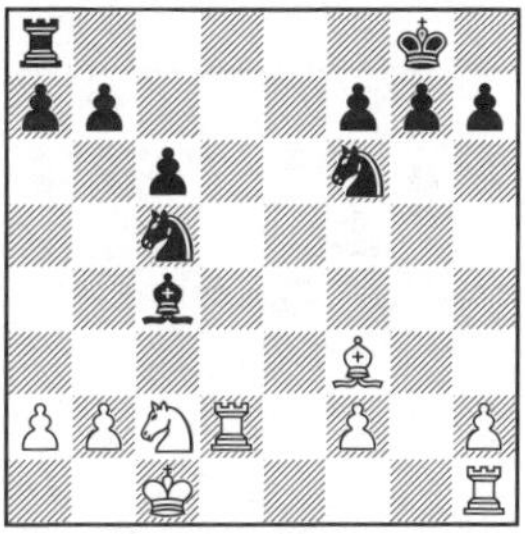

It may look that Black's game is easy, but you should know which pieces to trade. I think that we should be glad to exchange the bishops and leave the knights. I noticed an instructive example of bad strategic decisions:

chuckhar-perdurabo
gameknot.com 2012

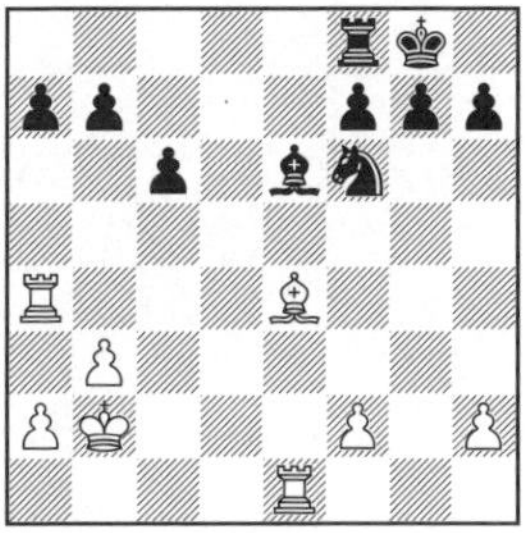

Black did not kill the right pieces, and even worse, he traded his only rook. That gave White a dark-squared path to the weak queenside pawns: 27...a6 28.♖b4 ♗c8?! (28...♘xe4) 29.♗g2 ♖d8 30.♔c3 ♔f8 31.♖d4 ♖xd4? 32.♔xd4 ♘g4 33.♔c5 ♘xf2 34.♔b6 and White eventually won.

21.♖hd1 ♘e6 22.♔b1 ♗d5 23.♗xd5 ♘xd5 24.♖d3 ♖d8 25.♘e3 ♘ef4 26.♖b3 ♖d7 27.♘xd5 ♘xd5

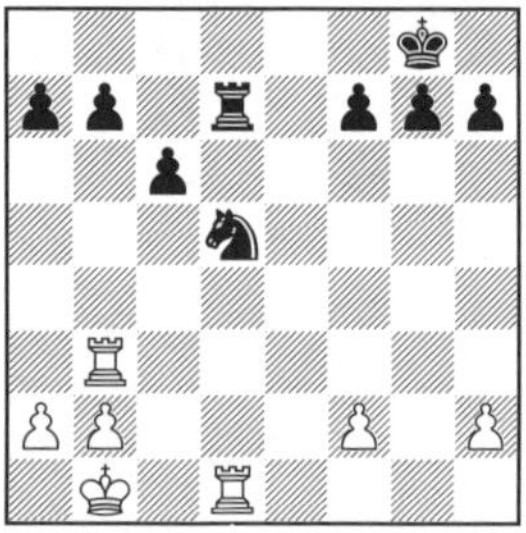

Black has built a firm fortress in the centre. White lacks any invasion squares along the central files. I would say that only Black could play for a win here.

28.♖e1 ♔f8 29.♖h3 h6 30.a3 f6 31.♔c2 ♔f7 32.♖h4 a6 33.♔b3 f5 34.♔c4 ♔f6 35.b4 ♖d8 36.♖d4 g5 37.♔c5 g4

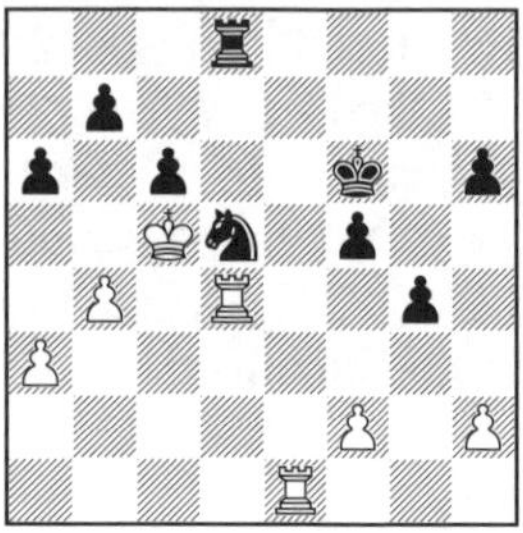

38.h3

White decides to eliminate as many pawns as possible. He still must be careful, as the h-pawn is too remote from his king. In an OTB game Black would have had practical chances.

38...h5 39.hxg4 fxg4 40.a4 ♖f8 41.b5 axb5 42.axb5 ♔g5 43.bxc6 bxc6 44.♖e5+ ♖f5 45.♖xf5+ ♔xf5 46.♖c4 ♔e5 47.♔xc6 ♘f4 48.♖c5+ ♔e4 49.♖c4+ ♔f3 50.♔d6 ♘d3 51.♖c3 ♔e4 52.♖c4+ ♔f5 53.♖a4 ♔g6 54.♖c4 ♘xf2 ½-½

Chapter 4. The Catalan Way

Main Ideas

1.d4 d5 2.c4 c6 3.♘f3 e6 4.g3 dxc4 5.♗g2 b5

This position has been topical lately owing to the renaissance of the Catalan. White sometimes reaches it via another move order – 3...♘f6 4.g3 dxc4 5.♗g2 e6, when 6.0-0 b5 7.a4 ♗b7 transposes to our line B. 1.d4 d5 2.c4 e6 3.♘f3 ♘f6 4.♘c3 c6 5.g3 dxc4 is even more topical. Then 6.♗g2 b5 7.0-0 ♗b7 8.b3! leads to line C.

White's main strategic goals

The following game is a model example of White's dream in this system:

Moiseenko-Postny
Tsaghkadzor 2015

1.d4 d5 2.c4 c6 3.♘f3 ♘f6 4.♘c3 a6 5.g3 dxc4 6.♗g2 e6 7.0-0 b5 8.♘e5 ♗b7 9.b3 cxb3 10.axb3 ♗e7 11.♗b2 0-0 12.♘e4 ♘xe4 13.♗xe4 ♖a7 14.♕c2 h6 15.♕c3 ♗f6 16.♕c5 ♖a8 17.♗a3 ♘d7 18.♕d6 ♘xe5 19.dxe5 ♕xd6 20.♗xd6 ♖fd8 21.♖ad1 ♖d7 22.♗c5 ♖xd1 23.♖xd1

Positional catastrophe 1

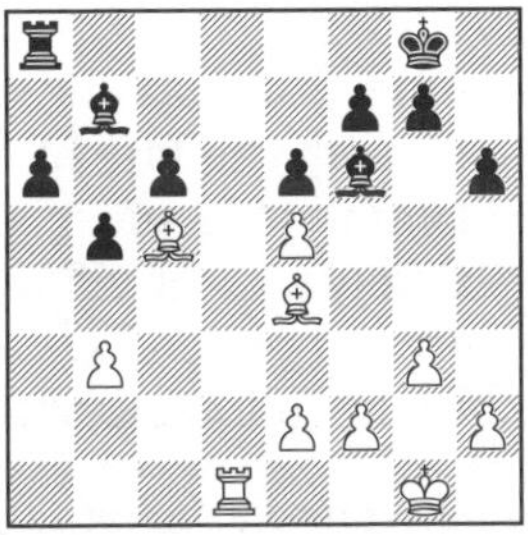

A study-like domination of White's light-squared bishop over the "big pawn" on b7:
23...♖d8 24.♗d3 ♖d5 25.exf6 ♖xc5 26.♗e4 ♖d5 27.♗xd5 exd5 28.e4 gxf6 29.exd5 cxd5 30.b4 ♗c6 31.♖a1 ♗b7 32.♖c1 d4 33.♖d1 1-0.

Positional catastrophe 2

Both 11...♘xe5 12.dxe5 ♘d5 13.♗xf8 ♔xf8 14.♘d2± (14.♘c3) and 11...♘d5 12.♗xf8 ♔xf8 13.♘d2 f6 14.♘xd7+ ♕xd7 15.♘e4± are hopeless for Black because of the weak dark squares.

Always activate the b7-bishop!

The above examples should teach us a lesson:

We do not take on c4 to gain a pawn! Our aim is to open the centre and achieve a dynamic unbalanced position with mutual chances.

For this aim we should always plan our actions with the fate of the b7-bishop in mind. We must activate it with a timely ...c5 or via the back door a6 after a previous ...a5. Remember the following patterns:

Gaehwiler-Sethuraman
Germany 2017

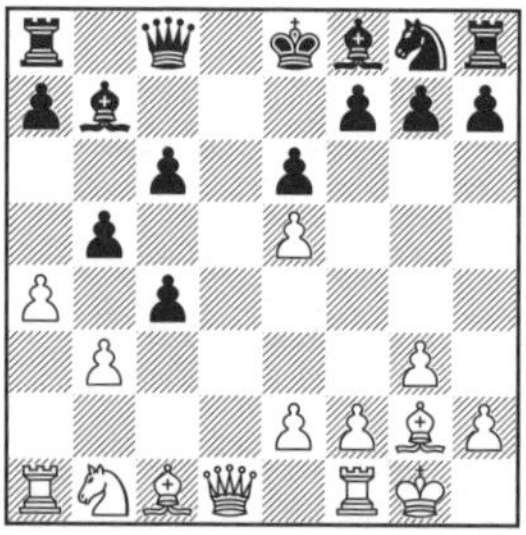

10...b4!, followed by ...c5, opens the b7-bishop and fixes the queenside in Black's favour. This example illustrates an important rule: It is better to play with equal pawns than struggling with a piece which lacks any prospects.

Again 7...b4 is a good move, although 7...cxb3 and 7...♗b4+ are viable alternatives.

Do not think how to keep the extra pawn. The b7-bishop's fate comes first!

Analysis

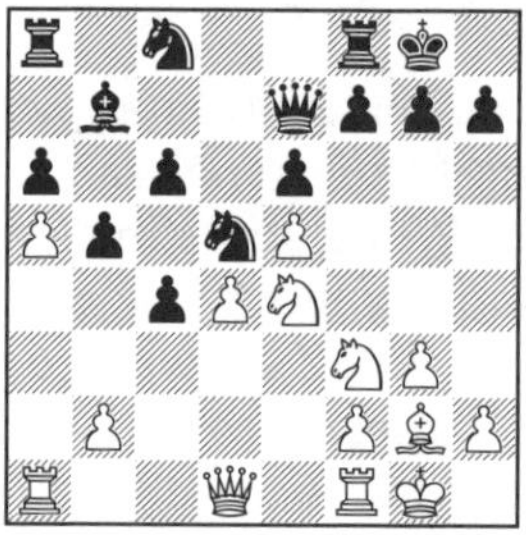

16...c5!=.

Analysis

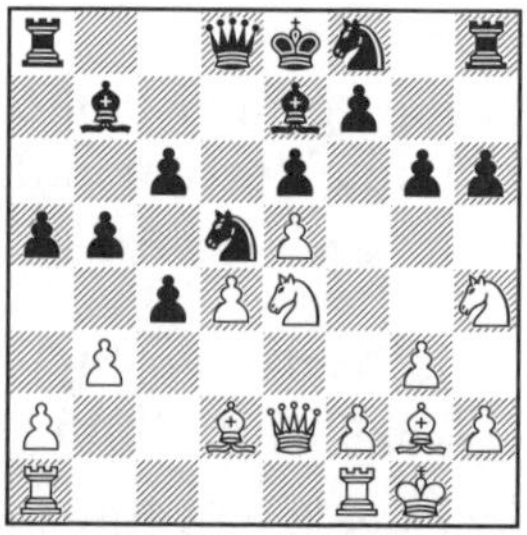

15...♗a6! – it is commonly safer to

keep the c-file closed. The bishop is rather useful on a6.

Now that we are heavily armed with strategic wisdom, let's consider White's main plans:

Plan with a4

The direct attack on our queenside pawns with **6.a4** does not pose any theoretical problems. We answer **6...♗b7**

Now **7.♘c3** allows the very sharp retort 7...b4!? 8.♘e4 c5! 9.♘e5! ♗d5:

White should play very ingenuously to keep the balance – 10.♗g5 f6 11.e3!! g6 12.h4!!, 10.♘xf7!? or 10.♗f4!. As you see, his best options are far from intuitive, while Black's play is easier since he does not have much of a choice.

I also consider the trivial 7...a6 8.0-0 ♘d7 with a decent game.

7.♘e5! is more restrictive, as the threat axb5 forces us to take a defensive stand: 7...a6 8.0-0 ♘f6 9.♘c3 ♕c8

We calmly complete our kingside development after 10.e4 ♗e7 11.d5 cxd5 12.exd5 b4 13.♘e4 0-0. White has to prove enough compensation.

Pawn structure with b3, ♕xb3

We have seen that the combination of a4+b3 allows ...b4, so White learned to avoid a4. His favourite approach lately has been **6.0-0 ♗b7 7.b3 cxb3 8.♕xb3 ♘f6 9.♘c3 ♗e7 10.♘e5**

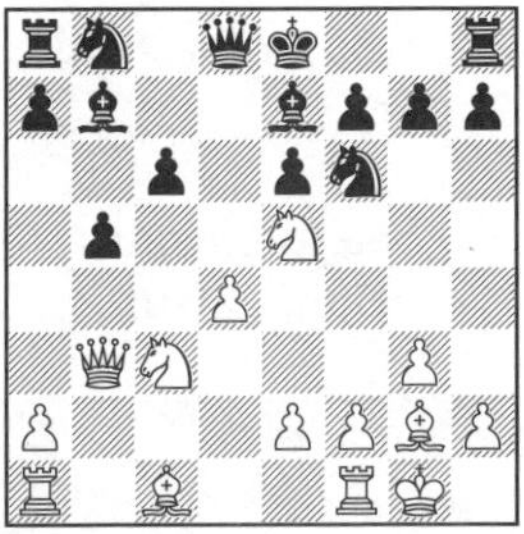

My recommendation here is to avoid passive defence with ...a6, but leave the a6-square for a piece – **10...b4!? 11.♘a4 0-0 12.♖d1 a5**.

I would like to warn you that other "natural" tries could easily lead to a debacle. Look what could happen if we linger with development:

Analysis

14.♖xd7! ♕xd7 15.♖d1 ♕c7 16.♘xb5+–.

Analysis

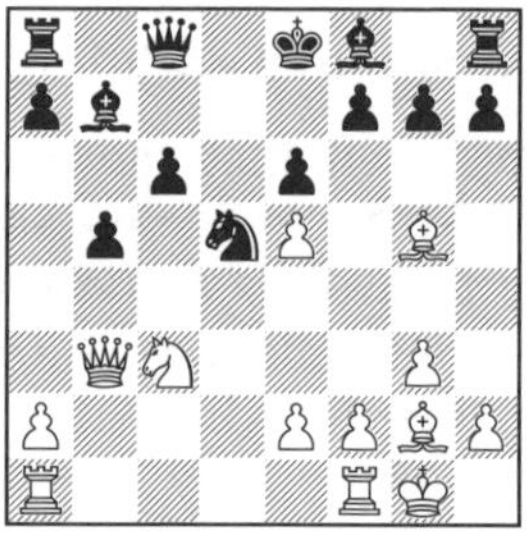

13.♘xb5!! cxb5 14.♖ac1 ♕d7 15.♖fd1 with an attack.

Salem-Gusain
Dubai 2016

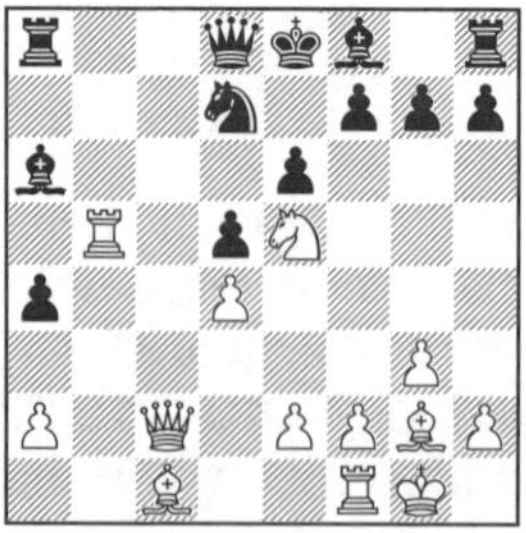

15.♖xd5!! exd5 16.♕c6!, when the threat ♗xd5 assures White of a terrible attack.

Attack through the centre

6.0-0 ♗b7 7.♘c3 ♘f6 8.e4 ♗e7 9.e5 ♘d5 10.♘e4 ♘d7

The big question here is whether to allow a trade of the dark-squared bishop. I believe that it is safer to refrain from h6. We can avoid positional vice with a timely ...c5 or an exchange sac as in the following example:

Analysis

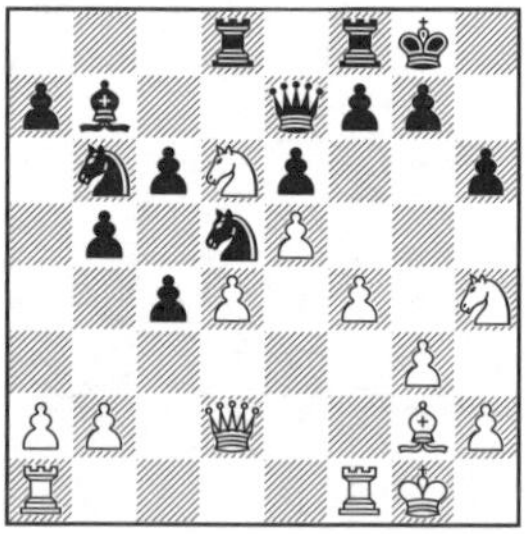

16...♖xd6!∓.

Pawn on h6

In this system we often face the dilemma: to play or not ...h6. There is no definite answer to it, but if we committed ourselves with this weakening, we should play very energetically and concretely to get adequate counterplay quickly. Otherwise we risk to be crashed.

Analysis

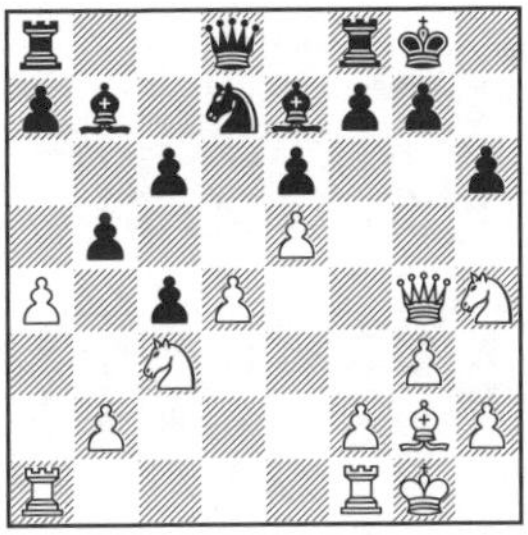

14...b4! 15.♘e4 ♖ab8 16.♖fd1 c5!∓.

Analysis

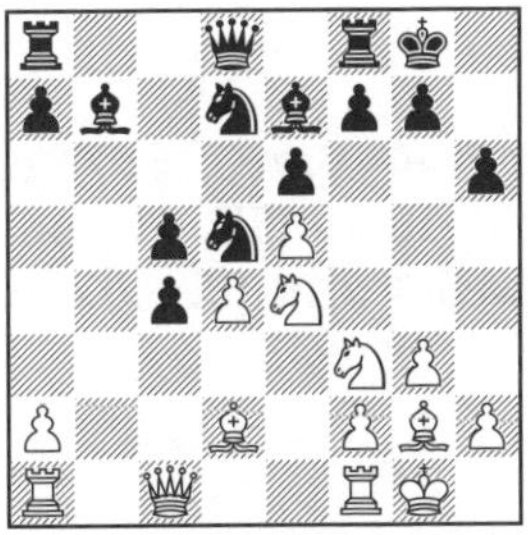

15.♗xh6? cxd4!∓.

Ipatov-Eljanov
Baku 2015

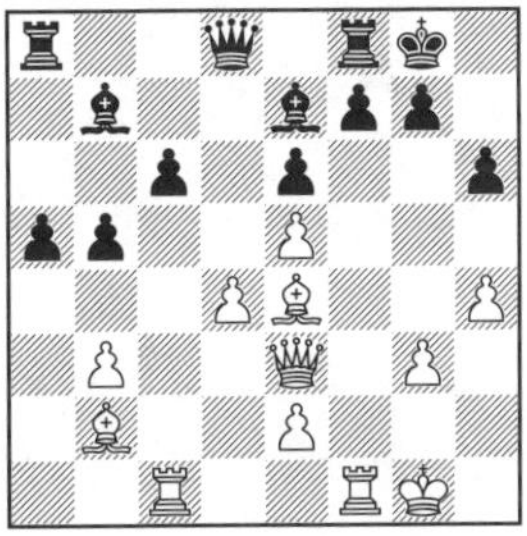

19...f5 is dubious. Instead 19...a4! 20.bxa4 bxa4 diverts the enemy forces from the kingside.

When we play ...a6

Since we do not want to defend passively, here is another useful rule:

Never play ...a6 if it is not strictly necessary.

I would note 2 exceptions from this rule:
6.a4 ♗b7 7.♘e5 a6 (forced!) and:
6.0-0 ♗b7 7.♘c3 ♘f6 8.♘e5 a6, although we have fair alternatives in this case – 8...♘d5 or 8...♕c8.

Theoretical status

Krasenkow believes that the key position for this system is:

While I agree that returning the pawn with 9...♗e7 is a solid equaliser, I analyse in detail the more challenging answer 9...♕c8!?.

My blitz practice suggests that the plan with b3 without a4 is more popular and not well covered in theory. Perhaps you should pay more attention to it.

Step by Step

1.d4 d5 2.c4 e6 3.♘f3 c6 4.g3

4.b3 is a rare attempt to drag Black into the Closed Catalan after 4...♘f6 5.g3

We have several ways to escape this scenario:

a) 5...dxc4 6.bxc4 c5 7.♗g2 (7.e3 cxd4 8.exd4 e5) 7...cxd4 8.♕xd4 ♗d7∞;

b) 5...♘e4 6.♗g2 ♗b4+ 7.♘bd2 ♗c3 8.♖b1 e5 (8...♕a5!? 9.0-0 ♕xa2 10.e3 f5∞) 9.dxe5 ♗f5 with excellent compensation.

4...dxc4 5.♗g2

5.♘c3 (or 5.a4 b5) 5...b5 6.a4 is seldom seen, but it hides a lot of venom. I suggest to transpose to line A1 with 6...b4 7.♘e4 c5!?

8.♘e5

8.♗g5 f6 9.♗e3 ♗b7 10.♘xc5 ♗xc5 (10...♗d5!? 11.♗h3 ♗xc5) 11.dxc5 ♕xd1+ 12.♖xd1 ♘e7.

8...♗b7 9.♗g2 ♗d5.

5...b5

5...♘d7!? 6.0-0 b5 7.a4 ♗b7 8.♘c3 a6 transposes.

A. 6.a4; **B.** 6.♘e5; **C.** 6.0-0

6.♘c3 ♗b7 7.e4 ♘f6 8.e5 ♘d5 9.♘g5 defines White's plan too early and we can adjust our set-up accordingly.

Since the queen's knight is no longer needed on d7, Black can go 9...♘a6, intending to castle queenside after 10.♕h5 (10.0-0 ♕d7 11.♘e4 c5!?) 10...♕d7 11.♘xh7?! 0-0-0!. Petursson played against Scherbakov 11.0-0, when 11...♘ab4! activates this commonly passive piece. The most White can extract from his onslaught is to regain the pawn with 12.♘xh7 0-0-0! 13.♘xf8, but the endgame is pleasant for Black.

A. 6.a4 ♗b7 7.♘c3

We can answer 7.b3 with 7...b4!? 8.bxc4 c5.

7.♘e5 transposes to line B. 6.♘e5.

The flexible 7.0-0 is best met by 7...♘f6

7...♘d7 is less precise in view of 8.♘e5! (8.b3 cxb3 9.♕xb3 b4!) 8...♕c8 9.♘xd7! (practice has only seen 9.b3? when 9...♘xe5! 10.dxe5 b4! is excellent for Black) 9...♕xd7 10.b3 with a stable initiative.

8.b3!?

A typical method of fighting against ...dxc4.

8.♘e5 transposes to line B.

8...cxb3 9.♕xb3 b4!

In most cases I advise to avoid ...a6. Although 9...a6 is also possible here, I recommend to steer clear of this passive set-up. White retains lasting pressure after 10.♘c3 (10.♖d1) 10...♗e7 (10...♘bd7 11.♘e5! b4 12.♗g5!±) 11.♖d1 ♘bd7 12.♘e5, e.g. 12...♘d5 13.♘e4±.

10.♘e5

10.a5 immediately allows the freeing 10...c5, e.g. 11.♗e3 ♗d5 12.♕a4+ ♕d7 13.dxc5 ♕xa4 14.♖xa4 ♘a6 15.♖c1 ♘d7∓.

10...♕c8!

It is best to enable ...c5 as quickly as possible. 10...♗e7 11.♗b2 ♘fd7 12.♘d3 a5 is risky as it hands the initiative to the opponent. Even with best play Black is on the brink of falling under attack – 13.♘d2 0-0 14.♖ac1 ♗a6 15.♘c4 ♖a7 16.♖fd1 ♘b6 17.♘ce5 ♖c7

18.♘c5!? (18.h4 ♗d6) 18...♗xe2 19.♖e1 ♗h5 20.h4 ♗xc5 21.dxc5 ♘d5 22.g4 f6 23.♘xc6 ♘xc6 24.gxh5 ♘e5 25.♕g3 h6 26.c6≌.

In two games Black took a second pawn and won, but White's attack is in fact very strong. The trick is not to hurry, but methodically suffocate the opponent – 10...♕xd4? 11.♗b2 ♕d8 12.♖d1 ♕c7 13.♘d2 ♗e7 14.♘xf7 ♔xf7 15.♘f3 ♘d5 16.♗e5!! (16.♘e5+) 16...♕a5 17.e4 ♘d7 [17...♘c7 18.♕b2 ♖g8 (18...♘e8 19.♗h3) 19.♖ac1! ♗f6 (19...♗c8? 20.h4 ♘d7 21.♖xc6 ♕xa4 22.♕c1 ♘b5 23.♖xe6+–) 20.♗xf6 gxf6 21.♕d2 ♖g6 22.h4!!±] 18.♗h3 ♖he8 19.♖d4±.

11.a5 c5 12.♕a4+ ♘bd7

Black gets rid of his weak bishop on b7 and completes development:

13.♘xd7

13.dxc5 ♗xc5 14.♖d1 ♗xg2 15.♔xg2 a6 16.♘xd7 ♘xd7 17.♗b2 (17.f3 ♖a7 18.♘d2 0-0 19.♘e4 ♗e7 20.♗f4 ♘c5! 21.♕xb4 ♘d3=) 17...♗e7 18.♗xg7 ♖g8 19.♗h6 e5∞; 13.♗xb7 ♕xb7 14.♗b2 a6 15.♘d2 ♕b5=.

13...♘xd7 14.♗xb7 ♕xb7 15.a6 ♕b6 16.♘d2 ♖c8

After 16...cxd4? 17.♘c4 ♕c5 18.♘a5 ♕d5 19.e4!! ♕xe4 20.♗b2+– the pin of the d7-knight decides the outcome.

17.dxc5 ♕c6 18.♕xb4 ♗xc5 19.♕g4 0-0 20.♗b2 e5. White's attack is over, the pawns are symmetrical. Play might continue 21.♖fc1 ♕b5 22.♖ab1 ♘f6 23.♕f3 ♗b6 24.♖xc8 ♖xc8 25.♕b7 ♖c7 26.♕b8+ ♕e8 27.♕xe8+ ♘xe8 28.♗xe5 ♖c2 29.♘f3 ♖a2 30.♖c1 f6 31.♗d4 ♖xa6 32.♔g2=.

A1. 7...b4!? **A2.** 7...a6

A1. 7...b4!?

My general principle after taking on c4 is to avoid spending a tempo on ...a6. So I checked 7...b4!? to discover that nobody has played it yet! Perhaps everybody quickly discarded it owing to:

8.♘e4 c5! 9.♘e5!

9.♘xc5? ♗xc5 10.dxc5 ♕xd1+ 11.♔xd1 ♘d7∓. After the knight leap the only way to avoid heavy positional pressure on the queenside is:

9...♗d5, and the ball is in White's court:

I'd be amazed if your opponent does not spend here half of his remaining time! He has at least 6 plausible continuations, but 10.a5 cxd4 11.0-0 could only enter the AI brain of neural net engines, so we could discard it. Besides, 11...♘e7 12.♗g5 ♘bc6 does not look dangerous.

The same can be said about 10.♗g5 f6 11.e3!! g6

12.h4!! fxg5 13.♕f3 ♕e7 14.♘d6+ ♕xd6 15.♕f7+ ♔d8 16.♗xd5 exd5 17.♕b7 with a ...draw!

10.0-0 f6 11.♘xc4 ♗xc4 12.♘xc5 ♗xc5 13.♗xa8 is possible, but after 13...♗d6 14.♗d2 ♘e7 15.♖c1 ♗d5 16.♗xd5 exd5 17.e4 dxe4 18.♕g4 ♔f7 19.♕xe4 ♕a5∓ White's rooks have no invasion squares.

However, other 2 options deserve our full attention as they are closer to human thinking and are based on typical tactical patterns:

a) 10.♘xf7!? ♔xf7 11.♘g5+ ♕xg5 12.e4!

> 12.♗xg5 ♗xg2 13.♖g1 ♗d5 14.e4 ♗xe4 15.♕e2 ♗d5 16.0-0-0 ♘d7 should be slightly in Black's favour. Without a knight, White's queen is not too dangerous.

12...♕e7 13.exd5 cxd4 14.0-0 e5 15.d6 ♕xd6 16.♕f3+ ♘f6 17.♕xa8. At first I thought Black's pawns should prevail here, but the computer finds threats all the time. So with best play it is probably a draw – 17...♘bd7 18.♗g5 ♕c5 19.♗h3 h6 20.♗xf6 ♘xf6 21.♖ae1 c3 22.f4 d3+ 23.♔h1 d2 24.♖xe5 ♗d6 25.♗e6+ ♔e7 26.♕xh8 ♗xe5 27.fxe5 ♕c6+ 28.♔g1 ♔xe6 29.exf6 ♕c5+ 30.♔g2 ♕d5+=.

b) 10.dxc5!? f6 11.♘xc4 ♗xc4 12.♘d6+ ♗xd6 13.cxd6 ♘d7 14.♗e3 f5 15.♖c1 ♗d5 16.♗xd5 exd5 17.♕xd5 ♘gf6 18.♕e6+ ♔f8 19.♕xf5 ♕e8 20.♗d4 ♕e4 21.♕xe4 ♘xe4 22.♖c7 ♔e8 23.0-0. The dust has settled, and an equal endgame has arisen. I would feel slightly anxious because of the rook on c7, but the computer easily neutralises it after both 23...a5 24.♖d1 ♖g8= and 23...♘xd6 24.♖d1 ♖f8 25.♗xg7 ♖f7 26.♖xd6 ♖xg7 27.a5 ♖e7.

c) Finally, **10.♗f4!!** is an altogether incredible idea, which leads to roughly balanced, but marvellously chaotic play:

10...f5

10...cxd4 is more solid – 11.0-0 f5 12.♘g5 ♗xg2 13.♔xg2 ♕d5+ 14.♘gf3 ♗c5 15.♖c1 c3 16.bxc3 bxc3 17.a5! ♘e7 18.♕a4+ ♘bc6 19.♖fd1

White regains both pawns – 19...0-0 20.♖xc3 ♖ac8 21.e3 (or 21.♘xc6 ♘xc6 22.♕b5 ♗b4 23.♕xd5 exd5 24.♖b3 ♗xa5 25.♘xd4 ♘xd4 26.♖xd4 ♖cd8 27.♖b5=) 21...♘xe5 22.♗xe5 g5 23.♗xd4 g4 24.♔g1 ♗xd4 25.♖xc8 ♖xc8 26.♘xd4 ♔f7 27.♘b5 ♖c4 28.♕b3 ♖b4 29.♖xd5 ♖xb3 30.♖c5 ♔f6 31.♘xa7 ♖a3=. The choice is a matter of taste, but 10...cxd4 gives Black less chances to win in my opinion. White just presses in the centre with natural moves.

11.♘xc5 ♗xg2 12.♘xe6 ♕b6 13.d5 b3! (an only defence against ♘xc4) 14.f3!! (14.♖g1 ♗b4+ 15.♗d2 ♗xd5 16.♘xg7+ ♔f8 17.♗xb4+ ♕xb4+ 18.♔f1 ♕d6 19.♘xc4 ♕d7)

14...♘d7

The most difficult part is, of course, to assess that White's attack is devastating after 14...♗xh1 15.♔f1. He is a ton of material down, but Black cannot set up coordination.

15.a5 ♕b4+ 16.♗d2 ♕b7 17.a6 ♕c8 18.♘xd7 ♕xd7 19.♖g1 ♘f6 20.♗c3 ♗h3 21.♕d4 ♘xd5 22.♘xf8 ♖xf8 23.♕e5+ ♘e7 24.♖d1 ♕a4 25.♕xg7 ♕xa6 26.♕xh7 ♕b6 27.♕h5+ ♘g6 28.♗d4 ♕e6 29.♗c3 (29.♕xh3 0-0-0∞) 29...♕b6∞.

If you seek lively play based mostly on calculation, 7...b4 is an excellent choice.

A2. 7...a6 8.0-0

8.♘e5 is seldom seen, probably because of 8...f6 – see line B.

8...♘d7

Another topical set-up arises following 8...♘f6 9.e4 ♗e7 10.e5 ♘d5 11.♘e4 ♘d7 12.♗g5 0-0 13.♗xe7 ♕xe7 14.♘d6

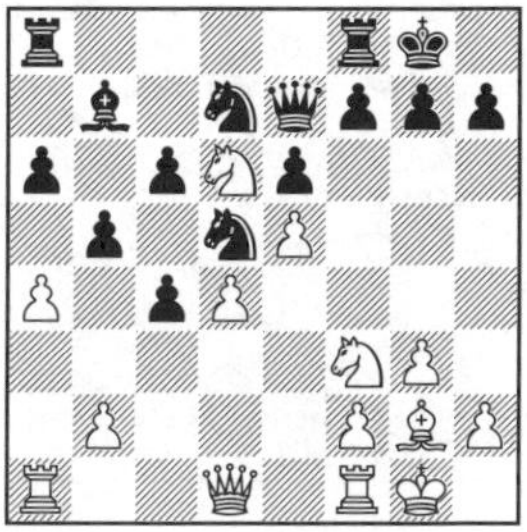

White has accomplished his strategic plan, but that does not promise him an advantage. Provided that we open up our bishop with ...c5! Thus I recommend 14...♘7b6

A solid, but passive defence is 14...♖ab8 15.axb5 cxb5 16.♘d2 ♖fd8 17.♘2e4 f6.

15.a5 ♘c8 16.♘e4 c5! 17.♘xc5 ♗c6 18.b3 ♖d8 19.♕c2 c3 with mutual chances. Black's knight enters play via a7-c6.

9.e4

9.♘e5 ♘xe5 10.dxe5 ♘e7 11.axb5 axb5 12.♗g5 h6 is about equal – 13.♘e4 ♕xd1 14.♖xa8+ ♗xa8 15.♖xd1 ♘d5 16.♖a1 ♗b7 17.♖a7 hxg5 18.♖xb7 f6=.

9...h6!?

It is better to prevent 9...♘gf6 10.e5 ♘d5 11.♘g5 h6 12.♘xe6 with unclear complications. Note that this variation became possible because of the early ...♘d7. Instead ...♘f6+... ♗e7 effectively prevents it.

10.d5! e5 11.♕e2 ♘gf6

11...♕b8!?= avoids the following stab and leaves more chances to both opponents.

12.♘d4!?

White also gets sufficient compensation with 12.♖d1 ♕b8=.

After the text Vinchev-Perry, ICCF 2015, went 12...cxd5 13.exd5 ♗c5 14.♘c6 ♕b6 15.♘e4 0-0 16.♘xc5 ♕xc5 17.♖d1 ♖fe8 18.d6 e4 19.♘e7+ ♔h7 20.♗e3 ♕e5 21.♗h3 ♖ed8 22.♗f4 ♕c5=.

B. 6.♘e5 ♗b7 7.a4

7.0-0 ♘f6 8.a4 (for 8.b3 – see line C) 8...a6 transposes to the main line.

Scherbakov recommends instead 8...♕c7? 9.♗f4 ♘h5 10.♗d2 ♘d7, missing altogether 11.♘c3!. White regains the material with a stable positional edge since 11...b4 12.♘e4 ♘xe5 13.dxe5 ♕xe5 14.♕c2 ♗e7 15.♕xc4 a5? stumbles into 16.♘f6+!.

7...a6

Of course I would like very much to save this move, but 7...♕c8 prematurely removes the hit on d4 and gives White a free hand on the queenside:

8.0-0 ♘d7

8...♘f6 9.b3! cxb3 10.♘d2! also promises White nice pressure. This line became possible because of the early ...♕c8.

9.♘xd7 ♕xd7 10.b3 assures White of the initiative, as mentioned in line A.

8.0-0

Nobody has tried 8.b3 exactly at this point, although 8...cxb3 9.♕xb3 ♘f6 10.0-0 ♕xd4 11.♗b2 ♕b4 12.♕c2 ♕c5 is not that bad for White. For instance, a correspondence game saw 13.♕xc5 ♗xc5 14.♖c1 ♘bd7, draw!

White does not have a convenient way to preserve the queens anyway – 13.♕b3 ♗e7 14.♖d1!

14.♖c1?! ♕b6 favoured Black in Alaverdyan-Tregubov, Yerevan 2014.

14...0-0 15.♗d4 ♕b4 16.♕xb4=.

8.♘c3 f6 (Although 8...♘f6!?, followed by ...♗d6 is perfectly sane.) 9.♘f3 b4 10.♘e4

Or 10.♘a2 c5 11.0-0 a5 12.dxc5 ♕c8∓.

10...c5! 11.♘ed2 c3 (or 11...cxd4 12.♘xc4 e5 13.0-0 ♗d5∞) 12.bxc3 bxc3 13.♘c4 cxd4 14.0-0 ♗b4 15.♗f4 ♘e7∞.

8...♘f6

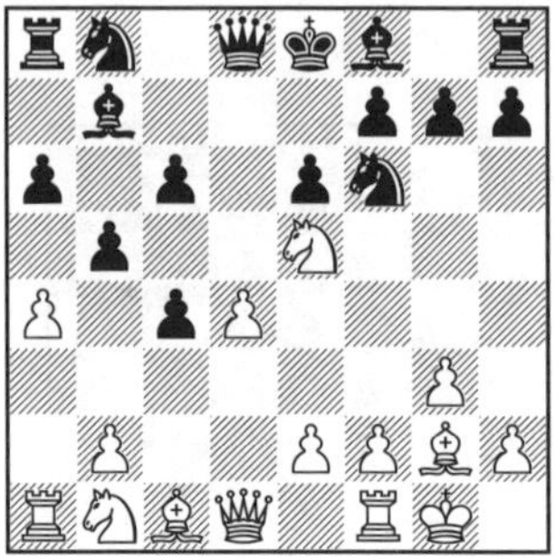

9.♘c3

9.b3 cxb3 10.♗b2

10.♕xb3 ♕xd4= – see 8.b3.

10...♘bd7 11.♕xb3 ♘xe5 12.dxe5 ♘d7!?

12...♘d5 is also good, but the text offers Black a clear plan – to undermine White's outpost on e5.

13.♘d2 ♗e7 14.♘e4 0-0 15.♘d6

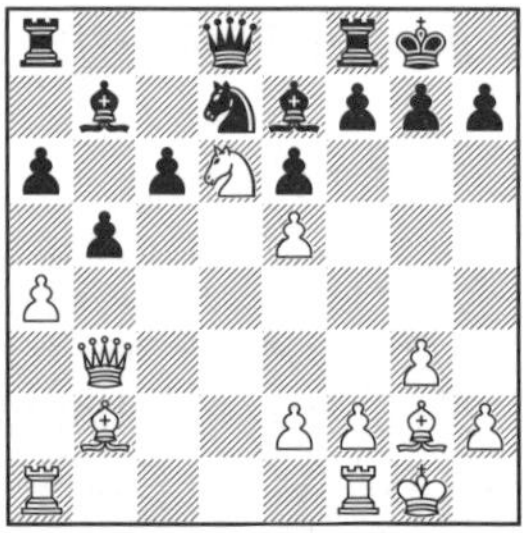

Play is equal. Now simplest is 15...♕b8, threatening 16.♖fd1 ♘c5. If 16.♕c3, then 16...♘xe5 is a dead draw, while 16...♗xd6 17.exd6 f6= would be an attempt to play on.

9...♕c8!?

9...♗e7!? discharges the tension. Play it if you forgot the main line –

10.axb5 axb5 11.♖xa8 ♗xa8 12.♘xb5 cxb5 13.♗xa8 0-0 14.♗g2 ♘d5

14...♗d6 15.♗g5 h6 16.♗xf6 ♕xf6 17.♘g4 ♕e7.

15.♗d2 ♕c7 16.e4 ♘f6=

16...♘b4 17.♕g4 (17.♗h3 ♗d6 18.d5=) 17...♘c2 18.♘f3 g6∞ is more challenging.

17.♗f4 ♗d6 18.♕e2 ♖c8 19.♖a1=.

10.e4

After 10.♗g5 normal answers are 10...♗e7 11.♗xf6 gxf6! or 10...♘bd7 11.♘xd7 ♘xd7 12.e4 b4! (repulsing the knight from the centre) 13.♘b1 a5 14.♘d2 ♗a6 (14...c3!?), although the engines assess highly Black's chances after 10...h6!? 11.axb5 cxb5 12.♗xf6 gxf6.

10...♗e7!?

10...♘bd7 may be a decent alternative, but the delay of castling offers White more chances to fight for the initiative:

11.♘xd7 ♘xd7

11...♕xd7?! 12.e5 ♘d5 13.♘e4 a5 (This aims to enable ...♗a6. 13... h6 14.♗d2 ♗e7 15.♕g4!↑ disrupts the connection between Black's rooks.) 14.♗d2 b4 (14...♗e7 15.♕g4 ♔f8 16.♗g5±) 15.♕f3 ♗a6 16.♖fd1 ♗e7 17.♕g4 ♔f8 18.h4 is unclear, but Black is practically a rook down.

12.d5 ♘c5 13.d6

13.♗e3 b4 14.dxe6 ♕xe6 15.♘e2 ♘b3 16.♖b1 a5 17.e5 ♗c5 18.♗xc5 ♘xc5 19.♕d4 ♘xa4 20.♘f4 ♕e7 21.♕xc4 0-0 22.e6 ♘b6 23.exf7+ ♖xf7 24.♕c5 ♘d5=.

13...b4 14.♘b1 e5 15.♗e3 ♘b3

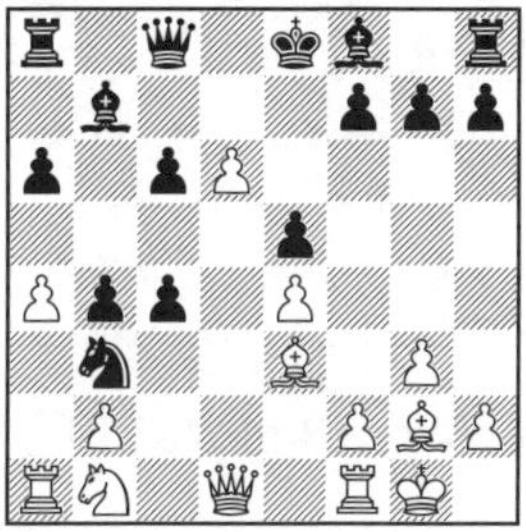

16.♘d2!

16.f4 exf4 17.♖xf4 ♕e6 18.d7+ ♕xd7 19.♕xd7+ ♔xd7 20.♖xf7+ is also balanced. For instance, 20...♗e7 21.♘d2 ♘xa1 22.♗c5 c3 23.bxc3 bxc3 24.♖xe7+ ♔d8 25.♖xb7 cxd2 26.♗f3 ♔c8 27.♖xg7 h5 28.♗b6 a5 29.♖c7+ ♔b8 30.♖d7 ♔c8 31.♖xd2 ♖b8 32.♗e3 ♘b3=.

16...♘xa1 17.♘xc4 ♕e6 18.♗b6 a5 19.d7+ ♕xd7 20.♕xd7+ ♔xd7 21.♖xa1. Amazingly, despite the queens trade, White's attack remains strong and Black has to make a few only moves – 21...f6 22.♘xa5 ♔c8 23.♗h3+ ♔b8 24.♘xb7 ♔xb7 25.a5 ♗e7 26.♖d1 ♖ad8=.

11.d5

It looks consistent to open the centre.

White has also tried to attack with pieces – 11.♘g4!?, when 11...0-0 12.♘xf6+ ♗xf6 13.e5 ♗e7 14.♕g4 ♔h8 15.♘e4 ♕c7 16.♗g5 ♗xg5 17.♘xg5 h6 leads to a typical position where we should open our b7-bishop:

18.♘e4 c5! or 18.f4 ♕e7 19.♘e4 c5!.

Grischuk played against Aronian 11.g4?!, but I do not understand the aim of this move. Black was fine after 11...♘fd7 12.♘f3 0-0 13.♗f4, when 13...b4 14.♘e2 c5 takes over the initiative.

11.f4?! 0-0 12.f5 exf5 13.♖xf5 ♘bd7 14.♗g5 occurred in two games. Although 14...♘xe5 was good enough, even stronger is 14...♕d8∓.

11...cxd5

The engines also defend easily after 11...0-0 12.d6 ♗d8∞.

12.exd5 b4 13.♘e4

The spectacular 13.♘xf7? fails to 13...0-0.

13...0-0

13...♘xe4 14.♗xe4 0-0 allows a forced draw after 15.♕h5 (15.♗f4 ♗f6 16.♖c1 ♗xe5 17.♗xe5 ♘d7 18.♗xh7+ is also a perpetual.) 15...g6 16.♘xg6.

14.dxe6 ♘xe4 15.exf7+ ♔h8 16.♕h5 ♕e6 17.♖e1 ♘d6 18.♗xb7 ♘xb7 19.♗f4 ♘d7 20.♘xd7 ♕xd7 21.♖ad1=

It transpires that White regains the piece, but there is still some life left in the position – 21...♗d6 22.♗e5 ♕xf7 23.♕xf7 ♖xf7 24.♗xd6 a5!?.

C. 6.0-0 ♗b7

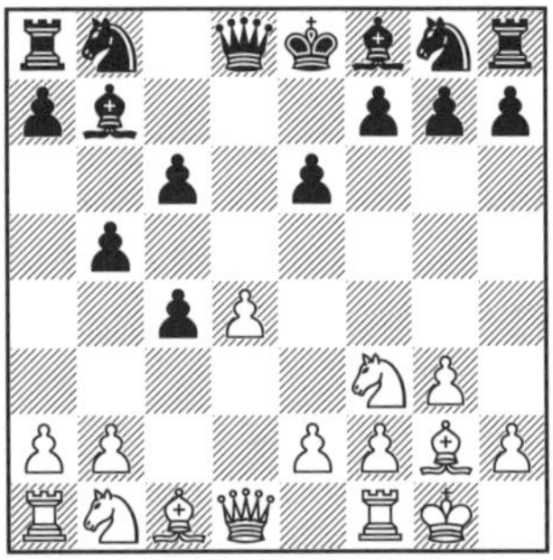

I will consider here the plan with **C1.** 7.b3, and with e4 – **C2.** 7.♘c3

7.a4 ♘f6 – see line A.

7.♘e5 ♘f6 8.b3 is an independent line.

Instead 8.a4 a6 transposes to line B.

For 8.♘c3 – see line C2 7.♘c3 ♘f6 8.♘e5.

8...cxb3 9.axb3 ♗e7 10.♘c3

After 10.♗a3 ♗xa3 11.♘xa3 ♕b6 12.♘c2 we play for ...c5, e.g. 12...♘bd7 13.♘xd7 ♘xd7 14.♕d2 0-0 15.♕a5 ♖fb8 16.♖fc1 c5.

10...a6 11.♗b2 0-0 12.♘e4 ♘xe4 13.♗xe4 a5 – see **Game 17** Ipatov-Eljanov, Baku 2015.

C1. 7.b3 cxb3 8.♕xb3 ♘f6

I recommend playing ...♘f6 before ...♘d7 in almost all cases. The reason is that 8...♘d7 is typically met by 9.♘e5, hitting c6. Of course Black could ignore the threat with 9...♘f6, but White could put more pressure with 10.♘c3, 10.a4 or 10.♗g5.

9.♘c3

9.a4?! only provokes the useful move 9...b4 – see line A, 7.0-0.

9.♖d1 does not threaten anything, so we can complete development –9...♗e7 and castle.

9...♗e7 10.♘e5

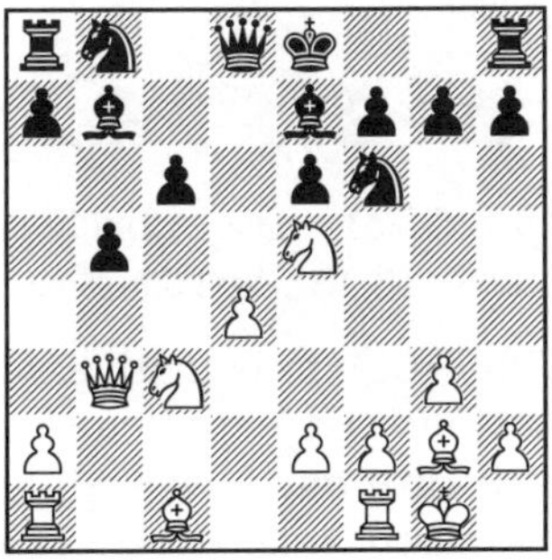

10...b4!?

Once again I promote this approach before 10...a6. In that case 11.♖d1 0-0 12.♘e4 promises White ample compensation for the pawn. See the instructive **Game 16** Nakamura-Lenderman, Saint Louis 2016.
The text diverts the knight towards the queenside since 11.♘e4?? would drop a piece.

10...♕b6 is not the best place for the queen and Black had to adjust it very soon – 11.♖d1 0-0 12.♘e4 a5 13.♗g5 ♕c7. Nevertheless, the game Florea-Coklin, ICCF 2018 eventually ended in a draw:

14.♕c2 ♘xe4 15.♗xe7 ♕xe7 16.♗xe4 g6 17.♖ac1 ♖d8 18.h4↑.

14.♗xf6 gxf6 15.♘g4 is more unpleasant. White's pieces are rather threatening, the point being 15...f5? 16.♘ef6+ ♔g7 17.♕e3+–.

11.♘a4

11.♖d1 0-0 12.♗g5 a5 13.♘a4

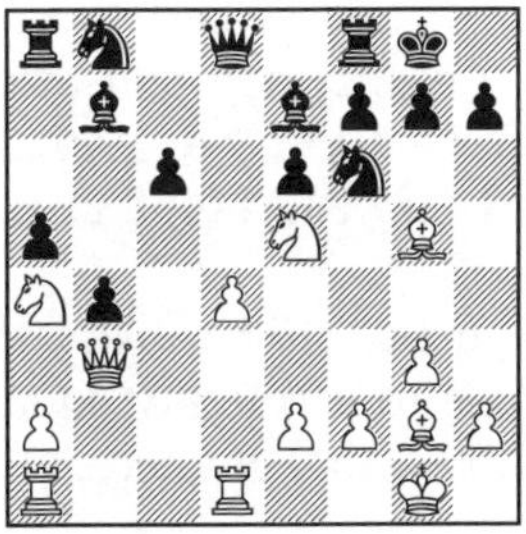

13...♗a6 14.♗xc6 ♘xc6 15.♘xc6 ♕e8 16.♘xe7+ ♕xe7 17.♕f3 h6= did not change anything in Houdini-Stockfish, 2018.

11...0-0 12.♖d1 a5

The idea is to activate the b7-bishop, e.g. 13.a3 ♗a6 14.♕c2 ♗b5.

13.♘c5 ♗xc5 14.dxc5 ♕e7 15.♗e3

Play is also balanced after 15.♕c2 ♘bd7 16.♘xd7 ♘xd7 17.♗e3 ♘f6 18.a3 ♘d5 19.♗d2 ♖fd8 20.♖db1 (20.e4 ♘c3) 20...h6 21.axb4 axb4 22.♖xa8 ♖xa8 23.e4 (23.♗xb4 ♗a6=) 23...♘c7 24.♖xb4 ♗a6 25.♖a4 e5=.

15...♘d5 16.♗d4 ♗a6 17.e4

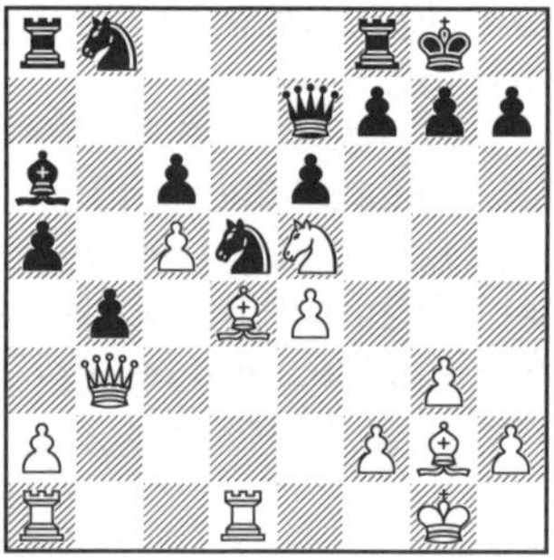

17...♘f6=

17...♘c7 is more risky and gives White decent compensation for the pawn – 18.♗e3 f6 19.♘c4 ♗xc4 20.♕xc4 ♘d7 21.f4 ♘b5 22.a4∞.

After the text 18.a3 bxa3 19.♖xa3 ♗b5 leads to a roughly equal position with mutual chances.

C2. 7.♘c3 ♘f6 8.e4

8.♘e5 a6

I'm not sure that 8...♘d5 or 8...♕c8 are more useful moves, although they are often seen in practice.

9.a4

9.b3 cxb3 10.♕xb3 transposes to line C1, but I would gladly grasp the chance to put a pawn on c3 with 9...b4 10.♘a4 c3.

9...♕c8 – see line B.

8...♗e7 9.e5

9.a4 is still a decent option.

Then 9...a6 10.e5 ♘d5 is of course a normal continuation, but my preferred approach dictates to look for more active options, if we had a choice at all. So I'd hesitate between 9...0-0 10.axb5 cxb5 11.e5 ♘d5 12.♘xb5 ♕b6 13.♘c3 a5 14.♘g5 ♘xc3 15.bxc3 ♗xg2 16.♔xg2 ♘d7 17.♘e4 f6∞ and:

9...b4 10.e5 ♘d5 11.♘e4 0-0 12.♗g5 ♘d7 13.♗xe7 ♕xe7 14.♖c1

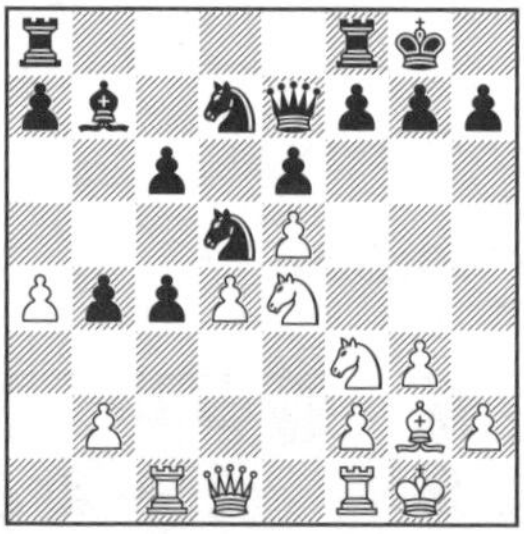

14...c5 15.♖e1 c3 16.bxc3 ♘xc3 17.♘xc3 bxc3 18.♖xc3 ♖ac8=.

9.♗g5 h6 10.♗xf6 is toothless since it is obvious that White cannot seriously disturb our king without his dark-squared bishop – 10...♗xf6 11.e5 ♗e7 12.♘h4 ♘d7 13.♕g4 0-0

14.a4 b4 15.♘e4 ♖b8 16.♖fd1 c5∓.

White has also tried to keep the centre fluid:
9.♕e2 0-0 10.♖d1 ♘bd7 11.♗f4

We can prepare a queenside offensive with:
11...a5 12.♖ac1 a4! 13.a3 ♕b6∓. The queen has found a stable place on b6, next follows ...♖fd8, ...c5, reviving the b7-bishop (or 14.e5 ♘d5 15.♗g5 ♖ae8, again followed by ...c5).
The immediate 11...b4 12.e5 (12.♘b1 c5!) 12...♘h5 13.♘e4 ♘xf4 14.gxf4 ♘b6 is also possible.

9.♖e1 does not make much sense in conjunction with 9...0-0 10.e5 – 10...♘d5 11.♘e4 – White certainly had more useful moves than ♖e1 in this structure. We could answer thematically – 11...♘d7 12.♗g5 c5.

9...♘d5 10.♘e4 ♘d7

The main line is 10...h6 – see **Game 15** Iskusnyh-Yakovich, Krasnoyarsk 2007. In line A with a4 a6 inserted, I recommended in this pawn structure to avoid weaknesses on the kingside, so I decided to be consistent.

11.♗g5 0-0 12.♗xe7 ♕xe7 13.♘d6 ♘7b6

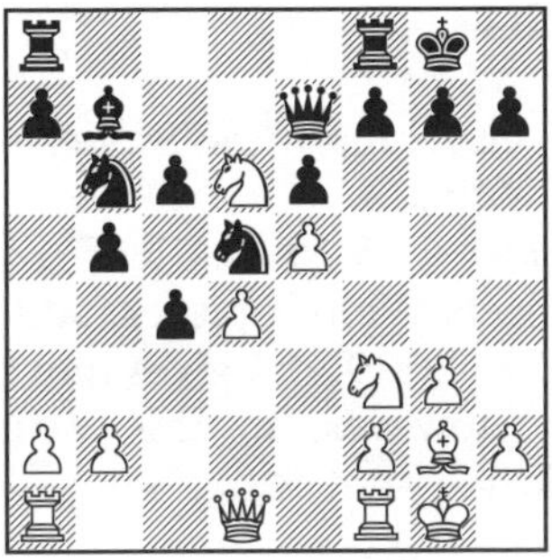

The knight looks pretty on d6, but on the other hand, it does not participate in the attack. It is not easy to prove enough compensation for the pawn.
14.b3 does not work owing to 14... c3.
After 14.♕c2 we answer 14...a5 – with the idea to stabilise the queenside with ...a4 and follow up with ...c5:
15.♘xb7 ♕xb7 16.♘g5 g6 17.h4 a4 18.a3. Black's position is quite resilient. He can even choose different defensive set-ups. One of them is ...♕e7, ...♘d7, ...♔g7, ...h5. Or he could transfer his d5-knight to f5 – 18...♘e7 19.h5 ♘f5 20.hxg6 hxg6 21.♖ad1 ♔g7 22.g4 ♘h4 23.f4 ♖h8, when White's attack has been stalled.

Another safe approach is to sac the exchange on d6. I explore it in the main line.

14.♕d2 h6

The plan with ...a6-a5-a4, followed

by ...♘c8 is also an option, if you want to avoid 15.♕a5.

15.♘h4

What else?! 15.♖fe1 a5 16.♖e4 is parried by 16...f5.
15.♕a5!? ♘c8 16.♘e4 ♕d8 17.♕d2 a5 rejects White's pieces, although 18.b3 ♘cb6 19.♖fc1 gives him some play. However, in this variation Black does not fear a kingside attack.
The text at least enables f2-f4-f5.

15...♖ad8! 16.f4 ♖xd6!

The safest solution. Now Black's better central pieces dominate the board.

17.exd6 ♕xd6∓

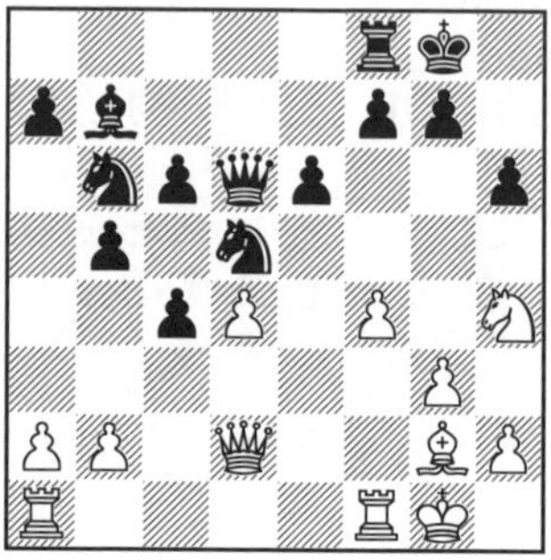

Black's main positional aim is ...b4, followed by ...c3. 18.f5 ♗c8 19.f6? is not a threat – we simply take the pawn.
19.fxe6 ♗xe6 20.♘f5 is also harmless in view of 20...♗xf5 21.♖xf5 ♘b4 22.♖af1 ♘d3 23.♕e3 f6.

Chapter 4. The Catalan Way

Annotated Games

15. Iskusnyh – Yakovich
Krasnoyarsk 03.09.2007

1.d4 ♘f6 2.c4 e6 3.g3 d5 4.♘f3 dxc4 5.♗g2 c6 6.0-0 b5 7.♘c3 ♗b7 8.e4 ♗e7 9.e5 ♘d5 10.♘e4 h6!?

11.♘h4

White may try to discourage long castling with 11.♗d2 ♘d7 12.b3. As always in such cases, I recommend to return the pawn in order to get counterplay – 12...0-0! 13.bxc4 bxc4 14.♕c1 c5!∓. It suddenly transpires that the sac on h6 is not that dangerous since capturing is not obligatory! In fact, 15.♗xh6? cxd4! is disastrous for White!

11...♘d7

11...g5 12.♘f3 ♘d7 13.a4 a6 14.h4 gxh4 15.♘xh4 c5?! (Krasenkow) 16.♕h5! gives White an attack.

12.♕h5

12.a4 is a double-edged move as it weakens White's queenside.

Then 12...♘7b6 13.a5 is unclear. Our most challenging retort would be:

12...a5!? 13.♕h5 ♘7b6 14.axb5

14.♗g5 hxg5 15.♕xh8+ ♔d7 16.♕xg7 ♕g8!! is similar, but Black will eat the a4-pawn.

14...cxb5 15.♗g5 hxg5! 16.♕xh8+ ♔d7 17.♕xg7

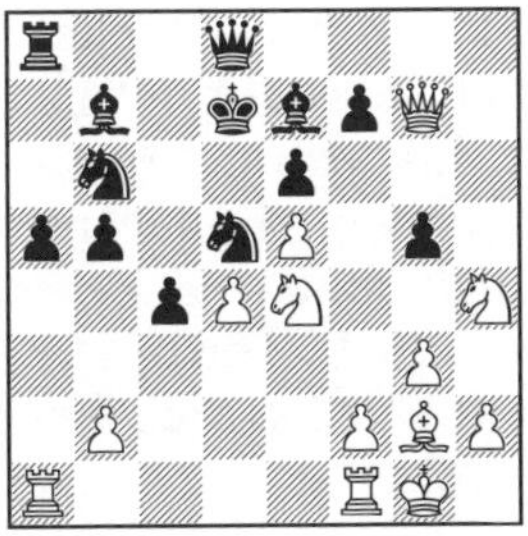

17...♕g8!! Underlying the power of Black's position. After 18.♕xg8 ♖xg8 19.♘f3 a4 20.♘c5+ ♔c7 White cannot tame the queenside pawns, e.g. 21.♘xb7 ♔xb7 22.♘d2 ♖c8 23.♖fb1 ♔a6 24.♖c1 c3 25.bxc3 ♘xc3 26.♗f1 ♔a5.

12...♘f8?!

When Black plays ...h6 in such positions, he should contemplate a long castle. Therefore, 12...♕b6! is a logical move – preparing ...0-0-0 with a tempo. White must defend d4 as:

13.♗g5 ♗xg5 14.♘xg5 allows 14...0-0. White lacks a bishop to sacrifice it on h6. The attempt to attack with 15.♗xd5 cxd5 16.♘gf3 ♕d8 17.g4 is well parried by 17...♕e8 18.g5 f6. Now let's consider:

13.♗e3 ♖f8 14.a4 0-0-0 15.♘f3 ♘xe3 16.fxe3 ♔b8

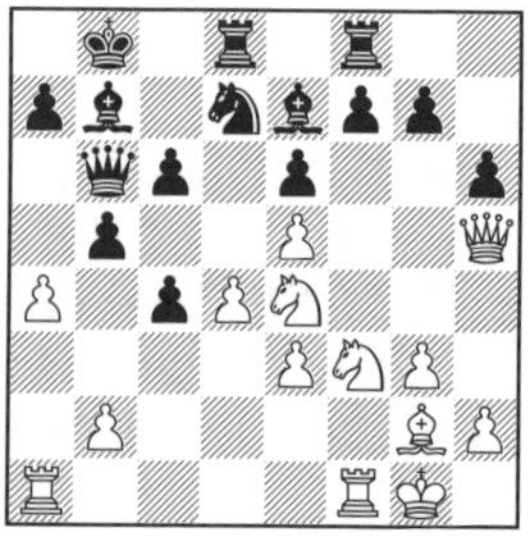

Black's king's pawn shelter is very solid, but he would not be able to convert his extra pawn without opening lines on the queenside. The game might follow:
17.♘d6 ♗xd6 18.exd6 bxa4!? 19.♘e5 f6 20.♘xc4 ♕b5 21.♕e2 ♘b6∓ or: 17.♘fd2 f6!∓.

13.♗d2 g6 14.♕e2

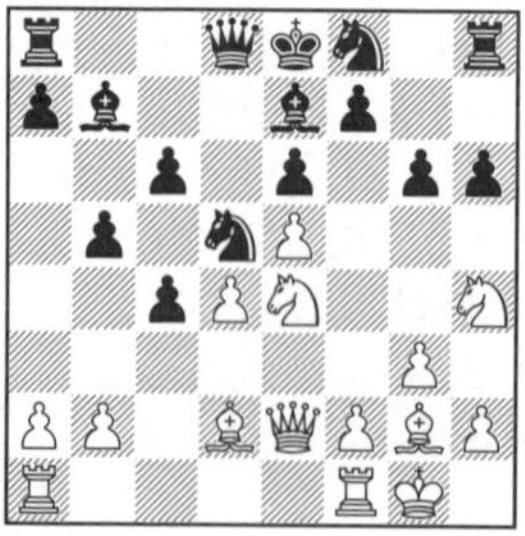

14...♘d7?!

This move is still not a mistake, but it betrays a wrong judgement. If Black had realised that he must meet b3 by ...♗a6, he would have found 14... a5!, intending 15.b3 ♗a6!.

15.b3 cxb3?

A typical strategic mistake. Now it is a one-way road as Black can only dream for a draw. 15...♗a6 was still the correct answer.

16.axb3 b4 17.♘d6+!

An excellent decision! 17.♖fe1, followed by ♖ac1, would have been also in White's favour, but Iskusnyh prefers to convert one advantage into another one. He weakens the dark squares and opens files for his heavy pieces.

17...♗xd6 18.exd6 a5

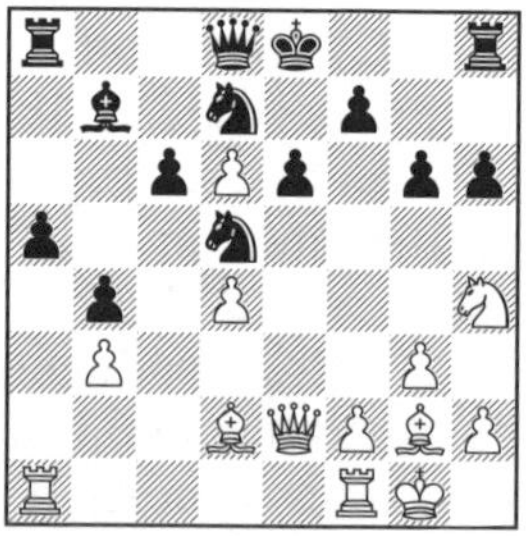

19.♖fe1?!

A first imprecision by White so far. 19.♗xd5! cxd5 20.♖fc1 would have given White an access to c7, to add to the threats on g6 and h6.

After the text Black could hide his king with 19...♔f8! although White keeps the initiative following 20.♕d3.

19...♗a6?! 20.♕e4 ♔f8?!

20...♘f8! was the most resilient defence. The knight may stay passively, but it neutralises all the sacrifices on g6 and e6, e.g. 21.♕e5 f6 22.♕e4 ♔f7 23.♕c2 ♗b5 24.♗e4 f5 25.♗xd5 cxd5 26.♕c5±.

21.♗h3??

Obviously some miscalculation. 21.♘xg6+ fxg6 22.♕xe6 was winning, albeit not that simply:

22...♗d3 23.♗xd5 cxd5 24.♕xd5 and Black is helpless against the threat ♖e7 – 24...♘f6 25.♕f3.
Now Black escapes and even shows some teeth.

21...g5 22.♘g6+ fxg6 23.♗xe6 ♔g7 24.♗xd5 cxd5 25.♕e7+ ♕xe7 26.♖xe7+ ♔f6 27.♖xd7= ♗d3 28.♖e7 ♖hd8 29.♖e3 ♗c2 30.g4 a4 31.bxa4 b3 32.♗c3 ♖xd6 33.a5 ♖c6 34.♗b2 ♖ca6 35.♗c3 ♖b8 36.♖ae1 ♗e4 37.f3 ♗c2 38.♖e8 ♖xe8 39.♖xe8 ♖c6 ½-½

16. Nakamura – Lenderman
USA-ch Saint Louis 14.04.2016

1.d4 d5 2.c4 e6 3.♘f3 ♘f6 4.♘c3 c6 5.g3 dxc4 6.♗g2 b5 7.0-0 ♗b7 8.b3 cxb3 9.♕xb3 ♗e7 10.♘e5 a6

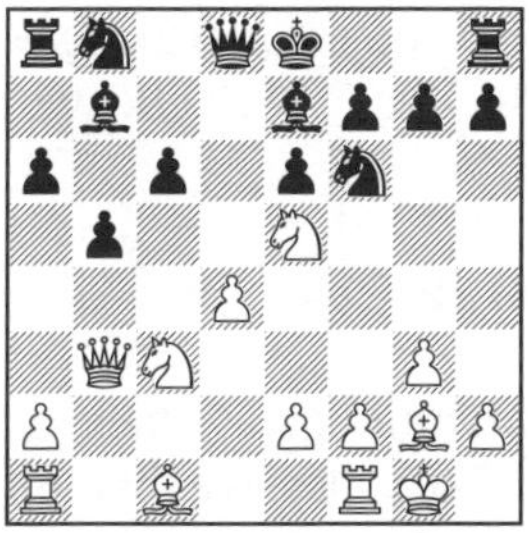

11.♖d1

Play is not forced, so White has a wide choice. Spassky defended the d4-pawn against Zinn in 1962 with 11.♗e3 0-0 12.♘e4 ♘d5 and put the king's rook on an open file – 13.♖fc1 a5 14.♗d2 ♕b6?!. The problem with this move is not only that White would take on c5 with a tempo, but that Black does not have the idea ...♘d7. Correct was 14...♕c7 15.♘c5 ♗xc5 16.♖xc5 ♘d7=, trading the active knights. Spassky got a winning position after 15.♕b2 ♖c8 16.♘c5 ♖a7? (16...♘a6! defended everything) 17.e4 ♘f6. Although he missed the best 18.♘c4!+–, his attacking set-up was the prototype of Nakamura's play – 18.♗e3 ♗xc5 19.dxc5 ♕c7 20.♖d1 ♘e8

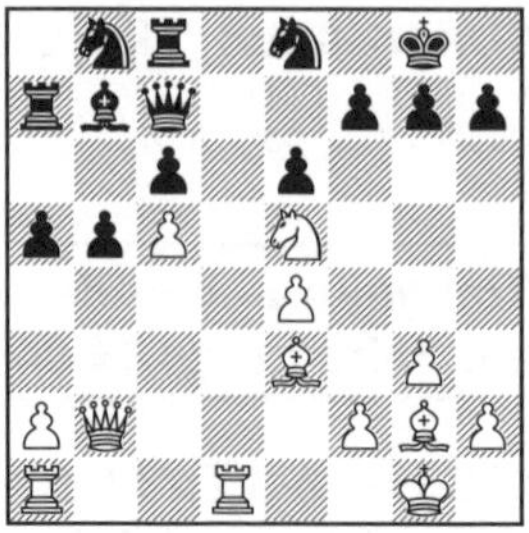

21.♗h3!? – a piece attack on e6 and f7. 21...♕e7 22.♖d6! ♗a6 23.♖ad1 ♖b7 (23...b4 24.♘xf7!) 24.♘xf7! ♔xf7 25.♗xe6+ ♕xe6 26.♖xe6 ♔xe6 27.♕b3+ ♔e7 28.♕g8! with curtains.

11...0-0 12.♘e4

12.♗g5 would give Black a tempo to trade the passive bishop at b7 – 12...h6! 13.♗f4 ♕c8 14.♖ac1 c5!? (The simplest solution. 14...♘bd7 is more ambitious.) 15.dxc5 ♗xg2 16.♔xg2 ♘c6=.

12...♕c7?!

In these positions it is risky to leave the enemy knights alive. Therefore, 12...♘xe4! 13.♗xe4 ♕c8 is logical.

Roiz considers here only 14.♗a3 ♗xa3 15.♕xa3 ♘d7 16.♘xd7 ♕xd7 17.♖ac1=. White does not have a convenient way to break through. If he captures on c6, the rook endgame would be absolutely equal.

White should aim to destroy the kingside with:

14.♕c2! h6 15.♗f4.

This position appears to be critical for the evaluation of 10...a6.

It is difficult for Black to unload the tension because of the weakness on h6:

15...♗f6

15...♖a7 16.a4! ♘d7 17.♘xc6 promises White some pull.

16.♖ac1 ♗xe5 17.dxe5 ♘d7 18.♕d2 ♖d8 19.♗xh6 ♕c7. Here White can develop his initiative with 20.♕g5 ♕xe5 21.♕e3 or 20.♗g5 ♘f6 21.♗e3.

13.♘g5! a5

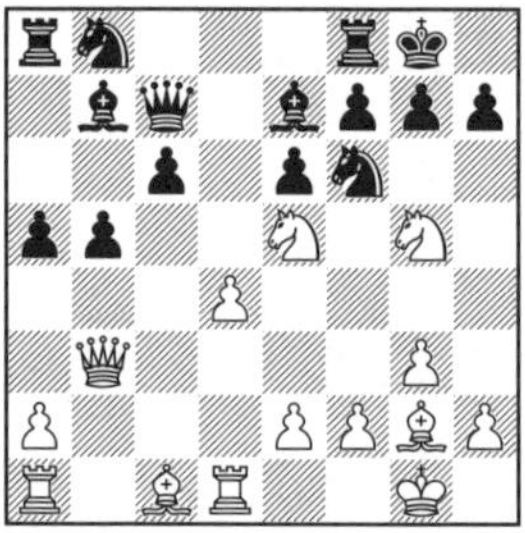

14.♗h3

It is useful to know this attacking pattern. However, White had better versions of the same idea:

14.♘exf7 ♖xf7 15.♗h3! ♗c8 16.♘xe6 ♗xe6 17.♗xe6 ♗d6 18.a4 b4 19.♖e1 ♘e4 20.♕d3 ♘c3 21.♗d2 ♔h8 22.♗xf7 ♕xf7 23.e4 ♘a6 24.♗xc3 bxc3 25.♕xc3±;

14.a4! b4 15.♗b2 ♕d8 16.♘exf7!±.

14...a4?!

14...♗c8 is more resilient. White retains the initiative with 15.a4 b4 16.♘exf7! ♖xf7 17.♘xe6, but objectively the play is about equal.

15.♕c2 ♗c8 16.♗f4 (16.♘g4 ♘bd7) **16...♕d8 17.♘g4**

White has full positional compensation for the pawn. Perhaps the biggest challenge is to choose the best move among many tempting alternatives. The sacrifice on f7 looms in many lines, but it is difficult to assess them. For instance:
17.♘exf7!? ♖xf7 18.e4 (threatening e5);
17.e4!? ♘h5 18.♘gxf7;
The positional 17.♖ac1 h6 18.♘gf3 – in all of them White conducts the play.

17...g6?

It seems that Nakamura had prepared 17...♘bd7! 18.♗e5 h6 19.♘xh6!+ gxh6 20.♗xe6! hxg5 21.♕g6+ ♔h8 22.♕h6+ ♔g8 23.♕xg5+ ♔h8 24.♗f5

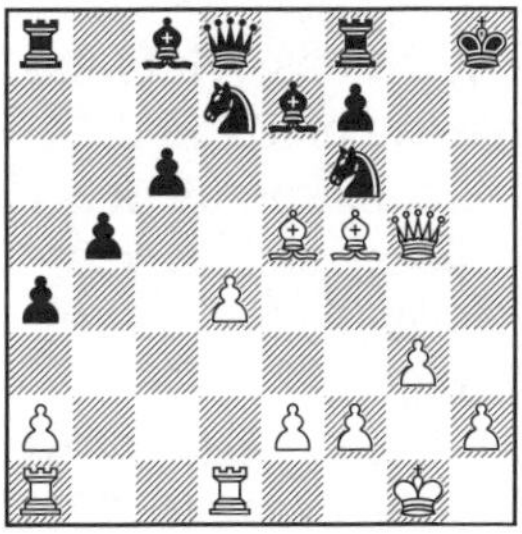

The engines claim that White is slightly better after 24...♘xe5 25.dxe5 ♘h7 26.♕h5 ♗xf5 27.♖xd8 ♖axd8 28.♕xf5, but this was Black's best option anyway, as the game course is much worse for Black.

18.♘xf6+ ♗xf6 19.♘e4 ♗g7 20.♗g2!

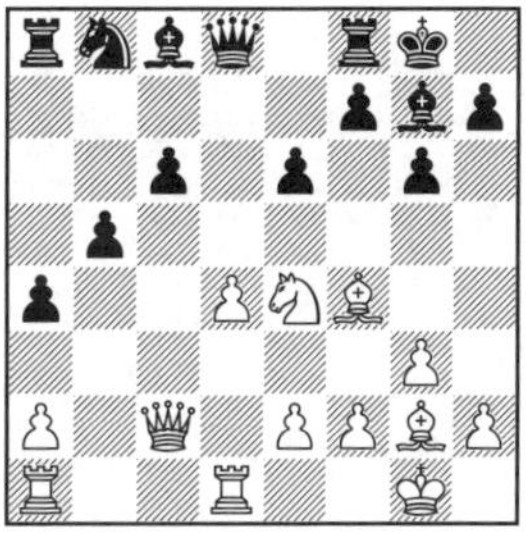

Suddenly White returns to the roots! Although the stabs on the kingside did not earn material gains, they hampered Black to complete development. The c8-bishop is as passive as ever. Even the most stubborn defence 20...♗d7 21.♖ac1 ♘a6 22.♕d2 ♘c7 23.♘c5 ♘d5 24.♗d6 ♖e8 is strategically hopeless after e2-e4-e5.

20...♕b6 21.♗d6 ♖e8 22.♖ac1 ♕d8

It transpires that 22...♗xd4 only opens the file for White's rook – 23.♕d2! ♗g7 24.♗c5 ♕a6 (24...♕a5 25.♕xa5+–) 25.♘d6 ♖f8 26.h4 when Black is virtually stalemated.

23.♗c5 ♗a6 24.♗b4 ♕c7 25.d5! exd5 26.♘d6 ♕d7 27.♘xe8 ♕xe8 28.e4 d4 29.e5 h5 30.f4 f6 31.♖xd4 fxe5 32.fxe5 ♗c8 33.♖cd1 ♗d7 34.♖d6 ♕xe5 35.♕xg6 ♕f5 36.♗c3 ♕f7 37.♖f1 ♕xg6 38.♖xg6 1-0

17. Ipatov – Eljanov
FIDE World Cup Baku 2015

1.d4 d5 2.c4 c6 3.♘f3 ♘f6 4.♘c3 a6 5.g3 dxc4 6.♗g2 b5 7.♘e5 ♗b7 8.0-0 e6 9.b3 cxb3 10.axb3 ♗e7

This pawn structure is less dangerous than the one arising after ♕xb3. It is easier for Black to generate counterplay as he often gets a passed pawn on the a-file. Besides, the queen is more active on b3, supporting hits on f7 and e6.

11.♗b2

If 11.♗g5, it would be safer to refrain from h6. Instead we could aim for ...c5 – 11...0-0 12.e3 ♖a7 13.h4?! c5!∓, Li Chao-Tomashevsky, St Petersburg 2012.

11...0-0 12.♘e4

Removing a defender of the kingside and aiming for an attack. Kramnik beat Giri with 12.♕c2 ♘fd7?! 13.♘d3 ♕b6 14.♘e4, with a firm grip on c5. Black should not be clutching for the extra pawn. After 12...♘bd7! 13.♘d3 (13.♘xc6 ♗xc6=) 13...♕c7 14.♘e4 ♘xe4 15.♗xe4 h6 Black has traded a knight like in the main game, but White lost two tempi on the not-so-useful manoeuvre ♘f3-e5-d3.

12...♘xe4 13.♗xe4 a5

This move might seem incomprehensible at first sight. To understand it, we should foresee White's strategic aims.

His main compensation for the pawn is the passive stand of the b7-bishop. However, Black can always counter-sac a pawn, either by giving up c6 or pushing ...c6-c5. To prevent it, White commonly puts a knight on c5, transforming the pawn structure in the following way:

Tashkov-Hiltunen
ICCF 2013

In such positions White has practically an extra piece on the kingside. Even in correspondence chess it is not an easy task to keep the balance. The game had a very instructive ending:

23...♕d7 24.h5 ♕e6 25.♕f5 ♕xf5 26.♗xf5 ♔f8 27.g4 f6 28.♗c3 ♔f7 29.♔g2 ♔e7 30.♗e4 ♔f8 31.e3 ♔f7 32.♔g3 ♖f8 33.f4 exf4+ 34.exf4 ♖d8

35.♖e1 ♔f8 36.♗g6 ♗c8 37.♔f3 ♗d7

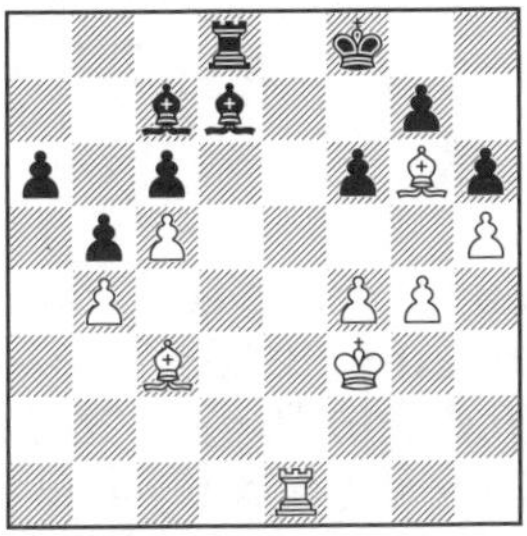

38.g5!! fxg5 39.f5 ♖c8 40.♗xg7+ ♔xg7 41.♖e7+ ♔g8 42.♖xd7 ♗e5 43.♔e4 ♗c3 44.♗f7+ ♔h8 45.♗e6 ♗xb4 46.f6 ♖f8 47.♔f5 ♗c3 48.f7 ♗b4 49.♔g6 1-0.

Returning to our game, a similar scenario could unfold after:
13...♗d6 14.♕c2 h6 15.♖fd1 ♕c7 16.♘d3 ♘d7 17.♘c5 ♘xc5 18.dxc5 ♗e5 19.♗xe5 ♕xe5 20.b4

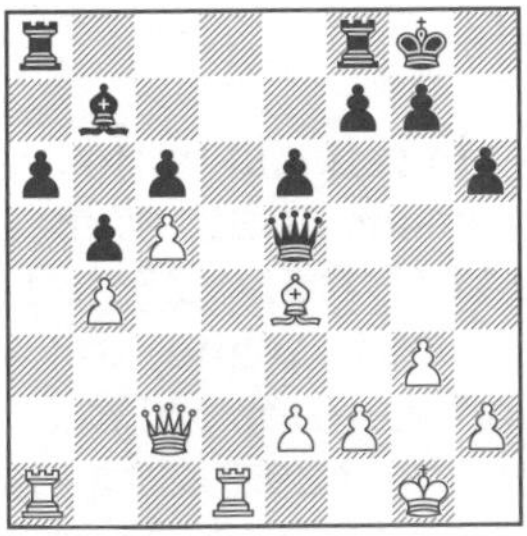

Without the dark-squared bishops Black is obviously struggling.
It transpires that the pawn at a5 is an indispensable asset in Black's set-up. It is a future passer!

14.♕d3 h6 15.f4

White's only constructive plan is to open the f-file and both grandmasters chose it in practice. However, it might be better just to hold the position without weakening the kingside. For example:
15.♖fc1 a4 (or 15...♕c7 16.♕f3) 16.bxa4 ♖xa4 17.♕f3=;
15.♕e3 (preparing the battery ♗c2+♕e4) 15...♗d6 16.♖fc1 ♕e7 17.♗c3 ♗xe5 (17...b4 was the normal move, but Black prefers to get rid of the bad bishop at once.) 18.dxe5

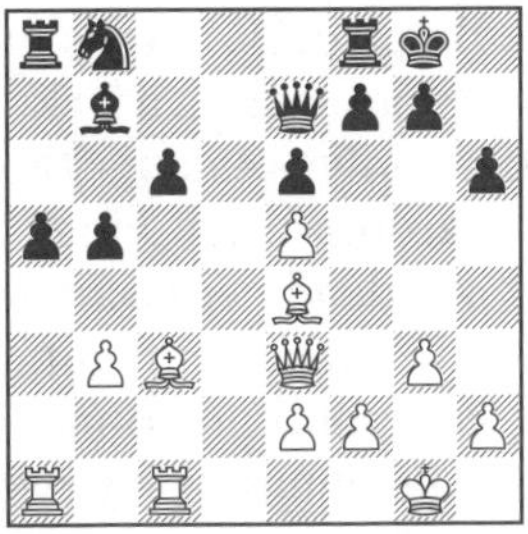

18...c5! 19.♗xa5 ♗xe4 20.♕xe4 ♖a6 21.♕d3 c4! 22.bxc4 b4 23.c5 ♕a7 24.♗b6 ½-½, Bochev-Malchev ICCF 2013.

15...♗d6 16.♕e3 ♘d7!

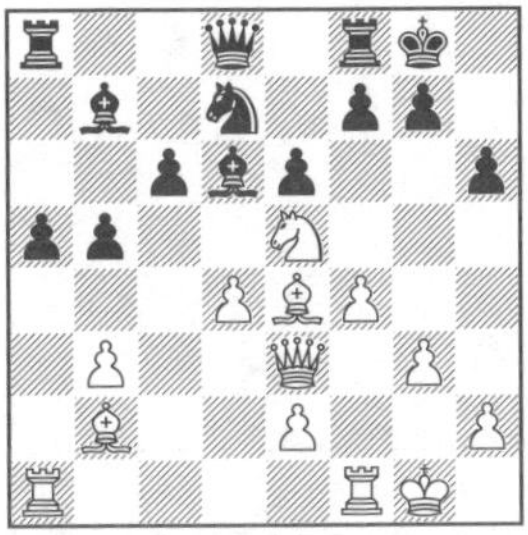

An excellent solution! It turns out that neither 17.♘xc6 ♕b6∓ nor 17.f5 exf5∓ suit White. Perhaps 17.♘d3 ♘f6 18.♗g2 ♘d5 19.♕f2 ♕e7 20.♘c5 ♗c8 21.♖fc1 f6∓ was the lesser evil.

17.♖ac1 ♘xe5

This is not bad, but Black could better exploit the weakness of the enemy kingside with a knight. So 17...♘f6! 18.♘xc6 (18.♗xc6 ♗xc6 19.♘xc6 ♕b6∓) 18...♕e8 gives him a clear edge.

18.fxe5 ♗e7 19.h4 f5?

A typical error in such positions. Fear has large eyes, a Russian proverb says. Black makes a jerky movement that only weakens the lights squares around his king. Sometimes it is indeed necessary to eliminate White's space advantage, but in the concrete position Eljanov had obvious counterplay with 19... a4! 20.bxa4 bxa4 and only precise calculation could tell how substantial White threats are. Let's check:

21.♖f4 a3 22.♗a1 a2 23.♖g4 ♔h8 24.♗d3

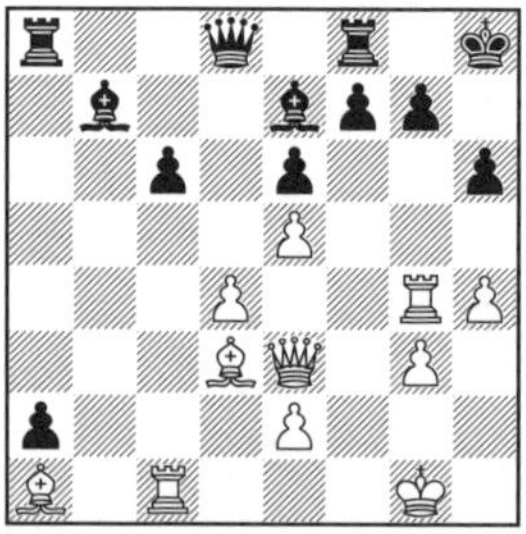

Now both 24...c5 and 24...♕d5 deny ♕e4, so White is simply lost. A glorious fate for the a-pawn!

20.exf6 ♖xf6 21.d5!

The passive white bishop wins now material, but the worse news for Black is that he remains under attack.

21...exd5

21...cxd5 deserved attention. 22.♗xf6 ♗xf6 23.♗d3 ♕d6 24.♖xf6 gxf6 25.♕xh6 ♕xg3+ 26.♔f1 ♖c8 should most probably end with a perpetual.

22.♗b1

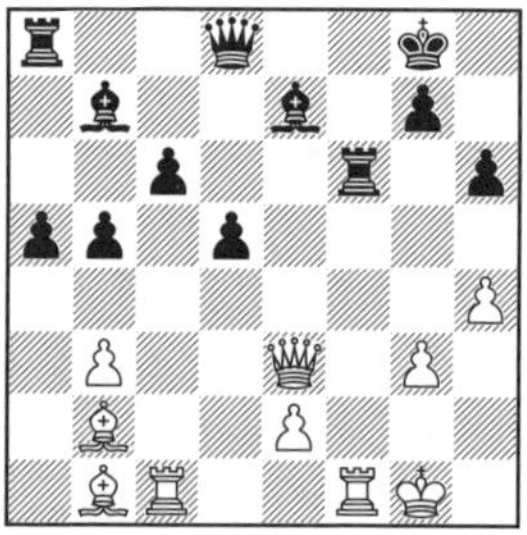

22...d4?

Black's king should try to escape to the queenside – 22...♕d6 23.♕d3 ♔f8! 24.e4! ♖xf1+ 25.♖xf1+ ♔e8 26.exd5 ♔d8. White still retains strong pressure after 27.♗xg7 ♕xd5 28.♗xh6 ♕xd3 29.♗xd3 a4 30.bxa4 bxa4 31.h5 ♖a5 32.g4±. His connected pawns run more smoothly.

23.♗xd4 c5 24.♗xf6 ♗xf6 25.♕e6+ ♔h8 26.♕f5?!

26.♖cd1! was winning on the spot, intending 26...♕g8 27.♖xf6 or 26... ♕b8 27.♖d6. The text retains an advantage, but Black is still kicking.

26...♕g8

27.♖f4?

This simply gives back the exchange. 27.♔h2!± was best, and if 27...♗d4, then 28.e3 ♗xe3 29.♖ce1 unleashes White's rooks.
In the subsequent tense fight the higher rated player prevailed. The a-pawn became the hero of the day.

27...♗d4+ 28.♖xd4 (28.♔h2 ♗e3) **28...cxd4 29.♖c7 ♖f8 30.♕xb5 ♗d5 31.♕c5 ♗xb3 32.♕xd4 ♖d8 33.♕b2 a4=**

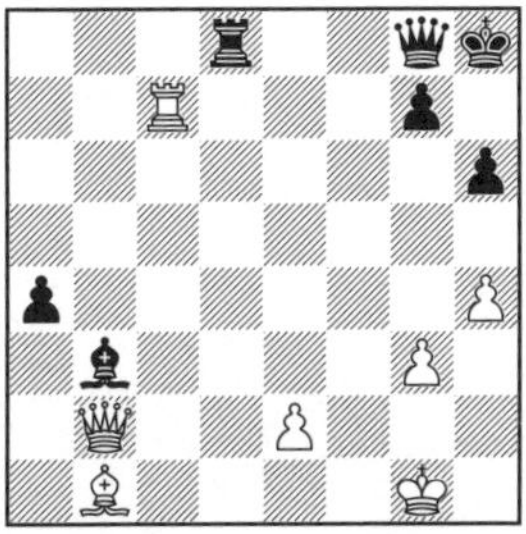

34.♖c6? ♖d1+ 35.♔h2 ♖h1+ 36.♔xh1 ♕d5+ 37.♔h2 ♕xc6 38.♕e5 ♗g8 39.♕a5 ♕c1 40.♗e4 ♕c4 41.♗f3 ♕b3 42.g4 a3 43.g5 hxg5 44.hxg5 a2 45.g6 ♕e3 46.♔g2 ♕c1 47.♕h5+ ♕h6 48.♕e5 ♕xg6+ 49.♔f2 ♗e6 50.♕b8+ ♔h7 51.♕h2+ ♕h6 52.♕e5 ♕h4+ 53.♔e3 ♕f6 54.♗e4+ ♔h8 0-1

Chapter 5. The Cunning 4.♘bd2

Main Ideas

1.d4 d5 2.c4 e6 3.♘f3 c6 4.♘bd2 ♘f6

The only other sensible retort is 4...f5, but I hate the Stonewall against g3. Facing a strong player, it is a one-way road even though White's knight is not on c3 to support b4-b5. Even if Black trades 3 minor pieces and remains with only his notorious light-squared bishop, it is often difficult to save the endgame.
In the diagram position White chooses between the Closed Catalan and the Meran.

The Closed Catalan

5.g3 has been effectively neutralised in the 80ies with the idea of developing Black's queen's knight on a6:
5...b6 6.♗g2 ♗b7 7.0-0 ♗e7 8.♕c2 0-0 9.e4 ♘a6!

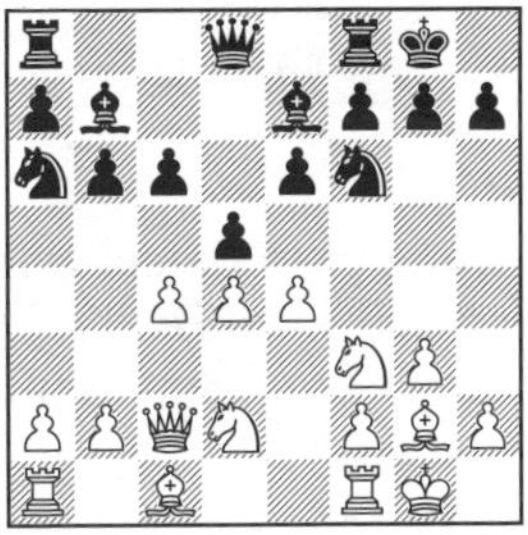

The trick is that 10.e5 ♘d7 11.cxd5 is met by 11...♘b4! 12.♕b3 ♘xd5. So White chooses **10.a3 c5 11.exd5 exd5 12.dxc5 ♘xc5 13.b4**

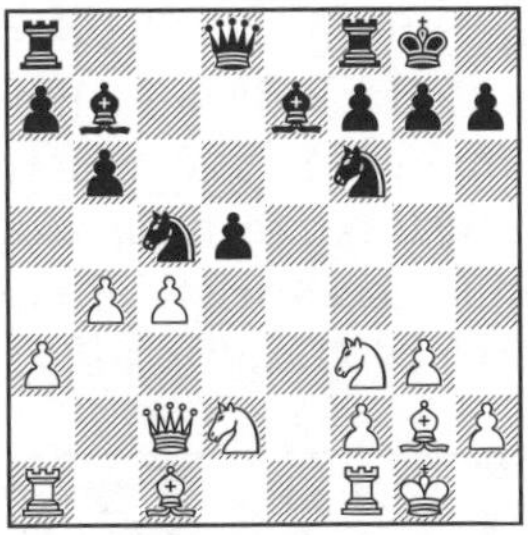

Here both 13...♘ce4 14.♘xe4 ♘xe4 15.♘d2 ♗f6 and 13...♘e6 lead to a symmetrical pawn structure with the corresponding high drawing chances.

Note that if White rejects the plan with ♕c2+e4 in favour of 8.b3, ♗b2, we should answer ...♘bd7, followed by ...c5.

The Meran

5.e3

5...♘bd7

Many strong players feel comfortable after 5...c5 6.cxd5 exd5. That is a matter of taste and experience with isolated pawns.

6.♗d3 ♗d6

Now White chooses between e4 and b3:

7.0-0 (or 7.e4 e5) 7...0-0 8.e4 e5 is known to even the chances. That is the price White has to pay for his "flexible" 4th move. The d2-knight does not attack d5 and Black can simply maintain the symmetry. One of the most extraordinary opening position in chess arises after 9.exd5 cxd5 10.c5 e4 11.cxd6 exd3=:

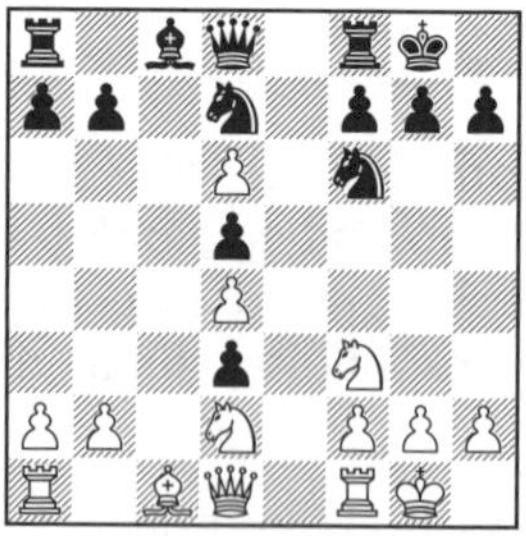

In the event of 9.cxd5 cxd5 10.exd5 exd4 11.♘e4 ♘xe4 12.♗xe4 ♘f6 or 10.♖e1 h6 11.h3 ♖e8 12.exd5 exd4 13.♖xe8+ ♕xe8 14.♘c4 Black temporary remains pawnless, but his active pieces allow him to keep the balance rather easily – see **Game 21** Nogga-Kraft, ICCF 2018.

Here is another thematic position where the extra pawn is not worth much:

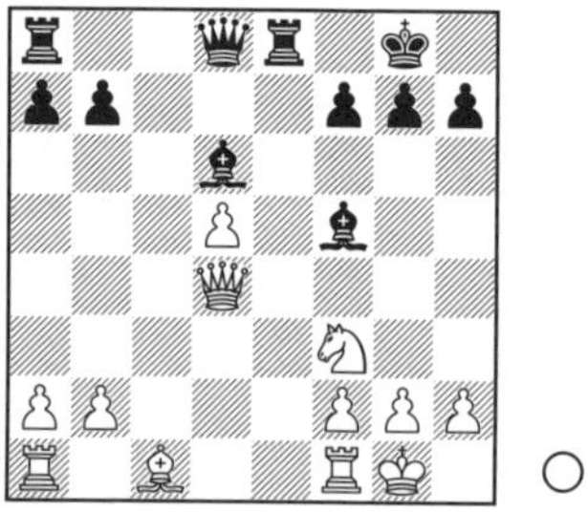

Black has excellent compensation after ...♕d7, ...♖e4, ...♖ae8.

7.b3!? offers us a wide choice.

The most popular answer is the Meran set-up 7...0-0 8.♗b2 b6 9.0-0 ♗b7. See **Game 21** Radjabov-Ding Liren, Moscow 2017.

I suggest to try 7...e5 8.cxd5 cxd5 9.dxe5 ♘xe5 10.♗b5+

10...♘c6!? with sharp play and chances for an attack.

Finally, I consider **5.♕c2 dxc4 6.♘xc4 c5 7.dxc5 ♗xc5 8.a3 0-0 9.b4**

The only thing you should remember of this line is not to retreat automatically to the passive square e7. Instead 9...b5!, aiming to enable ...♗d6, levels the game.

Theoretical status

In answer to 4.♘bd2 Scherbakov and Krasenkow suggest 4... f5, which I consider dull. In addition, Scherbakov also analyses the Closed Catalan 4...♘f6 5.g3, but here he does not mention at all the renown equaliser with ...b6, ...♗b7, ...♘a6, focusing on 5...♘bd7.

As a whole, Black does not have any theoretical problems after 4.♘bd2, but in practice he scores poorly. The same could be said about 4.♕c2 and 4.♕b3. It seems that Black players underestimate these seemingly unchallenging moves and often turn to be unprepared for them.

Chapter 5. The Cunning 4.♘bd2

Step by Step

1.d4 d5 2.c4 e6 3.♘f3 c6 4.♘bd2 ♘f6

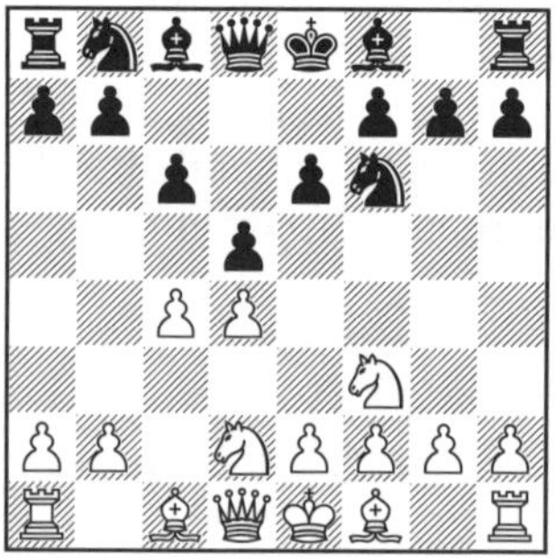

A. 5.g3; **B.** 5.e3; **C.** 5.♕c2

A. 5.g3 b6

The extended fianchetto 5...b5? leads to a very passive pawn structure after 6.c5. White will prepare e4 to open the centre.
It is possible to choose the move order with 5...♗e7 6.♗g2 0-0 7.0-0 b6.

6.♗g2 ♗b7 7.0-0 ♗e7 8.♕c2

We should meet 8.b3 by 8...0-0 9.♗b2 ♘bd7.

9...♘a6 is already dubious since Black cannot include his knight into play with ...♘b4. White can answer simply e3, ♕e2. On the other hand, I do not recommend to develop the knight to d7 against 8.♕c2 because I'm afraid of e2-e4-e5 with an attack. This argument is no longer valid with a bishop on b2.

10.♖c1

Or 10.e3 a5 11.a4 ♗b4 12.♘e1 c5.

10...♖c8

Black has completed development and I do not see any White's threats on the horizon. He can meet 11.e3 by 11...c5 or prepare it with 11...♖c7 12.♕e2 ♕a8.

8...0-0

Ponomariov chose once a set-up with 8...a5. It makes some sense against b3 as Black gets a plan with

...a4. I analysed it at length, but eventually discarded the whole idea since the pawn move costs a precious tempo in an open position if White chooses the standard plan: 9.e4 ♘a6 10.a3! (Ponomariov's opponent Studer opted for 10.e5 which is double-edged.) 10...0-0 11.♖d1 ♖c8 12.b3 c5 13.exd5 exd5 14.♗b2. In my opinion the tempo could tell, and White has more chances for a small advantage than in the main line. There would have been some reason to consider ...a5 if Black was okay after:

10.b3 0-0 11.♗b2 a4

11...♖c8 12.♖fe1 ♖c7 13.♖ad1 ♖e8 14.♕b1 ♕a8 15.a3 ♖cc8 16.♘e5±.

12.bxa4 ♘b4 13.♕b1 dxc4 14.♘xc4 ♖xa4 15.♖d1! b5 16.♘e3 ♕a8 17.a3 ♘a6 18.♘e5

My analysis convinced my that Black's king is in a bigger danger than it looks. The smallest mistake could lead to destruction of his pawn shelter. For instance, the waiting:

18...♖d8 19.♕c2 h6? (to make a *luft* before opening files) provides a target – 20.h4 ♘c7 21.d5 exd5 22.♘f5 ♗f8 23.exd5 ♘cxd5 24.♗xd5 ♘xd5 25.♘xh6+! gxh6 26.♕f5+–.

Therefore, he should quickly organise ...c5, while preventing d4-d5:

18...♘c7 19.♕c2 ♖d8!

19...c5? right away is bad owing to 20.d5! exd5 21.♘f5.

19...♖c8? fails to 20.h4 ♘ce8 (20...c5 21.d5 exd5 22.exd5 ♘cxd5 23.♘xd5 ♘xd5 24.♘xf7!) 21.h5 h6 (21...♘xh5 22.♘d7 ♖a6 23.♘c5±) 22.♘xf7! ♔xf7 23.e5±.

20.♖ac1

20.h4 is already ineffective due to 20...c5 21.dxc5 ♗xe4 22.♗xe4 ♕xe4 23.♖xd8+ ♗xd8 24.♕d2 ♗e7 25.♘d7 ♖a8=.

20...c5 21.dxc5 ♗xe4 22.♗xe4 ♕xe4 23.♖xd8+ (23.♕xe4 ♘xe4=) 23...♗xd8

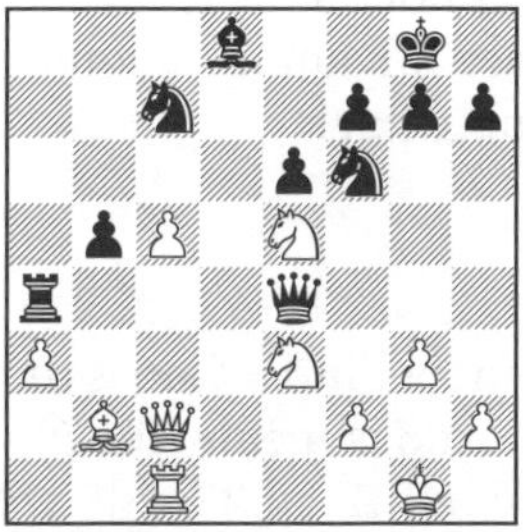

24.♕d2! ♗e7 25.♘d7 ♘fe8

Or 25...♖a8!? 26.♘xf6+ ♗xf6 27.♗xf6 gxf6.

26.♖e1 ♖a8 27.♘c2 ♕d5 28.♕xd5 ♘xd5 29.♘b4 ♘ec7 30.♘b6±. White still preserves some pressure as in many lines he remains with a distant a-passer.

To take stock: ...a5 is not worth the pain.

9.e4 ♘a6!

This plan was introduced in 1987 and quickly became the main equaliser against the set-up with ♘bd2, especially after the game Karpov-Tal, Brussels 1987.

The old move 9...♘bd7 took away the natural retreat square of the f6-knight and 10.e5 ♘e8 11.cxd5 cxd5 12.♖e1 assured White of lasting pressure. Even though the white bishop is not on the right square d3, the space advantage should enable a gradual attack.

10.a3

The point behind ...♘a6 is that 10.e5 ♘d7 11.cxd5 is met by the *intermezzo* 11...♘b4! 12.♕b3 ♘xd5 with 13...c5 to follow.

> 12...cxd5 13.a3 ♘c6 is also possible. Compare the c6-knight to the one on e8 in the line 9...♘bd7. Practice has proved that this difference is enough to even the chances, but the stable pawn structure in the centre could allow White to mount an attack against the black king.

White has also tried the logical 11.a3, when 11...c5! undermines White's centre.

12.dxc5

> Karpov decided to define the centre at once with 12.cxd5, obviously fearing that in some lines later Black could recapture by pawn. Tal answered 12...♗xd5 13.♕d3 ♕c8 (the AI engines value piece activity very highly, so they prefer to improve the placement of the a6-knight with 13...♘ab8!?) 14.♘e4 cxd4 15.♘eg5, when best is the calm 15...g6! with nice counterplay.

12...bxc5 13.♖e1

> 13.♖d1 is not logical as it shifts the focus from the kingside, where White has a space advantage, to the other flank, where Black feels confident. Correspondent players answer 13...♖b8 14.cxd5 exd5, but I do not see a reason to avoid the main set-up with 13...♘c7 14.cxd5 exd5 (14...♘xd5!?) 15.b4 ♘e6=.

13...♘c7 14.h4

> In the event of 14.♘b3 Black should open the centre with 14...dxc4 and seek counterplay on the b-file with ...♖b8.

14...a5 15.♘f1

> If 15.♘g5, we eat the pawn.

You see on the next diagram a critical position for 10.e5.

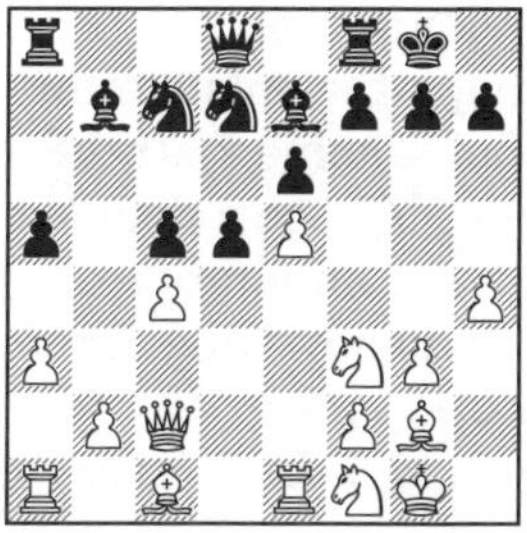

I analyse 15...h6!? in the annotations to **Game 19** Damljanovic-Dizdarevic, Zenica 1989. 15...♖e8 is also possible, when 16.h5 would provoke 16...h6 anyway. Black has clear counterplay with ...♖a6(a7), ...♕a8, ...♖d8.

10.b3 ♘b4 11.♕b1 dxe4 12.♘xe4 c5 13.♘xf6+ ♗xf6 requires precision from White.

14.♘g5 ♗xg5 15.♗xb7 ♖b8 16.♗xg5 ♕xg5 17.♗e4 f5 18.a3 ♘a6 19.♗d3 cxd4 leaves White pawnless although he has some compensation. More interesting is:

14.dxc5!?, when we should temper our natural greediness and find 14...♕d3! 15.♘e1 ♕d7 with a fine game.

10...c5 11.exd5

I prefer Black after 11.cxd5 exd5 12.e5 ♘e4 13.dxc5 ♘axc5 14.b4 ♘e6 15.♗b2 a5.

11...exd5 12.dxc5

It is tempting to oppose a rook against Black's queen with 12.♖d1, but we return the favour – 12...♖c8 13.dxc5

13.b3 dxc4 14.♘xc4 cxd4 15.♘xd4 ♗xg2 16.♔xg2 ♕d5+ 17.f3 ♖fe8 18.♘f5 ♕c6=.

13...♘xc5 14.b4 ♘e6 15.♗b2

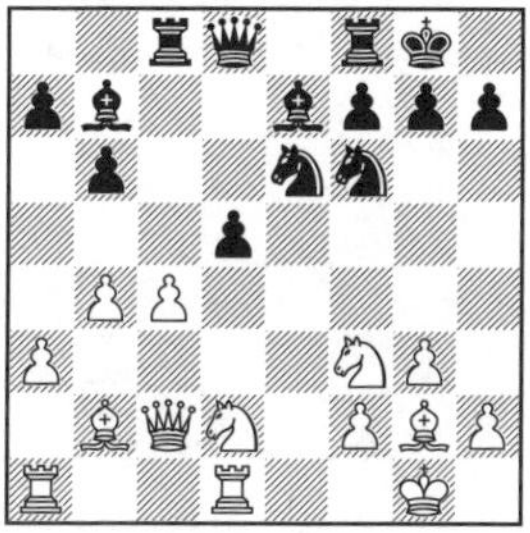

Black is close to full equality and 15...dxc4 should serve the goal. Even simpler is:

15...♖c7 16.♘d4 ♘xd4 17.♗xd4 ♕c8 18.♗e5 ♖c6. The trick is that Black can always take on c4 since it would be suicidal for White to take the rook. So play may continue 19.♕d3 dxc4 20.♘xc4 ♖e6 21.♗xb7 ♕xb7 22.♗b2 ♖e8=.

12...♘xc5 13.b4 ♘e6

The only way to alter the symmetry is 13...♘ce4!? 14.♘xe4 ♘xe4 15.♘d2 ♗f6

15...f5 is an extra weakness. After 16.♘xe4 (16.cxd5 ♖c8) 16...dxe4 17.♗e3 ♕e8 18.♖fd1 ♗c6 19.♕e2 White's chances are slightly better.

16.♗b2 ♖c8 17.♘xe4 ♗xb2 18.♕xb2 dxe4 19.♖ac1 ♕e7

Perhaps you have some chances to outplay a weak player here – he might allow tricks with ...e3 or ...g5 and ...f7-f5-f4. Objectively the pawn majority on the queenside makes

White's position a bit more pleasant. Black keeps the balance by exchanging rooks:

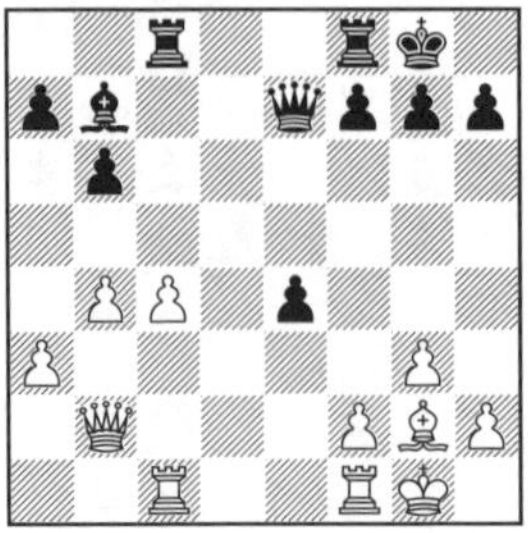

20.♕b3 ♖fd8 21.♖fd1 h6 22.♗f1 ♖xd1 23.♖xd1 ♖d8 24.♖xd8+ ♕xd8 25.♕c3 ♕d6 26.h4 a5=.

The text has been well tested. It aims to suck all the life out of the position.

14.♗b2

14.cxd5?! ♖c8 puts Black ahead in development.

14...a5

Perhaps this is the simplest path to full equality. See **Game 18** Helbich-Fenwick, ICCF 2014.

B. 5.e3

This timid variation poses only one problem – it is really difficult to win with Black. The simplest equaliser is:

5...♘bd7 6.♗d3 ♗d6 7.0-0

7.e4 e5 8.cxd5 cxd5 9.exd5 0-0 10.0-0 transposes.

7.b3!? allows 7...e5.

Perhaps the main retort is the Meran scheme 7...0-0 8.♗b2 b6 9.0-0 ♗b7. See a detailed analysis in the annotations to **Game 21** Radjabov-Ding Liren, Moscow 2017.

8.cxd5 cxd5 9.dxe5 ♘xe5 10.♗b5+ ♘c6!?

I suggest you to try this double-edged move. It is virtually unexplored and leads to complex positions.

Not everybody likes IQP position arising after 10...♗d7 11.♗xd7+ ♕xd7 12.♕e2! (Shirov played against Karpov 12.0-0, but 12... ♘d3 13.♕e2 ♘xc1 is roughly equal).

11.♗b2 0-0 12.0-0

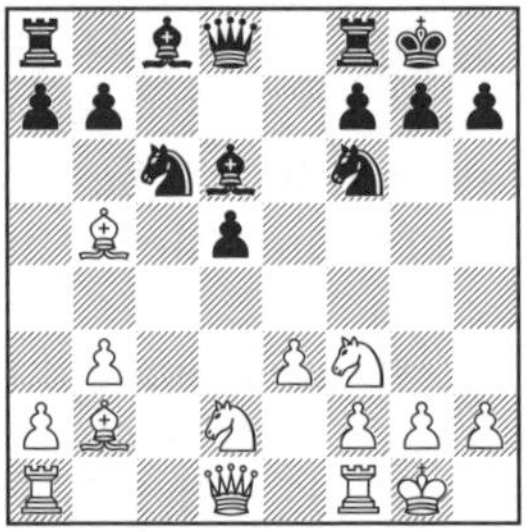

12...a6!?

I saw the position on the above diagram in the game Suba-Spraggett, Manresa 1993, where I also played. Suba won quite convincingly after 12...♖e8 13.♖c1 ♗d7 14.♗xc6 ♗xc6 15.♖c2 ♗b5 16.♖e1 ♗d3 17.♖c1 ♗b4 18.a3 ♗a5 19.b4± (the numeration of moves was different). The only other game I know is Karpenko-Malin, ICCF 2017: 12...♕e7 13.♖c1 ♗d7 14.♗d3 ♖ac8 15.♘d4

♗g4 16.♘xc6 ♖xc6 17.♕e1 ♗c7 18.h3 ♗h5 19.♖xc6 bxc6 20.♕c1 ♕d6 21.g3 ♖e8 22.♗a3 ½-½.

In both games Black took on c6 by piece. I propose to play with hanging pawns. They are famous with their dynamic "temper".

13.♗xc6

After 13.♗d3 ♖e8 14.♖c1 ♘e4 White will have to play against an IQP with an awkward knight on d2 and a passive pawn set-up on the queenside. (Things would have looked differently if White had an extended fianchetto with a3+b4.) Besides, he would not be able to exchange on c6 as in the above-mentioned games.

13.♗e2 ♗f5 puts the question what White could do with his knight at d2. (14.a3 does not help in view of 14...a5!) 14.♘d4 ♘xd4 15.♗xd4 ♖c8 16.♖c1 ♕e7 (16...♖xc1!? 17.♕xc1 ♕a5∞ practically wins the a2-pawn) 17.♘f3 ♗e4 is balanced, as well as 14.♖e1 ♕e7 15.♘f1 ♖ac8 16.♘g3 ♗e4 17.♘d4 ♗e5=.

13...bxc6 14.♖c1 c5∞

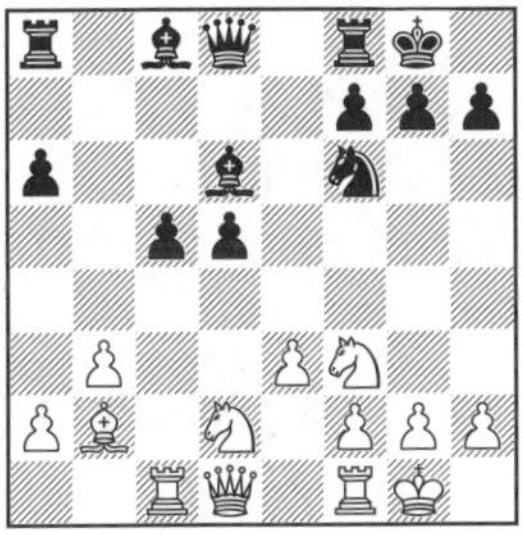

This structure is well known with a knight on c3 when the possibility of ♘c3-a4, ♗a3 ensures some pressure. In our case the knight on d2 is misplaced and Black could underline it with ...a6-a5-a4.

7...0-0 8.e4 e5 9.cxd5

9.exd5 cxd5 10.c5 e4 11.cxd6 exd3 leads to an amazing position which deserves a diagram:

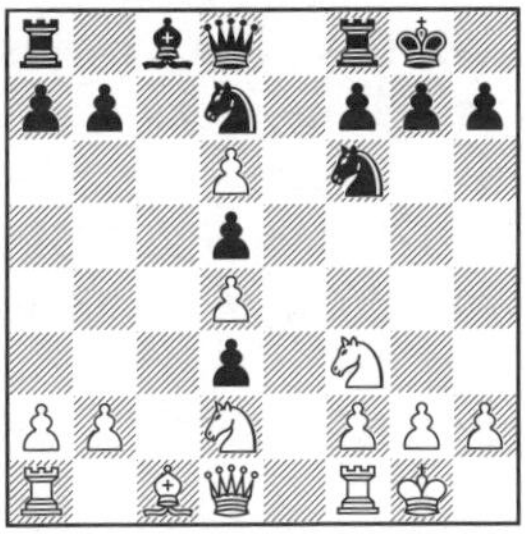

The whole d-file is stuck with pieces. The symmetry ends after 12.♖e1 ♖e8 ♘f1 ♕b6= or 12.♘b3 ♘e4= or 12.♘b1 ♘b6 13.♕xd3 ♘c4=.

9...cxd5 10.exd5

Or 10.♖e1 h6 11.exd5

The latest trend for White is to make another useful move before capturing on d5 – 11.h3 ♖e8 12.exd5 exd4 13.♖xe8+ ♕xe8 14.♘c4. Black then should not hurry to regain the pawn. His active pieces allow him to keep the balance rather easily – see **Game 20** Nogga-Kraft, ICCF 2018.

11...exd4 12.♘e4 ♘xe4 13.♗xe4 ♘f6 14.♕xd4 b6 15.♗d2 ♗c5 16.♕a4 ♖e8 17.♗c3 ♘xe4 18.♖xe4 ♗f5 19.♖xe8+ ♕xe8 20.♕xe8+ ♖xe8 21.b4 ♗d6= was tested in several correspondence games.

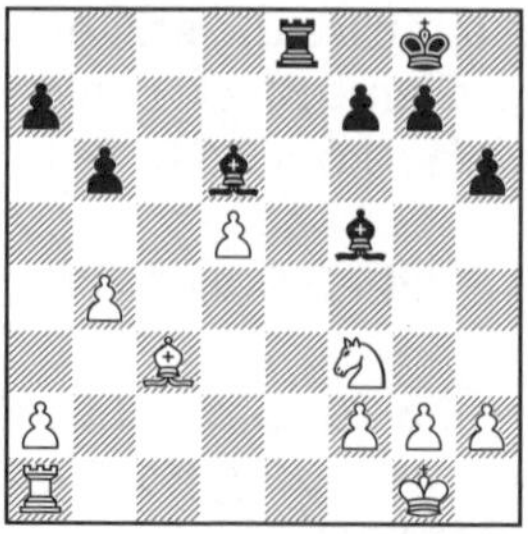

Black does not experience any difficulties. White's extra pawn is insignificant since he lacks a constructive plan:

22.♘d4 ♗d7 23.♘c6 ♖e4 24.b5 ♖c4 25.♗b2 ♖a4 26.a3 f6 27.h3 a6=.

10...exd4 11.♘e4

11.♘c4 ♗c5 is more complicated.

11...♘b6 12.♘xd6 ♕xd6 13.♘xd4 ♘bxd5 14.♘f5 may be "almost" equal for the engines, but still White has the bishop pair.

The critical position arises after 12.♗g5 h6 13.♗h4 ♘b6 14.♘xb6

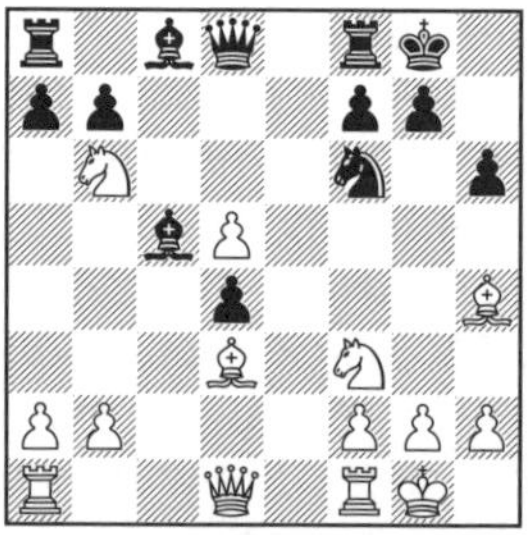

Now 14....♕xb6 15.b4 ♗e7 16.♖e1 ♗xb4 17.♖b1 ♕a5 18.♖e5 ♘d7 19.♖e2 ♘c5 20.♗e7 ♗g4! is double-edged. Perhaps it is easier to play after:

14...♗xb6 15.♗c4

Kiril Georgiev tried 15.♘d2 ♕d6 16.♖e1 ♘xd5 17.♘c4, when best is 17...♕c5 18.♕f3 ♗e6 19.♕e4 g6 20.♘e5 ♗f5 21.♕f3 ♘e3! 22.♗f6 ♗d8=.

15...g5 16.♗g3 ♘xd5 with tangled but balanced play. White can preserve tension with 17.♖c1 or 17.♖e1, while Korchnoi's 17.♘xd4 ♘f4 18.♘b5 is easily neutralised with 18...♕xd1 19.♖axd1 ♗g4=.

Nakamura opted for 11.♘xd4 in 3 blitz games of 2019, but nobody answered 11...♘e5.

Of course 11...♘b6 12.♘f5 ♗xf5 13.♗xf5 ♘bxd5 is close to a draw.

12.♘2f3 ♘xd3 13.♕xd3 ♘xd5=.

11...♘xe4 12.♗xe4 ♘f6

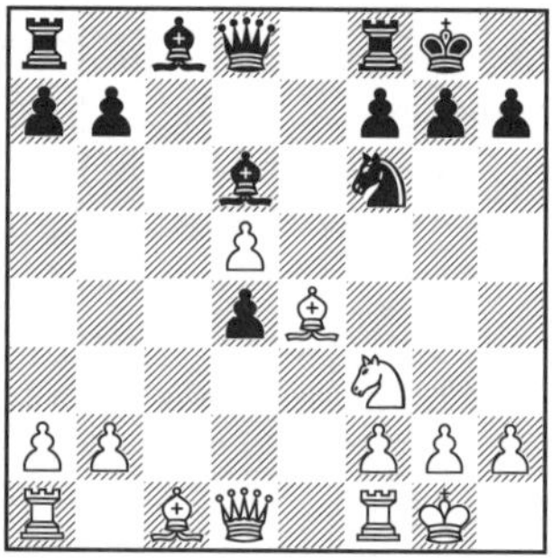

13.♕xd4

13.♗g5 ♗e7 14.♗c2

Or 14.♗xf6 ♗xf6 15.♘xd4 ♕b6=.

14...♘xd5 15.♗xe7 ♘xe7 16.♕xd4 ♗f5=.

13.♗c2 ♗g4 14.♗g5 h6 15.♗h4 g5 or 15...♖e8 16.♕d3 g5=.

13...♘xe4 14.♕xe4 ♖e8 15.♕d4 ♗f5 16.♗g5

Although White is a healthy pawn up, he can easily face difficulties since Black's bishop pair and the rook are very active. For instance, the passive 16.Be3 Qd7 17.Rfd1 Re4!

Kryakvin-Bukavshin, Moscow 2011, saw 17...Bc2 18.Re1 Qf5 19.Bd2 f6 20.Bc3 b6 21.Rxe8+ Rxe8 22.Re1 Rxe1+ 23.Nxe1 Bc5 24.Qd2 Be4 25.Bb4 Bxb4 26.Qxb4 Bxd5 with a quick draw.

18.Qd2, Gaifullin-Mokshanov, Samara 2015, offers Black an initiative after 18...Rae8! 19.Nd4 Bg4 20.Re1 R4e5.

16...f6 17.Bh4 Re4=

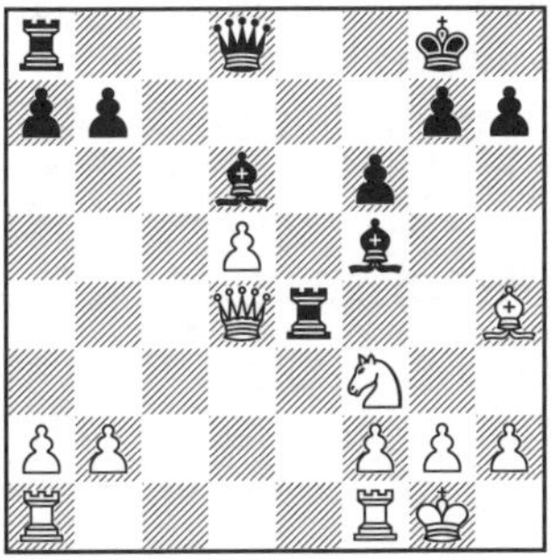

The d5-pawn is practically doomed. Many games finished in a draw in the next 5-10 moves. For instance: 18.Qd3 Bg6 19.Bg3 Bxg3 20.hxg3 Re6 21.Qc3 ½-½, Leitao-Matsuura, Sao Paulo 2007.

C. 5.Qc2 dxc4

The immediate 5...c5 also eliminates the centre, but gives White tempi after 6.cxd5!

Or 6.dxc5 Bxc5 7.cxd5 Qc7!=.

6...cxd4! 7.Nxd4 Nxd5

7...exd5 8.b3 Na6 9.a3 Bd7 should be roughly balanced, but my rule is to avoid IQP positions with Black.

8.e4, when best is 8...Nb6.

6.Nxc4

After 6.Qxc4 simplest is 6...b6 7.e4 Bb7, followed by ...Be7 and ...c5.

6...c5 7.dxc5 Bxc5

8.a3

In Sofia 2009, Carlsen played against Ivanchuk 8.g3 b5 9.Nce5 Qc7 10.Qb3 a6 11.Bg2 Bb7 12.0-0 Bd5 13.Qc3 with a slight pull due to the misplaced black queen. Black could improve with 9...Nbd7 10.Bg2 Bb7 11.Nxd7 Nxd7 12.Qd3 Qb6. In 2016 the same opponents met with reversed colours and Ivanchuk opted to fianchetto the queen's bishop.

8...0-0

8...b5 9.Nce5 Be7

On 9...Bd6 Black should reckon with 10.♗f4 0-0 11.♘xf7! ♔xf7 12.♖d1 ♘d5 13.♗xd6 ♕xd6 14.♕xh7 with an initiative.

10.e3 0-0 11.♗d2! a6 12.♘g5 ♕e8 13.♗c3 g6 14.h4 gives White tangible pressure.

9.b4

Or 9.e3 b5 10.♘cd2 (10.♘ce5 ♗d6!) 10...♕b6 11.b4 ♗d6 12.♗b2 ♘bd7=.

9...b5!

Ivanchuk-Carlsen, rapid Doha, 2016, went 9...♗e7?! 10.♗b2 ♕c7 11.♖c1 ♘bd7 12.e4 b5 13.♘a5 ♕xc2 14.♖xc2 ♘xe4 15.♗xb5±. The c6- and c7-square are open to White's pieces.

10.bxc5 bxc4 11.e3

The key of Black's design is that 11.♕xc4 ♗b7 offers excellent compensation. He will regain the pawn with comfortable play.

11...♗a6

12.♗b2

12.♗xc4 ♕a5+ equalises on the spot. The idea of the text is that 12...♕a5+ 13.♗c3 ♕xc5? would lose the exchange, although 13...♕c7= is enough.

12...♕c7 13.♗d4 ♕a5+=.

Annotated Games

18. Helbich – Fenwick
ICCF 2014

1.d4 ♘f6 2.c4 e6 3.g3 c6 4.♗g2 d5 5.♘f3 ♗e7 6.0-0 0-0 7.♕c2 b6 8.♘bd2 ♗b7 9.e4 ♘a6 10.a3 c5 11.exd5 exd5 12.dxc5 ♘xc5 13.b4 ♘e6 14.♗b2

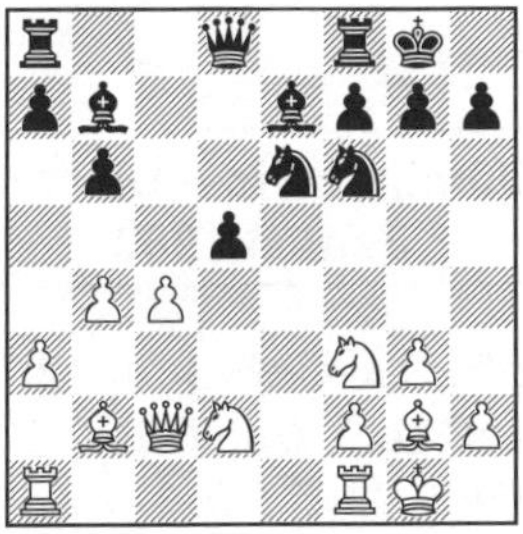

14...a5

Black fixes the enemy queenside pawns to limit their mobility. We'll see that in some alternative lines White can produce a passer with c4-c5 or attack the a7-pawn in an endgame. The main move is:

14...♖c8 15.♘e5 ♕c7, protecting the b7-bishop. My friend Kiril Georgiev is very confident in his endgame technique, so after 16.♖ac1 he traded queens with:

16...dxc4 17.♕xc4 ♕xc4 18.♘dxc4 ♗xg2 19.♔xg2 ♖c7 and signed a draw against Atakisi in Paracin 2016. Black still needs precision though – 20.♘e3 ♖fc8 21.♖xc7 ♖xc7 22.♖c1 ♖xc1 23.♗xc1 ♗d6 24.♘c6 a6=.

Eljanov tried to create imbalances with 16...d4, but this pawn could become a constant source of concern in future after 17.♗xb7 ♕xb7 18.♕f5 (18.f4!?) 18...g6 19.♕f3 ♕c7 20.♘d3, although 20...♘d7 should keep the balance.

Even the most timid answer 18.♕d3 ♘d7 19.♘ef3 a5 20.♘xd4 was enough to kill any suspense – 20...♘xd4 21.♗xd4 axb4 22.axb4 ♗xb4 23.♖fd1 ♘c5 24.♗xc5 ♗xc5 25.♘e4 ♖fe8 ½-½, Donchenko-Eljanov, Biel 2018.

15.b5

15.♖ad1 axb4 16.axb4 occurred in Tripp-Pinchon, ICCF 2016.

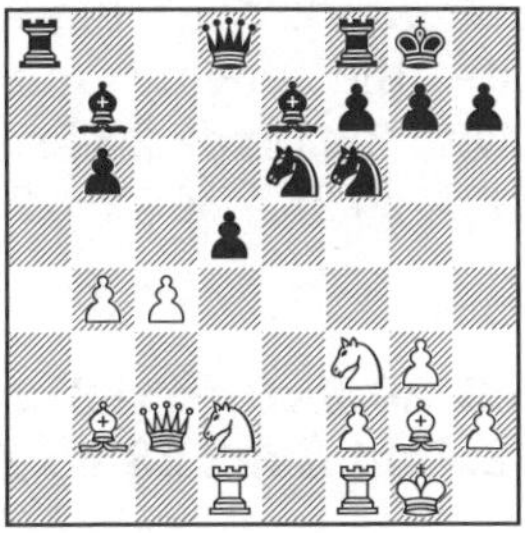

It went 16...♗xb4 17.♘h4 ♕c7 18.♗xf6 gxf6 19.♕f5 ♘g7 20.♕xf6 ♗e7 21.♕h6 ♖a6 22.cxd5 b5 23.♕e3 ♗xh4 24.gxh4 ♖g6 to end in a draw, but OTB Black would probably choose the solid:

16...♕c8 17.♕b3 ♖d8=.

15.bxa5 bxa5 16.♖ad1 dxc4 17.♘xc4 ♕c7 18.♖c1 ♖ac8 is obviously equal.

15...dxc4 16.♖ad1

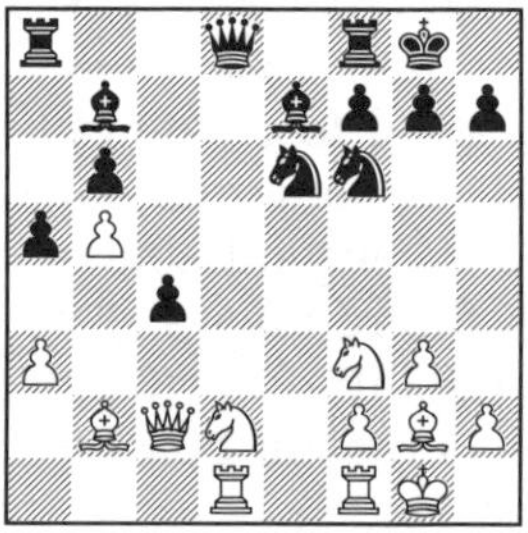

16...c3!

The last finesse, to uncoordinate White's pieces. After 17.♕xc3 ♗c5 18.♕c2 ♕e7 19.♘c4 ♗xf3 20.♗xf3 a draw was signed in Dugushov-Sugonyak, ICCF 2018. The main game lasted only a little longer:

17.♕xc3 ♕e8 18.a4 ♗b4 19.♕e3

After 19.♕c2 ♖c8 20.♕b1 ♕e7 21.♘e5 ♗xg2 22.♔xg2 Black could eliminate the enemy queenside pawns with 22...♗xd2 23.♖xd2 ♕b4 24.♖dd1 ♕xa4 25.♘c6 ♖xc6 26.bxc6 ♕xc6+=.

19...♘c5 20.♗xf6 ♕xe3 21.fxe3 gxf6 22.♘d4 ♗xg2 23.♔xg2

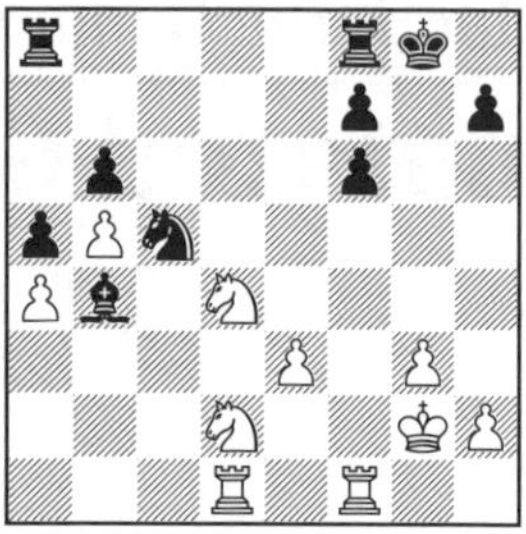

23...♗xd2

Now all the weak pawns swiftly disappear:

24.♖xd2 ♖ad8 25.♖c2 ♖fe8 26.♖xf6 ♖xe3 27.♖xb6 ♖xd4 28.♖xc5 ♖xa4 ½-½

19. Damljanovic – Dizdarevic
Zenica 1989

1.d4 ♘f6 2.c4 e6 3.♘f3 b6 4.g3 c6 5.♗g2 ♗e7 6.0-0 0-0 7.♘bd2 d5 8.♕c2 ♗b7 9.e4 ♘a6 10.e5 ♘d7 11.a3 c5 12.dxc5 bxc5 13.♖e1 ♘c7 14.h4 a5 15.♘f1

15...♖e8

It is understandable that Black

would like to refrain from ...h6, but this game shows that White can provoke it anyway. Therefore, I put **15...h6!?** under the microscope. The benefits of this move are obvious: White lacks ♘g5; Black might save a tempo on the set-up ...♖a6, ...♕a8, ...♖b8, doubling rooks on the b-file.

I do not see direct counter-indications, connected with a sacrifice on h6. For instance:

16.♗f4 ♖a6 17.♕d2 ♖b6 18.♗xh6? gxh6 19.♕xh6 ♘e8. Black always has ...f5 to include the rook in the defence.

Besides, taking on h6 is not obligatory and we could ignore it in some lines, e.g. 18.♘1h2 d4

18...a4 is also thematic. Then 19.♗xh6 gxh6 20.♕xh6 ♘e8 21.♘g5 ♗xg5 22.hxg5 ♘g7 saves the day:

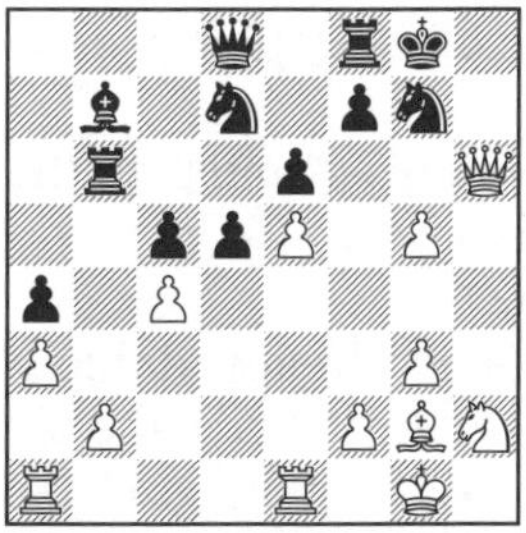

23.♘g4 ♘f5 24.♕h5 ♔g7 25.♘h6 ♕e7.

19.b4

19.♘g4? stumbles into 19...♕a8. The text aims to distract the rook from the defence of the e6-pawn and to open the a-file. The latter enables tactical hits as ♖a7 and ♖xd7.

19...axb4 20.axb4 ♖xb4 21.♗xh6

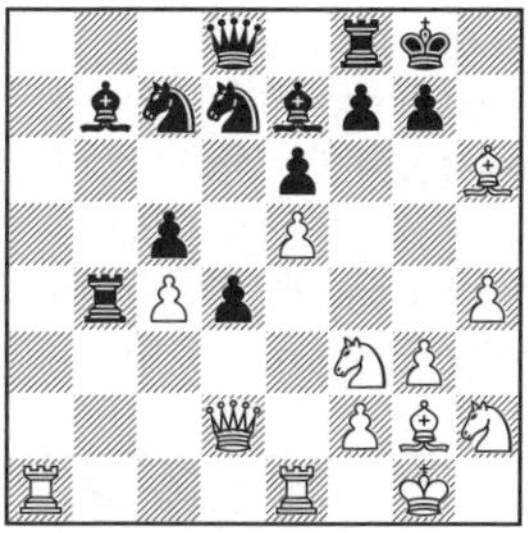

21...♘b6!

21...gxh6 22.♕xh6 ♘e8 23.♘g5 ♗xg5 24.hxg5 ♘g7 25.♖a7! ♗xg2 (25...♘f5 26.♕h5 ♗xg2 27.g6=) 26.♖xd7! ♕xd7 27.♘g4 f5=.

22.♗g5 ♘xc4 23.♕e2 d3∓.

16.h5!?

The obvious ways to exploit the absence of ...h6 is to put a piece on g5: 16.♗g5 h6 17.♗xe7 ♖xe7 (or 17... ♕xe7 18.♖ad1 ♖ab8) 18.cxd5 ♗xd5 19.♖ad1 ♖b8 20.♘1d2 ♘b5. In principle Black does not mind to trade the bishop, which was hitting his own pawn on c5. More testing is:

16.♘g5 ♘f8 17.♕e2 ♕d7 18.♕h5 ♗xg5 19.♗xg5 ♖eb8 20.♕g4 ♔h8∞.

16.h5 forces ...h6. In Radovanovic-J.Horvath, Zalakaros 2019, White delayed this move in favour of:

16.♗f4 and Black chose a set-up with 16...♘f8 (16...♖a6!? was more ambitious) 17.♖ad1, when Black committed the tactical mistake:

a) 17...♖a6?!, leaving the b7-bishop unguarded.

White could have exploited it with 18.♗g5! d4?! (18...h6 19.♗xe7 ♕xe7 20.cxd5 already favours White. Compared to the above-mentioned line, we have the inclusion of ♖ad1 ♘f8.) 19.♘xd4 ♗xg2 20.♘xe6±. White missed his chance and the game went:

18.h5 h6 to reach the following instructive position:

19.♘1h2

19.g4 seems more logical to me. I analysed 19...♕a8 20.g5 (Or 20.♘g3 ♖b6 21.g5 dxc4 22.♘e4 c3 23.bxc3 ♗xe4 24.♖xe4 ♖b2 25.♕xb2 ♕xe4 26.♗g3 hxg5) 20...dxc4 21.♘1h2 hxg5 22.♗xg5 ♗xg5 23.♘xg5 ♗xg2 24.f3 ♗xf3 25.♘hxf3 ♘d5 26.♘e4. White has sufficient compensation for the pawn after 26...f5= or 26... ♖d8 27.♕g2 ♖a7∞.

19...♕a8 20.♘d2

Now instead of the passive 20... ♘h7 which is balanced after 21.♘g4 ♔h8!, Black can try:

20...a4 21.♘g4 ♖b6 22.♕c1 ♖d8. It turns out that sacrifices on h6 are not that dangerous. I analysed the idea of bringing the light-squared bishop on d3 and discovered that Black could close the centre and counter-attack with ...f5. An illustrative line is:

23.♗f1 ♘e8 24.♗e2 ♖d7 25.♗d3 ♕d8 26.♗c2 ♖a6 27.♗d3 d4 28.♘e4

28...f5! 29.exf6 ♘xf6 30.♘gxf6+ gxf6 31.g4 (31.♗xh6 f5 32.♘d2 ♗g5 33.♗xg5 ♕xg5–+) 31...♘h7 32.♗xh6 ♗f8 33.♗xf8 ♕xf8 34.♕f4 ♔h8 35.♕g3 ♖g7 36.♔f1 e5↑.

To take stock, I determined a good set-up for Black after ...h6 and ...♖e8 – ...♘f8, ♖a6-b6, a4, ♕a8, ♖d8. In the event of danger Black could also include ...♔h8, ♘e8.

---

b) 17...♖a7! 18.h5

Or 18.♘1d2 ♕a8;

18.♗g5 d4;

18.cxd5 exd5 19.♗g5 d4 20.♗xe7 ♕xe7.

18...h6. Play is similar to the above analysis:

19.♘1h2

19.g4 is already dubious since the rook defends the 7th rank after 19...♕a8 20.g5?! dxc4 etc.

19...♕a8 20.♘d2 a4 21.♘g4 ♖d8∞.

16...h6 17.♘1h2 ♖b8?

According to the above analysis, the best set-up should be 17...♖a6 in order to enable ...♕a8. After 18.♘g4 Black has at least 3 solid set-ups:

a) 18...♘f8!? 19.♗f4 ♖b6 20.♖ab1 ♔h8 21.♕d2 dxc4∞;

b) 18...♗f8 19.♗f4 ♕a8 20.♖ad1 d4= – we cannot break in here;

c) 18...♖f8 19.♗d2 ♕a8 20.♘xh6+ (20.♕c1 dxc4) 20...gxh6 21.♗xh6 f5 (21...d4 may be safer) 22.exf6 ♖xf6 23.♗g5⩱.

18.♘g4 ♗f8 19.♗d2

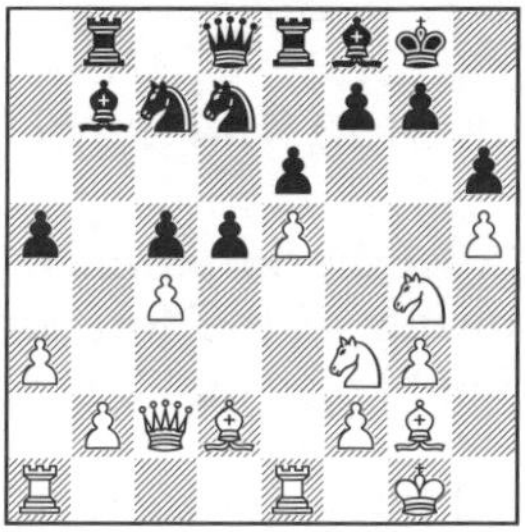

19...♗a6

A little strange way to trade light-squared bishops, which loses a pawn. Perhaps Black should have defended a5 with 19...♖a8 – 20.♖ad1 ♖a6 21.♘h4 ♗e7. Then 22.♗xh6 promises a strong initiative. The point is that after 22...♗xh4 23.gxh4 ♕xh4 24.♖d3 ♕xg4 25.♖g3 ♕xg3 26.fxg3 gxh6 27.♕d2 ♔h7 28.♗e4+ (28.♖f1) 28...♔g7 29.♗c2 White retains a lot of threats. However, the position remains complex, while after the text White is clearly better.

19...a4 also leaves White on top – 20.♕xa4

20.♕c1 ♗c6 (preparing ...♖b6) 21.♗xh6 fails to 21...gxh6 22.♘xh6+ ♗xh6 23.♕xh6 ♕e7 24.♘g5 f5.

20...♘b6 21.♕d1 dxc4

21...♘xc4 loses to 22.♗xh6!.

20.♗f1 ♗xc4 21.♗xc4 dxc4 22.♗xa5 ♘b6

Or 22...♖a8 23.♗xc7 ♕xc7 24.♘d2.

23.♖ad1 (23.♘e3!±) **23...♘cd5**

23...♘bd5 is also difficult – 24.♘e3 ♖b3 25.♘d2 ♘xe3 26.fxe3 ♖b7 27.♘xc4 ♕g5 28.♔g2 ♘d5 29.♕f2±, threatening e4 and ♘d6.

24.♘e3 ♕c8 25.♗xb6 ♘xe3 26.♖xe3 ♖xb6 27.♘d2 ♖b8 28.♘xc4 ♕b7 29.♕e4 ♕e7 30.♖ed3 ♕g5 31.♕f3 g6 32.♖d7 ♖e7 33.♖xe7 ♗xe7 34.hxg6 ♕xg6 35.♖d7 ♔f8 36.♕d3 ♕g4 37.♖xe7 1-0

20. Nogga – Kraft
ICCF 2018

1.d4 d5 2.c4 c6 3.♘f3 ♘f6 4.e3 e6 5.♘bd2 ♘bd7 6.♗d3 ♗d6 7.0-0 0-0 8.e4 e5 9.cxd5 cxd5 10.♖e1 h6 11.h3 ♖e8 12.exd5 exd4 13.♖xe8+ ♕xe8 14.♘c4

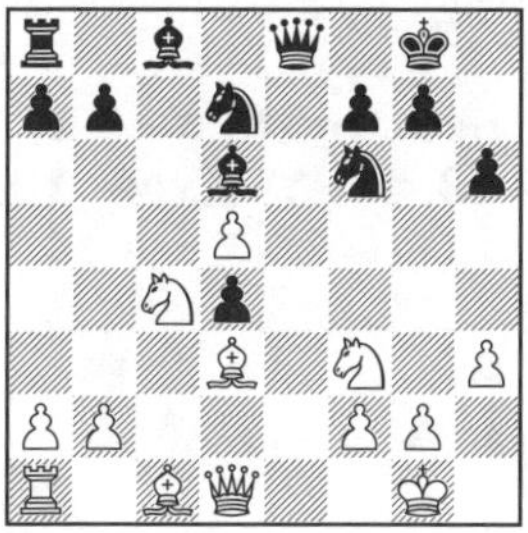

14...♗f8

The passive defence 14...♗c5!? is enough to make a draw. The game

Dunlop-Kupsys, ICCF 2018, went on 15.d6 b6 16.a3 a5 17.♗d2 ♗b7 18.b4 axb4 19.axb4 ♗xf3 20.gxf3

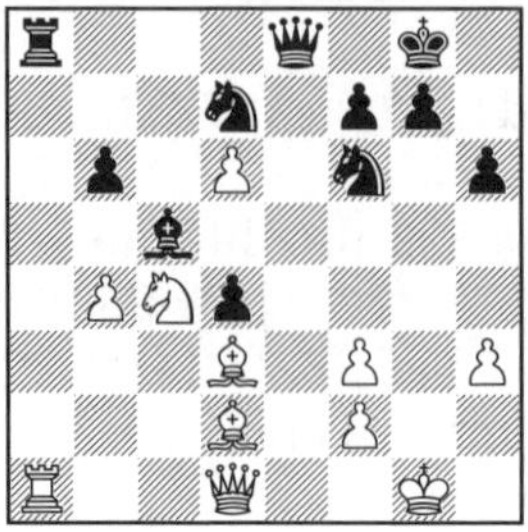

20...b5 21.♘a3 ♗xd6 22.♘xb5 ♗f8 23.♘xd4 ♖xa1 24.♕xa1 ♘e5 25.♗e2 ♘g6 26.b5 ♕e5, when White's extra pawn cannot be converted. He even should be cautious with his disrupted kingside.

Next year Dunlop unsuccessfully tried to improve with:

15.a3 b5 16.♘a5 ♘e5 17.b4 ♘xd3 18.♕xd3 ♗b6 19.♗b2 ♕d7 20.♘xd4 ♕xd5 21.♕xb5 ♗xd4 22.♕xd5 ♗xf2+ 23.♔xf2 ♘xd5 24.♖d1 ♗e6 ½-½, Dunlop-Dias, ICCF 2019.

I chose to comment 14...♗f8 because Black's play looks easier to remember – on every move he attacks something.

15.d6 ♘c5 16.♗f4 ♗e6 17.♘xd4 ♘xd3 18.♕xd3 ♗xc4 19.♕xc4 ♕e4

20.♗h2

20.♗g3 ♘h5 (20...♖d8!? 21.♕c7 ♖d7 22.♘b5 ♕b4=) 21.♗h2 ♘f4 22.♗xf4 ♕xf4 23.d7 retains the extra pawn, but no winning chances – 23...♖d8 24.♕c8 ♗e7 25.♘f3 ♕a4 26.♘e5 (26.♕xb7 ♖xd7 27.♕b8+ ♖d8 28.♕b3 ♕xb3 29.axb3 ♖d7 30.♘e5 ♖b7=) 26...♕a5 27.f4 ♕b4=.

20...♖d8 21.f3 ♕h4 22.♕c5

After 22.♖c1 the d6-pawn is still immune owing to the fork from f5. Black should play first 22...♕g5!.

22...♘e8 23.♕xa7 ♕g5!

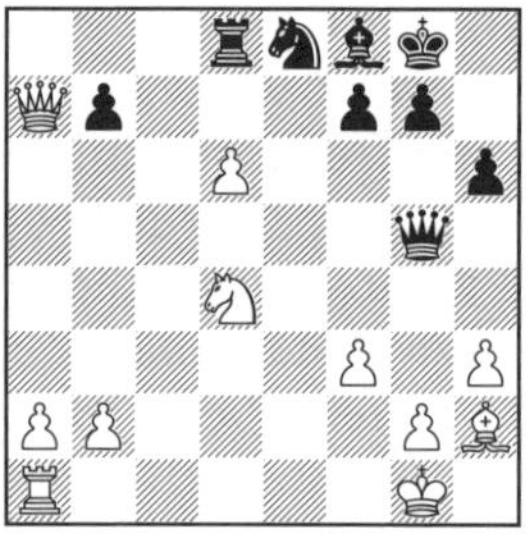

White's weak dark squares and the unstable knight on d4 ensure a long-term compensation. On the other hand, White's knight cannot leave d4 since that would allow ...♘f5 and ...♖d2. So both sides just stay on:

24.♕a4 ♘xd6 25.♔h1 ♕h4 26.b3 ♕g5 27.♗g1 g6 28.♖e1 ♕d2 29.♖e2 ♘f5!

A rare perpetual device!

30.♖xd2 ½-½

21. Radjabov-Ding Liren
Moscow 12.05.2017

1.d4 d5 2.c4 c6 3.♘f3 ♘f6 4.e3 e6 5.♗d3 ♘bd7 6.b3 ♗d6 7.♗b2 0-0 8.♘bd2 b6 9.0-0 ♗b7

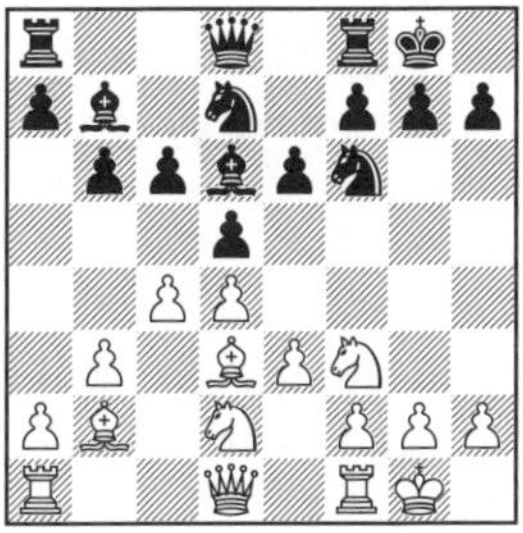

The "mirror" fianchetto is one of the main Black weapons against the plan with b3. If White treats it with ♘c3 and ♕c2, Black commonly tries to push ...e5. In our case the ♘d2 does not have an impact on the centre. That encourages the plan with ...c5, followed by ...♘e4.

10.♕e2

White has 3 sensible approaches:
1. To play ♘e5, f4 and aim for g4 or f5.

2. To open the centre with e4, followed by a piece attack on the black king.

3. To wait for ...c5 and play against hanging pawns.

He often starts with 10.♘e5, when safest is to prepare ...♘e4 by 10...c5. Play commonly continues:
11.cxd5

11.f4 cxd4 12.exd4 ♘e4! 13.♕e2 ♘xd2 14.♕xd2 f5! is even slightly better for Black since his b7-bishop has better prospects than the one at b2.

11...exd5

11...♗xd5!? is more simple, but Black does not have serious chances to complicate things in the arising symmetrical pawn structure.

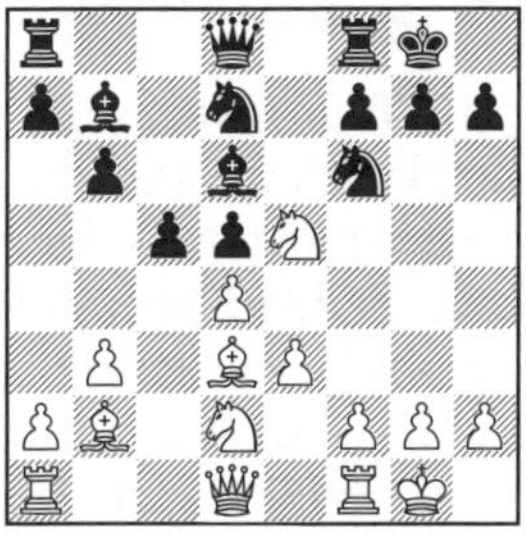

12.f4 (12.♘xd7 ♘xd7 13.dxc5 bxc5) 12...cxd4 13.exd4 ♘e4 14.♘xe4 dxe4 15.♗c4 ♘f6 16.♕e2 ♖c8 17.♖ac1 ♖c7∞

Black simply ignores the e5-knight. The rook lift 18.♖c3 ♘d5 19.♖g3 is senseless after 19...f5. 18.g4?! ♘d5 19.♕xe4 is more than risky. Perhaps best is:

18.♔h1 ♕c8 (preparing ...a6) 19.f5 a6 20.a4. This position occurred in two correspondence games which were drawn. A logical continuation is 20...♕a8 21.♖c3 ♖fc8 22.♖g3 ♗d5 23.♗c1 b5 24.axb5 axb5 25.♗h6 ♗f8 26.♕e3 bxc4 27.♖xg7+ and White forced a perpetual in Krauss-Bär, ICCF 2019. Black could have posed practical problems with a speculative pawn sac – 21...b5!? or 23...e3!? 24.♕xe3 ♘e4.

10.e4 dxe4 11.♘xe4 ♘xe4 12.♗xe4 ♘f6 13.♗c2 c5 14.dxc5 (14.♘e5 ♕c7

15.♕e2 cxd4) 14...♗xc5 15.♕e2 ♕e7 is another typical position.

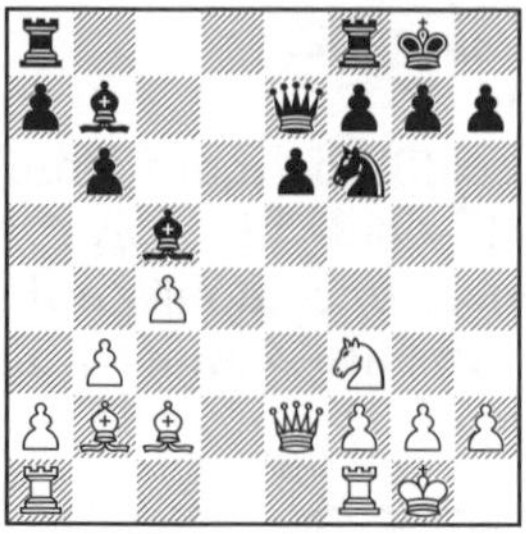

Although White's pieces are targeted on the black king, the open d-file and the extra pawn in the centre assure Black of adequate counterplay. The most obvious attempt:

16.♘g5?! stumbles into 16...♖fd8! 17.♗xf6?! ♕xf6 18.♗xh7+ ♔f8 19.♗e4 ♕xg5 and Black's rook invades the second rank. The more solid:

16.♖ad1= apparently keeps the balance according to the engines, but in practice White scores the meager 25%. Black's play is too easy. He trades both rooks and brings his king to e7.

10...c5!

Black prepares ...♘e4. This is a universal method of meeting b3, ♘bd2. It is much riskier to postpone serious strategical decisions with some "noncommittal" move like:

10...♕e7 11.♖ad1 ♖fe8 since White takes the initiative with 12.♘e5 c5 13.f4 cxd4 14.exd4. Black cannot block the d3-bishop anymore and have to defend passively. On the contrary, White has several active plans, for instance, g4-g5.

11.♖ad1

White still hopes to build up a kingside attack with f4, g4. Major alternatives are:

11.e4 dxe4 12.♘xe4 ♘xe4 13.♗xe4 ♗xe4 14.♕xe4 ♘f6 15.♕e2 cxd4 16.♘xd4 a6 17.♖ad1 ♕c7. Black has a comfortable equality, **provided that he keeps the queens!** He should seek to trade rooks and reach something like the position on the following diagram:

18.h3 (18.♘f3 ♖fd8) 18...♖ad8 19.♖d3 ♗c5 20.♕f3 ♖d7 21.♖fd1 ♖fd8 22.♘e2 ♖xd3 23.♖xd3 ♖xd3 24.♕xd3

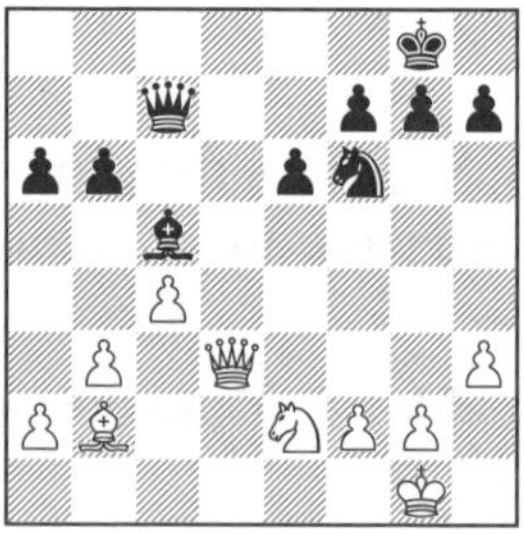

Now 24...♘d7 or 24...h6 are okay, while 24...♕d7? as in Kempinski-Piorun, Warsaw 2011, is a strategic mistake. Without queens White's

king could help his pawn majority on the queenside and establish lasting pressure.

11.♖fd1 shifts the battle focus to the centre. Although most games feature 11...♖e8 in response, I propose to define the pawn structure at once:

11...cxd4!? 12.♘xd4

> 12.exd4 ♖c8 13.♘e5 ♕e7 14.f4 g6 15.♖f1 has no venom with two tempi less. We can double the rooks on the c-file and threaten ...♘e8, ...f6 – 15...♖c7 16.♖ad1 ♖fc8, when 17.g4? fails to 17...dxc4 18.bxc4 b5! 19.c5 ♘xc5.

12...♖c8 13.cxd5 ♘xd5

White's extra tempo is not worth much. For instance, 14.♘c4 ♗b8 15.g3 ♕e7.

11...♘e4 12.cxd5 exd5

13.♗a6

White chooses to play against the d5-pawn, so he removes its defender. 13.♘e5 cxd4 14.exd4 ♘df6 15.f3 ♘xd2 16.♕xd2 is completely equal – 16...a5 17.♕e2 (17.♖c1 b5=) 17...♖e8=.

13...♗xa6 14.♕xa6 ♖e8

14...♕e7 was also possible – 15.dxc5 ♘dxc5 16.♕e2, when Black could choose 16...♖ac8 17.♘d4 g6 or 17...♗e5, or even a new set-up of his knights – 16...♘e6 17.♕d3 ♕b7 18.♘d4 ♘4c5.

15.dxc5

15.♕e2 ♕e7 16.dxc5 allows 16...bxc5=.

15...♘dxc5 16.♕e2

16...♖c8

Black opts for a passive set-up and holds it confidently. He had a more interesting possibility though:

16...♕d7!? 17.♖c1 f5!, aiming for ...f4.

> The key is that 18.g3 does not stop it, e.g. 18...f4! 19.b4 ♘e6 20.♕d3 fxe3 21.fxe3 ♕b7 with counterplay.

Bleker-Alexeyenko, ICCF 2017, saw 18.♖fd1 ♖ad8 19.g3 ♕f7 20.b4 ♘e6 21.♘e5 ♗xe5 22.♗xe5 ♕e7 23.a3 ♘6g5

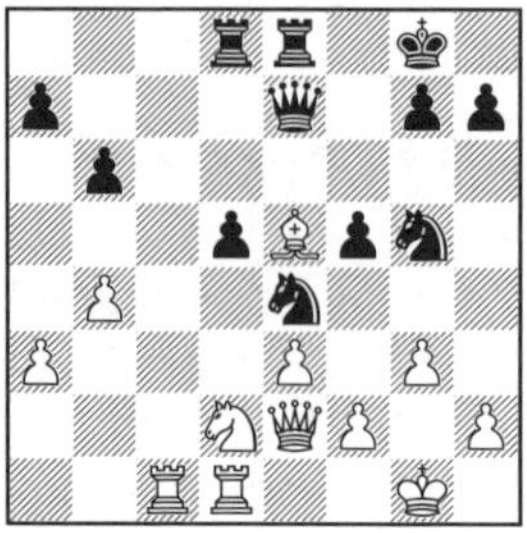

24.f4 (the only move!) 24...♖c8 25.♔g2 ♘f7=.
Let's now see the instructive defence of the isolated pawn Ding Liren presents.

17.♖c1 ♗f8 18.♖fd1 ♕e7 19.♘b1 ♕b7 20.♘c3 ♖ed8 21.♖c2 a6 22.h3 b5 23.♖dc1 ♘e6

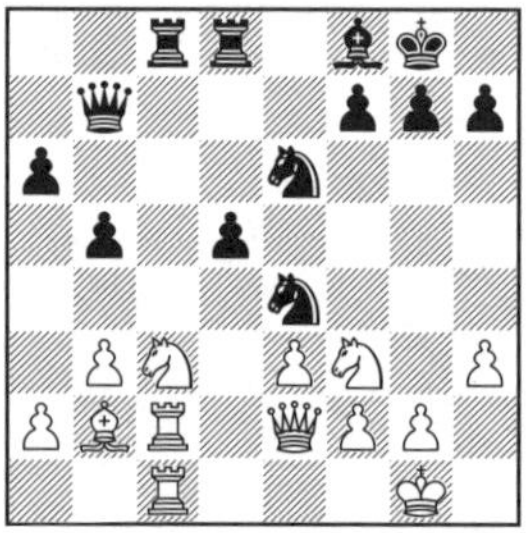

Black has only one weakness – d5. It is essential to defend such positions patiently, without jerky movements.

24.♕d3 ♖c5 25.♘e2 ♖dc8 26.♘fd4 ♖xc2 27.♖xc2 ♘4c5

The decision to keep the rooks is incomprehensible to me. 27...♖xc2 28.♕xc2 ♘4c5 was absolutely safe.

28.♕d1 ♘xd4 29.♗xd4 ♘e6 30.♖d2 a5 31.♗b2 ♖c5

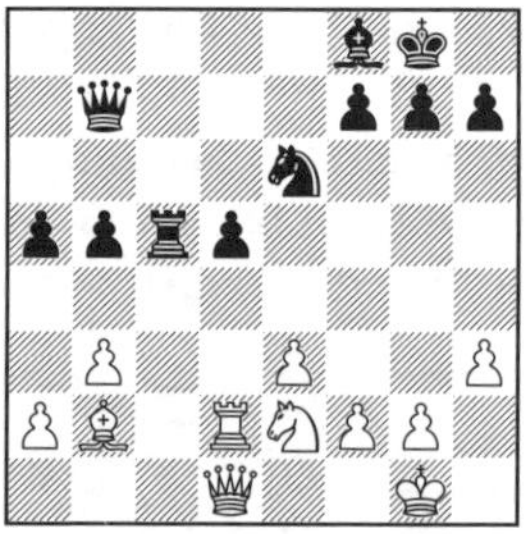

When defending an isolated pawn, the key is to do it from the side, to avoid e4. It is obvious now that White cannot improve from here. For instance, 32.h4 g6 33.h5 b4 or 32.♘c3 ♘c7.

32.♘d4 ♘xd4 33.♗xd4 ♖c6 34.♗b2 ♖c5 35.♗d4 ♖c6 36.♗b2 ♖c5 37.a3 ♕c6 38.♔h2 h6 39.g3 b4 40.a4 ♗e7 41.♗d4 ♖c1 42.♕g4 ♗f6 43.♗xf6 ♕xf6 44.♔g2 ♖c5 45.♕f3 ½-½

Chapter 6. 4.♕c2

Main Ideas

1.d4 d5 2.c4 e6 3.♘f3 c6 4.♕c2

This modest-looking move is in fact White's best-scoring option on move 4. We should have a clear idea of what we want to avoid, in order to treat it adequately.

Move orders

I definitely exclude the Stonewall as a viable option. I'm not a fan of the QGD either. Finally, I do not want to play against a Closed Catalan with ♘c3.

In principle I would like to take on c4 to open the centre.

However, 4...dxc4 5.♕xc4 b5 6.♕c2 ♗b7 gives White a free hand in the centre after 7.e4 ♘d7 8.♗e2. Therefore, I propose the flexible **4...♘f6** to pass the ball in White's court.

Now 5.♗g5 h6! dodges the QGD in favour of the Moscow Variation after 6.♗xf6 ♕xf6 7.♘c3 dxc4.

6.♗h4 dxc4 also suits me perfectly.

5.♘bd2 dxc4 is line C from the previous chapter.

5.e3!? ♘bd7 is the Anti-Meran with ♕c2. That is not a problem since White can choose 4.e3 ♘f6 anyway.

At last, 5.g3 dxc4! 6.♕xc4 b5 is real fun for Black.

Main lines

We should remember 2 positions from the Moscow Variation:

5.♗g5 h6 6.♗xf6 ♕xf6 7.e3 ♘d7 8.♘c3 g6 9.cxd5 exd5 10.♗d3 ♗g7 11.b4 0-0 12.0-0 ♕d6!

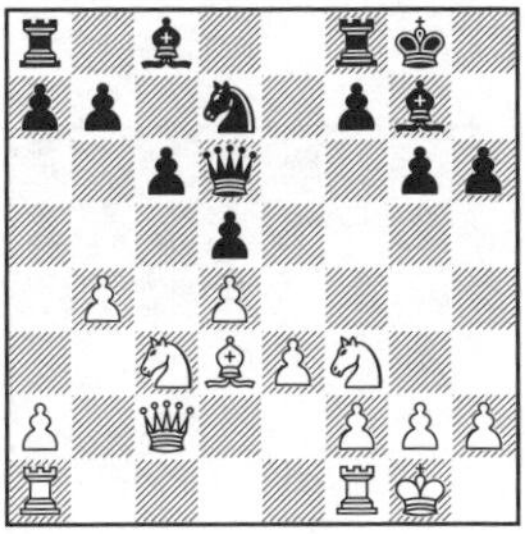

We follow up with ...♘b6, ...♗e6 and always meet b4-b5 by ...c5.

If White avoids the Carlsbad structure and plays e4, we take on c4 and undermine the enemy centre with ...c5:

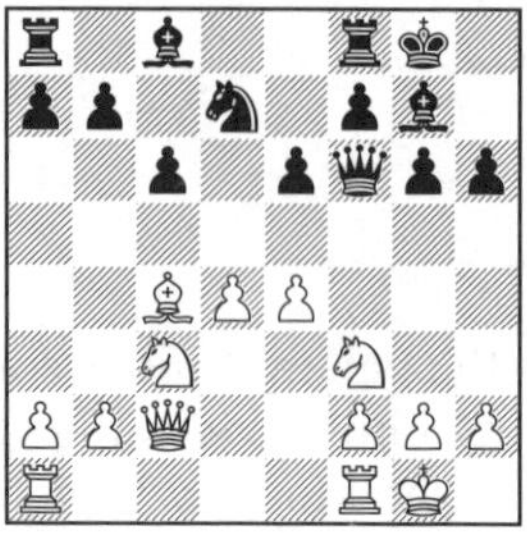

12...c5!? (12...e5 is also possible).

Our game is easy after **5.g3 dxc4 6.♕xc4 b5**

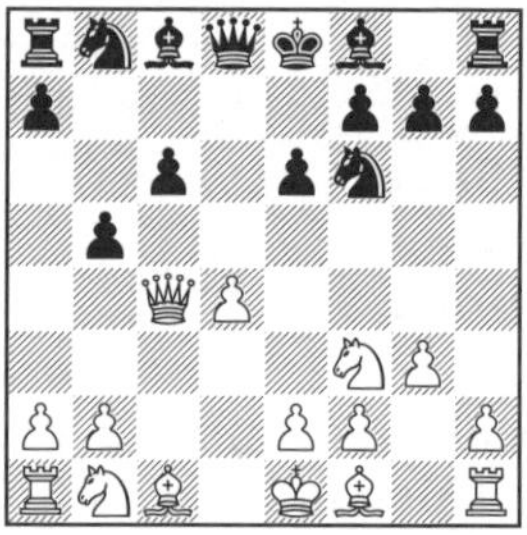

White has two ways to hinder somehow the freeing break ...c6-c5:
7.♕d3 ♗b7 8.♗g2 ♘bd7 9.0-0 a6 10.♘fd2!?

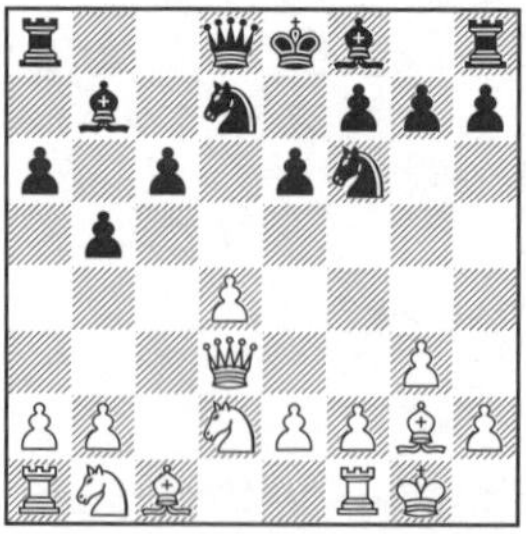

The point here is 10...♕b6! 11.a4 ♗e7 12.axb5 cxb5!=. Do not fear White's centre! It is not mobile.

The other principled line is 7.♕c2 ♗b7 8.♗g2 ♘bd7 9.♘e5

I recommend here 9...♘xe5 10.dxe5 ♘d5 11.0-0 ♗e7 12.♘c3 0-0 13.♖d1 ♕b8!=. See **Game 24** Hess-Wojtaszek, Douglas 2018.

Theoretical status

With 4.♕c2 White seeks to avoid theoretical discussions in the Marshall or the Noteboom. He cannot expect to obtain an advantage – Black's best plans have been well known for decades. Scherbakov has a detailed survey in his book, and Dreev mentions the sub-line of the Moscow Variation.
I only disagree with Krasenkov, who chooses the 4...dxc4 move order. He had no choice though, as 4...♘f6 5.♘bd2 would throw him out of the rest of his repertoire, based on the Stonewall.
The key to good results against 4.♕c2 is to know several typical position and, most of all, to play good positional chess.

Chapter 6. 4.♕c2

Step by Step

1.d4 d5 2.c4 e6 3.♘f3 c6 4.♕c2

4...♘f6

A. 5.♗g5; **B.** 5.g3

5.♘bd2 dxc4 is line C from the previous chapter.

5.e3 ♘bd7 belongs to the Meran domain.

5.♗f4 does not change our plan – 5...dxc4 6.♕xc4 b5 7.♕c2 ♗b7 8.e3

Or 8.e4 ♘bd7 9.♘bd2 (9.♘c3 b4 10.♘a4 c5) 9...a6 10.a4 ♗b4 11.♗d3 c5=, Ponomariov-Nakamura, rapid, Saint Louis 2011.

8...♘bd7 9.♗e2 a6

Or 9...♗e7 10.0-0 0-0 11.♘e5 c5 12.♗xb5 cxd4.

10.0-0 ♖c8 11.a4 ♗e7 12.♘bd2 0-0 13.♖fc1 ♘d5 14.♗g3 c5 15.♕b3 cxd4 16.exd4 ♖xc1+ 17.♖xc1 b4 18.h3=.

A. 5.♗g5 h6

I want to extract the maximum from White's particular move order. You can also switch to the QGD with 5...♘bd7, but you should reckon with 6.cxd5. Besides, the Cambridge-Springs plan does not work as 6.e3 ♕a5+ is met by 7.♘bd2.

A1. 6.♗xf6; **A2.** 6.♗h4

A1. 6.♗xf6 ♕xf6

A11. 7.♘c3; **A12.** 7.e3

7.g3 is harmless. The temporary weakness of the c4- and d4-pawn can be underlined with concrete play:

7...♘d7 8.♗g2 ♗b4+!? 9.♘bd2 ♘b6!

10.b3

Or 10.c5 ♘c4 11.e3 e5=.

10...c5!?

10...♗xd2+ 11.♕xd2 dxc4 12.0-0 cxb3 is also possible of course.

11.a3 ♗xd2+ 12.♕xd2 dxc4 13.bxc4 0-0 14.♖c1 ♖d8=.

7.♘bd2 ♘d7 8.e3 (8.g3 ♗b4 transposes to 7.g3) offers Black an ample choice. For consistency sake I suggest 8...g6 9.♗d3 ♗g7 10.0-0 0-0

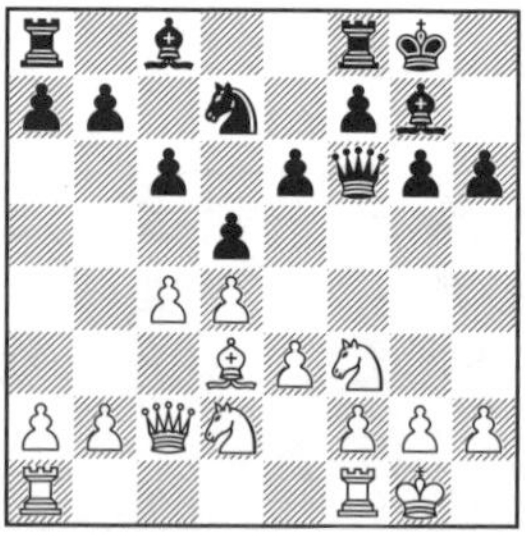

Now 11.cxd5 exd5 12.b4 is similar to **Game 22**. The d2-knight does not attack d5, so besides 12...♕d6 we could also play 12...♕e7!, preparing to meet b5 by ...c5.

11.e4?! e5 12.cxd5 cxd5 13.exd5 exd4 favours Black.

The most interesting option is:

11.♕b3 ♕e7 12.♖ac1

12.e4? stumbles into 12...dxe4 13.♘xe4 c5 14.d5 f5!.

12...a5. We can continue the waiting game with ...♖d8, ...♕d6, and choose between ...e5 or ...b6.

A11. 7.♘c3

This transposes to the Moscow Variation, where 7.♕c2 is seldom seen, although it scores better than any other 7th move.

7...dxc4

Dreev also considers 7...♘bd7 in his book on the Moscow Variation, but the text is simpler and more in the spirit of the Triangle System.

8.e3 b5

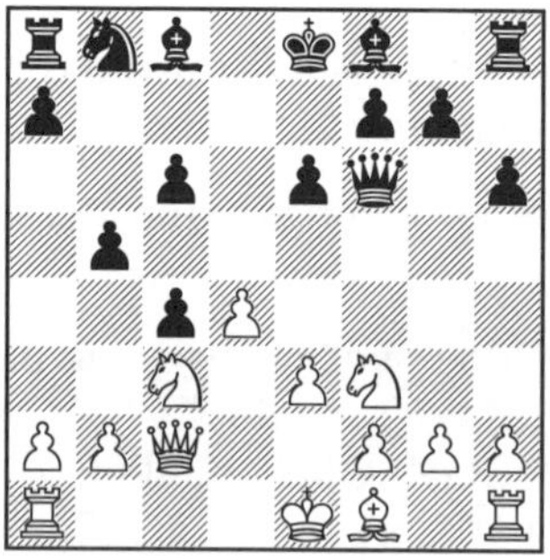

9.a4

It is not easy to assess that Black has a winning attack after 9.♘xb5? cxb5 10.♕e4 ♗b4+ 11.♔d1 0-0 12.♕xa8

♗d7. For instance: 13.♕e4 ♗c6 14.♕g4 ♘d7∓; 13.♕xa7 ♗c6 14.♗e2 ♗xf3 15.♗xf3 ♕f5–+.

9...♗b7 10.axb5

10.♘e5 ♗b4 11.axb5 cxb5 12.♗xc4? is incorrect – 12...bxc4 13.♕a4+ ♔f8 14.♕b5 ♕e7 15.♖b1 ♗c8 16.♘c6 a6!, Khlopov-Konstantinov, ICCF 2012.

10...cxb5 11.♘xb5 ♗b4+ 12.♘c3 0-0 13.♗e2

13.♗xc4 ♗xf3 14.gxf3 ♕xf3 15.0-0 is about equal, while the ambitious 15.♖g1 ♘d7 16.♗e2?! (16.♕e2 ♕c6!?) 16...♕h3 favours Black.

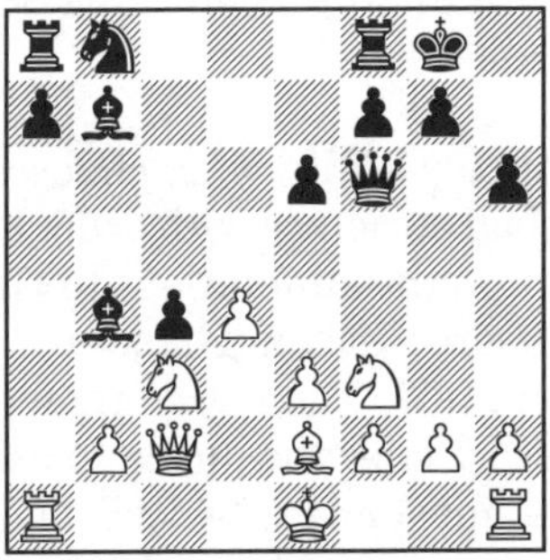

This position has been tested in more than 150 games. White does not have any weaknesses and should be at least not worse, but he scores less than 50%. Perhaps he tends to overestimate his chances and takes wrong decisions in the middlegame. Even if he won the c4-pawn, his winning chances would be minimal. Kramnik-Leko, rapid m. Miskolc 2007, went:
13...♘d7 14.0-0 ♖fc8 15.♖fc1 a5 16.♘a4 ♖ab8 17.♕d1 e5 18.♖xc4 (18.♗xc4 ♖d8) 18...♖xc4 19.♗xc4. Curiously, Kramnik had this position before, only he was Black against Beliavsky, and they signed a draw right here! With White he also drew, but on move 30 following 19...♗xf3 20.♕xf3 ♕xf3 21.gxf3 exd4 22.exd4 ♘b6 (22...♖d8!?=) etc.

A12. 7.e3 ♘d7 8.♘c3

This has never been considered dangerous, but the old plan with 8...♗d6, followed by ...♕e7, still allowed White to test the opponent without any risk. Then in the 90ies Black developed the provocative, but enterprising set-up:

8...g6!?

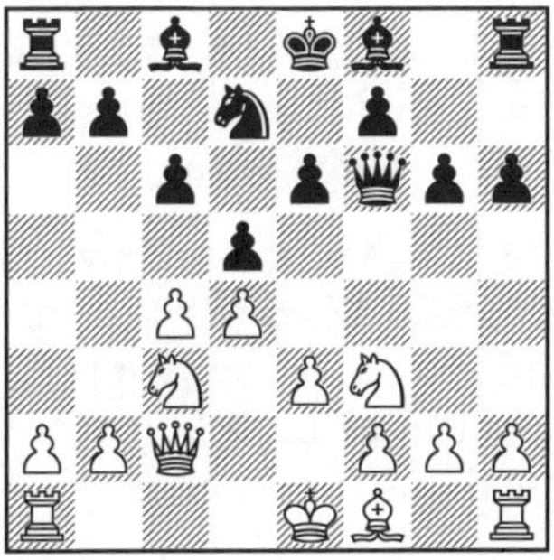

The idea is to castle and take on c4, followed by ...c5 or ...b6. White has tried 11(!) moves in this position, without much success.

9.♗d3

Topalov's 9.e4 dxe4 10.♘xe4 ♗b4+ 11.♔e2?! (11.♘c3 c5) had no followers. Black's king is safe after 11...♕g7! 12.c5 0-0 13.h4 e5.

Another attempt to punish Black is 9.0-0-0 ♗g7 10.h4. White's idea is to stabilise the centre with cxd5 and push h5, but it is difficult to advance from there: 10...0-0 11.♔b1 ♕e7 12.h5 (12.g4?! dxc4 13.♗d3 b5) 12...g5

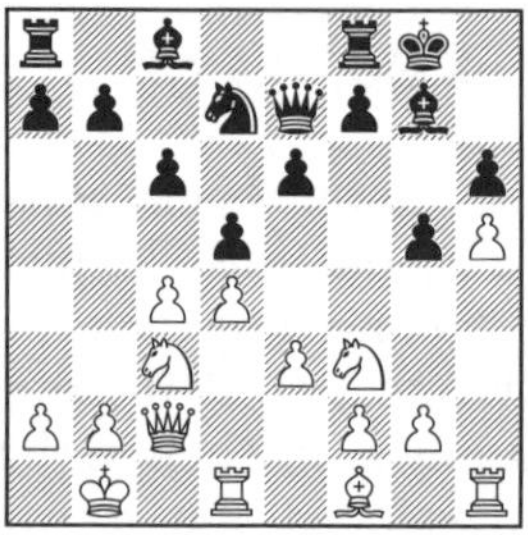

13.g4?!

If 13.cxd5 exd5 14.♗d3 ♘b6, and Black can even clamp on e4 by ...f5.

13...dxc4! 14.♗xc4 b5 15.♗d3 ♗b7∓. Nothing could stop Black from breaking through with ...c5.

9.a3 ♗g7 10.e4 is best met by 10...0-0 11.cxd5 exd5 12.e5 (or 12.exd5 ♖d8 with an active bishop pair) 12...♕e7 13.♘a4 (13.♗e2 c5) 13...f6↑.
A critical line for 8...g6 is:

9.♗e2 ♗g7 10.e4 dxc4! 11.e5

If White does not push e4-e5, again ...c5 is the best plan.

11...♕e7 12.♘e4 0-0 13.♕xc4 c5! 14.♘xc5 ♘xc5 15.dxc5 ♗d7 16.0-0 ♗c6. Black has full compensation as all the opponent's pieces are passive. Vallejo Pons-Hovhannisyan, Legnica 2013, went:

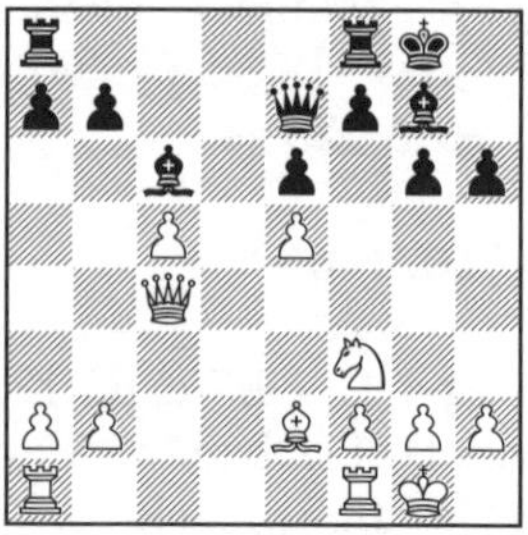

17.b4

If 17.♕c3 a5 18.♕e3 ♗d5 19.♖fc1 ♕c7 intending to double the rooks on the d-file.

17...a5 18.a3 ♕c7 19.♖ac1 axb4 20.axb4 ♗xe5 21.♘xe5 ♕xe5 22.♖fe1, when simplest is 22...♖a4=. In principle Black should gladly trade queens. Then he could bring his king to stop White's passer on the c-file.

In practice White often chooses the Carlsbad structure with cxd5. I consider it in the annotations to **Game 22** Bacrot-Kasimdzhanov, rapid, Mainz 2007. The key to remember is that we shift the queen to d6 and wait to meet b4-b5 by ...c5. Our minor pieces go ...♘b6 and ...♗e6.

9...♗g7

In this case I suggest to refrain from ...dxc4 as longer as possible. While it is playable, I feel it is a concession to offer the enemy the e4-square and the c-file. For instance, after 9...dxc4 10.♗xc4 ♗g7 11.0-0 0-0 12.♗b3 ♕e7 13.♘e4 e5 (13...♖d8 14.♖ac1) 14.♘c3 ♔h7 15.♖ad1 f5 White's pieces remain better coordinated.

10.0-0 0-0 11.♖ad1

Or 11.e4 dxc4 12.♗xc4 c5.

11...♕e7 12.♖fe1

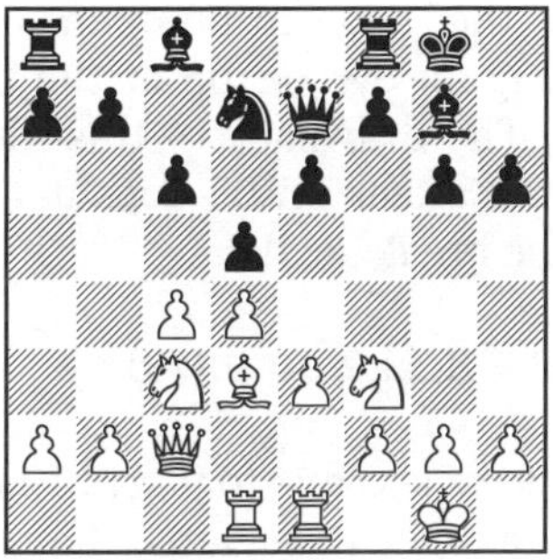

We have finished all our useful moves, and we should already define our plan. Since 12...f5 or 12...a6 contradict our general strategy to pursue positions with an open centre, the choice is easy:

12...dxc4! 13.♗xc4 ♖d8 14.a3

Now we have to think how to prepare ...c5. An obvious way is 14...b6 15.e4 c5 16.d5 ♘e5. The more sophisticated approach is:

14...a6!?

We could also gain space on the queenside first – 14...b5 15.♗e2 ♗b7 16.♘e4 (16.b4 a5, followed by ...e5) 16...a5!?.

15.♗a2 b6 16.e4 c5⇄.

A2. 6.♗h4 dxc4 7.♕xc4 b5 8.♕c2 ♗b7

9.e3

White's pieces are passive for an active approach as 9.♘bd2 ♘bd7 10.e4 (or 9.e4 ♘bd7 10.♘bd2). Black could pinpoint the weakness of d4 with 10...♕b6! 11.♗e2

11.a4 can hinder ...c5 only temporaryly – 11...♗b4 12.♗e2 0-0 13.0-0 ♖fc8 14.♖fd1 a6 15.♕d3 c5.

11...♘h5 12.♖c1 g5!? (12...♘f4 is fine, too) 13.♗g3 ♘xg3 14.hxg3 g4 15.♘h2 ♕xd4. In this chaotic position Black's bishop pair should be quite strong.

9.♗xf6 ♕xf6 10.e3 ♘d7 11.♘c3 a6 12.♗d3 ♗d6= (or 12...♖c8 13.0-0 ♕d8=).

9...♘bd7 10.♗e2

10.♗d3 does not protect f3, so Black could counter-attack with an early ...c5:

10...a6 11.a4 ♗b4+!? (he standard 11...♗e7 is also possible) 12.♘c3 c5 13.axb5 (13.♗xf6 ♘xf6=) 13...axb5 14.0-0 c4 15.♗e2 ♖xa1 16.♖xa1 ♕b6

17.b3 cxb3 18.♕xb3 ♗xc3 19.♕xc3 b4=.

10.♘bd2 a6 11.a4 ♖c8 12.♗e2 transposes to the main line.

10...a6 11.a4 ♖c8 12.♘bd2 c5

13.d5!? exd5 14.axb5 axb5 15.♗xb5 ♗e7=

Now the only way to pose some problems is 16.♗xf6 ♗xf6 17.♕f5, but after the cold-blooded 17...♔e7 (by the way, 17...♕c7 also equalises) 18.♖a7 ♖c7 19.0-0 ♕b8 20.♖a5 ♘f8!? (20...g6=) 21.♕c2 ♘e6 22.e4 g6 23.exd5 ♗xd5 Black's chances are at least not worse.

B. 5.g3 dxc4 6.♕xc4 b5

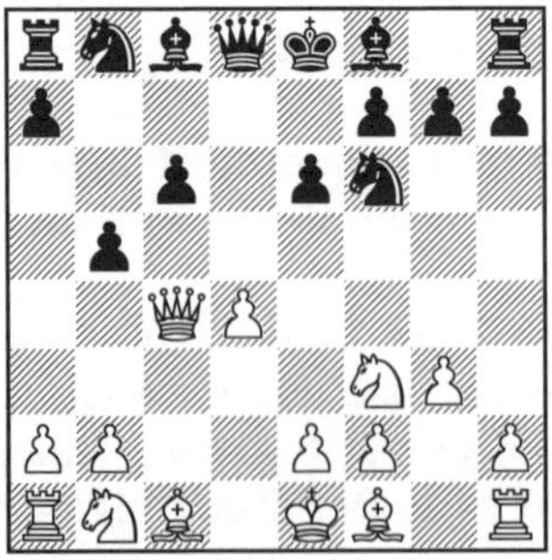

B1. 7.♕b3; **B2.** 7.♕d3; **B3.** 7.♕c2

B1. 7.♕b3

It is natural to remove the queen from the soon-to-be-open c-file, keeping an eye on b5 at the same time. The drawback of this idea is that the attack on b5 does not hinder the break ...c5!

7...♗b7 8.♗g2 a6 9.0-0

9.a4 is useless due to 9...c5! 10.dxc5

10.axb5 c4! regains the pawn – 11.♕d1 axb5 12.♖xa8 ♗xa8 13.0-0 ♗e7 14.b3 cxb3 15.♕xb3 b4= – see **Game 23** Caruana-Aronian, Saint Louis 2018.

10...♘bd7 11.♗e3

11.axb5 ♘xc5 12.♕c4 ♗d5 13.♕c2 axb5=.

11...♘xc5 (11...♘g4=; 11...♗xc5=) 12.♗xc5 ♗xc5 13.axb5

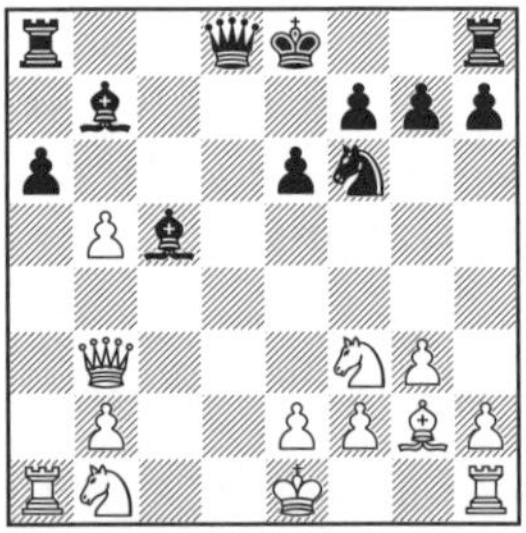

Black has a number of ways to even the chances, for instance:
13...♗xf2+ 14.♔xf2 ♘g4+ 15.♔e1 ♕b6 16.♖f1 ♘e3⩱;
13...♕b6 14.0-0 0-0.

9...c5 10.dxc5

10.a4 is already totally pointless as White cannot win a pawn.

For instance, 10...♘bd7 11.axb5 ♗d5 12.♕d3 ♗e4=. Black can also play on with:

10...c4 11.♕c2 ♘bd7∞.

10...♘bd7 11.♗e3 (11.♖d1 ♗xc5) **11...♗xc5 12.♗xc5 ♘xc5 13.♕b4**

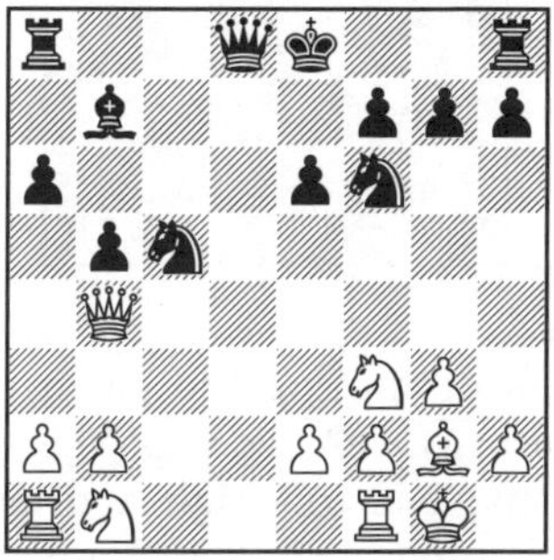

The last attempt to extract something out of the opening fails due to the weakness of the first rank:

13...♖c8 14.♖c1 0-0!

The endgame after 14...♘d3 15.♖xc8 ♘xb4 is also roughly equal.

15.♘bd2=

It turns out that 15.♖xc5? ♕d6 16.♖xb5 loses to 16...♕d1+ so White completes development and prepares for a balanced middlegame.

B2. 7.♕d3 ♗b7 8.♗g2 ♘bd7

This position often arises via the Catalan move order 1.c4 e6 2.g3 d5 3.♗g2 ♘f6 4.d4 dxc4 5.♕a4+ c6 6.♕xc4 b5 7.♕d3 ♗b7 8.♘f3 ♘bd7. The main difference to 7.♕b3 is that the queen protects the d4-pawn so White could try 8...a6 9.♘e5, although it is not too scary:

9...♘bd7 10.a4

10.0-0 ♘xe5 11.dxe5 ♕xd3 12.exd3 ♘d5 13.a3 0-0-0 14.♖d1 ♖d7 15.♘d2 ♘b6 16.♘e4 ♘a4=, Kiselev-Gerasimov, ICCF 2015.

10...♘xe5 11.dxe5 ♕xd3 12.exd3 ♘g4 13.axb5 ♘xe5 14.♔e2 axb5 15.♖xa8+ ♗xa8 16.♗f4 ♘g4 17.♘c3 ♗c5 18.♖a1 ♔d7 19.♘xb5 cxb5 20.♗xa8 e5=.

Of course White can opt for 9.0-0 ♘bd7 as in the main line.

9.0-0 a6

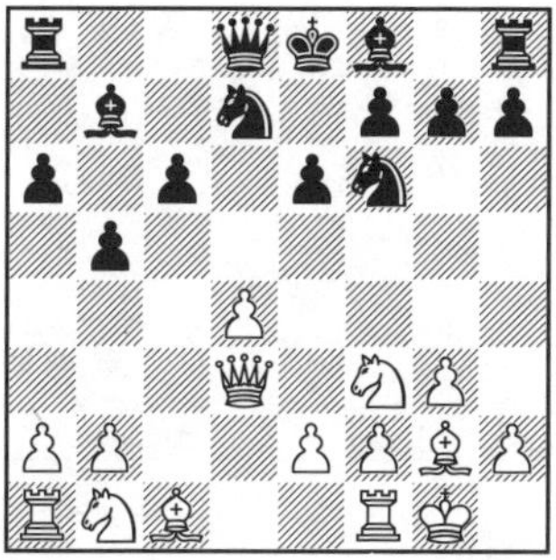

10.♘fd2!?

We have already seen 10.♘e5 ♘xe5.

The idea of 10.♘g5 is similar to the main line – White prevents ...c5. Accordingly, we could use the same receipt:

10...♕b6

10...♗e7 11.♘bd2 0-0 is a decent alternative.

11.♘c3

Or 11.a4 ♖d8 12.axb5 cxb5!=.

11...c5 12.♗xb7 ♕xb7 13.dxc5 ♘xc5 14.♕f3=.

10.a4 does not fare well. Black can still play 10...c5.

The only way to avoid repetition is 10...♗e7 11.♗g5 0-0 12.♘bd2 ♕b6∞.

11.axb5 ♗e4 12.♕d1 (12.♕d1 ♗d5 repeats) 12...axb5 13.♖xa8 ♕xa8 14.♘a3 ♕b7=.

10...♕b6! 11.a4 ♗e7 12.axb5

Black is well set for a waiting game – 12.♘c3 0-0 13.♘b3 ♖ac8 14.♖d1 ♖fd8=.

12...cxb5!

This recapture solves the opening problems. It is better to give up the centre, than to remain with a passive bishop after 12...axb5.

After the text 13.♗xb7= may be the best option since 13.e4 0-0 14.♘c3 ♖fd8 15.♘b3 ♘e5 16.♕e2 ♘c4 turned in Black's favour in Urban-B.Socko, Katowice 2010.

B3. 7.♕c2 ♗b7 8.♗g2

Gheorghiu won several games with 8.♘bd2 ♘bd7 9.♘b3, trying to clamp on c5. We question this idea with 9...♕b6 10.♗g2 a5!

11.a4

Self-disrupting the pawn chain with 11.♗e3 ♘d5 12.♖c1 ♘xe3 13.fxe3 is too high a price for stopping ...c5. The funny thing is that 13...c5 is still possible (although far from obligatory!) – 14.dxc5 ♗xc5 15.♘xc5 ♖c8 16.♕c3 ♖xc5 17.♕xg7 ♖xc1+ 18.♔f2 ♖xh1 19.♕xh8+ ♔e7 20.♗xh1 ♘f6 21.♕b8 ♘g4+ 22.♔e1 ♕c6 regains the pawn with an initiative.

11...bxa4 12.♖xa4 c5= (12...♕b5=).

8...♘bd7

9.♘e5

The only way to delay the freeing ...c5.
9.0-0 c5 has been extensively tested, and White scores below 35%. Black often takes over the initiative and his space advantage on the queenside becomes a weighty factor.

For 10.dxc5 ♗xc5 see **Game 24** Hess-Wojtaszek, Douglas 2018.

10.♗g5 ♖c8 11.dxc5 is imprecise.
The immediate 11.♗xf6! ♘xf6 12.a4 is more to the point – 12...b4 13.♘bd2 ♗e7 14.♕d3 0-0 15.♖ac1 ♘d7 16.♘g5 ♗xg5 17.♗xb7 ♖c7=.
11...♗xc5 12.♕d3 ♕b6

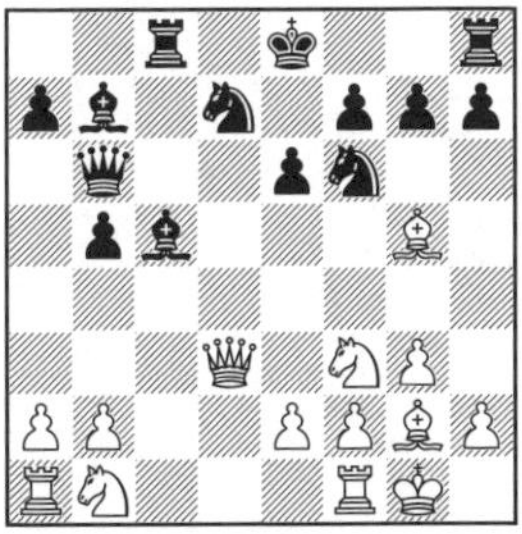

Here 13.♗xf6? is an instructive mistake, committed by the ultra-solid GM Andersson. His opponent Zvjaginsev also missed the splendid hit 13...♗xf2+!! 14.♖xf2 ♖c1+ 15.♗f1 ♘xf6 16.♕d2 ♕xf2+ 17.♔xf2 ♘e4+∓.
The lesser evil was 13.♘c3 a6 14.♗xf6 ♘xf6∓.

The inclusion of 10.a4 b4 does not change much – 11.♗g5 ♖c8 12.♘bd2 ♗e7 13.♖fc1 h6 14.♗xf6 ♗xf6!↑.

After 10.♘c3 b4 11.♘a4 ♖c8 12.♘xc5 ♘xc5 13.dxc5 ♗xc5 14.♕a4+ ♗c6 15.♕a6 0-0 Black is better developed.

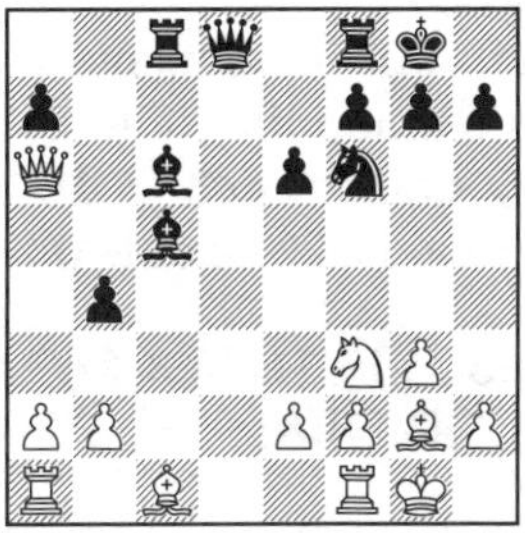

Most games feature 16.♗g5 h6 17.♖ad1 ♗d5∓, while 16.♗f4 ♕b6 17.♕xb6 axb6 creates a target on a2.

9...♘xe5!

9...♕b6 is not so smooth as White obtains a passed pawn on d5 – 10.♘xd7 ♘xd7 11.♘c3 c5 12.d5 ♘f6 13.e4 b4
After 13...♗e7 14.0-0 0-0 15.♖d1! is the most unpleasant set-up of White's rooks. The other one should attack the c5-pawn. 15...♖ad8 16.♗f4 exd5 17.♘xd5 ♘xd5 18.exd5 ♗f6 (Hoping to meet 19.♗e3 by 19...♗d4=. 18...♗d6 19.♗e3 b4 is ugly following 20.a4.) 19.♖ac1 c4 20.♗e3 ♕d6 21.♗d2 ♖fe8 22.♗a5 ♖c8 23.♕d2±.

14.♘a4!

Scherbakov considers only 14.♕a4+ ♘d7=.

14...♕a6 15.♘xc5 ♖c8 16.♕a4+ ♕xa4 17.♘xa4 ♗e7. Black will even the material, but his queenside pawns remain vulnerable – 18.0-0 exd5 19.exd5 ♗xd5 20.♗e3 h5 21.♖fe1 ♖c7 22.♖ec1 ♖xc1+ 23.♖xc1 0-0 24.b3±.

10.dxe5 ♘d5 11.♘c3 ♗e7 12.0-0 0-0 13.♖d1 ♕b8!

Play is balanced, e.g. 14.♘xd5 cxd5 15.e4 ♖c8 16.♕e2 dxe4 17.♗xe4 ♖c4=.

Delorme-Hammer, Helsingor 2017, saw 14.f4 a5!? (to ensure ...♖a6 or ...♗a6) 15.♘xd5 (15.e4?! ♘xc3) 15... cxd5 16.♗e3 ♖c8 17.♕d2 ♖c4 (17... ♖a6!? 18.♖dc1 b4) 18.♖ac1 ♗b4 19.♕d3 ♕c7= 20.b3

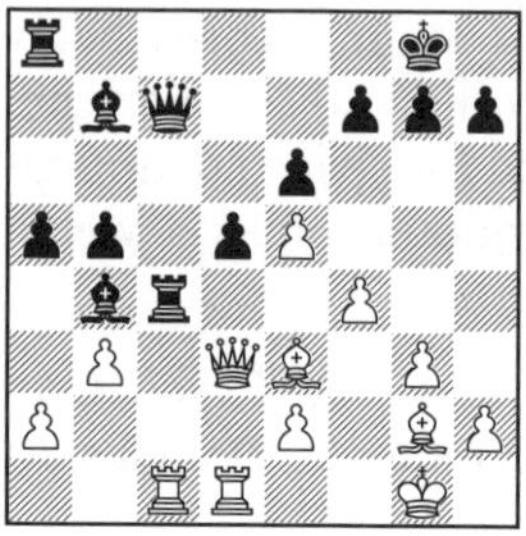

20...♖c3! 21.♖xc3 ♗xc3 22.♕xb5 ♗a6 23.♕b6 ♕xb6 24.♗xb6 ♗xe2 25.♖c1 ♖c8 26.♗e3 ♗a6 27.♗f1 ♗b7 28.♗d3 f6=.

Chapter 6. 4.♕c2

Annotated Games

22. Bacrot – Kasimdzhanov
rapid, Mainz 18.08.2007

1.d4 d5 2.c4 c6 3.♘c3 ♘f6 4.♘f3 e6 5.♗g5 h6 6.♗xf6 ♕xf6 7.e3 ♘d7 8.♕c2 g6 9.cxd5 exd5 10.♗d3 ♗g7

In the Carlsbad pawn structure after ♗g5xf6 ♗e7xf6 Black commonly tries to shift his bishop to d6. In our case the weakness of f6 casts a doubt on 10...♗d6 in view of 11.0-0 0-0 12.e4 dxe4 13.♘xe4±.

11.b4 0-0 12.0-0 ♕d6!

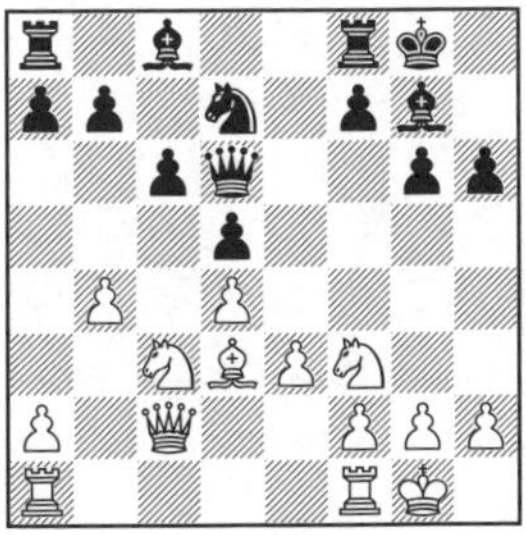

Black clearly shows his intention to meet the thematic 13.b5 by 13... c5, e.g. 14.dxc5 ♘xc5 15.♖ad1 ♗e6=. That puts under question the whole White's strategy. Indeed, I do not understand well what constructive plan he has from here. Of course he has no weaknesses, so he should be okay, but what sensible set-up to recommend for him?! Since he should be seeking some play on the queenside, he might put his king's rook on b1. However, after further a2-a4-a5 Black could answer ...a6, as Kasimdzhanov did in the commented game. Then White will clearly need his rook back on the kingside.

The majority of players prefer 13.♖ab1. That begs for the question what is White going to do against the standard set-up 13...♘b6, followed by ...♗e6 or even 13...a6 14.a4 ♖e8 15.h3 ♘f8 16.b5 axb5 17.axb5 c5 as in Ruck-Cheparinov, Dresden 2007? Basically, nothing:

Roiz-Karjakin, Sochi 2007: 13... ♘b6 14.♘d2 ♗e6 15.♘e2 ♖fc8 16.♖fc1 ♘d7 17.♘b3 b6 18.♘f4 ♖c7 19.♘xe6 ♕xe6 20.♗b5 ♖ac8 21.♗a6 ♖d8 22.♗e2 ♖dc8 23.♗a6 ♖d8 24.♗e2=;

Harikrishna-Dreev, Dos Hermanas 2005: 13...♘b6 14.♘d2 ♗e6 15.♘e2 ♖fc8 16.♖fc1 ♖c7 17.♘f4 ♗d7 18.♕c5 ♗f8 19.♕xd6 ♗xd6 and Black is even slightly better.

White has yet another problem after 13.♖ab1. Black can try to actively exploit the absence of the rook from the a-file with the stab 13...

a5!? 14.bxa5 (14.a3 axb4 15.axb4 ♖a3 16.♕c1 ♖a8= or 15...♘b6) 14... ♖xa5 15.a4

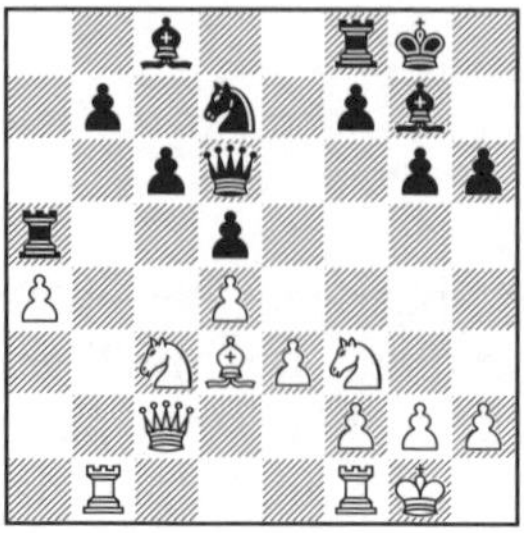

15...♖e8 16.h3 ♘f8=, Kamsky-Aronian, Sochi 2008.

Now we can better understand Bacrot's next move. He revives the positional threat b5 as c5 would be impossible:

13.♕b3 ♘b6! 14.a4 (threatening a5 and b5) **14...♗e6**

That's all! Black has neutralised b4-b5 and White is left without a plan. The first player should now design a solid set-up, which would allow him to maintain the balance. That is an easy task for the engines, but not for protein players. My database shows that White has scored only 1.5 points out of 6!

15.♘d2 ♘d7 16.a5

This is a purely defensive move. I.Sokolov-Dreev, Hastings 2000, saw instead 16.♖ab1 a5! 17.bxa5 ♖xa5 18.♕c2 b6 with an initiative.

16...♖fe8

Black does not need to equalise with 16...b6 17.♖fb1 c5.

17.♖fc1 a6 18.♘a4 ♖ad8

Perhaps 18...♖e7 was slightly more accurate – to enable 19.♘c5 ♘f8.

19.♕c3

I do not know why Bacrot rejected 19.♘c5.

Was he afraid of 19...♘xc5 20.bxc5 ♕c7, which is fairly drawish?! I would answer:

19...♕b8 20.♘f3 ♘f8, preserving some chances for an attack.

19...♘f8 20.♗c2?!

An introduction to a wrong set-up.

20...♖e7

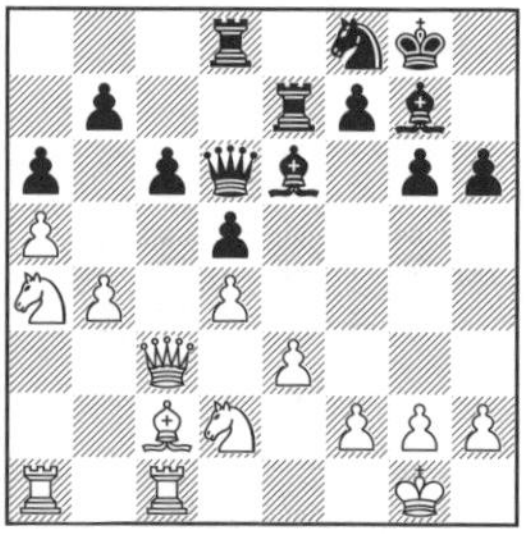

21.f4?

A horrible idea. Perhaps White hoped to put a knight on e5, but first of all, this does not work, and second, Black could repel it with ...f6. Something like 21.♖f1 ♖de8 22.♖ae1 ♗c8 23.♘b6 was still balanced.

21...♖de8 22.♖e1 g5

Black misses the killing 22...♗g4!! with the idea 23.h3 ♘e6! 24.hxg4 ♘xd4 25.♕d3 ♘xc2 26.♕xc2 ♗xa1–+. Alternatives do not save White from trouble:
23.♔h1 g5 24.f5 ♕f6 25.♕d3 ♕xd4; 23.♘c5 ♘e6 24.♘xe6 ♕xe6 25.h3 ♗f5 26.♘f3 ♗xc2 27.♕xc2 ♕d6 with positional pressure.

23.f5 ♗c8 24.♘f1?!

Again, White opts for a passive stand. He should have preserved the option of e3-e4. For instance: 24.♖e2 g4 25.♖f1 h5 26.♘c5 ♘h7 27.♔h1 ♕f6 28.♕d3, hoping for 28...♗h6?! 29.e4=.

24...♘h7 25.♘c5 h5 26.♕d2 g4 27.♕f2 ♕h6 28.♖ad1 h4

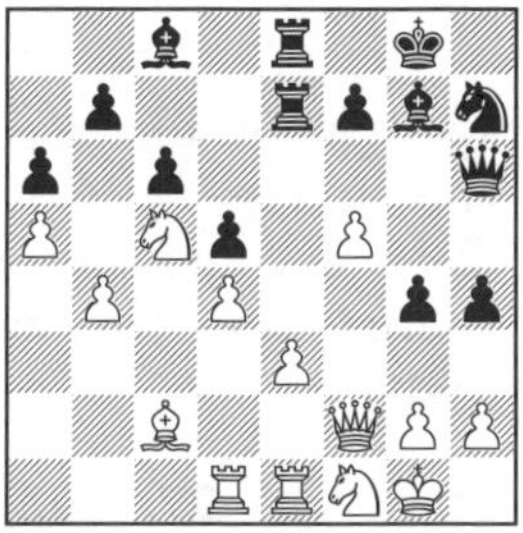

29.e4!?

Things were already bad enough, so this is a good practical attempt. If White waited any longer, he would not be able to prevent ...g3, e.g. 29.♖d2 ♘f6 30.♖de2 ♔h8 31.♗d3 ♕g5 32.♗c2 ♗h6 33.♗d3 g3 34.hxg3 hxg3 35.♕f3 ♖g8 36.e4 ♕h4.

29...dxe4 30.♘e3!?

30.♘xe4 opens the file and Black will trade queens at some point to reach a winning endgame. The queenside pawns on dark squares would be an easy prey for the black bishop – 30...♗d7 31.♖e3 ♘f6 32.♘xf6+ ♗xf6 33.♖xe7 ♖xe7 34.♘d2 (or Black will transfer his queen to d6) 34...♕e3.

30...♘f6 31.d5 cxd5 32.♘xd5 ♘xd5 33.♖xd5

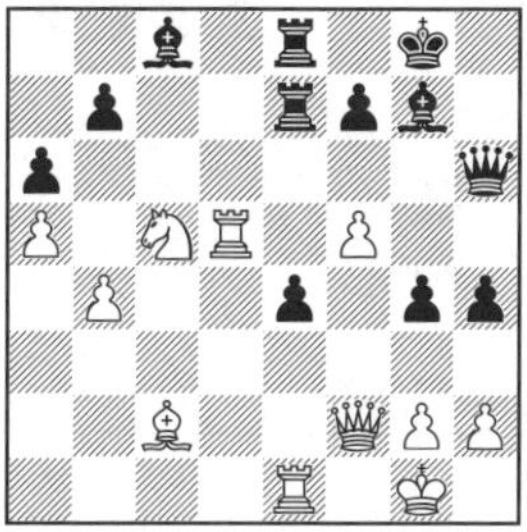

33...g3?!

The correct move order was 33...e3! 34.♕e2 g3.
After the text White misses to complicate things with 34.hxg3 e3 35.♕f4! hxg3 36.♕xg3 e2 37.♗d3. Black is still better following 37...♔f8!, but White could also err with

37...♖e3? 38.♕g4 ♔f8 39.♖xe2 ♗e5 40.♘e6+! fxe6 41.♖xe5 ♖xd3 42.♖f2 with sufficient compensation for the piece.

After 33...g3? the game is over.

34.♕e2? 34...♖e5 35.♖xe5 ♗xe5 (35...♖xe5!) **36.♕g4+ ♔f8 37.♖f1 e3 38.♔h1 gxh2 39.♗d3 ♗g3 40.♗c4 ♕g7 41.♕h5 ♖e5 42.♗xf7 e2 0-1**

23. Caruana – Aronian
Saint Louis 19.08.2018

1.d4 d5 2.c4 c6 3.♘f3 ♘f6 4.♕b3 e6 5.g3 dxc4 6.♕xc4 b5 7.♕b3 ♗b7 8.♗g2 a6 9.a4 c5 10.axb5 c4 11.♕d1 axb5 12.♖xa8 ♗xa8 13.0-0 ♗e7 14.b3 cxb3 15.♕xb3 b4

Sometimes White could be slightly better in this pawn structure, but only if he is able to push e4 and mount a kingside attack. For that aim his light-squared bishop should be on the b1-h7 diagonal. In our case play is balanced, and every exchange enhances the role of Black's passed pawn.

16.♗b2 ♘bd7 17.♘bd2 0-0 18.♖a1 ♕b8 19.♘e1

Fressinet chose another set-up for his knights – 19.♘c4 ♖c8 20.♘fd2 ♗xg2 21.♔xg2 ♘b6 22.♘e5 ♕b7+ 23.♔g1 ♘bd5 24.♘dc4 h6 25.♕d3. Now Black had to seek more exchanges – 25...♘d7! 26.♘xd7 ♕xd7 27.e4 ♕b5 with an initiative.

19...♗xg2 20.♔xg2 ♖c8 21.e4 h5

Aronian is true to his aggressive style, but perhaps 21...♕b7 22.f3 g5!? 23.♕d3 g4 24.fxg4 ♘xg4 had more chances to complicate things. For instance, 25.♕e2 could be answered by 25...f5. White should probably trade queens with 25.♕a6 ♕xa6 26.♖xa6 ♗g5=.

22.♘d3 h4 23.♖c1 ♖xc1 24.♘xc1 ♕b5

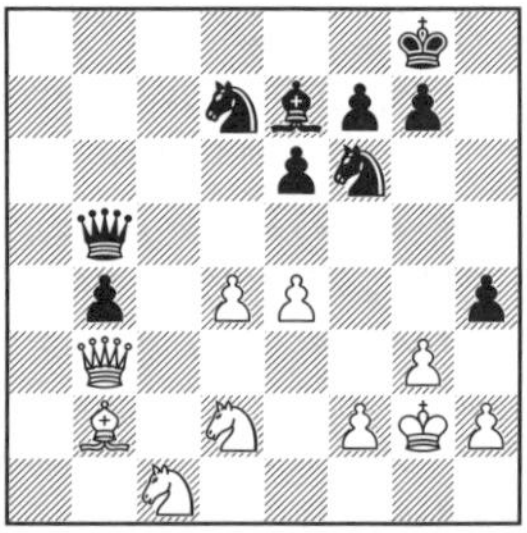

25.♕d3 ♕xd3

This move practically accepts a draw. The useless bishop at b2 should have encouraged Aronian to keep more tension with 25...♕c6 26.♘cb3 ♘b6.

26.♘xd3 hxg3 27.hxg3 ♘b6 28.♔f3 ♘fd7 29.♘b3 ♘c4 30.♗c1 e5 31.dxe5 ♘cxe5+ 32.♘xe5 ♘xe5+ 33.♔e2 ♔f8 34.f4 ♘g4 35.♔f3 ♘h2+ 36.♔g2 ♘g4 37.♔f3 ♘h2+ 38.♔g2 ♘g4 ½-½

24. Hess – Wojtaszek
Douglas 2018

1.c4 ♘f6 2.g3 c6 3.♘f3 d5 4.♕b3 dxc4 5.♕xc4 b5 6.♕c2 ♗b7 7.♗g2

♘bd7 8.d4 e6 9.0-0 c5 10.dxc5 ♗xc5

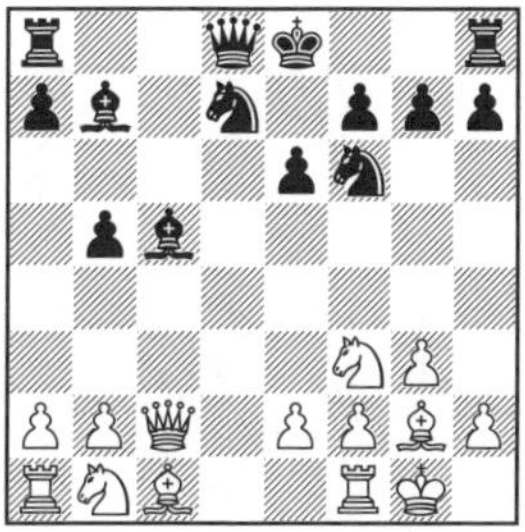

11.♘c3

11.♗g5 hands Black the initiative after 11...♖c8.

11.♕d3 a6 12.♗e3 looks logical – in principle White should try to weaken Black's dark squares on the queenside. That should be enough to keep the balance, although Black would have some initiative following 12...0-0 13.♖c1 ♕b6 14.♗xc5 ♘xc5 15.♕e3 ♖ac8 16.♘bd2 ♘d5. Play is similar to the main game.

11...♖c8 12.a3 0-0 13.♕d3

Fridman chose to secure his queen on e2 with 13.♗g5 h6 14.♗xf6 ♘xf6 15.e3 ♕b6 16.♕e2 and made a draw, although Black's pieces are obviously more active.

13...a6 14.♗e3 ♘b6

This allows White to trade too many pieces. 14...♕b6 15.♗xc5 ♖xc5, keeping the queens, was more testing.

15.♕xd8 ♖fxd8 16.♗xc5 ♖xc5 17.♖fd1 ♖dc8

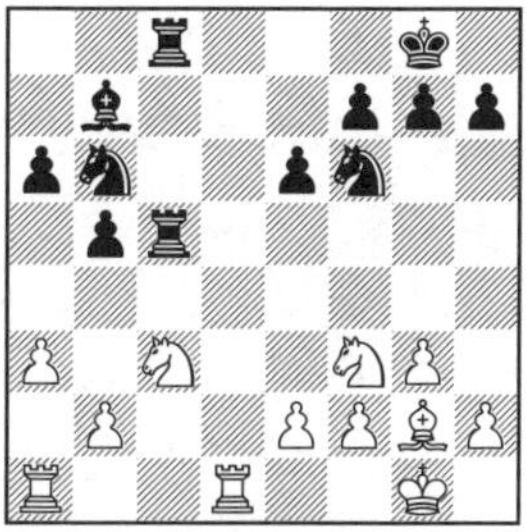

18.♘d2?!

18.♘e1! ♗xg2 19.♔xg2 ♘c4 20.♘d3 ♖5c7, Lenderman-Bhat, Saint Louis 2010, 21.♖ab1 was drawish.

18...♗xg2 19.♔xg2 ♖5c6 20.a4

Tight defence with 20.♖ab1 should hold, too. The text is good, but only in connection with 22.♘c1!.

20...b4 21.♘a2 a5 22.♘b3

22.♘c1! would have solved White's problems. The idea is 22...♘xa4 23.♖xa4 ♖xc1 24.♖xc1 ♖xc1 25.♘b3 ♖c2 26.♘xa5=. Hess' move leaves the a2-knight unemployed.

22...♘c4 23.♖ac1 e5

23...♘d5!, planning to check from e3, was more dangerous for White. The rooks are commonly very strong against passive knights.

24.♖b1

Another passive move. 24.♔g1 ♔f8 25.♖c2 was more resilient.

24...♔f8 25.♘ac1 ♔e7 26.♘d3 ♘d7

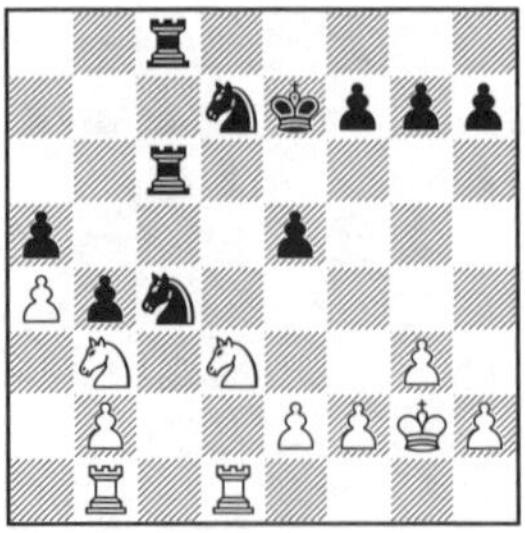

27.♘d2?

The decisive mistake. Both White's knights were essential for the defence. Now Black invades via the c-file.

27.g4 ♘db6 28.♖a1∓ kept the material balance in view of 28...e4 29.♘f4 ♘xb2 (29...♖d6!∓) 30.♘xa5.

27...♘xd2 28.♖xd2 f6 29.b3 ♖c3 30.♔f1 ♘f8 31.e3 ♘e6 32.h4 g5 33.hxg5 ♘xg5 34.♘e1 ♘e4 35.♖db2

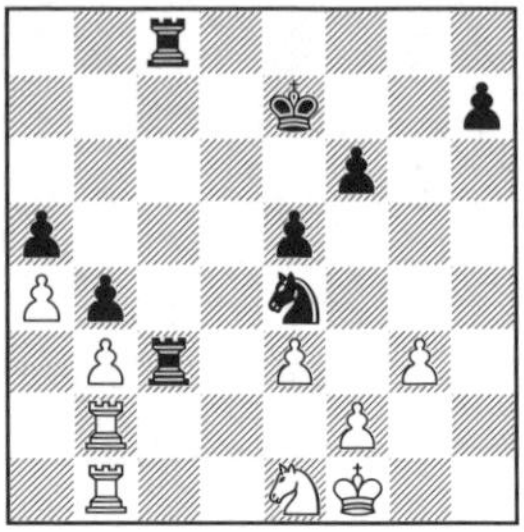

35...♖c1 36.♔g2 ♖xb1 37.♖xb1 ♖c3 38.♖d1 ♘c5 39.♖d5 ♔e6 40.e4 f5 41.f4 exf4 42.♖xf5 ♖xg3+ 43.♔h2 ♖c3 44.♘g2 ♘xe4 45.♖xa5 f3 46.♘f4+ ♔d6 47.♖d5+ ♔c6 48.♖f5 ♖xb3 49.a5 ♖b2+ 50.♔h3 f2 51.♘d3 ♖b3 0-1

Main Ideas

1.d4 d5 2.c4 e6 3.♘f3 c6 4.♕b3 ♘f6

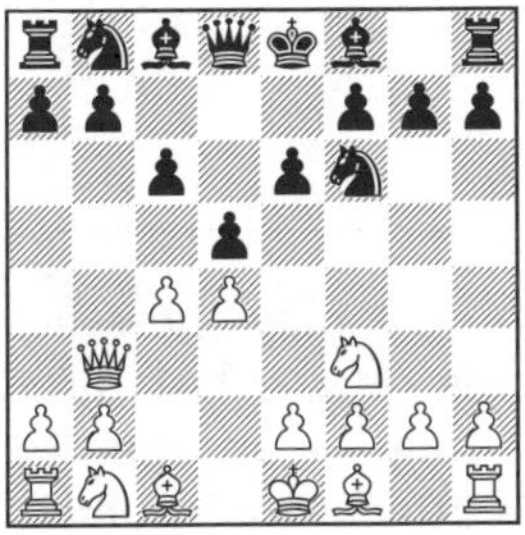

This line transposes to the previous chapter after 5.g3 dxc4.

The character of play in the other lines is very different because the c4-pawn is defended after ♘c3. Thus **5.♘c3** is not a sacrifice, compared to 4.♕c2 – **5...dxc4 6.♕xc4 b5**, and White faces an important choice.

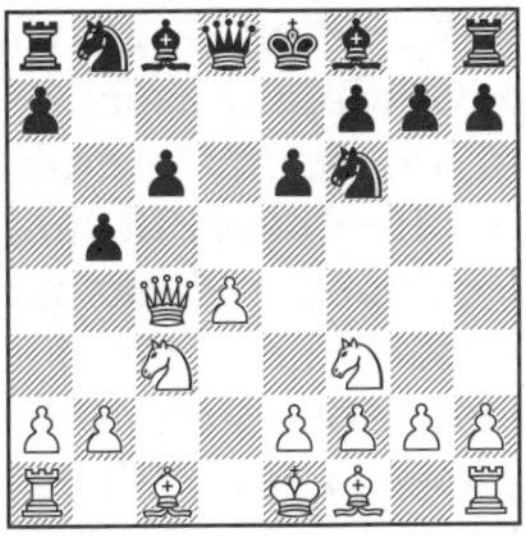

If he wants to build a perfect pawn centre with e4, he should retreat to d3:

7.♕d3 a6 8.e4 c5 9.e5 c4! with entertaining double-edged play. You should also remember the following position: 8.♗g5 c5 9.♗xf6 gxf6! 10.d5

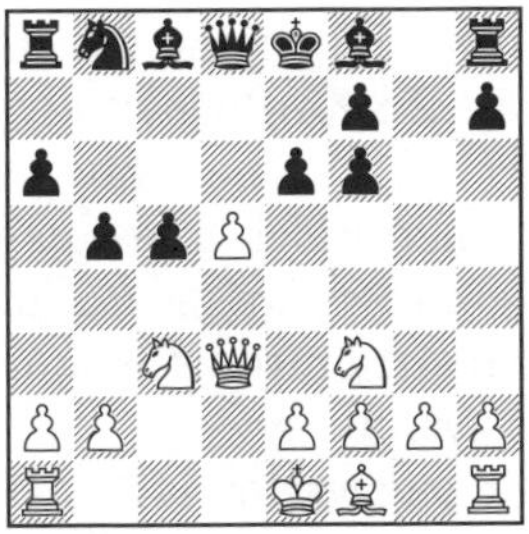

10...♗b7! with a strong bishop pair.

7.♕b3 does not threaten e4, so we can delay ...c5. If White fianchettoes his bishop, we use the a6-square to activate our bishop:

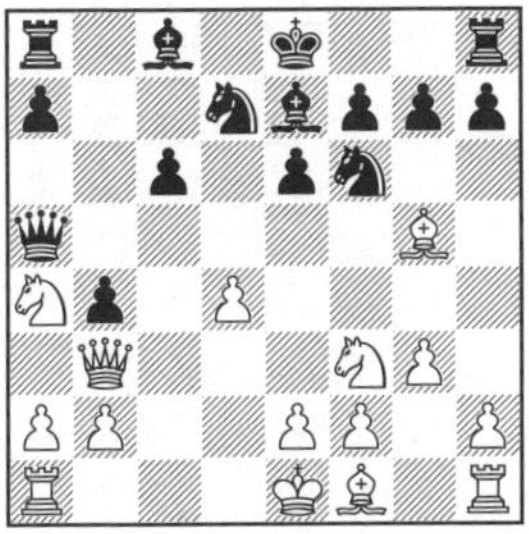

11.♖c1 0-0!, intending ...♗a6-b5.
In the event of e3, we return to the plan with ...a6 and ...c5.

5.♗g5 h6 6.♗xf6 ♕xf6 7.♘c3 is the Moscow Variation.

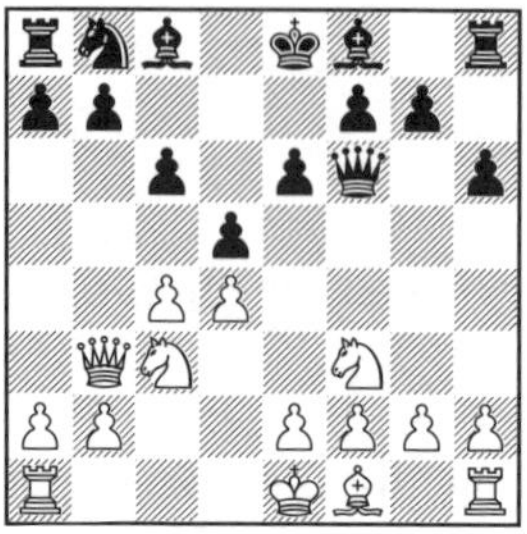

We cannot follow the receipt from the previous chapter since 7...♘d7 8.e4 leads to independent play. It is not bad for Black and I consider it in **Game 26** Kardashevskiy-Kezin, Moscow 2019. The only problem is that when Black frees his bishop with ...e5, there arises a symmetrical pawn structure with some initiative for White.
My main suggestion is **7...dxc4** (to drag the queen to c4) **8.♕xc4 ♘d7**. At least White has an ample choice here, therefore – more chances to mess things up. For instance, 9.0-0-0 a5 might turn into a race game, while the fianchetto 9.♖d1 g6 10.g3 ♗g7 11.♗g2 0-0 12.0-0

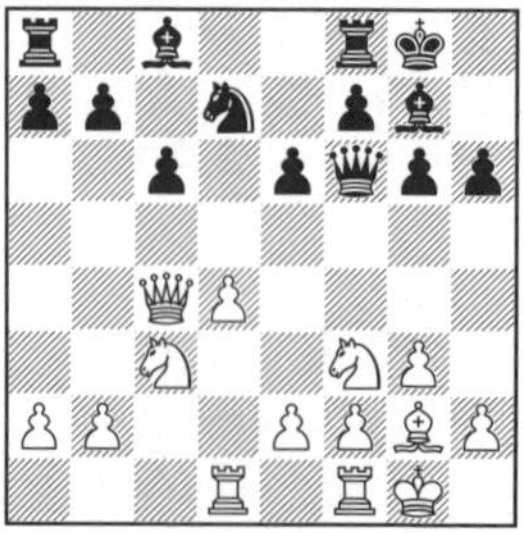

allows us to achieve the thematic break 12...e5 and pose concrete problems after 13.♘e4 ♕e7 14.d5 ♘b6!?.

The most solid set-up for White is 9.e3 g6 10.♗e2 ♗g7 11.0-0 0-0 12.♖fd1 ♕e7 13.♘e4

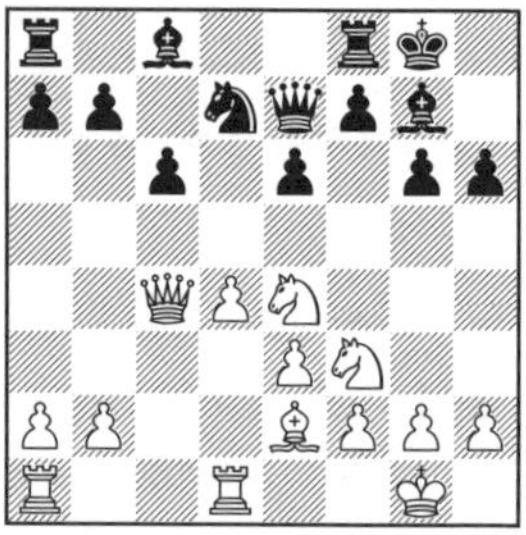

You can just play chess here, manoeuvring on the last three ranks and waiting for an opportunity to counter-attack. For instance, ...♖d8, ...♘b6-d5, ...b6, ...♗b7, with ...b5-b4 and ...c5 in mind.
The easiest solution is to push ...e5 – 13...♖d8 14.♕c2 e5!? 15.d5 cxd5 16.♖xd5 ♘b6=.

Theoretical status

I met only a partial coverage of this line. Krasenkow does not analyse it at all, and Scherbakov omits the Moscow Variation. Even when we overlap with him, I usually suggest different plans. My overall opinion is that the theory of this line is underdeveloped and has plenty of blank spots. The wide choice for both sides leaves ground for creativity. Nevertheless, White scores more than 60% in practice, so have a careful look at my propositions.

Chapter 7. 4.♕b3

Step by Step

1.d4 d5 2.c4 e6 3.♘f3 c6 4.♕b3 ♘f6

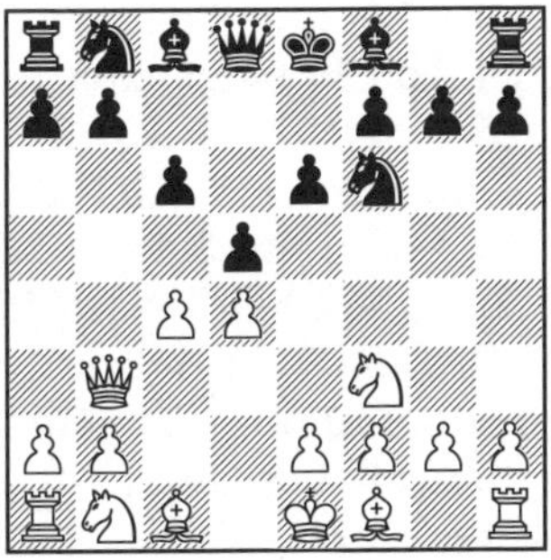

A. 5.♘c3; **B.** 5.♗g5

5.g3 dxc4 was covered in the previous chapter.

5.♗f4 does not change our plan – 5...dxc4 6.♕xc4 b5 7.♕c2 ♗b7 8.♘bd2 ♘bd7 9.e3 ♖c8. The idea is to push ...c5 after due preparation. A good set-up is:
10.a4

Or 10.♕b3 (to hinder ...♗b4) 10...a6 11.a4 ♗e7 12.♗e2 0-0 13.0-0 ♘b6 14.axb5 cxb5.

10...a6 11.♗e2

11...♘b6!? 12.b3 ♗b4 13.0-0 0-0 14.♗e5 ♕e7 15.♕b2 ♘fd7 16.♗g3

If 16.♖fc1 ♘xe5 17.♘xe5, we still play 17...c5 18.axb5 axb5 19.♗xb5 cxd4, when the queen is ready to leap to g5.

16...bxa4 17.bxa4 a5 with ...c5 coming.

A. 5.♘c3 dxc4

It is possible to keep control of the centre with 5...♘d7, but our repertoire is built around the concept of capturing on c4. Practical results confirm the soundness of this approach.

6.♕xc4 b5 7.♕d3

7.♕b3 is also seen. We answer 7...♘bd7.

Note the difference – I recommend 7...a6 against 7.♕d3 in order to meet 8.e4 by 8...c5. 7.♕b3 does not protect e4, so 7...♘bd7 8.e4 is a pawn sac – 8...b4 9.♘a4 ♘xe4 10.♗c4 ♘ef6 11.0-0. Although White has some positional compensation, he lacks imminent threats.

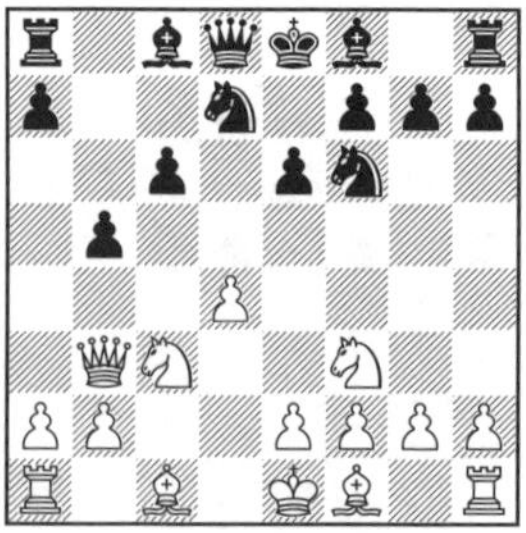

8.♗g5

Alternatively: 8.g3 ♗b7 9.♗g2 a6 (nobody has tried 9...c5!? 10.♕xb5 ♗xf3=) 10.♘e5 ♕c8 11.0-0 c5 12.♘xd7 ♕xd7 13.♗xb7 ♕xb7 14.dxc5 ♗xc5 15.♗g5, Ivanchuk-Nihal, Leon 2019. Now simplest is 15...♘g4 or 15...♗e7=.

8.♗f4 a6 9.♖d1 does not stop 9...c5!.

8...♗e7

This move aims to preserve the a6-square for the bishop.

8...a6 is a decent alternative – 9.e3 (9.e4 c5 10.d5 c4 11.♕c2 ♕b6; 9.♖d1 c5; 9.g3 c5) 9...c5 10.♗e2 ♗b7 11.0-0 ♗e7 transposes to 8...♗e7.

9.e3

9.g3 allows Black to show the idea behind 8...♗e7 – 9...b4 (or 9...0-0 10.♗g2 b4 11.♘e5 ♘xe5 12.dxe5 ♘d7=) 10.♘a4 ♕a5

11.♖c1 (11.♗xf6 gxf6 12.♘d2 ♗a6 13.♖c1 0-0 14.♗g2 ♗b5; 11.♗g2 0-0 12.0-0 ♗a6 13.♖fe1 ♗b5) 11...0-0 (11...♗a6?! 12.♗xf6! gxf6 13.e4 ♗b5 14.♗xb5 cxb5 15.♘c5 ♘xc5 16.dxc5 ♖c8 17.0-0 0-0=) 12.♗xf6 (12.♖xc6 ♗b7 13.♗xf6 ♘xf6 14.♖c1 ♖ac8–+) 12...gxf6 13.♗g2 ♗a6 14.♘d2 ♖ac8 15.0-0 (15.♘c4 ♕c7 16.♕c2 c5) 15...♗xe2 16.♖fe1 ♗b5∓. The common motif in all those lines is the manoeuvre ...♗c8-a6-b5.

9...a6

After e3 it is already senseless to push ...b4, so we turn to the general plan with ...c5.

10.♖d1

Or 10.♗e2 c5.

10...♗b7 11.♗e2 c5. Black has excellent chances. He could maintain the tension in the centre or display an aggressive frame of mind with 12.0-0 c4.

7...a6

The alternative is 7...♘bd7. The difference between the two moves is the way we meet e4. In the main line we answer it with ...c5, while 7...♘bd7 assumes to follow up with ...b4. For instance:

8.a3!? a6 9.e4 b4 10.axb4 ♗xb4 11.♗e2 ♗b7 12.e5 ♘d5 13.0-0.

8.e4

8.♗g5 c5 9.♗xf6

Or 9.a4 cxd4 10.♘xd4 b4 (10...bxa4!?=) 11.♘e4 (11.♗xf6 gxf6!∓) 11...♗e7 12.♖d1 ♗b7 13.♗xf6 leads to tangled play after both 13...♗xf6 14.♕c4 ♗xe4 15.♘xe6 ♕a5 16.♘c7+ ♔f8 17.♘xa8 (17.♕xe4 ♕xc7 18.♕xa8 ♗c3+=) 17...b3+ 18.♖d2 ♗c6 19.♕xb3 ♘d7 and 13...gxf6 14.♕f3 b3!!∞, Lautier-Bareev, Linares 1994.

9...gxf6! is a challenging line. 10.d5 looks very strong,

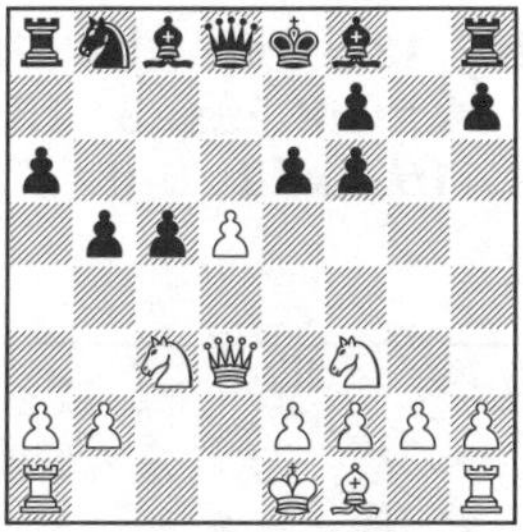

but 10...♗b7! puts White's activity to the question.

Aronian took on e6, when 11.dxe6 ♕xd3 12.exf7+ ♔xf7 13.exd3 ♗xf3 14.gxf3 ♘c6 is fine for Black, and 11...fxe6!? might be even stronger.

Grischuk gambled with 11.0-0-0 b4 12.♘a4, when 12...♗xd5! 13.e4 ♗h6+ 14.♔c2 b3+! 15.axb3 ♘c6 is winning. Remains:

11.e4 ♘d7 12.♖d1

White drew a correspondence game after 12.♗e2 ♕c7 13.0-0 0-0-0, when 14.♖ad1 transposed to 12.♖d1, while 14.a4? fails to 14...b4 15.♘d1 f5!.

12...♕c7! 13.♗e2 0-0-0 14.0-0

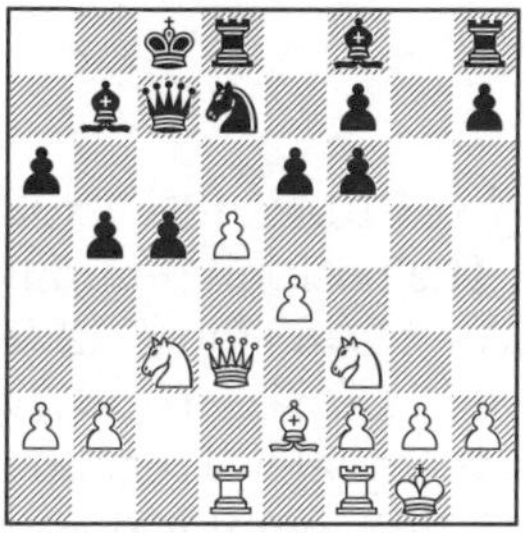

The game Le Quang Liem-Jumabayev, Zaozhuang 2012, finished with a miniature in White's favour after 14...♗d6? 15.dxe6 ♘b6 16.e5 fxe5 17.♘g5.

Correct was:

14...♔b8! (or 14...♖g8), when it is unclear how White could attack the black king:

15.a4 b4 16.dxe6

16.♘b1 f5! destroys the centre.

16...fxe6 17.♘b1 ♖g8 with a powerful attack, e.g. 18.♘bd2 f5! 19.exf5 ♗d6 20.fxe6 ♘b6−+.

8.g3 c5 9.♗g2 ♗b7 10.0-0 ♘bd7 may be equal, but Black's space advantage on the queenside could earn him an initiative in an endgame. See **Game 25** Bartel-Grachev, Moscow 2009.

8...c5

9.e5

9.dxc5 ♗xc5 10.♕xd8+ ♔xd8 is balanced. The position reminds me of the QGA – 11.♗d3 ♘bd7 12.0-0 ♗b7 13.e5 ♘d5 14.♘e4 ♔e7! 15.♗g5+

Ten years later Tregubov opted for 15.♗d2, but it is no improvement in view of 15...♗b4.

15...f6 16.exf6+ gxf6=, Tregubov-Gelfand, Sochi 2005.

9...c4!

9...cxd4 10.♘xd4 ♘d5 11.♕g3 looks more dangerous to me as White's pieces threaten our king – 11...♗b7 12.♗e2 ♘e7 13.♗e3 ♘bc6 14.♘e4 ♘g6 15.♘d6+ ♗xd6 16.exd6 ♘xd4 17.♗xd4 0-0 18.0-0.

10.♕b1

The reason behind this move is to target indirectly the b5-pawn. Nabaty-Umanec, Pardubice 2012, saw instead 10.♕c2 ♘d5 11.a4 ♗b7 12.axb5 ♘xc3 13.bxc3 axb5 14.♖xa8 ♗xa8. Black's queenside pawns plus the d5-square promise excellent chances.

15.♗e2 ♗e7 16.0-0 0-0 17.♘d2 ♗d5 18.f4 g6 19.♘e4 ♘c6 20.♗e3. Black has played well so far and 20...b4! 21.cxb4 ♘xb4 22.♕b1 ♕a8–+ would have been decisive.

10...♘d5 11.a4

It is difficult to mount an attack on the other flank since Black has not committed his king yet – 11.♗e2 ♘c6 12.0-0 ♗b7 13.♖d1 ♖c8 14.♗d2 ♗e7 15.h4 ♘a5 16.♘e4 h6. White lacks a target.

11...♗b7 12.axb5 ♗b4 13.♗d2 axb5 14.♖xa8 ♗xa8 15.♘xb5 ♗xd2+ 16.♘xd2 0-0 17.♘xc4 ♘c6

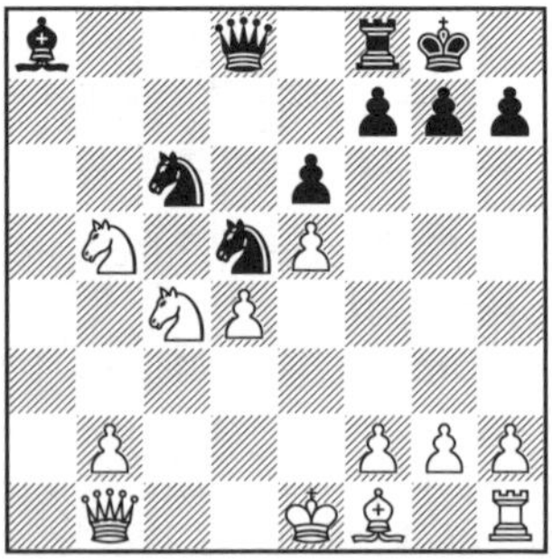

Black will open the f-file and his attack will become menacing. White must make only moves to hold on. The game Morrow-Tashkov, ICCF 2019, went on 18.♕d1 f6 19.exf6 ♕xf6⩲.

B. 5.♗g5 h6 6.♗xf6

6.♗h4 dxc4 is line A of the previous chapter.

6...♕xf6

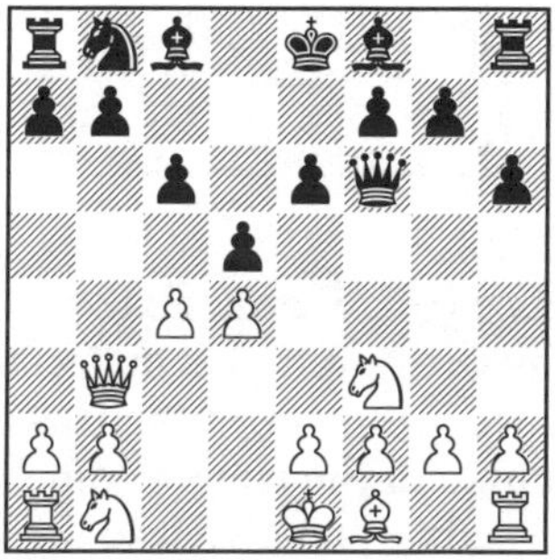

7.♘c3

This move steers the game into the Moscow Variation. Minor alternatives are:

After 7.♘bd2 ♘d7 8.e3 g6 9.♗d3 ♗g7 10.0-0 0-0 11.♖ac1 we have to find several waiting moves. White's only constructive plan is to push e4 at some moment, so we could anticipate it with 11...♕d8.

The idea is to counter 12.e4 with 12...dxe4 13.♘xe4 c5.

Another waiting move is 11...♖d8, intending to repel the queen with ...a5-a4 and open the centre with ...e5 or ...dxc4+...c5.

12.♖fe1 ♕b6 13.♕c3 ♖d8 14.h3 a5.

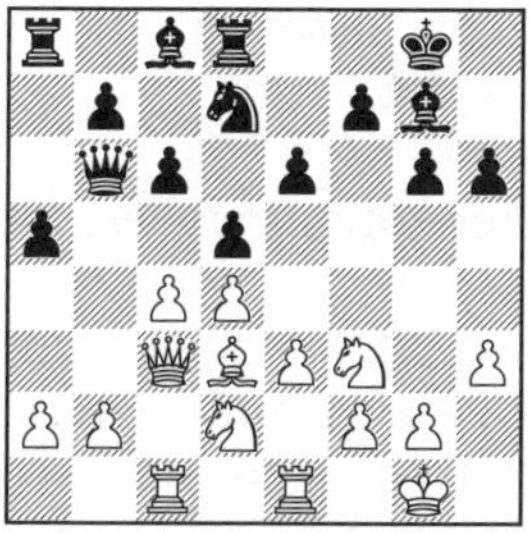

White cannot proceed with 15.e4? as 15...dxe4 16.♘xe4 c5 would be clearly worse for him.

7.g3 ♘bd7 8.♗g2 has never been seen.

Then the thematic plan 8...g6 9.♘bd2 ♗g7 10.0-0 0-0 11.e4 dxc4?! 12.♘xc4 c5 (The pawn sac 12...e5 13.♘fxe5 ♘xe5 14.dxe5 ♕e7 15.f4 is insufficient.) 13.e5 ♕e7 is bad because the fianchettoed bishop is very strong. We should apply direct pressure on the centre:

8...g5! 9.e3 dxc4 10.♕xc4 g4 11.♘h4 e5 12.0-0 exd4 13.exd4 ♘b6 14.♕e2+ ♗e6=.

7...dxc4

The main move has been 7...♘d7 8.e4 dxe4 9.♘xe4, when Black can choose between 9...♕f5!? and 9...♕f4. Both should lead to a symmetrical pawn structure with a strong drawish tendency. See **Game 26** Kardashevskiy-Kezin, Moscow 2019 for details.

The text is more complex strategically – for better or worse.

8.♕xc4 ♘d7

Now I'll pay more attention to:
B1. 9.e3; **B2.** 9.♖d1

The other options are less frequent:

9.0-0-0 is White's best scoring move. This is a logical and aggressive set-up, but the queenside is certainly not the safest haven for the white king. We can underline it with:

9...a5 10.e3 a4

This pawn sacrifice looks tempting, but it can lead to a repetition of moves.

Preparing ...a5 with 10...♕d8!? might be the best way of playing for a win. A model variation is 11.♔b1 (11.g4 ♗e7 12.♖g1 a4 13.a3 ♖b8 14.♕xa4 b5 15.♕c2 b4 16.axb4 ♖xb4≌) 11...♗e7 12.♘e4 a4 13.♕c2 a3 14.b3

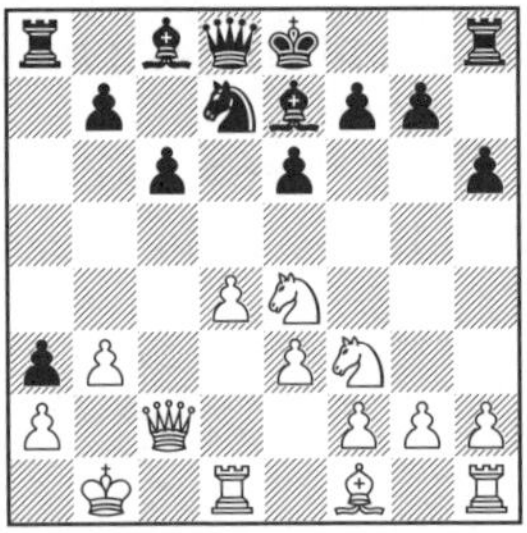

Now we have to develop the bishop – 14...♕c7 15.g4 b6 16.♘e5 ♗b7 (16...♘xe5 17.dxe5 ♕xe5 led to a drawish rook endgame after 18.♕xc6+ ♔f8 19.♖d2 ♕b8 20.♘d6 ♗xd6 21.♕xd6+ ♕xd6 22.♖xd6 ♗b7=, Tauber-Novák, ICCF 2016.) 17.f4 ♘xe5 18.dxe5 0-0 19.♗g2 ♖ad8. We trade both rooks to weaken the enemy first rank, and there is still a lot of play ahead.

11.♘xa4 g6 12.♘c3 ♗g7 13.h4

I'm following the game Ivanisevic-Aronian, Dresden 2008. Unfortunately, I do not see how to evade the draw after 13.♕b4 ♗f8 14.♕b3 ♗g7.

13...0-0 14.h5 g5≌ 15.♗d3

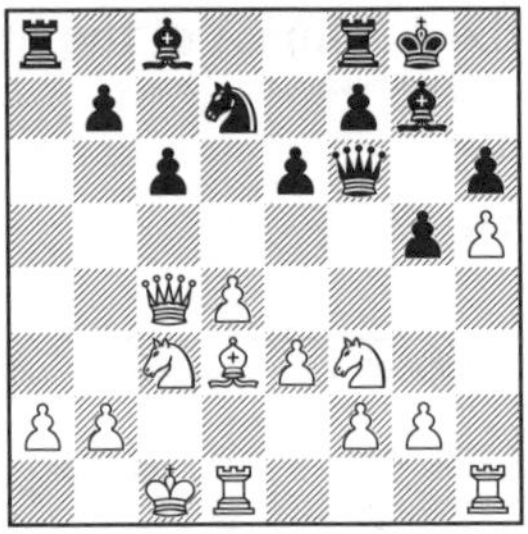

15...♘b6

15...g4!? 16.♘h2 ♕xf2∞ would have restored the material balance with fair chances. The course of the source game is instructive, so I give it to the end:

16.♕b3 ♘d5 17.♗b1 (17.♔b1) 17...♖d8 18.♘e5 c5 19.♕c2 cxd4 20.♕h7+ ♔f8 21.♘g4 ♕e7 22.♘xd5 (22.♖xd4) 22...exd5 23.♘xh6 ♕f6 24.♘g8 ♕c6+ 25.♗c2 ♖xa2 26.h6 ♗e5 27.exd4 ♖a1+ 28.♔d2 ♗f4+ 29.♔e1 ♖e8+ 30.♔f1 ♖xd1+ 0-1

9.e4 e5 10.d5 ♘b6 11.♕b3 ♗c5 12.♗e2 0-0 13.0-0 cannot be of any concern to Black. He can fight for an advantage with 13...♖d8 or 13...cxd5, while 13...♗g4 is "only" equal.

9.g3 e5 gives Black an easy game.

9...♕e7 10.♗g2 ♕b4 is solid, but I do not see a reason to spend two tempi just to swap the queens.

10.0-0-0 ♗e7 11.♘e4 ♕f5 12.♕c2 0-0. Black can continue with ...♖d8 or to transfer the queen to a5 after ...cxd4.

B1. 9.e3 g6

Dreev recommends 9...♕e7 10.♗e2 ♕b4, trading queens. Of course Black has no weaknesses, so this approach is perfectly viable – if you like to defend a somewhat cramped position.

10.♗e2

10.♘e4 ♕e7 11.♘e5 ♕b4+ 12.♕xb4 ♗xb4+ 13.♔e2 ♗e7=, Aronian-Giri, rapid, Zuerich 2016.

10...♗g7 11.0-0 0-0 12.♖fd1 ♕e7 13.♘e4

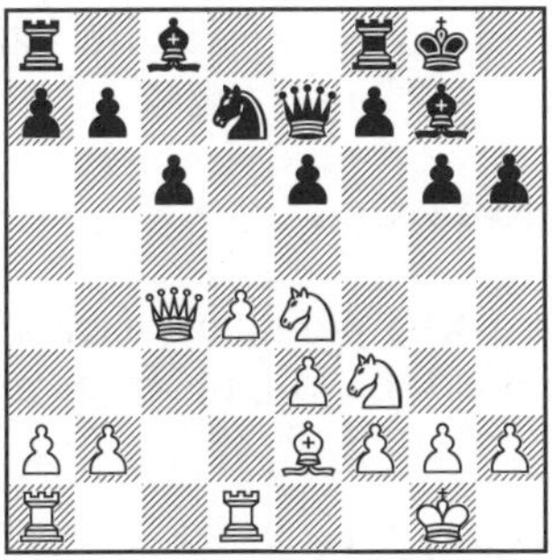

Black must choose a plan here.

Cheparinov opted for 13...♖d8 14.♕c2 f5 15.♘c3 e5 16.d5 e4 17.♘d4, when 17...♘e5 would have been roughly equal. The problem with his move order is that White could go to c5 – 15.♘c5! ♘xc5 16.dxc5 with an edge. So he should prefer the immediate:

13...f5

Now 14.♘c5!? is still possible, although less strong – after 14...♘xc5 15.dxc5 ♔h7 16.e4 ♗xb2 17.♖ab1 ♗a3 18.♖d6 fxe4 19.♕c3! exf3 20.♗xf3 e5 White's initiative just compensates the missing pawn. The other option is also unclear:

14.♘c3 ♔h8 15.♖ac1 e5 16.d5 e4 17.♘d4 ♘e5 18.♕b3 ♖d8

Black is holding following 19.dxc6 bxc6 20.♘a4 ♗d7 21.♕b7 (21.♘c5 ♗e8 22.♘ce6 ♗f7) 21...♖db8 22.♕c7 ♖c8 23.♕b7 ♖cb8=, but as a whole, I do not like Black's set-up. It provides the white knights with stable places in the centre.

Perhaps it is more prudent to refrain from ...f5, at least temporary:

13...♖d8 14.♕c2 e5!? 15.d5 cxd5 16.♖xd5

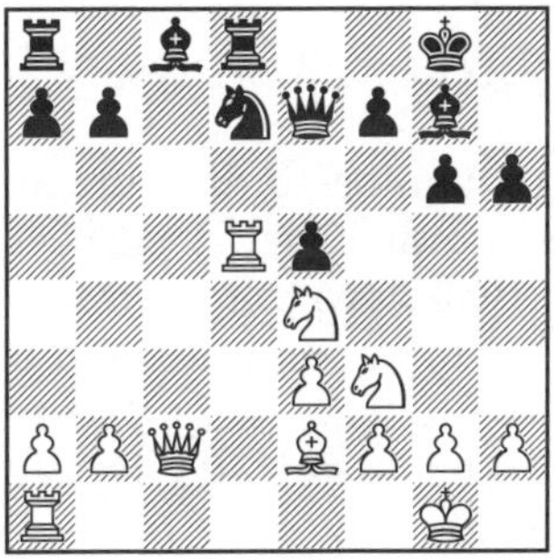

16...♘b6

This is cleaner than 16...f5 17.♘c5 ♘xc5 18.♖xd8+ ♕xd8 19.♕xc5 ♗e6 20.♗c4 ♗xc4 21.♕xc4+ ♔h7 22.♕f7, although 22...♖c8 should be enough for a draw.
16...♘f6 also deserves attention

17.♖xd8+ ♕xd8 18.♖d1 ♕e7 19.♕c5 ♕xc5 20.♘xc5 ♗f8 21.♖c1 f6

Two correspondence games from 2017 ended in a draw from here. For instance, Löfler-Just saw 22.♗d3 g5 23.h3 ♗xc5 24.♖xc5 ♗e6=.

B2. 9.♖d1 g6 10.g3

10.e4 e5 11.d5 ♘b6 12.♕b3 ♗c5 13.♗e2 0-0 14.0-0 ♗g4 assures Black of a comfortable equality thanks to his active dark-squared bishop. Moiseenko-Eljanov, Lvov 2014, went:
15.dxc6
After 15.♘d2 ♗xe2 16.♘xe2 ♖fd8 17.dxc6 Black could already recapture on c6 by queen.
15...bxc6 16.h3 ♗xf3 17.♗xf3 h5 18.♘e2 ♖fd8=.

10...♗g7 11.♗g2

11.♗h3, aiming to discourage ...e5, looks too artificial. I suspect that White will have to return the bishop later to its natural stand on g2. 11...0-0 12.♖d2 ♕e7 13.0-0 ♖b8 14.♕b3 b5 15.♖c1 ♖d8 16.♗g2 ♗b7 17.♘e4 f5.

11...0-0

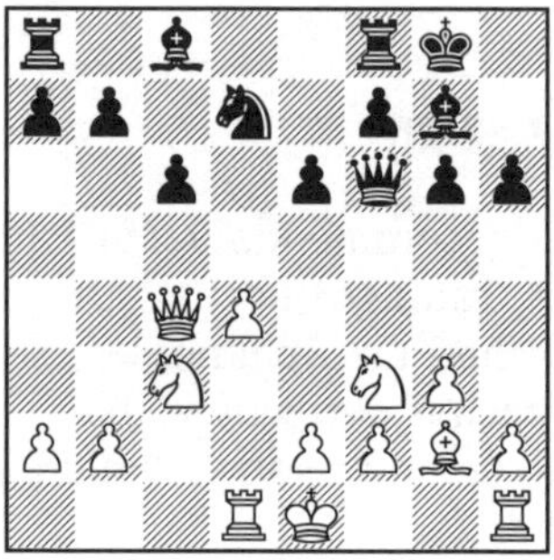

12.0-0

Ivanchuk beat Navara with 12.♕b3, but it was not the opening's fault at all. The idea is to meet 12...e5 by 13.d5. Although this break is still possible, 12...♕e7, followed up by ...b6 is more interesting. See **Game 27**. It shows an alternative plan to ...e5, which is possible in various lines.

12...e5 13.♘e4

The weakest points of Black are d6 and c5, so the knight takes aim at them.

13...♕e7 14.d5

14.♖d2 exd4 15.♘xd4= may be more realistic, but nobody has tried it.

14...♘b6!?

14...cxd5 15.♕xd5 ♘b6 16.♕c5 ♖e8!= is also possible since:
17.♕xe7 ♖xe7 18.♖d8+ ♔h7 is in Black's favour with his bishop pair. White should prefer:

17.♘d6 ♗e6 18.♘xe5 ♗xe5 19.♕xe5 ♘c4 20.♘xc4 ♗xc4=, hitting e2.

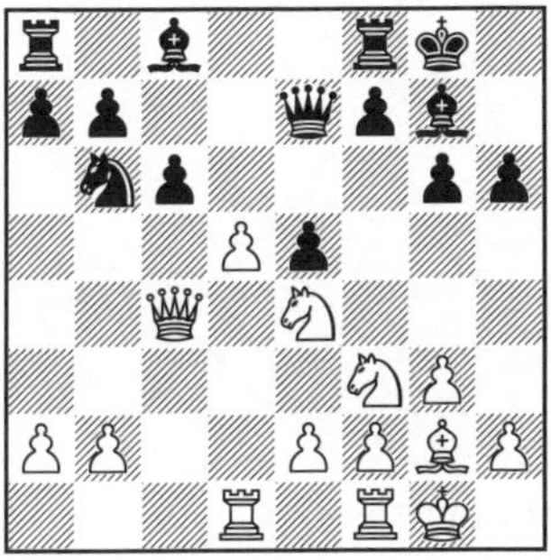

15.d6 ♕e8 16.♕c2 f5 17.♘c5 e4 18.♘d4 ♖f6 19.♘db3

All three correspondence games have finished in a draw, but it is clear that White is overextended.

19...a5 is probably not best as White obtains counterplay with 20.f3. Simpler is:

19...♘d5 20.d7 ♗xd7 21.♘xb7 ♗e6, going for f7. The d5-square is well fortified, so Black will retain his space advantage.

Chapter 7. 4.♕b3

Annotated Games

25. Bartel – Grachev
Moscow 18.02.2009

1.d4 d5 2.c4 c6 3.♘f3 ♘f6 4.♘c3 e6 5.♕d3 dxc4 6.♕xc4 b5 7.♕d3 a6 8.g3 c5 9.♗g2 ♗b7 10.0-0 ♘bd7

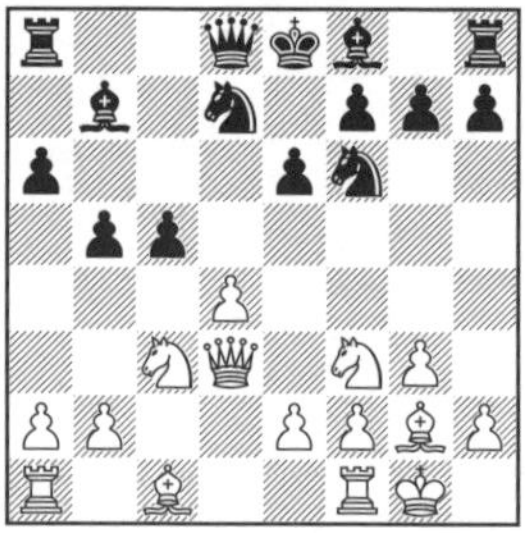

11.♗f4

It is not easy to assess the pros and cons of ...c4. We have been taught that central pawns were more important than flank ones, so our prejudices are against relieving the tension. However, computers shed different light on such positional factors. Pawn centre could be a strong asset if it allowed White to build an attack. In or case White's pieces are not placed properly for that. Thus:

11.♖d1 c4!? 12.♕c2

12.♕e3 ♗e7 13.a3 ♘d5.

12...b4!?

12...♗b4 13.a3 ♗xc3 14.bxc3 ♗e4 is also nice for Black.

13.♘a4?

13.♘b1∞ was the only move.

13...♗e4! 14.♕d2, Agdestein-Jussupow, Wolvega 2008, 14...c3! 15.bxc3 ♕a5∓.

11...c4!? also works after 11.♗f4 – 12.♕c2 ♗e7 13.a3 ♘d5 14.♘xd5 exd5∞.

Perhaps White should have chosen the move order 11.dxc5 ♗xc5 12.♗f4, transposing to the main game.

Also possible is 12.♗e3 ♖c8 13.♖fd1 ♕b6 14.♗xc5 ♘xc5 15.♕e3 0-0 16.a3 h6 17.♖ac1 b4=.

11...cxd4 12.♕xd4 ♗c5 13.♕d3 0-0 14.♖ad1

14.♗d6 ♗xd6 15.♕xd6 ♕b8 is fine for Black. The text might look strange, but the other rook must protect f2. Otherwise 14.♖fd1 ♕b6 would be awkward.

14...♕b6 15.a3

15.♗d6 does not disturb Black since he can answer 15...♖fc8.
15.♘g5 ♗xg2 16.♔xg2 ♖ac8 17.♕f3 was tried in 3 games.

Then 17...♗d4 18.♘ge4 is completely equal, but:

17...♗e7!? would pose some problems. For instance, 18.♘ge4 would not be enough due to 18...b4 19.♘xf6+ ♘xf6 20.♘e4 ♘d5, having 21.♖c1 f5! 22.♘d2 ♕d4 in mind.

15.♘g5 ♗xg2 16.♔xg2 ♖ac8 is in Black's favour – he does not need his bishop at b7.

15...♖fd8

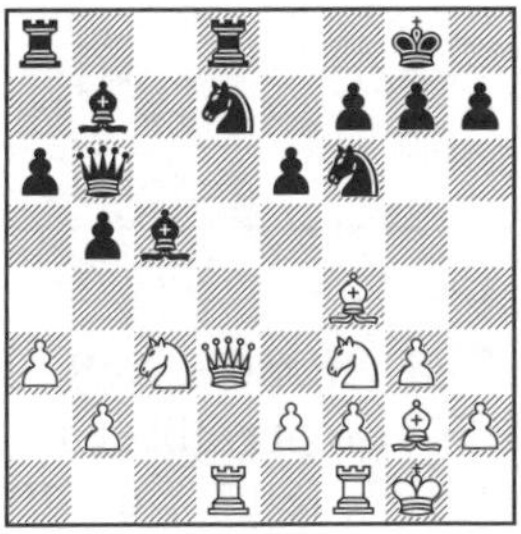

16.♕b1?!

Black's pieces are obviously more active, so Bartel should have sought exchanges. Agdestein understood that and played against Dizdar 16.♗d6! with roughly even chances. The text is the turning point of the game. Now Black's pressure becomes tangible.

16...♖ac8 17.h3 h6 18.g4

It was more resilient to play 18.♖d3, preparing ♘d2.

18...♕a7

Naturally, Black's only way to make progress is ...b4. The only question is whether to recapture on b4 by pawn or by piece. It seems that Grachev wants to preserve his bishop, but 18...a5! 19.♖c1 b4 was at least as good. 20.♘a4 ♕a6 21.♘xc5 ♘xc5 22.axb4 axb4

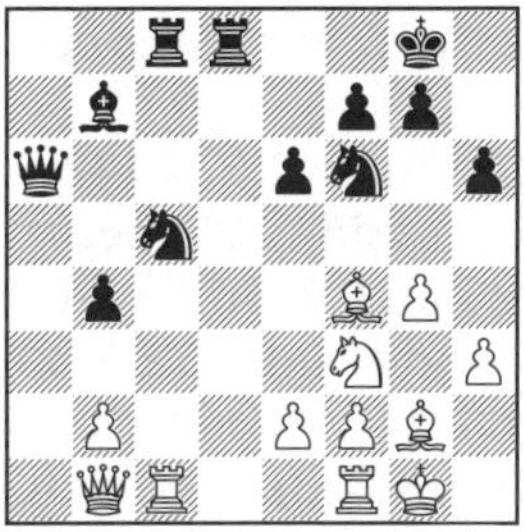

Black plays on domination – 23.♖fe1 ♗e4 24.♕a1 ♕b7∓.
After the text 19.♖d3, intending ♘d2, was probably the most stubborn defence.

19.♗d6

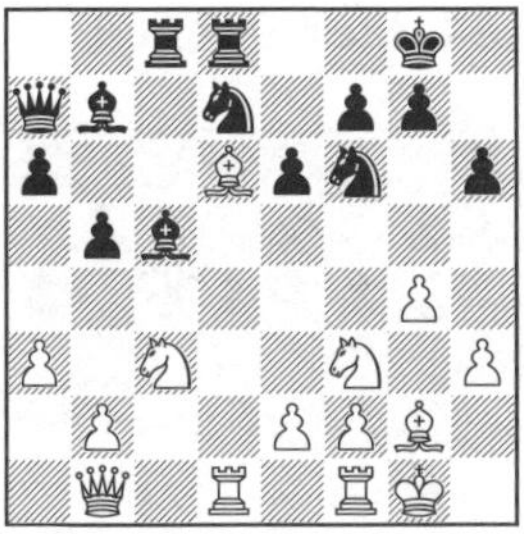

19...♗xd6

Grachev did not realise that he should preserve both rooks. With his next moves he allows the ex-

change of his heavy pieces and his advantage almost disappears.
19...♕a8 20.♗xc5 ♖xc5! was more unpleasant.

20.♖xd6 ♘b6?! 21.♖xd8+ ♖xd8 22.♖d1 ♕a8 23.♖xd8+ ♕xd8

The chances are already level and 24.♘e5 would have completed the mass exchanges. The rest of the game is irrelevant to the opening.

24.♕d1 ♕c7 25.♕d4?! ♘c4∓ 26.♘d1 ♗d5 27.♘e3 ♘xe3 28.♕xe3 a5 29.♕d2 ♘e4 30.♕d1 ♕c5 31.♘d4 ♘d6 32.♘b3 ♗xb3 33.♕xb3 a4 34.♕d1 ♕e5 35.♗f1 ♘c4 36.b3 axb3 37.♕xb3 ♘d2 38.♕d3= ♕b2 39.e3?? (39.♔g2=) **39...♘f3+ 40.♔h1 ♕xf2 0-1**

---

26. Kardashevskiy – Kezin
Moscow 02.02.2019

1.d4 d5 2.♘f3 ♘f6 3.c4 e6 4.♘c3 c6 5.♗g5 h6 6.♗xf6 ♕xf6 7.♕b3 ♘d7 8.e4 dxe4 9.♘xe4

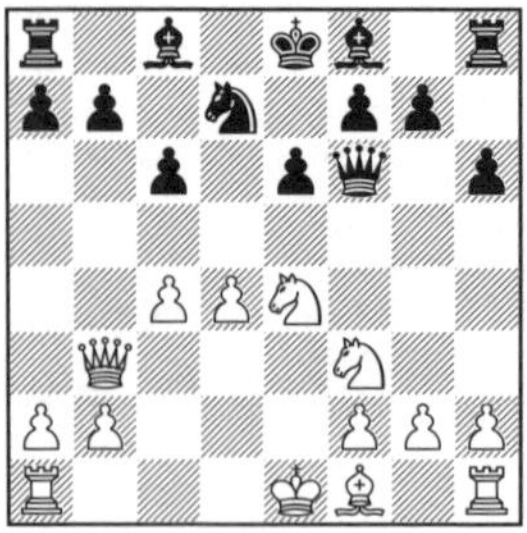

9...♕f5!?

The far more popular alternative is 9...♕f4 10.♗d3 e5 11.0-0 ♗e7.

White has tried many times 12.♖fe1 exd4 13.♘xd4 0-0=. 12.♖ad1 exd4 13.♘xd4 0-0 14.♗c2 ♘f6 also gradually equalises. In 2017 Aronian showed a new idea:

12.♖ae1 exd4 13.♗b1!?, intending to build a ♗+♕ battery against the black king. Although Black should be able to tame the attack, White preserves some initiative after 13...0-0 14.♘g3

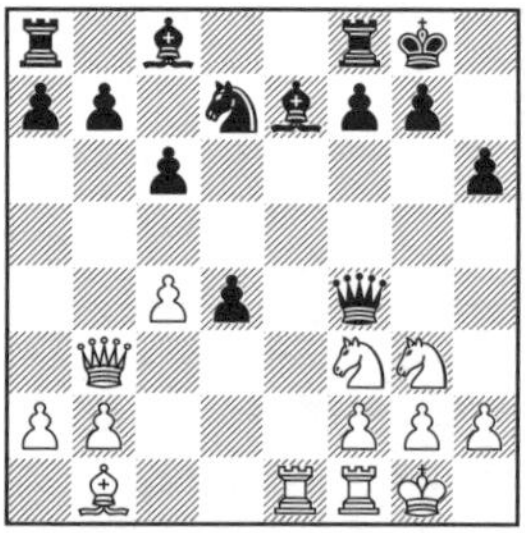

14...♗d8!?

14...♘c5 15.♕d1 ♖e8 16.♘h5 ♕g4! is also playable (16...♕d6?! 17.b3 ♘e6 18.c5 ♕d8 19.♘e5±, Cheng-Demuth, Melbourne 2017) 17.♖e5 d3 18.♖fe1 ♗e6 19.♗xd3 ♘xd3 20.♕xd3↑.

15.♕d3 g6 16.h4 h5!

Ding Liren played against Aronian in Tbilisi 2017 16...♘f6 17.h5 g5?! and was worse after 18.♘e5.

17.♘xh5

White can also attack with 17.♖e4 ♕f6 18.b4 ♗c7 19.♘xh5, but the paradoxical 19...♕h8 20.♘g3 ♘f6 21.♖xd4 ♗g4 takes over the initiative.

17...♕h6 18.♘g3 ♗xh4=.

10.♗d3 ♕a5+ 11.♘c3 e5! 12.0-0 exd4 13.♖fe1+

In several correspondence games White checked with the other rook, but there is no significant difference – 13.♘xd4 ♗e7 14.♖ae1 ♘c5.

13...♗e7 14.♘xd4 ♘c5 15.♕d1 ♕d8 16.♗f5 0-0 17.♗xc8 ♖xc8

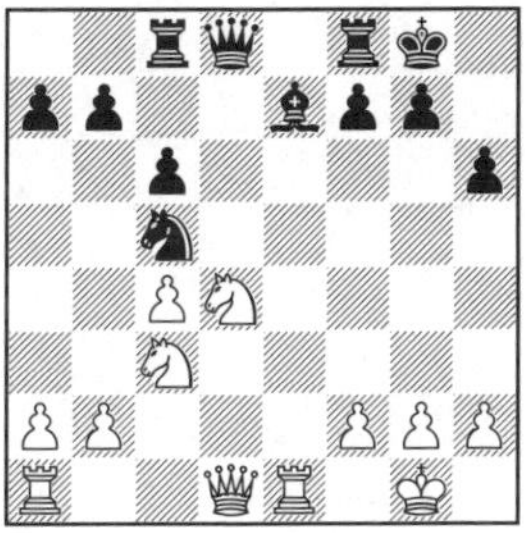

18.♘f5

After 18.♕g4 Black can answer 18... g6, but 18...h5! is more forced – 19.♕xh5 ♕xd4 20.♖xe7 ♖ce8 21.♕e2 ♖xe7 22.♕xe7 ♘d3 23.♕e2 ♕xc4 24.♖d1 ♖d8=.

18...♗f6?!

The bishop is unstable here. After ♕f3 White will threaten ♘xh6+. In this critical moment of the game Black showed laziness and apparently discarded the line 18...♗g5! 19.♕g4 g6 20.h4 gxf5 21.♕xf5 ♗e7 22.♖ad1 as "dangerous".

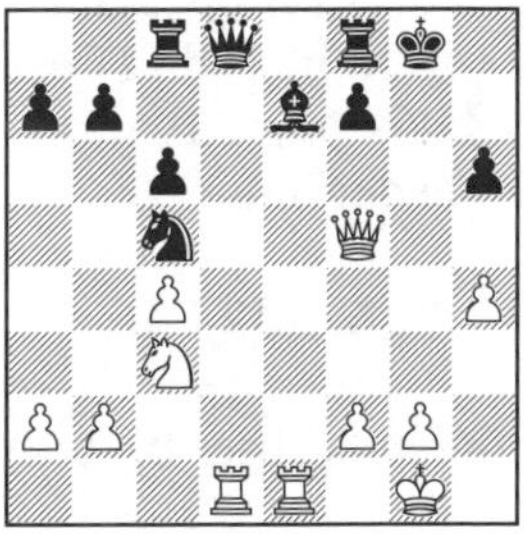

Yet further calculation shows that White has only a draw: 22...♕e8 23.♘e4

Or 23.♕g4+ ♔h8 24.♕h5 ♔h7=.

23...♘e6 24.♖e3 ♖d8 25.♖de1 ♕d7 26.♖g3+ (26.♘f6+ ♗xf6 27.♕xf6 ♔h7=) 26...♔h8 27.♕e5+ ♔h7=. Such course of the game would have made it even more theoretically important.

19.♕f3 ♖c7 20.♖ad1 ♖d7 21.♖xd7

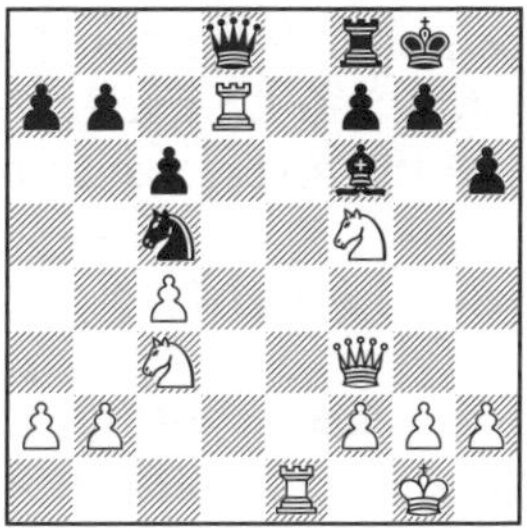

21...♘xd7?!

21...♕xd7 22.♘xh6+ ♔h7 was more resilient. Following 23.♘g4 ♗xc3 24.bxc3 ♖e8 25.♖e3 ♖xe3 26.♘xe3± Black is "only" a pawn down, but not worse positionally.

22.♖d1 ♖e8 23.h3?!

It was time to convert the initiative into material – 23.♘e4! ♖e6

23...♗xb2 24.♘ed6 ♖f8 25.♘xb7 ♕c7 26.♘xh6+ gxh6 27.♕g4+±.

24.♘c5 (24.g3±) 24...♖e5 25.♘xb7 ♕b6 26.♘bd6 ♕xb2 27.♘xh6+ (27.♘xf7±) 27...gxh6 28.♕g4+ ♗g7 29.♕xd7 ♕d2 30.♖f1 ♖e1 31.g3±.

After the text 23...♖e6! 24.♘e4 ♕e8± kept material balance, although 25.♔f1 maintained pressure.

23...♕c7? 24.♘e4

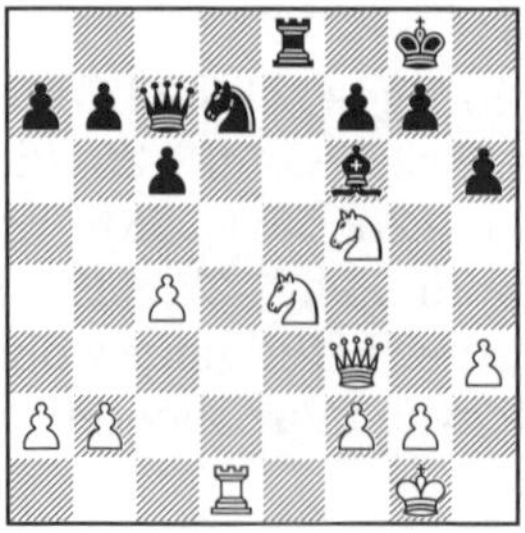

The knights are excellent team mates with a queen in attacking positions. 24...♔f8 25.♕a3+ c5 26.♘fd6 ♖e6 27.♕xa7 collects a pawn, but the text is even worse.

24...♗xb2 25.♘xh6+?

This complicates White's task. The "dumb" 25.♘ed6 ♖f8 (25...♖e6 26.♘xh6+ ♖xh6 27.♕xf7+ ♔h7 28.♘f5) 26.♘e7+ ♔h7 27.♘xf7 was curtains.

25...gxh6 26.♕g4+ ♗g7 27.♖xd7 ♕e5 28.♘d6?! (28.♘g3!±) **28...♖e7** (28...h5! 29.♕f3±) **29.♖xe7 ♕xe7 30.♘f5 ♕g5 31.♕e4?**

The final mistake. 31.♕xg5 hxg5 32.♘d6 b6 33.♘c8± was winning a healthy pawn.

31...♗f6 32.g3 h5 33.♘e3 ½-½

---

27. Ivanchuk – Navara
rapid, Prague 28.05.2009

1.d4 d5 2.c4 c6 3.♘f3 ♘f6 4.♘c3 e6 5.♗g5 h6 6.♗xf6 ♕xf6 7.♕b3 dxc4 8.♕xc4 ♘d7 9.♖d1 g6 10.g3 ♗g7 11.♗g2 0-0 12.♕b3

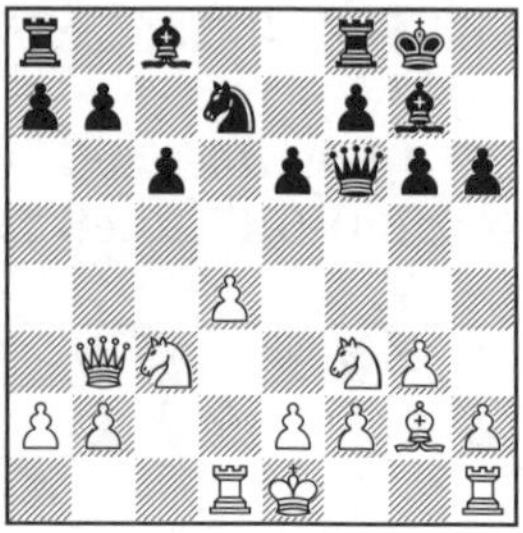

12...♕e7

In fact 12...e5 is possible – 13.d5 ♘b6 14.♘d2 cxd5 15.♘xd5 ♕d8 16.♘c4 ♘xc4 17.♕xc4 ♕a5+ 18.b4 ♕a4 19.0-0 ♗e6=. Black has completed development and he has no weaknesses, Serner-Zemlyanov, ICCF 2014. The only "drawback" of this line is the drawish symmetrical pawn structure. Navara shows that Black has nothing to fear if he refrains from the break in the centre.

13.0-0 b6

The plan with ...e5 remains an option, only Black should prepare first a retreat square for his queen at f8 – 13...♖d8 14.e3 e5

> Serper made a draw with 14...♘b6 15.♘e5 ♗d7, but this is a bit too passive for my taste.

15.♖fe1 ♕f8 16.h3 exd4 17.exd4 ♘b6 18.♘e5 ♗e6, when 19.d5= looks a reasonable decision.

14.e3 ♗b7 15.♘d2 ♘f6

Black defends the b7-bishop by

queen, obviously preparing ...c5. Fabri-Varkentin, ICCF 2019, saw a more active set-up: 15...♖ab8!? 16.♘c4 ♖fc8

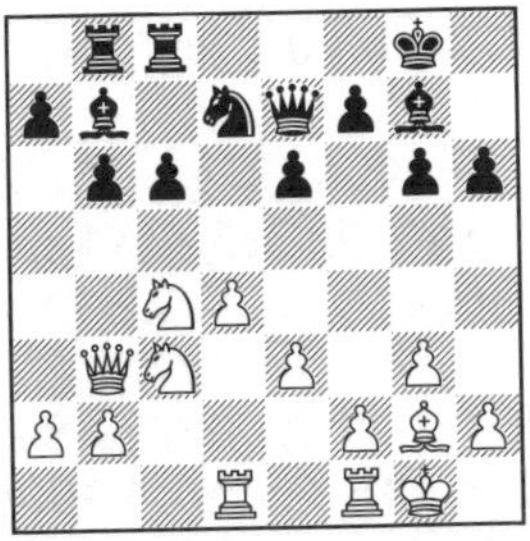

Black intends to advance on the queenside with ...b5 and ...c5 after ...♗a8 first. The game saw further: 17.♕c2 ♘f6 18.e4 ♗a6 19.♕a4 ♗xc4 20.♕xc4 b5 21.♕e2 b4 22.♘a4 ♘d7. ...c5 is coming, and the opponents signed a draw.

16.♖c1 ♖fd8 17.♖fd1 ♖ac8 18.♘c4

White could have hampered ...c5 by 18.♘de4 ♘xe4 19.♘xe4, when the other break in the centre takes over the initiative – 19...e5 20.dxe5 ♗xe5.
Or 18.♕a4 ♗a8 19.♘e2 ♘d5 20.a3 c5↑.

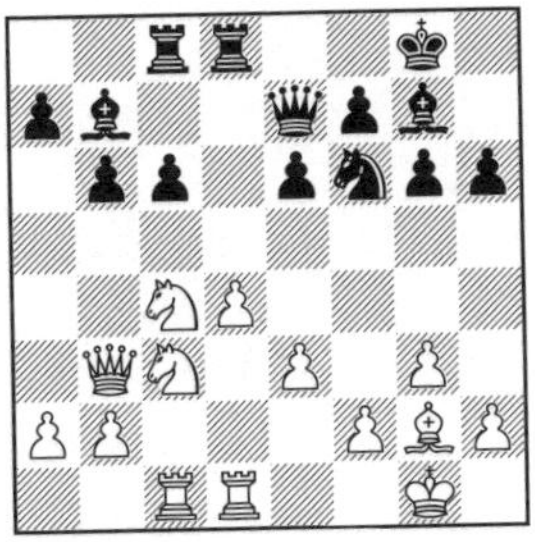

18...c5 19.♗xb7 ♕xb7 20.dxc5 ♖xd1+ 21.♕xd1 ♖xc5 22.b3 ♕c6

Black is already slightly better as he has a bishop vs a knight in an open position. His queen is fine on the main diagonal. He should now devise a plan how to repel the enemy knights from their stable stands. A good alternative to the game is 22...♗f8 (to control d6) 23.a4 a6.

23.♕d6 ♘d5 (23...♕f3!?) **24.♕xc6 ♖xc6 25.♘e2 b5 26.♘d2 ♖a6!∓**

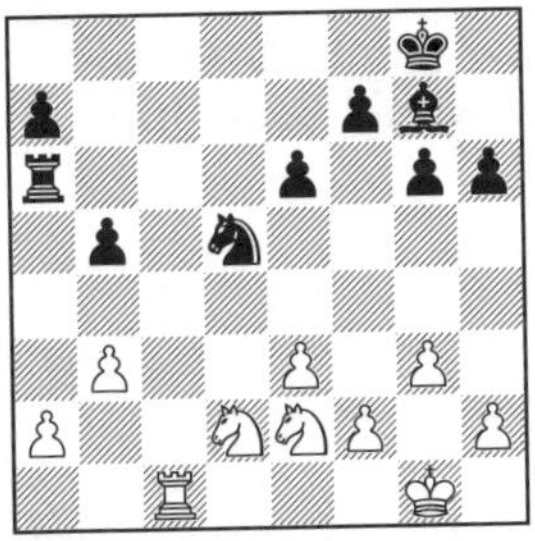

In principle when we have a bishop vs a knight we should aim to preserve a rook, but trade queens. So far Navara has played "by the book", and the reward is the a2-pawn.

27.♖c8+ ♔h7 28.♘c1 ♘c3 29.♔f1 ♘xa2 30.♘xa2 ♖xa2 31.♘e4 a5?

Black decides that the distant passed pawn guarantees him the win, but he underestimates White's counterplay. Since his only weakness is f7, the best practical choice, especially having in mind that it was a rapid game, was 31...g5, enabling ...♔g6.

32.♖c7

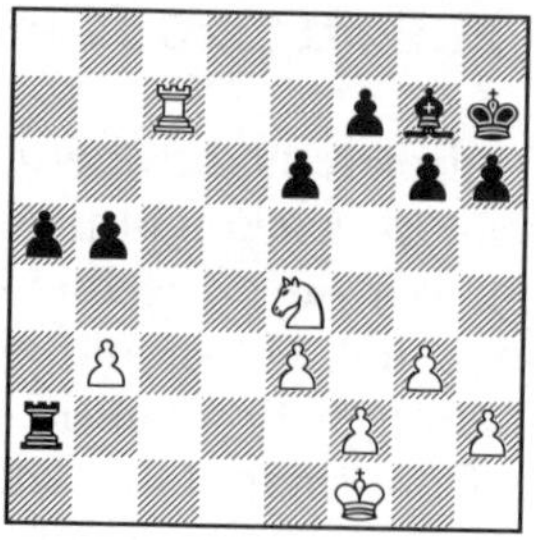

32...♖b2?

Perhaps here Navara realised that the straightforward 32...a4 33.bxa4 bxa4 34.♖xf7 a3 35.♖a7 g5 36.h4 gxh4 37.gxh4 ♖a1+ 38.♔g2 a2 39.♔f3 would lead him nowhere, but could not brace himself to play for a draw. So he completely abandons his king, hypnotised by his queenside pawns.

33.♖xf7 ♖xb3 34.♖a7 a4?

34...♖b1+ 35.♔g2 g5 36.♖xa5 b4 37.♖b5 ♔g6 38.♘c5 ♗f6 kept Black in the game.

35.♘f6+ ♔h8 36.♖a8+ ♗f8 37.♘d7 a3 38.♘xf8 b4 39.♘xe6+ ♔h7 40.♘d4 ♖b2 41.h4 a2 42.♔g2 ♖d2 43.♘b3 ♖b2 1-0 (44.♘c1+–)

Chapter 8. The Carlsbad Structure

Main Ideas

1.d4 d5 2.c4 c6 3.♘c3 e6 4.cxd5 exd5

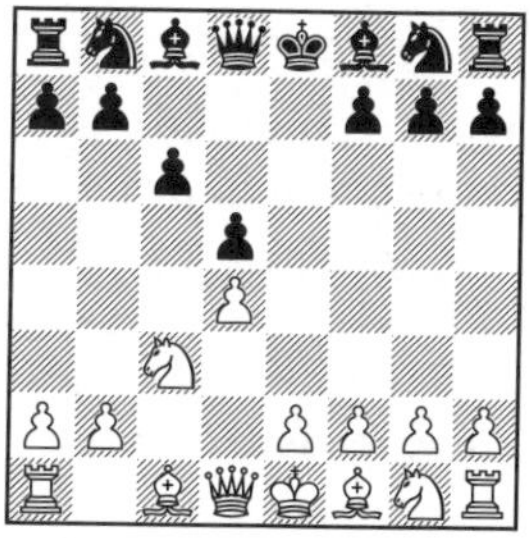

White must be very scared of ...dxc4 to opt for this totally harmless version of the Carlsbad structure. With this move order Black leads out his only problem piece to f5 without any positional concessions. Why is that so important? After all, White can trade it from d3 and attempt the same plan with b4-b5, known as a minority attack. The main reason is that Black obtains in his possession a very solid set-up, based on ...b5. Then without the bishops, e3-e4 would only lead to equality, at most. Our battle plan is to exchange both bishops and direct our knights to c4 (via b6 or d6) and e4.

White cannot prevent ...♗f5 with **5.♕c2** since we have **5...♗d6 6.♘f3 ♘e7**, e.g. 7.♗g5 h6 8.♗h4 ♕a5! 9.e3 ♗f5.

Other possibilities are **5.♗f4 ♗d6 6.♗xd6 ♕xd6 7.e3 ♗f5 8.♗d3 ♗xd3** and**:**
5.♘f3 ♗f5 6.♗f4 (6.♗g5 ♗e7) **6... ♗d6 7.♗xd6**.
In short, most games reach this type of positions:

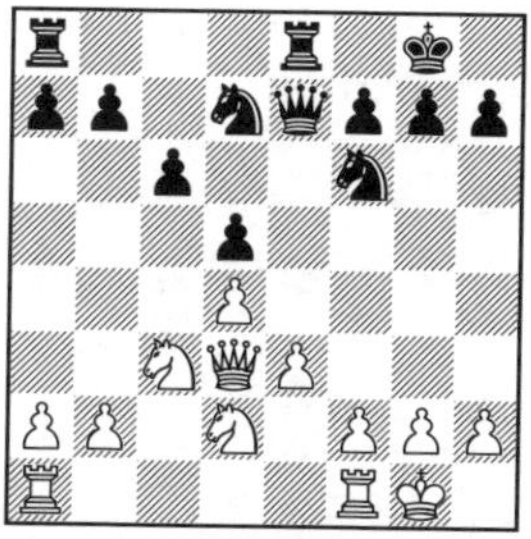

Depending on the way White traded the dark-squared bishop, our queen could be on e7 or d6.
Let's now investigate four scenarios in which White tries to execute b4-b5:

1. He thrusts 13.b4 without any preparation, exploiting the unprotected state of the b7-pawn. White's knight at d2 is passive and that encourages us to counter-attack in the centre – 13...a5 14.b5 (14.a3 axb4 15.axb4 b5∓) 14...c5=.

2. He starts with ♖ab1 and we "automatically" answer ...a5:

Note the manoeuvre ...♘d7-b6-c8-d6 – 15.a3 ♘c8! 16.♘a4 (16.b4 axb4 17.axb4 b5 18.♘e2 ♘d6) 16...♘d6 and White cannot achieve b4-b5.

3. He starts with a3. Again we answer ...a5 and after ♘a4 we get the following position:

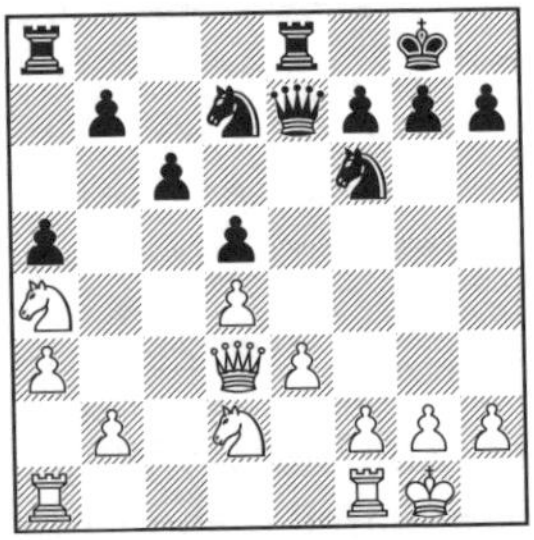

In that case we fix the queenside with 14...b5 15.♘c3 a4 16.♖ac1 ♘b6. The motif ...a5-a4 occurs with or without ...b5, but the result is the same – White cannot push b4 anymore. In the latter case Black might opt for the more flexible set-up with ...b6, as in **Game 29** Lesiege-So, chess.com 2017, although I believe that playing with ...b5 is easier.

Another variant of the same structure occurred in:

Carlsen-So
chess.com Speed 1m+1spm 2017

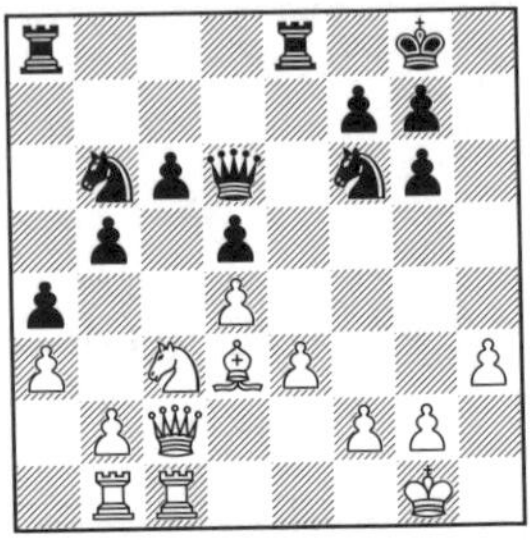

White has remained without a plan, so his game is practically unpleasant – 18.♘a2 ♘c4 19.♘b4 ♖e6 20.♕d1 ♖ae8∓.

4. White starts with ♘a4:

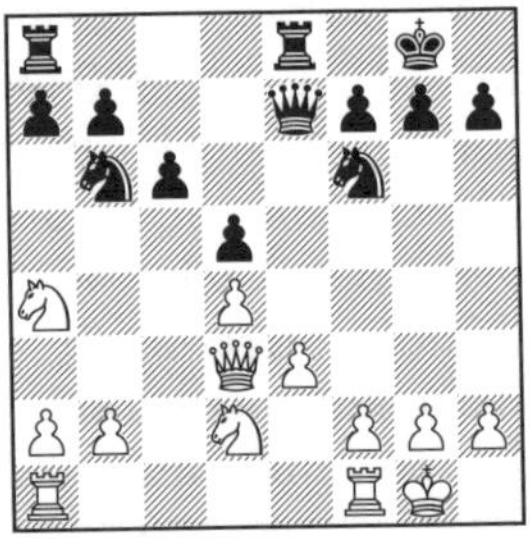

14.♘c5 ♘c8 15.b4. We have a choice now between 15...b6 and 15...a5 16.b5 cxb5 17.♕xb5 ♘d6 18.♕b6 ♖ec8 with play down the c-file.

In these examples White had played ♘d2 in order to prevent ...♘e4 or ...♘b6-c4. If he leaves the knight on f3, our knights reach comfortable places with ...♘e4, ...♘df6, eventually ...♘e4-d6.
Let's now consider what we could

do if White does not follow any constructive plan and chooses a waiting game. In this case we should firstly impose a firm grip on the centre. Then we could try a pawn storm with either the f- and g-pawn or with the h-pawn alone. Our aim should be something like this position:

Bratchenko-Korneev
Novgorod 1997

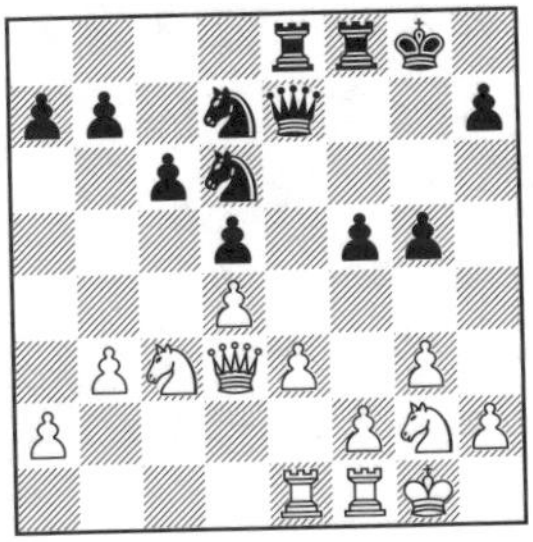

Now let's see what happens if our queen is on d6. From this square it hinders the manoeuvre ...♘b6-c8-d6. On the other hand, I see two advantages:
1. It protects the c6-pawn. This enables the following line:

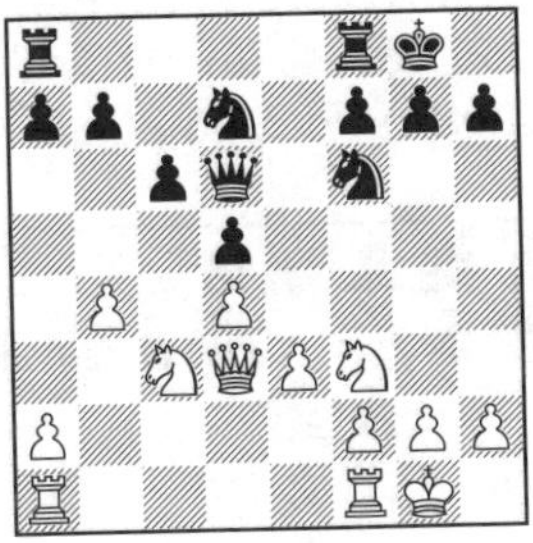

12...b5! 13.a4 a5 14.axb5? (14.bxa5 b4=) 14...axb4 15.bxc6 ♕xc6∓.
2. Whenever White plays ♘d2, we have ...♘g4, hitting h2.

Important decisions

The early sortie of our bishop to f5 leaves the b7-square unprotected. That may tempt White to attack it with ♕b3. We always sacrifice this pawn. For instance:

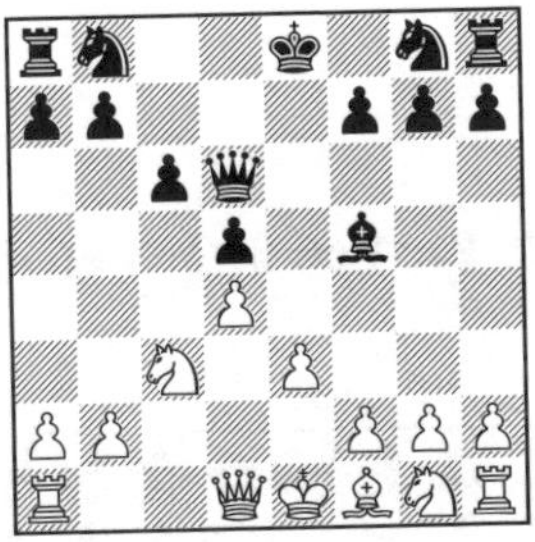

8.♕b3 ♘d7 9.♕xb7 ♖b8 10.♕xa7 ♖xb2 with compensation.

Another key moment arises when White tries to remove our bishop from the b1-h7 diagonal with ♘h4. I suggest to never retreat to e6 as we would remain with a passive bishop after ♗d3. Instead we should seek concessions from White with ...♗g4 or ♗e4. In some lines ...♗g6 is also okay.

Finally, I would like to bring your attention to ♗g3 instead of ♗xd6. We should not be scared to open the h-file by taking on g3. But it would be best to eat the bishop by knight with the manoeuvre ...♘g8-e7-f5. If White meanwhile plays ♕b3, we confidently take ...♗xg3 and sacrifice the b7-pawn with ...♘d7, as noted above. The open h-file is not dangerous since we have a good control of the centre. We simply play ...h6 later.

Chapter 8. The Carlsbad Structure

Step by Step

1.d4 d5 2.c4 c6 3.♘c3 e6 4.cxd5 exd5

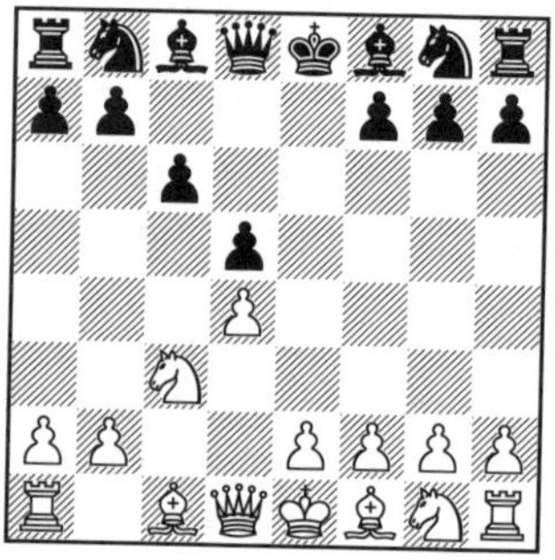

Now **A.** 5.♕c2 is the most challenging option while **B.** 5.♗f4 and **C.** 5.♘f3 are more flexible.

A. 5.♕c2 ♗d6

5...g6 has a good reputation as well, but White can fight for the initiative with:
6.♗f4 ♗f5 7.♕d2 ♘f6 8.f3 ♗g7 9.g4. The text is undoubtedly safer.

6.♘f3 ♘e7 7.♗g5

7.e4 dxe4 8.♘xe4 allows Black to trade bishops with 8...♗b4+ 9.♗d2 ♗xd2+ 10.♕xd2

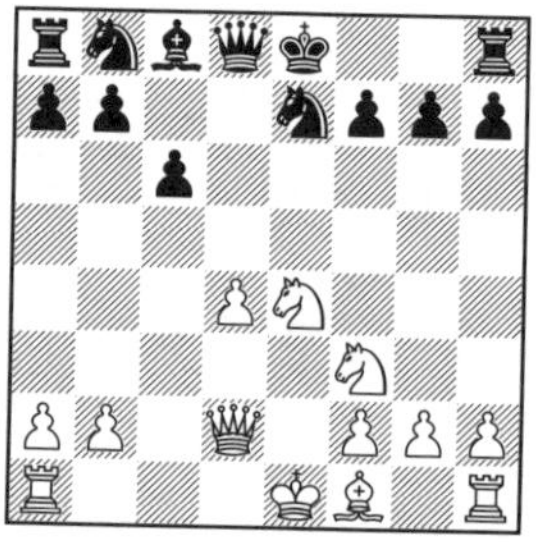

10...♗f5

10...0-0 11.♗c4 ♗g4 12.♘e5 ♗f5 is provocative. Although the engines confidently defend after 13.♘g5 ♘d5 14.g4 ♗e6 15.♗d3 g6 16.h4 ♘d7, the character of play is chaotic and double-edged.

11.♗d3 ♗xe4 12.♗xe4 ♕d6 13.0-0 ♘d7 14.♖fe1 0-0=. Obviously we do not risk anything here, e.g. 15.♖e2 ♘d5 16.♖ae1 ♘7f6 17.♗d3 ♖ad8 18.g3 ♖fe8 19.♘e5 g6 20.a3 ♘b6.

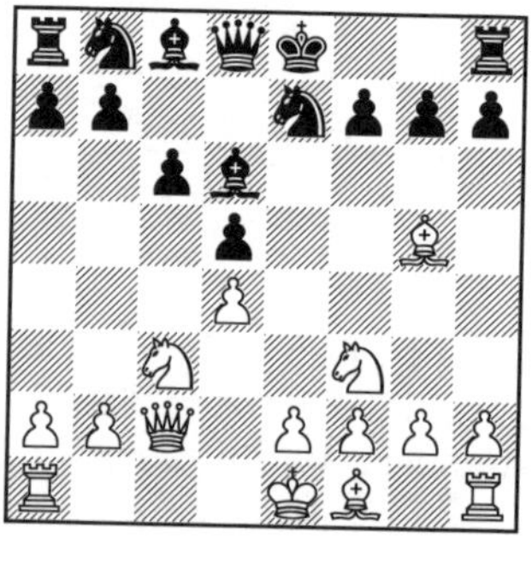

7...f6

Actually, I think that this move is ugly. An alternative way to enable ...♗f5 is 7...h6 8.♗h4 ♕a5! 9.e3 ♗f5 10.♗d3 ♗xd3 11.♕xd3 ♕a6 12.♕xa6 ♘xa6=. Abdyjapar-Nguyen, Tashkent 2016, saw further 13.0-0-0.

13.♗g3 ♘f5 14.♗xd6 ♘xd6 is also balanced.

13...♘f5 14.♗g3 ♘xg3 15.hxg3 ♘c7 16.g4=.

8.♗h4

Rapport and Ivanchuk recently chose 8.♗d2!?. After 8...♘a6 we have a split:

a) 9.e4 ♘b4 10.♕b3 a5! 11.a3 a4 12.♕d1 dxe4 13.♘xe4 ♘bd5 14.♗c4 ♗e6=, Ivanchuk-Kramnik, Tbilisi 2017. Now 15.0-0 allows 15...♘e3=, while 15.♕c2 0-0 16.0-0 ♔h8 17.♖fe1 (17.♘h4 g5) 17...♗g4 18.♘h4 g5 forces exchanges – 19.♗xd5 ♘xd5 20.♘xd6 ♕xd6 21.♘f5=.

b) 9.a3!? ♘c7 10.e4 dxe4 11.♘xe4 ♗g4

This position occurred in Rapport-Shankland, rapid, Saint Louis 2019. It is unclear and needs more tests, especially the plan with 0-0-0 for White. Instead Rapport played: 12.♕b3, when:

12...b6?! seriously weakened Black's queenside. Shankland's plan with long castling deserves attention and might work after:

12...♕d7!, having in mind 13.♕xb7? ♕e6. White should continue 13.♗c4 0-0-0! 14.0-0 ♗e6∞.

8...♗f5 9.♕d2 ♘d7

The knight goes to d6 via b6-c8.
9...g5 10.♗g3 h5 11.♗xd6 ♕xd6 12.h4 g4 13.♘g1± fixies the kingside in White's favour.

10.♗g3

10.e3 ♘b6 11.♗g3 transposes. The point is that White needs to play ♗g3 in order to enable ♘h4+♗d3.

10...♘b6 11.e3 ♘bc8

Of course Black has many other setups, but I suggest this manoeuvre since it is thematic for the Carlsbad structure. Thus you would not need to remember various plans.

12.♘h4 ♗e6 13.♗d3 0-0 14.♕c2 g6 15.♘f3 ♗f5

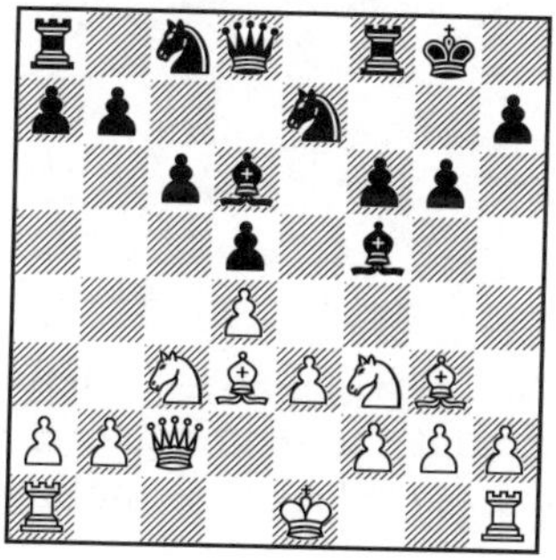

Once we trade the light-squared bishops, we can claim a comfortable equality. Our knight will soon land on its best square, d6. The only problem is the weakness of e6, but it is easily defended – 16.0-0 ♗xg3 17.hxg3 ♘d6 18.♘a4 ♗xd3 19.♕xd3 ♔g7 20.♘c5 ♕c8 21.♖fe1 (21.b4 h5) 21...♖e8. At this point 22.e4 is not dangerous in view of 22...dxe4 23.♘xe4 ♘xe4 24.♖xe4 ♘d5.

The only way to keep the position double-edged is 16.♗xf5 ♘xf5 17.0-0-0. However, Black has more chances to disturb the enemy king after 17...a5.

B. 5.♗f4 ♗d6 6.♗g3

6.♗xd6 ♕xd6 7.e3 ♗f5 8.♗d3

8.♕b3 ♘d7 9.♕xb7 ♖b8 10.♕xa7 ♖xb2 11.♕a8+ ♖b8 12.♕a4 ♘gf6 13.♘f3 0-0⩱.

8...♗xd3 9.♕xd3 ♘f6 10.♘f3 transposes to line C. An independent deviation is:

10.♘ge2 ♘bd7 11.0-0 0-0 12.f3 ♖fe8 13.♘g3

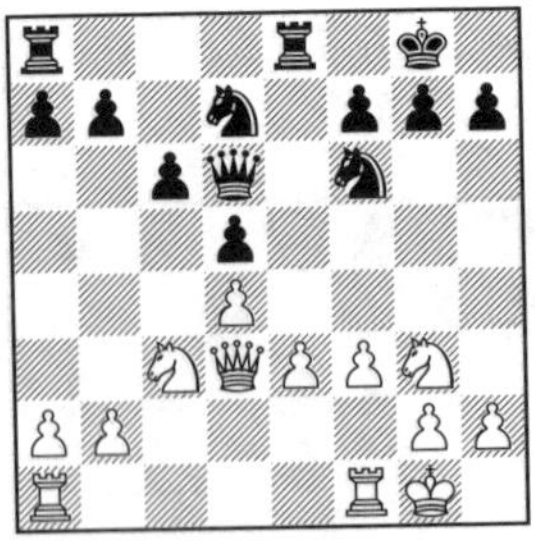

The idea e4-e5 is ineffective without the light-squared bishops, so Black has nothing to worry about. He can constrain the g3-knight with 13...g6, then put his second rook on d8 to prepare ...c5.

V. Inkiov played against me the strange move 6.g3 ♗xf4 7.gxf4. Perhaps the best set-up for Black is ...♘h6, ...♘d7-f6.

My choice 7...♘e7 8.♘f3 ♘d7 9.e3 ♘f6 10.♕c2 ♗f5 11.♗d3 ♗xd3 12.♕xd3 0-0 13.0-0-0 ♕c8 14.♖dg1 ♕f5 was also slightly better for Black.

6...♘e7

A simple positional solution. Black is planning to eat the g3-bishop by knight after ...♘f5.

6...♗f5 7.♕b3 ♗xg3 8.hxg3 ♕e7 9.f3!? is rather unclear. For instance:

9...♘d7 10.g4 ♗g6 11.♕xb7

11.♔f2 0-0-0 12.♖c1 ♔b8 13.e3 f5∞.

11...♖b8 12.♕xc6 ♕b4 13.♖c1 ♘e7 14.♕c7 0-0 15.e3 ♖b7 16.♕f4 ♕xb2 17.♘ge2 ♖c8 18.e4∞.

7.e3 ♘f5

8.♗d3

8.♗xd6 ♘xd6 is obviously fine for Black. His pieces hinder the minority attack, while he could try a pawn storm on the kingside, as in Bratchenko-Korneev, Novgorod 1997: 9.♗d3 ♗f5 10.♗xf5 ♘xf5 11.♕d3

Perhaps 11.♕g4 g6 12.e4 is the better option – 12...h5!? 13.♕f4 dxe4 14.♕e5+ ♔d7 15.♘xe4 ♔c8 16.0-0-0 ♖e8 17.♕f4 ♕c7 18.♕f3 ♘d7 with sharp play. Black is at least not worse here. He may hide his king on a7.

11...♘d6 12.♘ge2 0-0 13.0-0 ♘d7 14.♖ae1 ♕h4 15.g3 ♕e7 16.b3 ♖ae8 17.♘f4 g5 18.♘g2 f5↑.

8...♘xg3 9.hxg3 ♘d7 10.♕c2 ♘f6 11.0-0-0

I have been following P.Nikolic-Oll, Polanica Zdroj 1996, which went on 11...g6 12.♘f3 ♔f8 13.♘g5 ♘g4 14.♘h3 f5 15.♘f4 ♔g7 16.♔b1 ♗d7 17.♕d2 ♕e7 18.♖de1 ♘f6 19.f3 ♖ae8 20.♗c2 ♗c8 21.♕f2 ½-½.

It is more challenging to play **11... h6!?**, avoiding weaknesses. We should not fear any attack on the h-file since we are going to castle long. For instance:

12.f4 ♕e7 13.♘f3 ♗e6 14.♔b1 0-0-0∞.

C. 5.♘f3 ♗f5

5...♗d6 6.♗g5 ♘e7 has its fans, but I do not particularly like the position which arises after 7.♕c2 f6 8.♗d2 ♘a6 9.a3 as in game Rapport-Shankland from line A.

6.♗f4

6.♗g5 may bring about similar positions after 6...♗e7.

6...♕b6 is a fair alternative, provided that you do not take on b2 after 7.♕d2 ♘d7 8.e3 ♘gf6 9.♗d3 ♗xd3 (9...♘e4 10.♕c2 ♘xg5 11.♗xf5 ♘xf3+ 12.gxf3 g6 13.♗xd7+ ♔xd7 14.0-0-0 is strategically unbalanced and messy) 10.♕xd3. Instead Black should play 10...♗d6 11.0-0 0-0=.

7.♗xe7 ♕xe7 8.e3 ♘f6 9.♗d3

After 9.♘h4 both 9...♗e4 and 9... ♗g4 are possible.

9...♗xd3 10.♕xd3 ♘bd7 11.0-0 0-0 leads to a typical position:

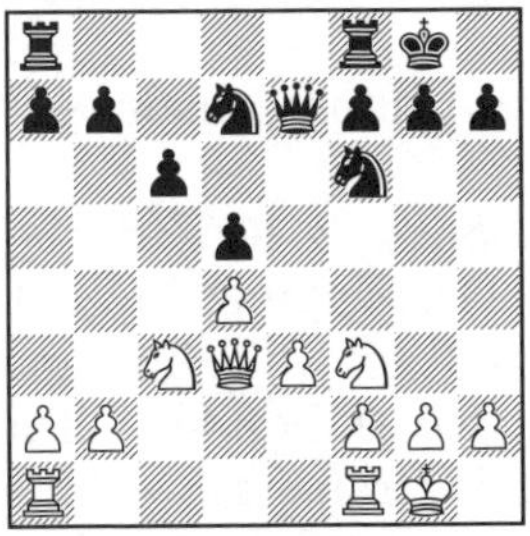

Be sure to look at **Game 28** Tan-Sadler, Daventry 2019.

6.h3 ♗d6 7.g4

7.♗g5 ♕b6 8.♕d2 h6 9.♗h4 ♘d7.

7...♗g6 8.♗g2 ♘d7 9.0-0 is a weird set-up, where Black has an ample choice, e.g. 9...h5 10.g5 ♘e7 or 9... ♘e7 10.♘h4 0-0.

6...♗d6

This looks simplest to me. Black often plays 6...♘f6 7.e3 ♕b6, but 8.♗d3 leads to unclear complications – 8...♕xb2 9.0-0 ♗g6! (9...♗xd3 10.♕xd3) 10.♗xg6 hxg6∞. 8...♗xd3 9.♕xd3 ♗e7 is safer, but then why have we played ...♕b6?!

7.♗xd6

Anastasian is the main protagonist of 7.♗g3 ♘f6 8.e3 (8.♕b3 ♗xg3 9.hxg3 ♕b6=)

We can calmly castle – 8...0-0 9.♘h4

9.♗d3 ♗xd3 10.♕xd3 is harmless. The engines love 10...♗xg3 11.hxg3 g6, while humans prefer 10...♖e8 11.♘d2 ♕e7. The latter should transpose to the main line when White takes on d6.

9...♗g4!?

9...♗e4 10.♗d3 ♖e8 fares well for Black, but 10.f3 ♗g6 11.♘xg6 might be slightly preferable for White.

10.♕b3

10.f3 is pointless here in view of 10...♗e6. I analysed further 11.♗xd6 ♕xd6 12.g4 c5 13.g5 cxd4 14.♕xd4 ♘e8 15.♗d3 ♘c6 16.♕f4 ♕xf4 17.exf4 d4↑.

10.♗e2 ♗xe2 11.♕xe2 ♘e4 12.♘f5 ♗b4 13.0-0 ♘xg3=.

10...♗xg3 11.hxg3 c5

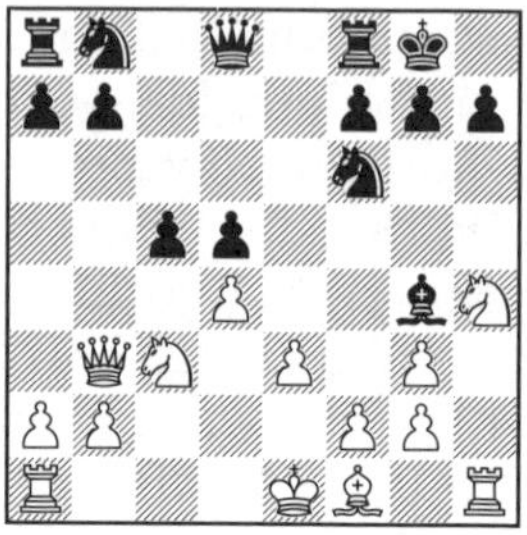

12.♘f3

12.♕xb7? cxd4 13.♕xa8 ♕b6.

12...cxd4 13.♘xd4 ♘c6. Black has enough threats. The battle for the d4-square might finish with a draw following 14.♕a4 ♕b6 15.♕b5 ♕c7! 16.♘xd5 ♘xd5 17.♕xd5 ♘xd4 18.♕xd4 ♖fd8 19.♕xg4 ♕a5+ 20.♔e2 ♕d2+ 21.♔f3 ♖d6 22.♕a4 ♖f6+=.

7...♕xd6 8.e3

8.♕b3 ♘d7 9.♕xb7 (9.e3 ♘gf6 10.♗e2 0-0) 9...♖b8 10.♕xa7 ♖xb2 11.♕a8+ could prove to be a storm in a teacup.

11...♔e7

This leads to a spectacular perpetual. We could play on with 11...♖b8!? 12.♕a4 ♘gf6 13.e3 0-0⩲. For instance: 14.♘h4 ♗e6 15.♗d3 ♘e4 16.♘xe4 dxe4 17.♗xe4 f5 18.♗d3 ♘e5 19.♗e2 ♖b2 20.0-0 ♘g4 21.♗xg4 fxg4 22.e4 ♖b4.

12.a3 ♕c7 13.♖c1 ♘gf6!! 14.♕xh8 ♕a5 15.e4 ♖b1 16.♖xb1 ♕xc3+ 17.♘d2 ♘xe4 18.♖d1 ♘xf2 19.♔xf2 ♕xd4+ 20.♔g3 ♕e5+ 21.♔f2 ♕d4+=.

8...♘d7 9.♗d3 ♗xd3 10.♕xd3 ♘gf6 11.0-0 0-0

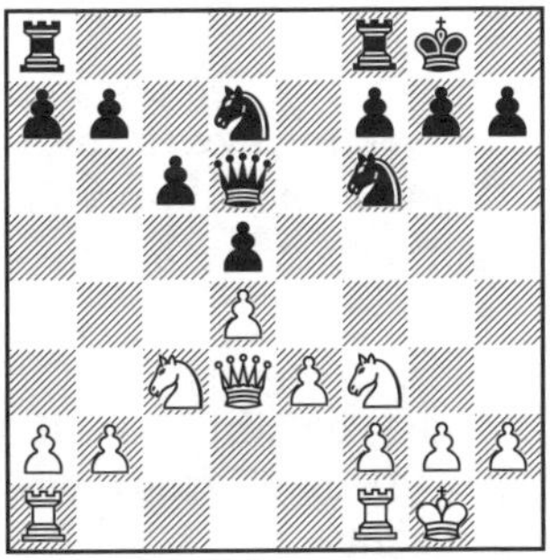

This is a critical position for the 4.cxd5 line. The only constructive plan for White is the minority attack, but Black's piece are well placed to meet it.

12.♖ab1

A key moment is that 12.b4 b5 13.a4 a5 14.axb5? (14.bxa5 b4=) fails to 14...axb4 15.bxc6 ♕xc6∓.

12.a3 does not threaten anything as 12....♖fe8 (Of course the standard answer to a3, 12...a5, is good, too.) 13.b4 b5 14.a4 a5 is the above line without a tempo.

12...a5! 13.♖fc1

13.a3 a4 immediately fixes the pawn structure on the queenside.

13...♖fe8 14.♘d2=

White hopes for ♘a4 and a3, but Black has at least two decent ways to neutralise it:

a) to manoeuvre the d7-knight to d6 – 14...♘b6!? 15.♕c2 ♘c8 16.♘a4 ♕e7 17.♘c5 ♘d6=;

b) to use the placement of the queen on d6 to harass the white king – 14...♘g4 15.♘f1 (15.♘f3 ♘gf6= is more reasonable) 15...♘gf6 16.♘a4 ♘e4 17.f3 (17.a3 b5) 17...♘g5 18.a3 ♘e6 19.♕c2 b5 20.♘c3 a4∓.

Look also at the instructive **Game 29** Lesiege-So, chess.com 2017.

Chapter 8. The Carlsbad Structure

Annotated Games

28. Tan – Sadler
Daventry 13.1.2019

1.d4 d5 2.c4 e6 3.♘c3 c6 4.cxd5 exd5 5.♘f3 ♗f5 6.♗g5 ♗e7 7.♗xe7 ♕xe7 8.e3 ♘f6 9.♗d3 ♗xd3 10.♕xd3 ♘bd7 11.0-0 0-0

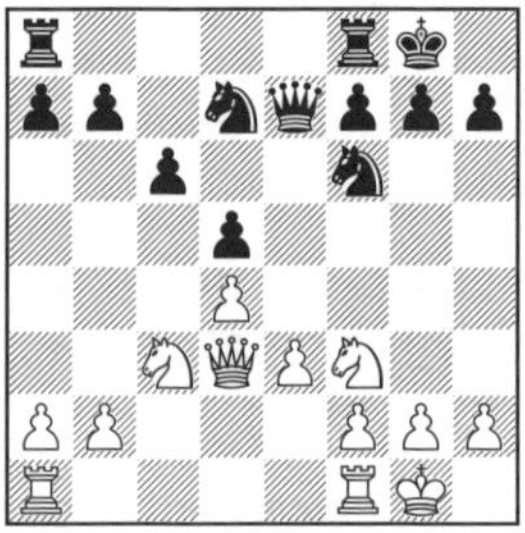

12.♘d2

White could already start the minority attack with:

12.b4, using the unprotected state of the b7-pawn.

If White's knight were on the passive square d2, b4 could be attacked with 12...a5 13.b5 c5. In our case that would offer White slightly the better chances.

The other thematic way of meeting b4 is 12...b5. Again, 13.a4 a6 14.♖fb1 is slightly more pleasant for White as Black's d7-knight cannot easily accomplish the manoeuvre ...♘d7-b6-c8-d6-c4.

Finally, 12...♘e4 13.b5 ♘xc3 14.bxc6! assures White of the better pawn structure without any dynamic compensation (for instance, pressure on the c-file). That leaves us the only other option:

12...a6

a) If now White revives the threat b5 by 13.a4, we should prepare for active counterplay on the queenside with:

13...♖fc8

13...♕xb4 14.♖fb1 ♕d6 15.♖xb7 c5 16.♕b1 c4 17.♕b4± was still insufficient.

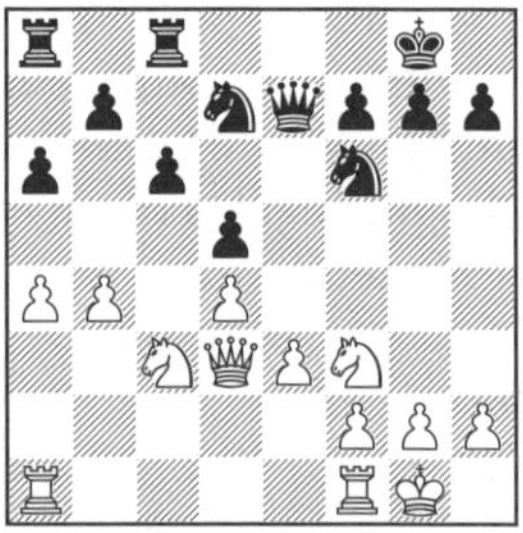

Now 14.b5 does not bother us due to 14...cxb5 15.axb5 a5∓, while:

14.♕b1 a5!? 15.b5 (15.bxa5 ♖cb8=) 15...c5 16.dxc5 ♖xc5= displays the reason behind 13...♖fc8.

The above variations suggest that b5 is ineffective without a good piece support.

b) 13.♖fc1 looks logical, but then we can activate our knight – 13...♘e4 14.a4 ♘df6

Another typical defence is 14...♘b6 15.h3 ♘xc3 16.♕xc3 ♘c4

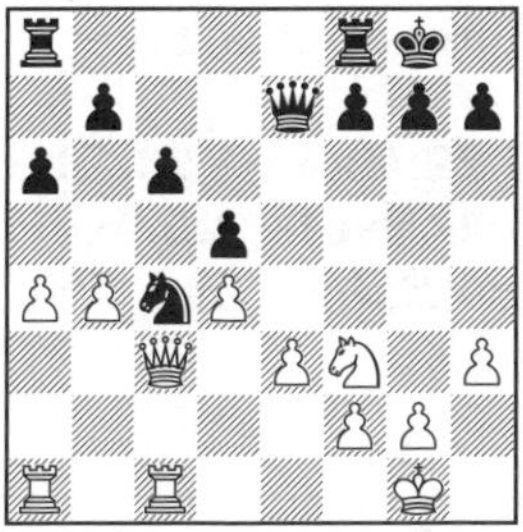

17.♕b3 (17.b5 axb5 18.axb5 cxb5 19.♕b3 ♕d7=) 17...♘d6, when b4-b5 is banned for good.

15.b5 axb5 16.axb5 ♖xa1 17.♖xa1 ♕b4 18.♘e2 (18.♖c1 ♕a3 19.♖c2 ♖c8) 18...♕xb5=.

Another preparatory move is 12.♖ab1. As a rule, we meet it by 12...a5.

Then 13.a3 is a strategic failure since 13...a4 would ban the minority attack for the rest of the game. By the way, 13...♘e4 is more challenging – 14.b4 (14.♖fc1 ♘d6) 14...axb4 15.axb4 b5.

13.♖fc1 ♘e4

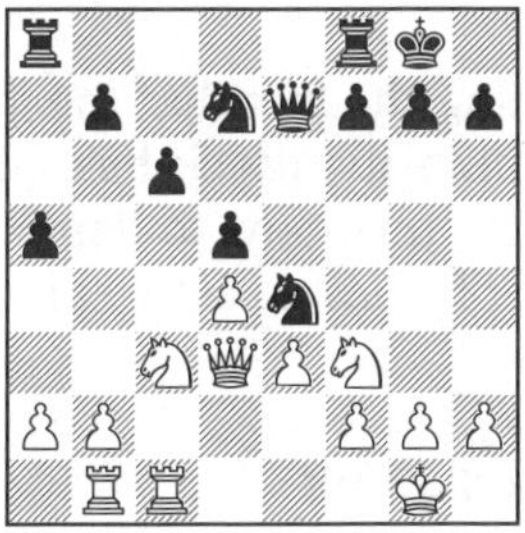

14.♘e2 g5 and 14.♕c2 f5 allow Black to launch his own attack, so let focus on:

14.a3 ♖fe8 15.b4

15.♘d2 offers a wide choice: 15...f5, or 15...♘d6 16.♕c2 f5, or 15...♘xd2 16.♕xd2 ♘b6 17.♕c2 ♖ad8 18.♘a4 ♘c4 19.♖a1 ♘d6.

15...axb4 16.axb4 b5 17.♘e2 ♘b6!? intending to trap the rook in the event of 18.♖xc6 ♘c4.

We see that if Black puts a knight on e4, his game is rather easy. Thus 12.♘d2 appears to be a sensible move.

12...♖fe8 13.♖ab1

Let's check again the other approaches to the minority attack and see what difference 12.♘d2 has introduced.

The passive knight already enables another method against 13.b4 – 13...a5 14.b5 (14.a3 axb4 15.axb4 b5∓) 14...c5=. Black's knights have the better control of the centre.

13.a3 a5 14.♘a4 b5 15.♘c3 a4 16.♖ac1 ♘b6 17.♘a2 ♘c4=.

13.♘a4 ♘b6 14.♘c5 ♘c8 15.b4 allows two solutions:

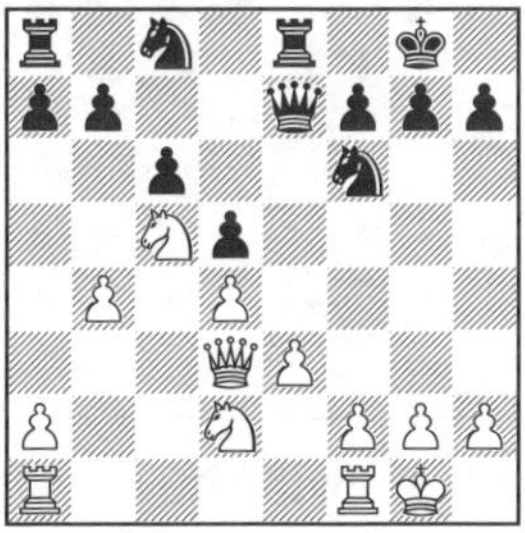

15...b6 or 15...a5 16.b5 cxb5 17.♕xb5 ♘d6 18.♕b6 ♖ec8 with play down the c-file.

13...a5! 14.♕c2 ♘b6!

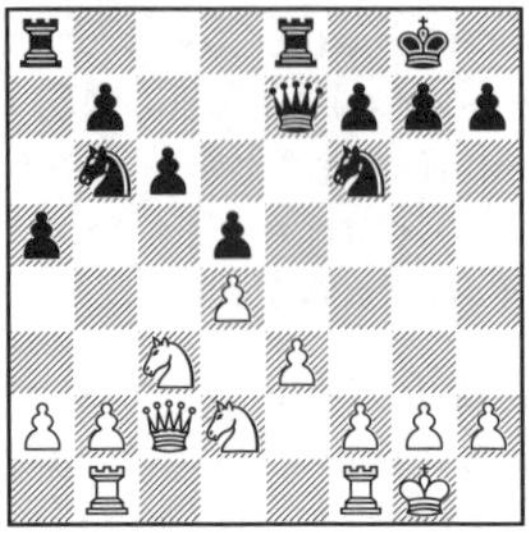

This is the modern way of fighting the minority attack. The knight goes to d6 via c8, and eventually to c4 after a preliminary ...b5. For instance: 15.a3 ♘c8 16.b4 axb4 17.axb4 b5 18.♘e2 ♘d6!. If White delays b4, he will never be able to push b4-b5 after 16.♘a4 ♘d6 17.♘c5 g6 or 17...♘d7. That leaves White with just one constructive plan – to open the centre:

15.♖fe1 g6 (15...♘c8) **16.h3 ♔g7 17.a3 ♘c8 18.e4**

18.f3 requires a little imagination – 18...♘d6 19.e4

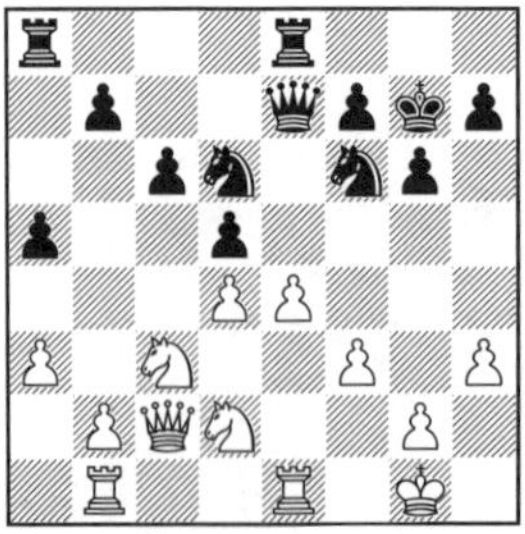

19...♘h5! 20.exd5 ♕f6=.

18...dxe4 19.♘dxe4 ♘d6 20.♘xf6 ♕xf6 21.d5

White takes course to the draw, which would be the logical outcome after 21...♖xe1+ 22.♖xe1 ♖c8. Sadler tries to keep the game going, but White forces exchanges:

21...c5 22.♘a4 c4 23.♘b6 ♖ad8 24.♘xc4 ♖xe1+ 25.♖xe1 ♘xc4 26.♕xc4 ♕xb2 27.a4 ♕b4 ½-½

29. Lesiege – So
chess.com 2017

1.d4 ♘f6 2.c4 e6 3.♘f3 d5 4.♘c3 c6 5.cxd5 exd5 6.♗f4 ♗d6 7.♗xd6 ♕xd6 8.e3 ♗f5 9.♗d3 ♗xd3 10.♕xd3 ♘bd7 11.0-0 0-0 12.♖ab1 a5 13.♕c2 ♖fe8 14.a3

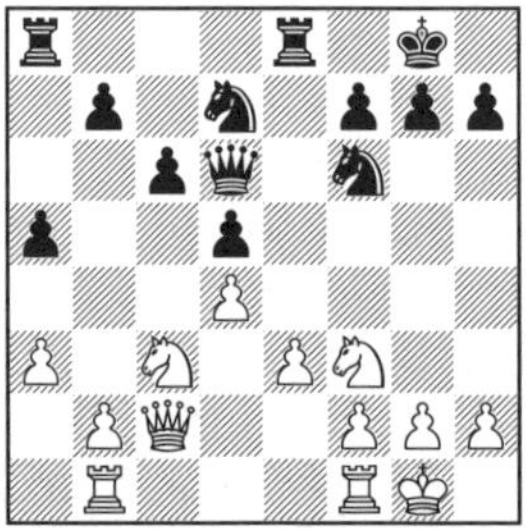

14...♘b6! 15.♘d2 ♘g4 16.♘f3

Admitting the fact that the attempt for a minority attack has failed. It is Black's turn now to demonstrate whether he has an active plan of his own.

16...♘c4 17.h3

17.e4 was possible – 17...♕g6 18.♘h4 ♕h5 19.♘f3 dxe4 20.♘xe4 ♖xe4 21.♕xe4 ♘d2=.

17...♘f6 18.♘d2 ♘xd2

It would have been a positional mistake to play 18...b5 when White's b-pawn is still on b2. After 19.a4 he would get the better pawn structure.

19.♕xd2 ♘d7 20.♖fc1 ♘b6 21.♕d3 a4 22.♕d1 ♖a7 23.♘a2 ♘c4 24.♘b4 ♖aa8 25.♘d3

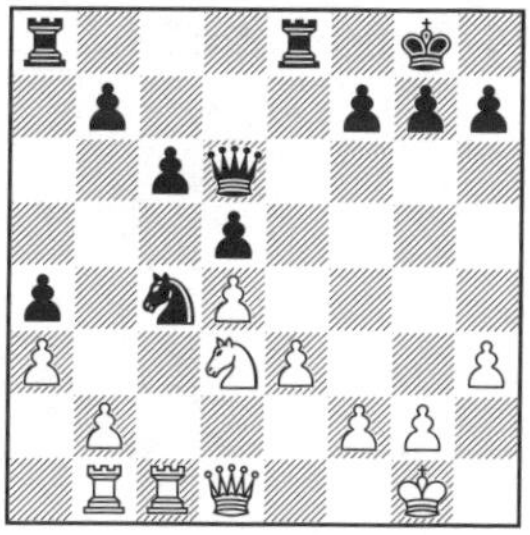

25...b6

Six months later in the same pawn structure (there were also ♗d3 vs ♘f6 and the h7-pawn was shifted to g6), So improved with ...b5 against Carlsen, and gained the upper hand. It is understandable that Black would like to stay flexible on the queenside, while attempting to create threats on the other wing. However, Lesiege quickly organises counterplay.

26.♖a1 ♖e7 27.♕c2 h6 28.♖a2 ♖e6 29.♕c3 ♖ae8 30.b3 axb3 31.♕xb3

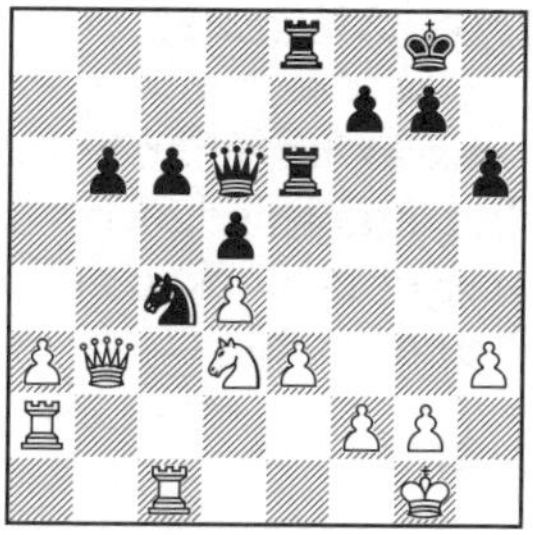

31...♖a8

So acknowledges the fact that he cannot do anything against the white king:
31...♕d8 32.a4 ♕h4 33.♘e5! ♘xe5 34.dxe5 ♖g6 35.♕xb6 ♕xh3 36.f4, or 31...♖g6 32.♘f4 ♖g5 33.a4 h5 34.♖e2 h4 35.♔h1 ♕f6 36.♘d3 ♖f5 37.♖ce1, and White is ready to open the e-file with e4.

32.a4 ♖ee8 33.♘b2 b5 34.axb5 ♖xa2 35.♕xa2 cxb5 36.♘d3

Black has two separate pawns to defend, so he should be careful. Perhaps he should stake on the passed b-pawn, move it forward and defend it tactically – 36...b4 37.♕a4 ♖b8 38.♖b1 ♕g6=.

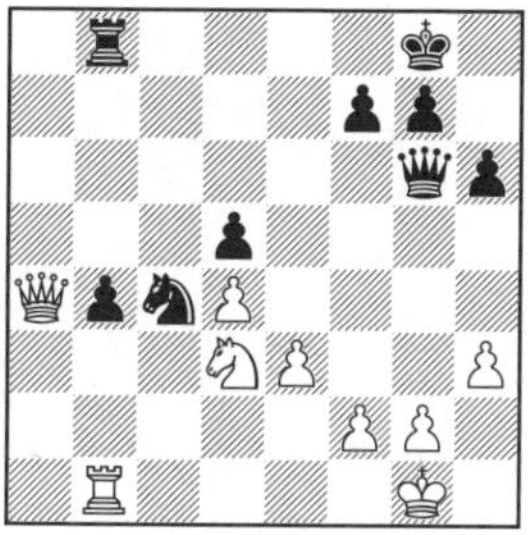

That would distract the opponent from the d5-pawn.

36...♕g6?! 37.♕e2?!

White misses his chance to take a slight but stable edge by 37.♘b4. The b-passer is blocked and the d5-pawn is under a hit.

37...♕e4!

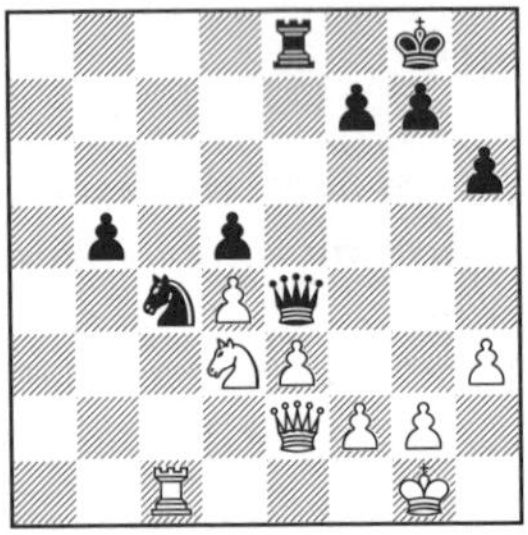

38.♖b1

The last attempt to play on is to escape from the pin with 38.♕c2. Black answers 38...♖a8 39.♘b4 ♕e6, and the active rook should keep him safe.

38...♕xd4 39.exd4 ♖xe2 40.♖xb5 ♖d2 41.♘f4 ♖xd4 42.♘xd5 ♖d1+ 43.♔h2 ♖d2 44.♖b4 ♘e5 45.♘e7+ ♔h7 46.♔g3 g6 47.♖b5 ♘d7 48.♖d5 ♖xd5 49.♘xd5 ♔g7 50.♔f4 ♘f6 51.♘xf6 ♔xf6 52.h4 ♔e6 53.♔e4 ♔d6 54.♔d4 ♔e6 55.♔e4 ♔d6 56.♔d4 ♔e6 57.♔e4 ½-½

Main Ideas

1.d4 d5 2.c4 e6 3.♘f3 c6 4.♗g5

With this move White avoids theoretical disputes and cools down Black's hopes to take on c4. The price he pays is the exchange of the bishop and the refusal to fight for an edge with an early e4.

4...♗e7 5.♗xe7 ♕xe7 6.e3 ♘f6 7.♘c3 0-0 8.♕c2

Black's only concern is what to do with his remaining bishop. His plan is to play ...dxc4 followed by ...c5. Then the bishop could go to d7. Therefore, it is logical for White to delay the development of his king's bishop in order to take on c4 in one step. To be fair, 8.♕c2 does not really hamper 8...dxc4!? 9.♗xc4 c5=, but I suppose that we would have more chances for a win in the asymmetrical pawn structure which arises after **8...♘bd7 9.cxd5** (or we take on c4) **9...exd5 10.♗d3 ♖e8 11.0-0 ♘e4**

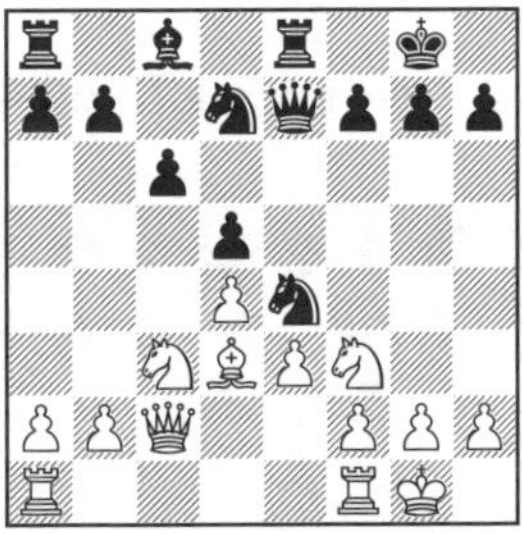

We know already this structure from the previous chapter. This position favourably defers from the QGD, where Black must put the d7-knight to the passive square f8 before trading dark-squared bishops with ...♘e4. In our case the knight can go directly to f6. That assures us of quick development and offers a simple way of fighting the minority attack – we completely ignore it! **12.b4 ♘df6 13.b5 cxb5 14.♗xb5 ♗d7=.**

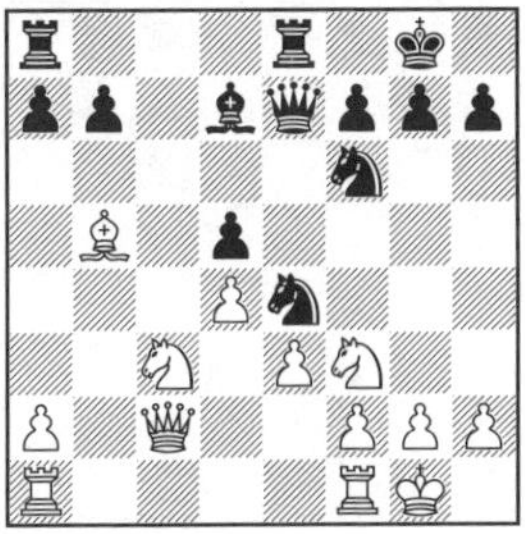

Chapter 9. 3.♘f3 c6 4.♗g5

Step by Step

1.d4 d5 2.c4 e6 3.♘f3 c6 4.♗g5

4...♗e7 5.♗xe7 ♕xe7 6.e3

6.♘bd2 ♘f6 7.g3 0-0 8.♗g2 ♘bd7 9.0-0 is harmless. The simplest solution is 9...e5 (9...b6!?) 10.dxe5 (10.cxd5 e4) 10...♘xe5 11.♘xe5 ♕xe5 12.cxd5, Wang Yue-Liang Chong China 2006,

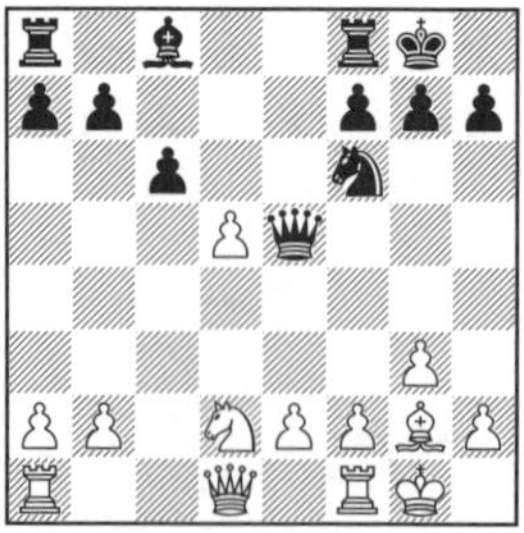

12...♘xd5 13.♘c4 ♕e7 14.e4 ♘b6 15.♕d6 ♖e8 16.♕xe7 ♖xe7 17.♘a5 ♗e6=.

6...♘f6 7.♘c3 0-0 8.♕c2

Black's main idea is to play ...dxc4 followed by ...c5, so White fights for a tempo. For instance:
8.♗d3 dxc4 9.♗xc4 c5 10.0-0 cxd4 would be fine for Black.

The other plausible waiting option is 8.♖c1, but the rook would be misplaced on that square in the event of a minority attack. Thus after 8...♘bd7 White would have to play 9.♗d3 (instead of cxd5 in the main line), when the simple 9...e5 levels the game at once – 10.dxe5 ♘xe5 11.♘xe5 ♕xe5 12.cxd5 ♘xd5=.

8...♘bd7

8...dxc4!? 9.♗xc4 c5 10.0-0 cxd4 11.exd4 ♕c7! is a simpler equaliser. Black's queen could not remain on e7 for long due to the threat ♖fe1. From c7 it can run further away to b6 or f4. Play might continue:

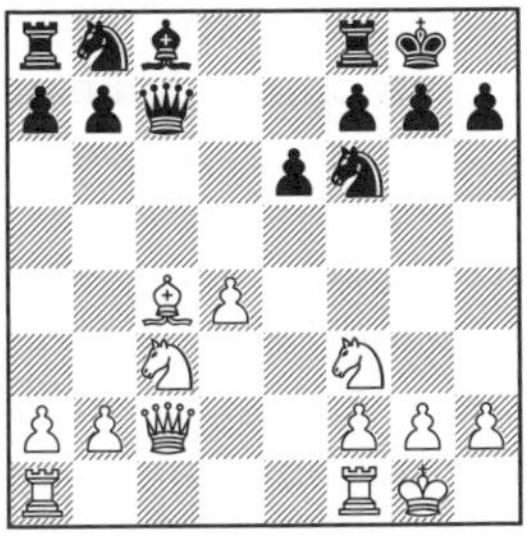

12.♕e2 (12.♗b3 ♘c6) 12...♘c6 13.♖ac1

13.♖fd1 ♗d7 14.d5 is harmless – 14...exd5 15.♘xd5 ♘xd5 16.♗xd5 ♖ae8 17.♕c2 h6 18.h3 ♕b6 19.a3 ♗e6=.

13...♗d7 14.♖fd1

Again 14.d5 exd5 15.♘xd5 ♘xd5 16.♗xd5 h6 is comfortable for Black.

Or 14.♘e4 ♕f4.

14...♖ac8 15.♗b3

15.d5 exd5 16.♘xd5? even loses to 16...♘xd5 17.♗xd5 ♘d4.

15...♕b6=.

The plan with 8...b6?! should be avoided in my opinion. Following 9.cxd5 cxd5 10.♘e5 ♗b7 11.♗d3 ♖c8 12.0-0 ♘c6 13.♘xc6,

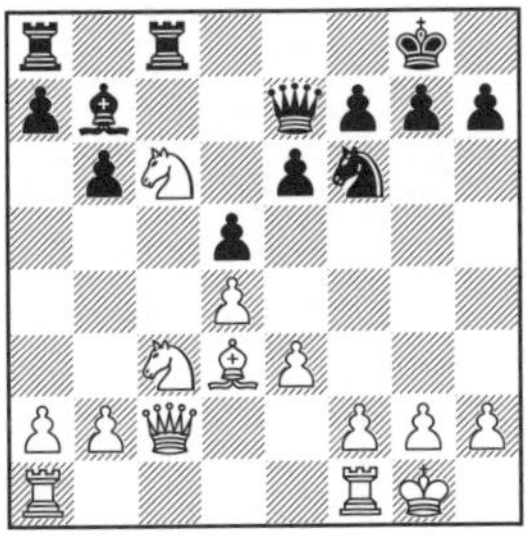

Dreev and Timofeev signed a draw, but White retains a lasting pull owing to his better bishop. Fischer-M.Horvath, ICCF 2016, went 13...♖xc6 14.f3 a6 15.♕f2 ♖c7 16.♕h4 h6 17.♖ac1 ♖ac8 18.♖c2 ♕d7 19.g4 ♕e7 20.♖g2 e5 21.♔h1 exd4 22.exd4 ♘h7 23.♕g3 b5 24.♖e1↑.

9.cxd5

It is senseless to continue the waiting game with 9.♖d1 because Black has the useful answer 9...a6 – this move would be handy against both the minority attack and 10.♗d3 dxc4 11.♗xc4 b5.

9...exd5 10.♗d3 ♖e8 11.0-0 ♘e4

Black still has to work to equalise as the opponent's bishop is obviously better. On the other hand, this position favourably defers from the QGD, where Black must put the d7-knight to the passive square f8 before trading dark-squared bishops. In our case it can go directly to f6.

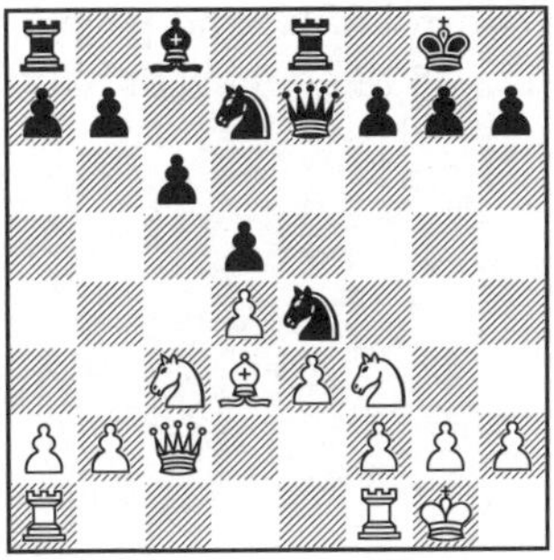

12.b4

White does not need a rook support to push b4-b5. Nevertheless 12.♖ab1 is often met. It is natural to answer 12...♘df6

If you play 12...♘b6 by analogy with the previous chapter, it is not a mistake – 13.♘d2 ♗f5.

13.b4

13.♘d2 ♗f5 14.♘dxe4 dxe4 15.♗e2 h5 16.♖fc1 h4 17.h3 g5 looks promising.

13...♗f5 14.♘a4 (14.b5?! ♖ec8) 14...♗g6 15.♘e5 ♘d6 reaches the set-up I recommended in the previous chapter.

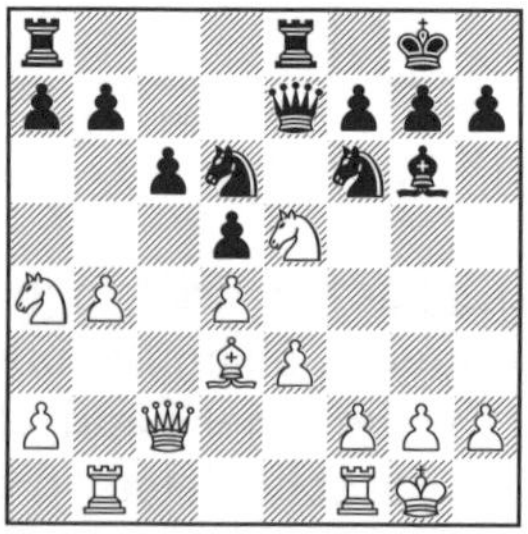

Now 16.♘xg6 hxg6 17.b5?! gives us play down the c-file after 17...cxb5 18.♗xb5 ♖ac8∓.

After 16.♗xg6 hxg6 17.♘c5 we could keep control of b5 and prepare ...f6 with 17...g5 18.a4 ♖ac8 or play in the centre with 17...♘fe4. See **Game 30** alcalaino-milne, gameknot.com 2013.

12.♗xe4 dxe4 13.♘d2 f5 14.♘c4 ♘f6∞ could be dangerous for White.

12...♘df6 13.b5 cxb5

Portisch played 13...c5 14.dxc5 ♘xc5 and easily held the draw. The text also opens the c-file and is probably more precise.

14.♗xb5 ♗d7

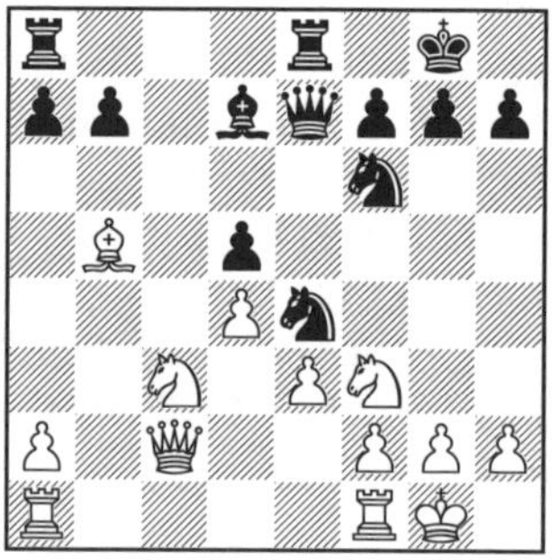

15.♗xd7 ♕xd7 16.♘xe4 ♘xe4 17.♘e5 ♕e6 18.♕b2 b6=.

Annotated Games

30. alcalaino – milne
gameknot.com 28.09.2013

1.♘f3 d5 2.d4 e6 3.c4 c6 4.♗g5 ♗e7 5.♗xe7 ♕xe7 6.e3 ♘f6 7.♘c3 0-0 8.♕c2 ♘bd7 9.cxd5 exd5 10.♗d3 ♖e8 11.0-0 ♘e4 12.b4 ♘df6 13.♖ab1 ♗f5 14.♘a4 ♗g6 15.♘e5 ♘d6 16.♗xg6 hxg6 17.♘c5

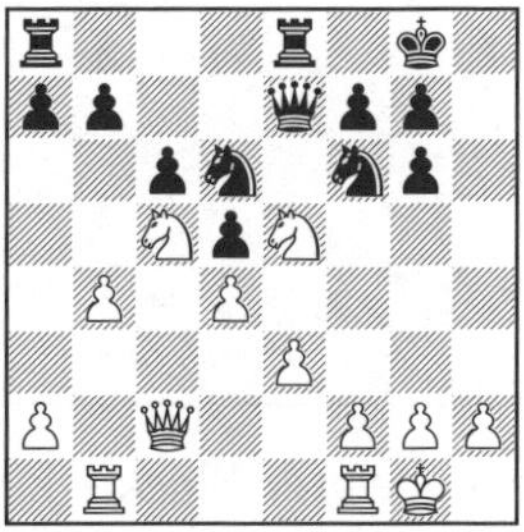

17...♖ac8

This move practically bans b4-b5, so Black can focus on the kingside.

18.a4 ♘fe4 19.a5

This move was not necessary. Instead 19.♖be1 g5 20.f3= was called for. 19.f3 ♘g5 20.f4 was premature since Black can open the centre with 20...b6 21.♘cd3 c5.

19...a6?

I understand Black's wish to fix the queenside, but that would have been a good idea only when he had gained space on the other wing. Until then Black needed the possibility of opening the centre with ...c5. After the text White could have taken the initiative on the kingside with 20.f3! ♘g5 21.f4! ♘ge4 22.♖f3, intending g4, f5. White's next move betrays poor understanding – he removes his rook from the vital f-file.

20.♖fe1 ♕g5!

The queen protects the g6-pawn and enables ...f6. 21.f4 would not help in view of 21...♕h5 and White lacks ♖f3.

21.f3 f6 22.fxe4 fxe5

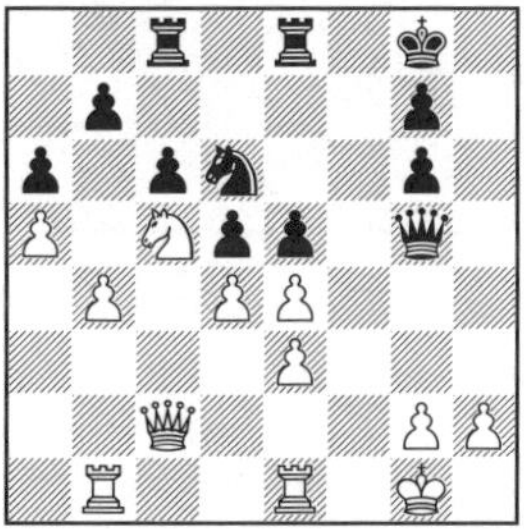

Now Black obtains enough counterplay to level the chances. For instance, 23.exd5 cxd5 24.♕b3 ♘c4.

23.♕b3 exd4 24.exd4 ♕h4 25.g3 ♕g4 26.h3

This may be analytically correct, but it is obviously impractical. White's king will be terribly weak for the rest of the game. 26.exd5 ♕xd4+ 27.♔h1 ♕xd5+ 28.♕xd5+ cxd5 29.♔g1=, followed by 30.♖bd1, was much safer. Without queens, the fixed queenside pawns and the active ♘c5 amply compensate for the small material deficit.

26...♕xh3 27.exd5 cxd5 28.♕xd5+ ♘f7 29.♕b3

Keeping the queen closer to the king looks safer. After 29.♕f3 Black could force a draw with 29...♘g5 30.♕d5+ ♘f7 or play on with 29...♖cd8! 30.♖xe8+ ♖xe8 31.♖f1 ♘h6.

29...♕g4

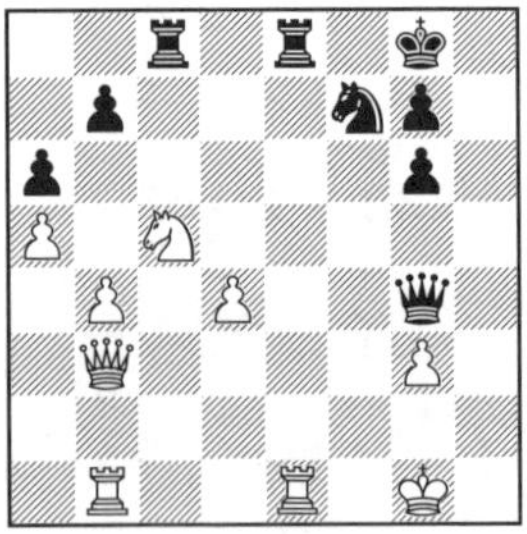

30.d5?!

30.♘e6! ♖c6 (30...♖c4=) 31.d5 ♖c4 32.♖bc1 trades a rook and keeps things under control.

30...♘g5 31.d6+ ♔h7 32.d7 ♖xe1+ 33.♖xe1 ♖f8 34.♘e6?

Decisive mistake. The only move was 34.♕e3 ♕f5 (threatening ...♕d5) 35.♘e4 ♘xe4 36.d8=♕! (36.♕xe4 loses to 36...♕f2+ 37.♔h1 ♕xg3) 36...♖xd8 37.♕xe4∓.

34...♘xe6 35.♖xe6 ♖f3 36.♕xf3 ♕xf3 37.d8♕ ♕xg3+ 38.♔h1 ♕h3+ 39.♔g1 ♕xe6 40.♕h4+ ♔g8 41.♕d8+ ♔f7–+

This is hopeless. Black's king can even move forward and eat the queenside pawns.

42.♕c7+ ♕e7 43.♕f4+ ♔e6 44.♕e4+ ♔d6 45.♕d3+ ♔c6 46.♕c4+ ♔d7 47.♕d5+ ♔c7 48.♕c4+ ♔b8 49.♕f4+ ♔a8 50.♕d4 g5 51.♔g2 ♕f6 52.♕d2 g4 0-1

Chapter 10. Fighting the Reti and the KI Attack

Step by Step

1.♘f3 d5

A. 2.c4 e6 3.g3; **B.** 2.g3

A. 2.c4 e6 3.g3

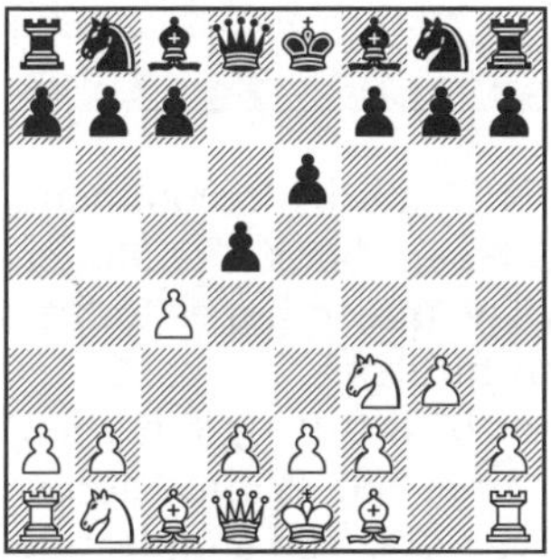

My advice is to avoid the Triangle set-up here, mostly because of:
3...c6 4.b3!

4.♗g2 dxc4 is in the spirit of the Triangle. Black has decent chances after 5.a4 ♘f6 6.0-0 ♘a6 7.♘a3 ♗xa3 8.♖xa3 (8.bxa3 ♘c5 9.♖b1 0-0 10.♕c2 ♘d5 11.♕xc4 ♕a5 12.d4 ♘xa4 13.♗d2 ♘db6 14.♕d3 ♕h5 15.♕c2 e5 16.♘xe5 ♕xe2) 8...♘b4 9.a5 0-0 10.b3 cxb3 11.d4 b6 12.axb6 ♕xb6 13.♖xb3 a5, or:

5.♘a3 ♗xa3 6.bxa3 ♘f6 7.♕c2 b5 8.a4 ♗b7 9.♗a3 ♘bd7

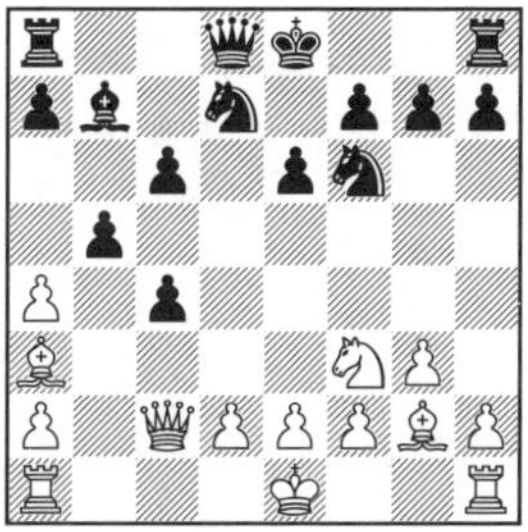

10.♕b2 (10.0-0 a6 followed by ...c5) 10...c5!? (10...♕a5 11.♗d6 ♕xa4∞) 11.♕xb5 ♗d5.

4...♘f6

The march of the a-pawn to a3 does not change the fact that White has more space in the centre.

5.♗g2 ♗e7 6.0-0 0-0 7.d4 b6 8.♕c2 ♗b7 9.♘c3 ♘bd7 10.♖d1

I do not like Black's position – it

is very passive. The key moment is that the knight on c3 has a strong impact on the centre. That is the big difference in comparison with the similar line 4.♘bd2 from Chapter 5. Instead of all this Black has a simpler way to obtain comfortable play:

3...dxc4! 4.♕a4+

4.♘a3 is seldom seen – 4...♗xa3 5.bxa3 b5

6.a4

6.♖b1 a6 7.a4 ♗b7! 8.axb5 ♘f6, and Black completes development.

6...a6 7.♗b2 ♘f6 8.axb5 axb5 9.a4 b4.

4.♗g2 a6 5.0-0

5.a4 ♘c6! 6.♘a3 e5, intending to meet 7.♘xc4 by 7...e4! is in Black's favour.

5...♘f6 6.♕c2

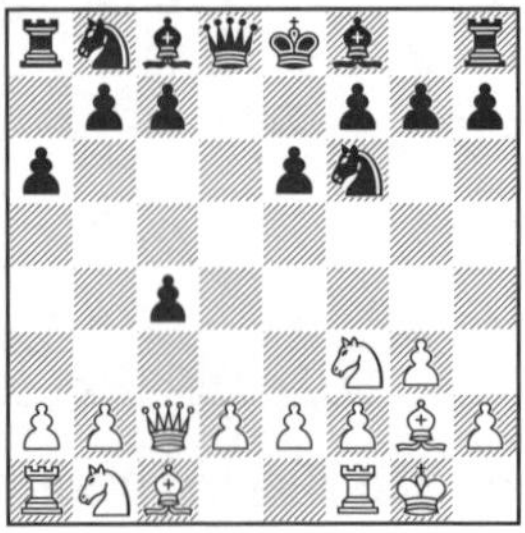

6...c5 7.♘e5 ♖a7!. Solving the only problem – the development of the c8-bishop.

8.a4 b6 9.♘a3 ♗b7 10.♘axc4 ♗xg2 11.♔xg2 ♗e7=, Wei Yi-Kramnik Moscow 2019

4...♘d7 5.♗g2 a6 6.♕xc4 b5 7.♕b3

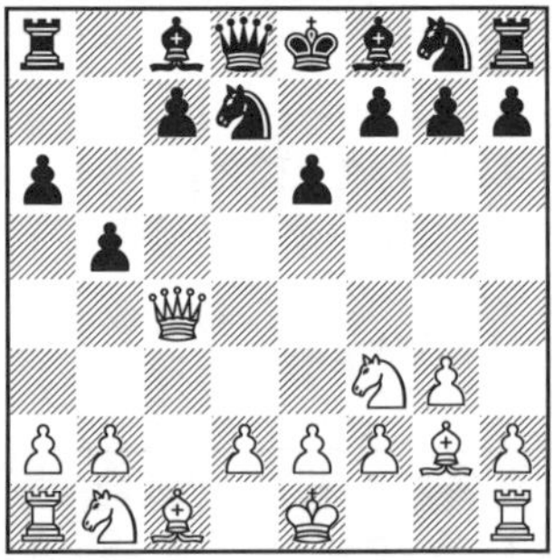

This is Demuth's recommendation in his recent book *The Modernized Reti*. The queen hopes to hit b5 after a future a4.

7.♕c2 ♗b7 8.0-0 ♘gf6 has been the main line, but White cannot even achieve 50%. The simplest defence is to refrain from ...b4. Black can guard the b5-pawn with ...♕b6 or ...♗c6. For instance:

9.a4 c5 10.♘c3 ♗c6

Or 10...♕b6 11.d3 ♗e7 12.♕b3 ♘d5 (12...0-0! 13.axb5 ♘d5=).

11.d3 ♗e7 12.♘d2 ♗xg2 13.♔xg2 0-0 14.♘f3 ♕b6 15.axb5 axb5 16.♖xa8 ♖xa8 17.♕b3 ♖a5 18.♗d2 h6 19.♖c1 ♔f8 20.♘b1 ♖a8 21.♘c3 ♖a5 22.♘b1 ♖a8 23.♘c3 ♖a5 ½-½, Laznicka-Vallejo Pons, Patras 2019.

7...♗b7 8.0-0 ♘gf6 9.♘c3 c5 10.d3 ♗e7 11.a4

11...c4! 12.dxc4 ♘c5 13.♕d1 b4 14.♘b1 ♕xd1 15.♖xd1 ♘fd7!

Demuth misses this move. 15...♘b3 16.♖a2 ♖c8 17.♗e3 is not too clear.

16.♗e3 ♗f6

Black regains the pawn, remaining with the more active pieces. See **Game 31** Hauser-Ruokokoski, ICCF 2018.

B. 2.g3 c6 3.♗g2 ♗g4

I consider this scheme in my book (with Delchev) *Attacking the English/Reti*. Let me note that the move order with 2...♗g4 is also possible. I would not like to repeat myself, so I will only focus on a set-up which I omitted:

4.d4 ♘d7 5.0-0 e6 6.c4 ♘gf6 7.♘c3

This is an original version of the Triangle. It may seem that Black should not have any problems with his bishop on g4 instead of c8, but my numerous blitz games with Gutman convinced me that we should act energetically:

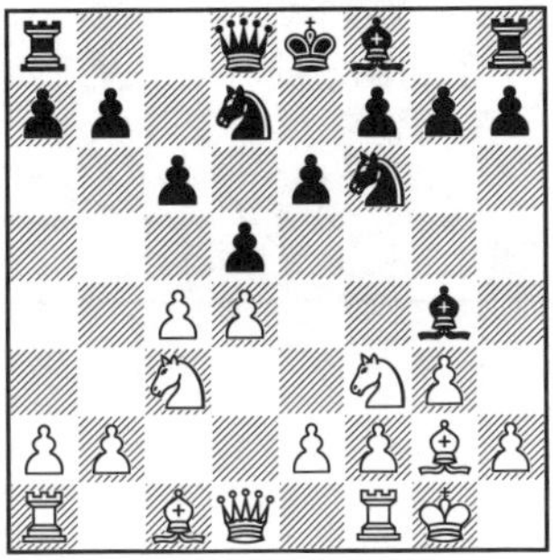

7...dxc4!

7...♗e7 8.h3 ♗h5 9.♘e5 ♘xe5 10.dxe5 ♘d7 11.cxd5 cxd5 12.f4 turns out to be in White's favour.

8.e4

The insertion of 8.a4 a5 offers Black the square b4. After 9.e4 (9.♕c2 ♕b6 10.♖d1 ♘d5! 11.♘e4 ♕a6∓; 9.h3 ♗xf3 10.♗xf3 ♗e7=) he can answer as in the main line – 9...e5. Even better is: 9...♕b6 10.h3 ♗xf3 11.♗xf3 e5 12.d5 ♗c5 13.♕e2 ♕a6∓ (13...♕b3!∓), Matnadze-Ortiz, San Cristobal 2012.

8...e5!? 9.♗e3

9.dxe5 ♗xf3 10.♗xf3 ♘xe5 11.♗e2 ♗b4 or 9.d5 cxd5 10.♘xd5 ♘xd5 11.♕xd5 ♕c7 is inferior for White.

9...exd4 10.♗xd4 ♘c5! 11.e5 ♘d5 12.♕e2

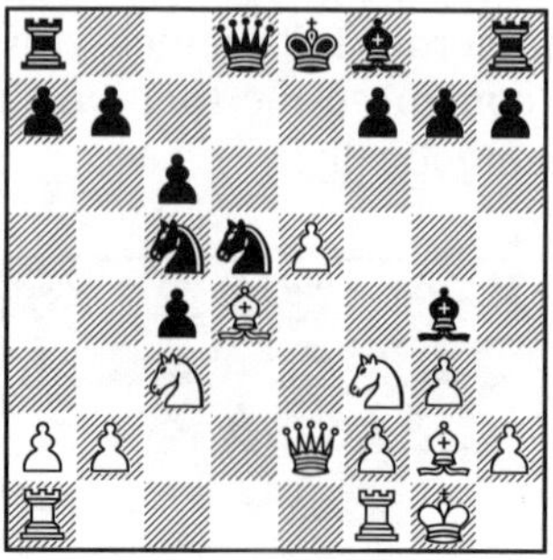

This sharp position has been untested so far. Although Black's play has been arrogant, I do not see how White could punish us. The engines consider 12...♘d3 and 12...♘b6, but I think that 12...♗f5 13.e6 ♘xe6 14.♕xc4 ♗e7 15.♖ad1 0-0 is safer. White can regain the pawn following 16.♖fe1 ♖e8 17.♗xa7 ♗b4 18.♘h4 ♗xc3 19.bxc3 ♗c2 20.♖d2 ♖xa7 with comfortable equality.

Annotated Games

31. Hauser-Ruokokoski
ICCF 2018

1.♘f3 e6 2.c4 d5 3.g3 dxc4 4.♕a4+ ♘d7 5.♗g2 a6 6.♕xc4 b5 7.♕b3 ♗b7 8.0-0 ♘gf6 9.d3 ♗e7 10.♘c3 c5 11.a4

11...c4! 12.dxc4 ♘c5 13.♕d1 b4 14.♘b1 ♕xd1 15.♖xd1 ♘fd7! 16.♗e3 ♗f6 17.a5

17.♘e1 ♗xg2 18.♔xg2 allows Black to protect his b4-pawn with 18...a5. He could also target c4 – 18...♘b3 19.♖a2 ♘e5.

17...♗xb2 18.♖a2 ♗f6 19.♘d4 ♗xg2 20.♔xg2 0-0 21.♘d2

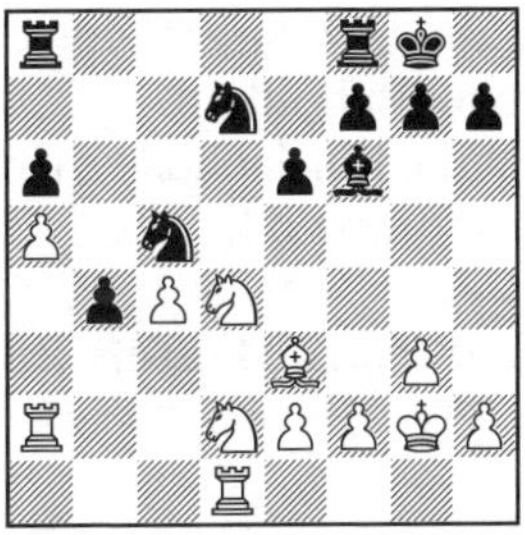

Now Black must decide the set-up of his rooks. Since the b4-pawn is his main trump, but also his main weakness, it would be natural to double the heavy pieces on the b-file: 21...♖ab8 22.♖b1 ♖b7 23.♖ab2 ♖fb8 24.♘c6 ♗xb2 25.♘xb8 ♖xb8 26.♖xb2 b3 with some pressure. However, White can improve with 23.♘4b3 ♖c8 24.♘xc5 ♘xc5 25.♗xc5 ♖xc5 26.♘e4 ♖c6 27.♖a4 ♗e7 28.c5. Although Black remains with an active rook, the game should be drawn.
This line shows that the b4-pawn is difficult to defend. Then Black could think about targeting the c4-pawn. In that event he should double the rooks on the c-file:

21...♖a7 22.♘4b3 ♖c7 23.♖b1 ♗c3 24.♘c1 ♖fc8 25.♘d3

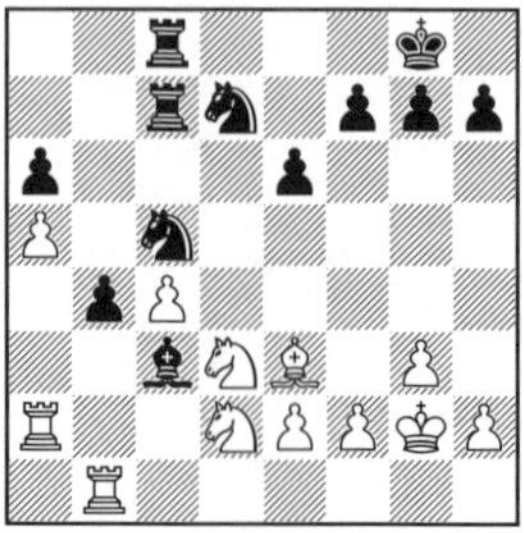

25...♘xd3 26.exd3 f5. The b4-pawn is protected, at least for now, and Black has a new target – on d3. Still White should hold on.
In the game Black chose a third set-up, abandoning b4:

21...♖ab8 22.♖b1 ♖fc8 23.♖ab2 e5

23...♗d8 24.♘c2 ♗xa5 25.♖a2 ♗d8 26.♘xb4 a5 27.♘d3 ♖xb1 28.♘xb1 was also level.

24.♘4f3 e4 25.♘d4 ♘e6 26.♘xe4 ♗xd4 27.♗xd4 ♘xd4 28.♖d2

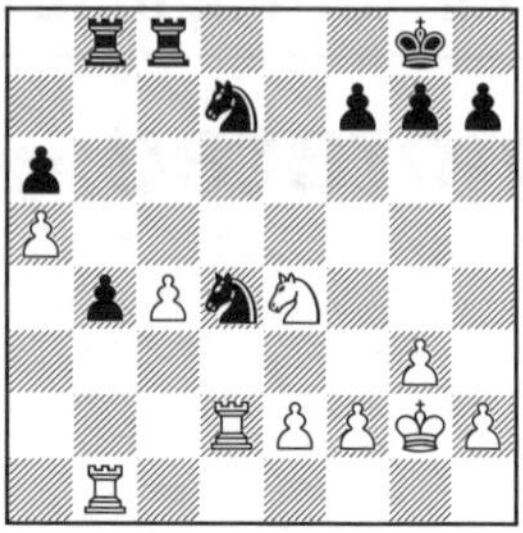

This pin saves the day.

28...♘xe2 29.♖xd7 ♖xc4 30.♘d6 ♖d4 31.♖e1 ♖d2!

Black must be careful. 31...♘c3?? failed to 32.♘c8!.

32.♖b1 h5 33.♖b7 ♖xb7 34.♘xb7

Black cannot defend both his queenside pawns, so White evens the material.

34...♘c3 35.♖xb4 ♘d1 36.♖f4 g5 37.♖f6 ♔g7 38.♖xa6 ♖xf2+ 39.♔g1 ♖a2 40.♘d6 ♘e3 41.♘e4 h4 42.gxh4 gxh4 43.h3 ♘d5 44.♘d6 ♔g6 45.♘c4+ ♔f5 ½-½

Index of Variations

Chapter 3. The Marshall Gambit
1.d4 d5 2.c4 e6 3.♘c3 c6 4.e4 (4.♗f4 77)

Chapter 4. The Catalan Way
1.d4 d5 2.c4 e6 3.♘f3 c6 4.g3 (4.b3 *106*)

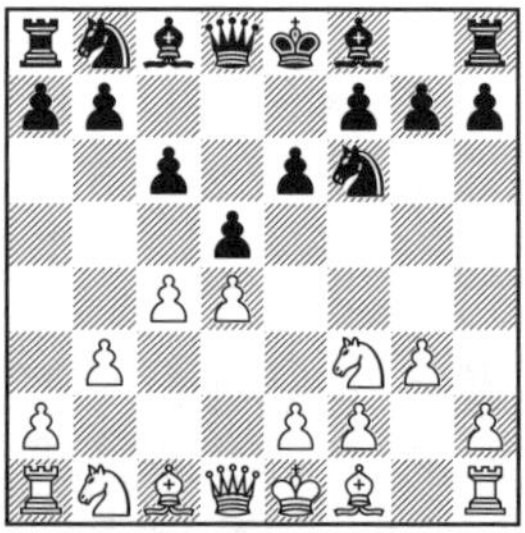